Rethinking Clusters

Research on the topic of clusters and industrial districts is very extensive. However, most of it has focused more on understanding the past than on trying to map out the future. The aim of this book is to fill this gap by identifying and discussing the main research topics that populate the current scientific debate and highlight the emergent lines of research that will constitute the future research agenda. It does so by drawing on the debate started with the "rethinking clusters" workshops, which in a short time have become a rich place for discussion among cluster scholars around the world.

Rethinking Clusters: Towards a New Research Agenda for Cluster Research collects contributions from authoritative colleagues, who cover a number of relevant and timely issues, such as the territorial roots of radical innovation processes, new ways of understanding and measuring the role of place in economic development, path renewal, internationalization and entrepreneurship. The final section is devoted to the critical analysis of policies that support smart specialization.

The chapters in this book were originally published as a special issue of the journal *European Planning Studies*.

Luciana Lazzeretti is Full Professor in Management in the Department of Economics and Management at the University of Florence, Italy.

Francesco Capone is Assistant Professor of Management in the Department of Economics and Management at the University of Florence, Italy.

Annalisa Caloffi is Associate Professor of Applied Economics in the Department of Economics and Management at the University of Florence, Italy.

Silvia Rita Sedita is Associate Professor of Management in the Department of Economics and Management at the University of Padova, Italy.

Rethinking Clusters
Towards a New Research Agenda for Cluster Research

Edited by
Luciana Lazzeretti, Francesco Capone, Annalisa Caloffi and Silvia Rita Sedita

LONDON AND NEW YORK

First published 2021
by Routledge
2 Park Square, Milton Park, Abingdon, Oxon OX14 4RN

and by Routledge
52 Vanderbilt Avenue, New York, NY 10017

Routledge is an imprint of the Taylor & Francis Group, an informa business

Introduction, Chapters 1–4, 6–10 © 2021 Taylor & Francis
Chapter 5 © 2019 Cristina Chaminade, Marco Bellandi, Monica Plechero and Erica Santini. Originally published as Open Access.

With the exception of Chapter 5, no part of this book may be reprinted or reproduced or utilised in any form or by any electronic, mechanical, or other means, now known or hereafter invented, including photocopying and recording, or in any information storage or retrieval system, without permission in writing from the publishers. For details on the rights for Chapter 5, please see the chapter's Open Access footnote.

Trademark notice: Product or corporate names may be trademarks or registered trademarks, and are used only for identification and explanation without intent to infringe.

British Library Cataloguing in Publication Data
A catalogue record for this book is available from the British Library

ISBN 13: 978-0-367-67202-7

Typeset in MinionPro
by Newgen Publishing UK

Publisher's Note
The publisher accepts responsibility for any inconsistencies that may have arisen during the conversion of this book from journal articles to book chapters, namely the inclusion of journal terminology.

Disclaimer
Every effort has been made to contact copyright holders for their permission to reprint material in this book. The publishers would be grateful to hear from any copyright holder who is not here acknowledged and will undertake to rectify any errors or omissions in future editions of this book.

Contents

Citation Information	vii
Notes on Contributors	ix
Dedication	xi
Preface	xii

Introduction: Rethinking clusters. Towards a new research agenda for cluster research 1
L. Lazzeretti, F. Capone, A. Caloffi and S. R. Sedita

1 Radical or not? The role of clusters in the emergence of radical innovations 26
Nils Grashof, Kolja Hesse and Dirk Fornahl

2 Radical vs incremental innovation in Marshallian Industrial Districts in the Valencian Region: what prevails? 46
Jose-Luis Hervas-Oliver, Francisca Sempere-Ripoll, Sofia Estelles-Miguel and Ronald Rojas-Alvarado

3 Place-based innovation in industrial districts: the long-term evolution of the iMID effect in Spain (1991–2014) 62
Rafael Boix-Domenech, Vittorio Galletto and Fabio Sforzi

4 Rereading industrial districts through the lens of entrepreneurship 81
Roberto Grandinetti

5 Understanding processes of path renewal and creation in thick specialized regional innovation systems. Evidence from two textile districts in Italy and Sweden 100
Cristina Chaminade, Marco Bellandi, Monica Plechero and Erica Santini

6 Local or global? Does internationalization drive innovation in clusters? 117
Marco Bettiol, Maria Chiarvesio, Eleonora Di Maria and Debora Gottardello

7 Clusters and internationalization: the role of lead firms' commitment and RIS proactivity in tackling the risk of internal fractures 137
Mario Davide Parrilli

8 Growth in regions, knowledge bases and relatedness: some insights from the Italian case 156
Niccolò Innocenti and Luciana Lazzeretti

9 Six critical questions about smart specialization 171
Robert Hassink and Huiwen Gong

10 In response to 'Six critical questions about smart specialization' 188
Dominique Foray

Index 201

Citation Information

The chapters in this book were originally published in the journal *European Planning Studies*, volume 27, issue 10 (August 2019). When citing this material, please use the original page numbering for each article, as follows:

Introduction
Rethinking clusters. Towards a new research agenda for cluster research
L. Lazzeretti, F. Capone, A. Caloffi and S. R. Sedita
European Planning Studies, volume 27, issue 10 (August 2019), pp. 1879–1903

Chapter 1
Radical or not? The role of clusters in the emergence of radical innovations
Nils Grashof, Kolja Hesse and Dirk Fornahl
European Planning Studies, volume 27, issue 10 (August 2019), pp. 1904–1923

Chapter 2
Radical vs incremental innovation in Marshallian Industrial Districts in the Valencian Region: what prevails?
Jose-Luis Hervas-Oliver, Francisca Sempere-Ripoll, Sofia Estelles-Miguel and Ronald Rojas-Alvarado
European Planning Studies, volume 27, issue 10 (August 2019), pp. 1924–1939

Chapter 3
Place-based innovation in industrial districts: the long-term evolution of the iMID effect in Spain (1991–2014)
Rafael Boix-Domenech, Vittorio Galletto and Fabio Sforzi
European Planning Studies, volume 27, issue 10 (August 2019), pp. 1940–1958

Chapter 4
Rereading industrial districts through the lens of entrepreneurship
Roberto Grandinetti
European Planning Studies, volume 27, issue 10 (August 2019), pp. 1959–1977

Chapter 5
Understanding processes of path renewal and creation in thick specialized regional innovation systems. Evidence from two textile districts in Italy and Sweden
Cristina Chaminade, Marco Bellandi, Monica Plechero and Erica Santini
European Planning Studies, volume 27, issue 10 (August 2019), pp. 1978–1994

Chapter 6
Local or global? Does internationalization drive innovation in clusters?
Marco Bettiol, Maria Chiarvesio, Eleonora Di Maria and Debora Gottardello
European Planning Studies, volume 27, issue 10 (August 2019), pp. 1995–2014

Chapter 7
Clusters and internationalization: the role of lead firms' commitment and RIS proactivity in tackling the risk of internal fractures
Mario Davide Parrilli
European Planning Studies, volume 27, issue 10 (August 2019), pp. 2015–2033

Chapter 8
Growth in regions, knowledge bases and relatedness: some insights from the Italian case
Niccolò Innocenti and Luciana Lazzeretti
European Planning Studies, volume 27, issue 10 (August 2019), pp. 2034–2048

Chapter 9
Six critical questions about smart specialization
Robert Hassink and Huiwen Gong
European Planning Studies, volume 27, issue 10 (August 2019), pp. 2049–2065

Chapter 10
In response to 'Six critical questions about smart specialization'
Dominique Foray
European Planning Studies, volume 27, issue 10 (August 2019), pp. 2066–2078

For any permission-related enquiries please visit:
www.tandfonline.com/page/help/permissions

Notes on Contributors

Marco Bellandi, Department of Economics and Management, University of Florence, Italy.

Marco Bettiol, Department of Economics and Management, University of Padova, Italy.

Rafael Boix-Domenech, Departament d'Estructura Econòmica, Facultat d'Economia, Universitat de València, Spain.

Annalisa Caloffi, Department of Economics and Management, University of Florence, Italy.

Francesco Capone, Department of Economics and Management, University of Florence, Italy.

Cristina Chaminade, Department of Economic History, Lund University, Sweden; Department of Business and Management, Aalborg University, Denmark.

Maria Chiarvesio, Department of Economics and Statistics, University of Udine, Italy.

Eleonora Di Maria, Department of Economics and Management, University of Padova, Italy.

Sofia Estelles-Miguel, Department of Management, Universitat Politècnica de València, Spain.

Dominique Foray, Ecole Polytechnique Fédérale de Lausanne, Switzerland.

Dirk Fornahl, Centre for Regional and Innovation Economics, University of Bremen, Germany.

Vittorio Galletto, Institut d'Estudis Regionals i Metropolitans de Barcelona, Universitat Autònoma de Barcelona, Spain.

Huiwen Gong, Department of Geography, Kiel University, Germany.

Debora Gottardello, Faculty of Business and Economics, Universitat Rovira I Virgili, Tarragona, Spain.

Roberto Grandinetti, Department of Economics and Management, University of Padova, Italy.

Nils Grashof, Centre for Regional and Innovation Economics, University of Bremen, Germany.

Robert Hassink, Department of Geography, Kiel University, Germany.

Jose-Luis Hervas-Oliver, ESIC Business and Marketing School, Madrid, Spain; Department of Management, Universitat Politècnica de València, Spain; Universidad de la Costa, Barranquilla, Colombia.

Kolja Hesse, Centre for Regional and Innovation Economics, University of Bremen, Germany.

Niccolò Innocenti, Department of Economics and Management, University of Florence, Italy.

Luciana Lazzeretti, Department of Economics and Management, University of Florence, Italy.

Mario Davide Parrilli, Department of Accounting, Finance and Economics, Bournemouth University, UK.

Monica Plechero, Department of Economics and Management, University of Florence, Italy.

Ronald Rojas-Alvarado, Gestión Organizacional, Univesidad ICESI, Cali, Colombia; UNAD, Escuela de Ciencias básicas, tecnología e ingeniería, Colombia.

Erica Santini, Fondazione per la Ricerca e l'Innovazione, Florence, Italy.

Silvia Rita Sedita, Department of Economics and Management, University of Padova, Italy.

Francisca Sempere-Ripoll, Department of Management, Universitat Politècnica de València, Spain.

Fabio Sforzi, Dipartimento di Scienze Economiche e Aziendali, Università degli Studi di Parma, Italia.

In memory of Giacomo Becattini

Preface

This volume collects a number of relevant contributions that were presented at the workshop "Rethinking Clusters: Critical Issues and New Trajectories of Cluster Research" in Florence, Italy (2018), which brought together cluster scholars from all over the world.

This workshop was the first in a series of events that ignited a movement that has continued over the years from Florence and Padua, Italy, to Valencia, Spain, and is still in development. This initiative has established a community of scholars interested in cluster/industrial districts research and enables them to meet yearly at the annual international event.

Launched by three universities of Florence, Padua and Valencia, and by the PhD in Development Economics and Local System (DELOS)[1], the "Rethinking Clusters" project[2] has, in fact, progressively expanded to include a community of researchers from many institutions discussing a number of issues related to clusters, industrial districts and geographical agglomerations.

The present volume mainly deals with the new research agenda on clusters/industrial districts research according to eight main themes. These range from cluster life cycles, creativity, innovation, networks, cluster policy, internationalization and sustainability, to cluster variety and relatedness.

Luciana Lazzeretti
Francesco Capone
Annalisa Caloffi
Silvia Rita Sedita

Notes

1. University of Florence and University of Trento
2. www.rethinkingclusters.org

INTRODUCTION

Rethinking clusters. Towards a new research agenda for cluster research

L. Lazzeretti, F. Capone, A. Caloffi and S. R. Sedita

ABSTRACT
Notwithstanding the wide research on clusters and industrial districts, most of the preceding contributions tried to analyse and investigate past research and rarely tried to critique or propose any future trajectories of this stream of research. The aim of this special issue is to identify and discuss the main themes of research that populate the current scientific debate and highlight the emergent lines that may well set the future research agenda. In order to provide a scenario for better understanding the content of this special issue, in this work, we encouraged a mix of quantitative and qualitative approaches. In particular, to identify the most important themes of current and future research, we present a bibliometric analysis of the papers that were presented at the international workshop 'Rethinking Clusters', which took place in Florence in 2018, with more than 100 participants. This exercise together with a wider literature review permits us to propose a new research agenda on cluster research according to eight main themes. These range from cluster life cycles, through creativity, innovation, knowledge networks, cluster policy issues, internationalization, sustainability, finally to cluster variety and relatedness.

1. Introduction

Cluster research has attracted major interest in several disciplines and many contribution along the years have tried to investigate and rationalize this stream of research (Caloffi, Lazzeretti, & Sedita, 2018; Cruz & Teixeira, 2010; Hervas-Oliver, Gonzalez, Caja, & Sempere-Ripoll, 2015; Lazzeretti, Sedita, & Caloffi, 2014; Sedita, Caloffi, & Lazzeretti, 2018, etc.).

Notwithstanding the wide research on clusters and industrial districts (as in the earlier formulations of such research), most of the contributions tried to analyse and investigate past research and rarely tried to critique them or propose future trajectories of this stream of research. The aim of this special issue is to identify and discuss the main themes of research that populate the current scientific debate and highlight the emergent lines of research that will constitute the future research agenda.

In order to provide a scenario for better understanding contents of this special issue, we developed a mix of quantitative and qualitative approaches. In particular, to identify the most important themes of the current and future research, we present a bibliometric analysis of the papers that were presented at the international workshop 'Rethinking Clusters', which took place at the University of Florence in 2018, with more than 100 participants. We chose this conference because it had a specific focus on new trajectories of cluster research, and it was participated in by a large population of experts in the field. Often research presented at a conference or a workshop is professionally unpublished. Nevertheless, as with any scientific work, workshop proceedings often contain original advances beyond the published literature. Therefore, the Special Issue's analysis of the papers presented at the workshop informs EPS readers of emergent issues and methods under discussion (Glänzel, Schlemmer, Schubert, & Thijs, 2006; Lisée, Larivière, & Archambault, 2008).

Our departure point from previous research on the evolution of the cluster literature (Lazzeretti et al., 2014) involved gaining new insight from the bibliometric analysis. In particular, previous research identified the founding works of the cluster literature, as well as the main keywords – taken by 8381 Web of Science articles, published in 829 journals – around which the cluster literature had recently developed. We then analysed the abstracts of the contributions presented at the workshop, matching and comparing the main keywords in cluster research with the content of the abstracts. We highlighted the most recurring research trajectories and the most relevant emerging themes. This exercise allowed us to identify eight main themes, which are: (i) cluster life-cycles, (ii) clusters and creativity, (iii) agglomeration, innovation and firm performance, (iv) knowledge networks, innovation and clusters, (v) policy and social issues, (vi) internationalization and global value chains, (vii) environmental issues and sustainability, (viii) other issues. Out of this analysis, we present a new research agenda for cluster research stemming from the eight themes that emerged. Finally, we illustrate the structure of the Special Issue.

2. The analysis of the papers presented at the workshop

2.1. Methods

We analysed all the papers that were presented at the Rethinking Clusters workshop in 2018; in particular, we collected information on paper titles, keywords, abstracts, as well as authors and their affiliations. All these data are publicly available on the workshop website (www.clusters.unifi.it). The workshop launched a call for papers where presenters were requested to submit an extended abstract of around 300–500 words to attend the conference. The workshop was organized around tracks whose contents were related, but not limited, to key themes on cluster research.[1] A total of 71 papers were presented in the parallel sessions.

As a first step, we performed a textual analysis (Capone, 2016; Feldman & Sanger, 2006) on the titles and abstracts of the 71 papers presented at the workshop. The analysis was performed using the Semantria software, which helps identify the potential presence of the most recurring and significant words in the title and abstracts' text. This step ends up with the identification of a number of keywords that characterize the recent development of cluster research.

As a second step, we compared the keywords identified by looking at the workshop papers with those that Caloffi et al. (2018) and Sedita et al. (2018) previously identified (also from the analysis of a set of 8381 Web of Science articles on cluster literature, published in 829 journals).

Such analysis helped us putting into the broader context of the cluster literature the themes discussed in the conference, and understanding similarities and differences between keywords coming from different sources. At the end of this step, we identified several keywords, which – thanks to the comparison with the previous literature – we grouped into a smaller number of meaningful macro-themes. The latter are the main streams of research that have been identified by the previous analyses on the trajectories of the cluster research.

In the third and final step, we transformed our database into a matrix that puts into relation papers to topics. In particular, we considered that a paper is connected to a macro-theme when the former cites one or more keywords that belong to such a theme. As shown in the following Section 3, the database thus transformed was used to perform social network analysis (Wasserman & Faust, 1994).

Table 1 displays the macro-themes and the keywords used for the bibliometric analyses.

2.2. Results

To investigate the main themes of the workshop we performed an analysis of the titles and abstracts of the papers. Such analysis, which was carried out with the NVIVO software (Bazeley & Jackson, 2013), was aimed at identifying the most cited words in the titles and abstracts of the papers.

Figure 1 presents the word cloud of the most cited words[2] in the contributions submitted to the conference. Cluster is the most important word at the centre of the figure as expected, while there are other frequently cited words like innovation, industry, knowledge, regions, firms, network and development. In general, this figure confirmed our expectation of the analysis.

The subsequent analysis was based on keywords. It was also carried out with the Semantria software (Capone, 2016; Feldman & Sanger, 2006) and aimed at identifying

Table 1. The macro-themes and keywords used for the bibliometric analysis.

Macro-theme	Keywords
Cluster life cycle	Cluster life cycle, cluster emergence, cluster evolution
Culture and creativity	Culture, creativity, creative city, creative class, creative economy, creative industries, cultural industries, culture, cultural heritage
Developing and emerging countries	Emerging countries, developing countries
Entrepreneurship	Entrepreneurship, entrepreneur
Environmental issues	Resilience, multi-hazard, natural disasters, sustainable, sustainability
Innovation	Innovation, radical innovation, incremental innovation, R&D, exploration, exploitation, DUI, open innovation, regional innovation system
Internationalization/MNEs	Foreign direct investment, FDI, global value chains, MNEs, multinationals, internationalization
Networks	Inter-firm, collaboration, network, knowledge networks, brokerage, inter-organizational
Policy	Smart specialization strategy, cluster policy, cluster initiatives, policy
Relatedness/diversity	Relatedness, diversification, variety, related variety, unrelated variety
Social issues	Social enterprises, social entrepreneurship, human rights, social issue, inequality

Source: Own elaboration starting from Lazzeretti et al. (2014).

Figure 1. Word cloud of the most cited words in the presented papers on cluster research. Source: Own elaborations.

the most cited 'keywords' in the conference papers, as indicated in Table 1. Figure 2 displays the percentage of papers that cite a specific keyword.

Innovation and networks are the macro-themes that collect the majority of citations. Respectively about 25% and 20% of conference papers cited at least one keyword that is included in these macro-themes. As already shown by Caloffi et al. ((2018) and Sedita et al. (2018), network-related and innovation-related keywords (hence: concepts) are strictly interlinked to the development of the cluster literature. The network soon becomes the centre of interest of scholars willing to understand the governance structure of the production and the social process that occurs in clusters. Networks are also the locus of innovation and internationalization. Also, the debate on innovation is pervasive. On the

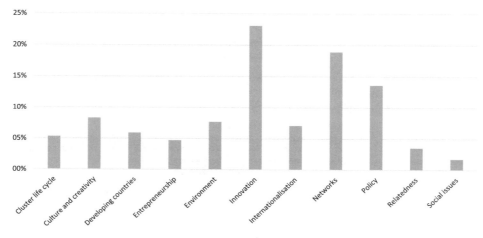

Figure 2. The most important macro-themes cited in the conference papers. Source: Our elaborations.

one hand, the cluster is regarded as a tool to generate and diffuse innovation. On the other hand, scholars try to understand what impacts on cluster production and innovation processes are generated by the presence of disruptive changes (e.g. in technologies, markets, etc.) (see, for instance, the works of Bellandi, De Propris, & Santini, 2019; or Hervas-Oliver et al., 2019).

Policy-related keywords were also popular among conference presenters. About 14% of the conference papers cite the policy macro-theme. More generally, the debate on policies has always gone together with the debate on clusters. In recent years, as shown by the conference papers we analysed, scholars have focused on the relationship between clusters and the Smart Specialization Strategies promoted by the European Union, as well as on place-based development strategies.

Internationalization-related keywords, as well as culture and creativity ones, emerge later in the cluster debate, but they have grown rapidly (Sedita et al., 2018). Environment-related keywords are very recent, but are also gaining momentum (see, for instance, De Marchi, Di Maria, & Gereffi, 2017; or Bettiol, Chiarvesio, Di Maria, & Gottardello, 2019).

Relatedness/variety and entrepreneurship are cited by 4% of the conference papers. Finally, social issues collect about 2% of the citations.

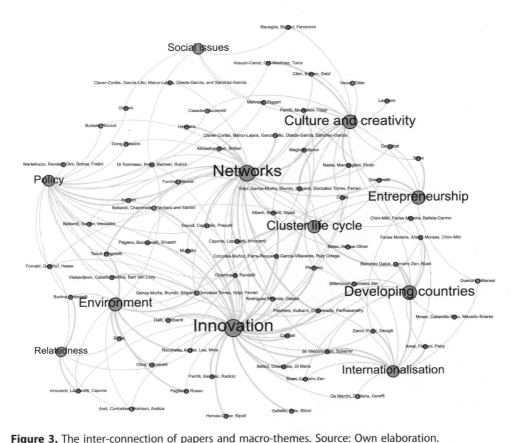

Figure 3. The inter-connection of papers and macro-themes. Source: Own elaboration.

Note: Node's size: degree of total citations of keyword in the paper; Big (red) nodes: main topics; small (blue) nodes: contributions.

To analyse the connections between macro-themes, we started from the matrix between macro-themes and papers that is described in the previous Section 2.1. This matrix was transformed into a network by using social network analysis tools. In particular, we used the UCINET-Netdraw software to draw the network and the UCINET to analyse it (Borgatti, Everett, & Freeman, 2002). The graph we obtained is displayed in the following Figure 3. The graph is a two-mode network.

The big (red) nodes in Figure 3 represent the macro-themes, and the smaller (blue) ones the conference papers. Macro-themes are linked to papers when the latter cite one or more keywords that are grouped into such macro-themes. The size of nodes quantifies relevance, measured by the number of citations received by the contributions.

Innovation is the macro-theme that has most connections with others. Innovation connects strongly with policy, relatedness, entrepreneurship, internationalization and developing countries.

Policy is also connected to a variety of macro-themes. Papers discuss not only innovation policy, but also internationalization policy, social policy, entrepreneurship policy, relatedness and smart specialization strategies, policies supporting culture and creativity (see, for instance, the work of Hassink & Gong, 2019; or Grandinetti, 2019). Network is also well connected to culture and creativity, entrepreneurship and cluster life cycle.

In the next section according to these results, we present a specific literature review to each macro-theme and we will discuss an ensuing research agenda.

3. A discussion on the future trajectories of cluster research

3.1. Cluster life cycle

The cluster life cycle argument is not new, but received renewed attention after the publication of a special issue, titled 'Cluster life cycles', edited by Ron Boschma and Dirk Fornahl (2011), which collected a variety of qualitative and quantitative case studies that generally shed light on the validity of the model. The contribution is also noted of Martin and Sunley (2011), who critically addressed the validity of the model, proposing a new way forward to look at the evolution of clusters, rooted in complexity thinking. They acknowledge the complex nature of the unit of analysis and suggest considering the cluster as a complex adaptive system, following a four stage adaptive cycle: exploitation, conservation, release, reorganization. Each phase is characterized by different levels of (1) potential resources available to the system, (2) internal connectedness of system components, and (3) resilience (or the capacity to face internal/external shocks). Their deep discussion on the evolution of clusters does not contradict at all the idea of a cluster life cycle, but it has the merit to alert us against bio-evolution-type stereotypical models. As promised, the special issue opened up a large debate among scholars. Li, Bathelt, and Wang (2012) marked an important step forward in the analysis of cluster evolution, by linking the cluster life cycle model to network dynamics. They recognized the relevant role of social and business networks in clusters, and proposed an analytical framework whose main components are: context (economic and institutional structures), action (related to the ability of individuals and organizations to explore learning opportunities and make strategic decisions) and network (social and economic relations between organizations). Following Belussi and Sedita (2009a), Elola, Valdaliso, Lopez, and

Aranguren (2012), by means of a meta-study on four Basque clusters, also accurately analysed the factors that accounted for their origin, development and maturity.

What generally emerges from previous research is that there is a heterogeneity of cluster life cycles, each one influenced by the triggering factors which intervene in the local system's genesis – the so called cluster existence argument (Maskell & Kebir, 2006) – and in its evolution-exhaustion, which refers to the factors explaining the decline and pathology of clusters, as it has been authoritatively described by Loasby (2004) for the British shoes industrial district or by Sunley (1992) for the historical decline of Lancashire cotton.

Even if we acknowledge the limitation of the adoption of the biological metaphor to illustrate cluster evolution, we agree on the need for further scientific effort in search of the most proper model to be applied while also recognizing the complex system of actors that shape the evolution of clusters. A relational perspective is appropriately adopted, where the complex network of relationships between government, local firms, start-ups, vocational training institutions, universities, MNEs (multinational enterprises) and foreign clients/suppliers is under scrutiny.

3.2. Clusters and creativity

The topics of creativity, culture and local development have been for long time a relevant strand of literature for the study of cluster research (Cooke & Lazzeretti, 2008). Shared issues between both disciplines have been analyses of place-based innovation processes, studies of innovative and creative networks of artists and cultural industries, research on technologies, enlarging the discussion of product and process innovations to topics of copyright and the impact of new information and communication technologies (ICT).

Even the rediscovered focus on the strategic role of territories is a shared topic. Creative cities, smart cities but also green and resilient cities represent privileged units of analysis and assume a key role for the economic growth of industrialized countries. In Europe, they become important for the development of strategies based on Smart Specialization. But 'smart' has become a 'trigger' term in the analysis and critique of 'Surveillance Capitalism' by the likes of Zuboff (2019)

Creativity, culture, cluster and district have been largely considered as 'fuzzy' concepts (Markusen, Wassall, DeNatale, & Cohen, 2008). They have a multidisciplinary nature with a local and global dimension, typical of the transition of our century. These aspects have emerged clearly in recent bibliometric analyses conducted on themes of cluster research (Cruz & Teixeira, 2010; Hervas-Oliver et al., 2015; Sedita et al., 2018; etc.), creative economy, cultural and creative industries (Lazzeretti, Capone, & Innocenti, 2017). Such analyses reaffirm the deep bond between the two strands of literature.

Traditionally, studies on creative economy research are developed around three fundamental pillars: the analysis of creative class, creative cities and cultural and creative industries (CCIs) (Pratt, 2008).

If the announcement of the creative economy is often bracketed with the work of Richard Florida on the rise of creative class (Florida, 2002), recently themes of CCIs have become central (Jones, Lorenzen, & Sapsed, 2015). This area of study comprises many differentiated themes but also with elements of strong fragmentation. Nevertheless, it has many possibilities for further development. In summary, we can conclude that, nowadays, creative economy research represents a successful multidisciplinary paradigm, born and developed in English-speaking countries and applied at global level (Lazzeretti et al., 2017). This paradigm is still in a developmental phase and represents a possible area of connection with the development of cluster research as a proven pioneer of cross-strand research by Lazzeretti, Boix, and Capone (2008) and Boix, Hervás-Oliver, and De Miguel-Molina (2015).

Among the main topics that can be identified for a future research agenda, we may distinguish the following. The first line of research, not yet sufficiently developed, concerns the CCIs in the global world, particularly, in the 'Global South'. While much has been discussed concerning CCIs of the first-generation countries, such as those in North America and Europe (Boix, Capone, De Propris, Lazzeretti, & Sanchez, 2016), this topic applied to the study of emerging countries is still under-researched (UNESCO, 2013). The typical forms of local development are combined with those of the informal economy and cultural and creative activities are one of the involved sectors.

A second important line concerns the digitization of cultural and creative resources and their linkages with other sectors. The combination of ICT and cultural goods represents an important trajectory of development, including the development of the videogame industry, robotics sector, industry 4.0 and 5.0 and the growth of the so-called cultural and creative tourism (Richards, 2011).

Related to the latter there is another important area of study that deals with so-called 'creative entrepreneurship' (Lazzeretti & Vecco, 2018). This corresponds to the study of entrepreneurial activities in the cultural and creative sectors, characterized by forms of self-entrepreneurship and networking both in private and public sectors.

Finally, we report a new and emerging line of research concerning the societal function of culture (Heidenreich & Plaza, 2015). Following the increasing worries related to recovery from the economic crisis, the issue of migration and the growth of natural calamities, the role played by culture for society is coming back to be central. In this way, initiatives are linked to various forms of social innovation and social enterprises, which also have cultural and creative activities as a core.

3.3. Agglomeration, innovation and performance in agglomerations

There is an exciting yet unsolved ongoing debate on agglomeration and firm performance (e.g. Gilbert, McDougall, & Audretsch, 2008; Hervas-Oliver, Sempere-Ripoll, Rojas-Alvarado, & Estelles-Miguel, 2018; Knoben, Arikan, van Oort, & Raspe, 2016; Rigby & Brown, 2015) with very different inconclusive results and directions. The first debate, on the one hand, presents the objective of deciphering whether agglomeration exerts positive or negative effects on a firm's performance, with a tension of findings that point out both negative (e.g. Gilbert et al., 2008; Myles Shaver & Flyer, 2000; Sorenson & Audia, 2000) and positive effects (e.g. McCann & Folta, 2011). This debate mixes different types of agglomerations, firms and uses different performance measures with a variety of insights.

Different but related to the first one is the second debate, on the other hand, focused on disentangling 'performance asymmetries' due to agglomeration effects (e.g. Crescenzi & Gagliardi, 2018; Lee, 2018). Put differently, this line of research investigates 'who really gains within agglomerations', questioning the previous assumption that all firms gain the same from co-location. Again, the discussion presents rather inconclusive results, with studies pointing out that best capability-based firms gain the most (e.g. McCann &

Folta, 2011), while others show that strong capability-based firms are not the ones gaining the most. The latter effect is explained by the fact that 'spillovers' from these are captured by weaker co-located firms that gain the most and contribute the least to agglomerations (Hervas-Oliver, Sempere-Ripoll, et al., 2018), showing an interesting tension that deserves further attention by scholars.

Complementary to those lines of research and going one step further, a third sub-field of inquiry is devoted to generating evidence on a more fine-grained related issue: are agglomerations influencing the generation of radical vs incremental innovation (e.g. Gilbert, 2012; Ostergaard & Park, 2015)? As a matter of fact, most research on Marshallian Industrial Districts (MIDs) has traditionally assumed incremental or continuous innovation (e.g. Garofoli, 1991; Robertson & Langlois, 1995). As a result, the analysis of the occurrence of radical innovation in MIDs has been reduced to specific case studies (see Hervás-Oliver, Albors-Garrigos, Estelles-Miguel, & Boronat-Moll, 2018) or restricted to show how radical innovation was unable to occur, producing instead decline from inertia (e.g. Glasmeier, 1991; Grabher, 1993; Isaksen, 2018; Ostergaard & Park, 2015). This line of research constitutes a promising research avenue, along with the above sub-lines of inquiry explained.

3.4. Knowledge network, innovation and clusters

Knowledge networks have received considerable attention in clusters and industrial districts research since the early reviews (Breschi & Malerba, 2005; Tallman, Jenkins, Henry, & Pinch, 2004). The first contributions on knowledge networks began with the work of Powell, Koput, and Smith-Doerr (1996) (Powell & Grodal, 2005) on inter-organizational collaborations on how knowledge spreads in networks (Burt, 2004; Coleman, 1988; Granovetter, 1973) and in narrow geographical areas (Bathelt, Malmberg, & Maskell, 2004; Maskell & Malmberg, 1999).

More recently, however, the idea that knowledge is equally widespread in clusters and industrial districts has been widely criticized (Fitjar & Rodriguez-Pose, 2017), highlighting that it is also relevant to consider the structure of local networks and the firm's capability to benefit from a central position in networks (Giuliani & Bell, 2005; Giuliani, 2013).

In this context, the proximity approach (Boschma, 2005) has received more and more attention in recent years (Capone & Lazzeretti, 2018). The strand of research focuses on which are the drivers of similarity / dissonance that promote the establishment of collaborations between organizations, evaluating not only geographical proximity, but also organizational, institutional, social and cognitive proximity. Many of these studies have also developed an empirical and evolutionary approach on how the impact of these drivers changes over time (Balland, 2012; Balland, De Vaan, & Boschma, 2012; Capone & Lazzeretti, 2017; Lazzeretti & Capone, 2016; etc.), using advanced methodology like SAOM / SIENA and ERGM models.

It is then possible to highlight some multidisciplinary themes of growing interest in the future that range among Management, Regional Sciences and Evolutionary Economic Geography.

The first one concerns the fact that most contributions on inter-organizational networks and proximity, mainly consider 'formal' relationships, such as R&D partnerships (D'Este, Iammarino, Savona, & von Tunzelmann, 2012), EU projects (Autant-Bernard,

Billand, Frachisse, & Massard, 2007), patents (Ter Wal, 2013) or publications (De Stefano & Zaccarin, 2013). Accordingly, 'informal' relationships are still under-researched due to the difficulty of collecting informal network data.

Secondly, among the few contributions that analyse informal relationships, most of them focus on business relationships and undervalue the role of social ties and personal bonds in innovation. Notwithstanding the fact that since Granovetter's work (1973), the importance of considering the social context in which people and firms are embedded has been emphasized (Broekel & Boschma, 2011). More recently, some authors for instance (Ooms, Werker, & Caniëls, 2018) have investigated personal relationships and proximity in collaborations and have shown that firms' relationships are strongly grounded in the relations 'between persons' and that personal proximity is still widely under-investigated. Such 'microgeographies' are subjects of interest to economic sociologists (MacKenzie, 2008).

Third, although there is a tradition of studying informal relationships (Salavisa, Sousa, & Fontes, 2012; etc.), most authors focus on each relationship separately. In fact, few contributions have attempted to analyse the influence of the 'co-evolution' of multiple network relationships on innovation (Capone & Lazzeretti, 2018; Ferriani, Fonti, & Corrado, 2013). This seems to be particularly interesting thanks to recent advancements of the statistical methodologies that permit analysis of multilevel (relationships) networks or multiplex networks (Lazega & Snijders, 2015; Snijders, Lomi, & Torló, 2013; Wang, Robins, Pattison, & Lazega, 2013).

Some open questions for the future regard the role of knowledge networks in localized geographical contexts, such as clusters and industrial districts, Faced with the challenges and opportunities of the pervasive processes of globalization and digitization. In an era of artificial intelligence and 4.0 Industry, knowledge is becoming more and more chaotic and could these processes overcome social dynamics and the role of localities?

3.5. Policy and social issues

After great enthusiasm and just as much disappointment, the time has come to highlight some possible future prospects for cluster policy theory and practice. Many authors have already performed this exercise, as the story of cluster policies is studded with declines and subsequent revivals (Andersson, Hansson, Schwaag-Serger, & Sorvik, 2004; Benneworth, Danson, Raines, & Whittam, 2003; Fromhold-Eisebith & Eisebith, 2005; Hospers, 2005; Koschatzky, 2012; Martin & Sunley, 2003). We build on those contributions, as well as on more recent scholarly reflections, to put forward the legacy that the reflection on clusters (and industrial districts) has left in contemporary policies and, in particular, in the future development of policies for responsible innovation.

As literature has shown, the initial era of great enthusiasm has sometimes led policymakers to uncritically adopt the concept of cluster, which have made many initiatives fail (Becattini, 2000; Hospers, 2006). However, these failures have not wiped out cluster policies, which still survive in many countries. More important than the presence of these experiences is, however, the fact that the concept of clusters has left an important legacy in policy design and implementation. Some aspects of that legacy have become an integral part of many approaches to innovation policies, and are likely to remain so for a long time; others could become increasingly important in the future.

Firstly, the reflection on clusters and industrial districts has helped policy makers in many countries and regions to realize that territorial contexts, with their peculiar networks of social relations, skills, attitudes and established institutions can either boost or prevent development and innovation (Becattini, 1979; Becattini, Bellandi, Del Ottati, & Sforzi, 2003; Cooke & Morgan, 1998; Koschatzky, Schnabl, Zenker, Stahlecker, & Kroll, 2014; Wolfe & Nelles, 2008). The regional innovation system has paved the way for these concepts in the field of politics (Cooke, Heidenreich, & Braczyk, 2004; Cooke & Memedovic, 2001). Such concepts then entered the idea of platforms and, more recently, smart specialization and place-based policies (Asheim, Boschma, & Cooke, 2011; Barca, McCann, & Rodríguez-Pose, 2012; Foray, David, & Hall, 2009).

Secondly, and more generally, thanks to the reflection on clusters and on regional innovation systems the concept of system has gradually entered the toolbox of innovation policy and is now a fundamental aspect of almost any approach to innovation policy (Metcalfe, 1994; Woolthuis, Lankhuizen, & Gilsing, 2005).

Thirdly, the idea that the cluster (an, in particular, the industrial district) is a place of life, and is inhabited by a community of people – grouped in various organizational forms – that have an influence on local innovation and development, could be further enhanced in the design and implementation of future policies (Becattini, 2015a, 2015b; Cooke & Morgan, 1998). Indeed increased attention to civic society is required, if we want policies to promote responsible innovation. Civic society, in its various local organizational forms, can contribute to the democratic government of the objectives of research and innovation and to the orientation of policies towards achieving these objectives (Cooke, 2018; Owen, Macnaghten, & Stilgoe, 2012). It will be interesting to see if cluster-based civic communities will be able to deal with this problem better than other types of social groups. 'Surveillance Capitalism' is the major contemporary indicator of 'irresponsible innovation', perhaps not quite in the same league as climate change or nuclear weapons, but in the upper reaches of civic infamy.

3.6. Internationalization and global value chains

The internationalization of clusters is a renowned phenomenon, at least after the fall of the Berlin wall, which favoured international commerce and the mobility of human and financial capital. What is interesting to observe is how internationalization processes changed over time, moving from a pure export to a global sourcing activity, from a relocation process to massive investments of foreign companies in local production systems (Belussi & Sammarra, 2009; Gordon & McCann, 2000; Markusen, 1985). In some specific cases, internationalization takes the form of an inverse relocation, as in the case of Arzignano, the leather tanning district in the Vicenza province (Italy) – Belussi and Sedita (2009b). The variety of forms of internationalization still co-exist, sometimes even within the same cluster. What we observe now is a complex picture where sectoral analogies are difficult to find. Which are the new rules of the game (if any)?

Recent empirical research has pointed out the increasing involvement of clusters in global value chains (GVCs) (De Marchi et al., 2017; Gereffi, 1999; Gereffi & Bair, 2001; Gereffi, Humphrey, & Sturgeon, 2005; Gereffi & Kaplinsky, 2001; Gereffi & Korzeniewicz, 1994), where the international division of labour might even give rise to symbiotic relationships between distant districts/clusters (Belussi & Rita Sedita, 2008). This evidence opened up a stream of inquiry over the identification of the proper unit of analysis and the search for foundational works that might be considered the shoulders of the giants upon which to build a new research field (Hervas-Oliver, Belussi, Sedita, Caloffi, & Gonzalez, 2018). In particular, the majority of work focused on the relationship between MNEs and clusters, being investigated either under the lenses of the economic geography literature (Iammarino & McCann, 2013) or of international business studies (Cantwell & Mudambi, 2011). The perspective of analysis is clearly different, since on the one side the research question is mainly related to potential benefits or detrimental aspects of the entry of MNEs in clusters, on the other side the research question is mainly addressed to investigating the locational benefits for MNEs in clusters as part of a scarce resource seeking strategy (Dunning, 2009). We feel the need to push forward a new interpretative model that can fill the gaps in this literature, providing new taxonomies and cross-country empirical evidence, as in the first attempt made by Belussi, Caloffi, and Sedita (2017). Probably a radical change in the unit of analysis is due. The relational dimension appears crucial and actor-network theory might inform analyses of the complex dynamics underpinning the evolutionary trajectories of clusters.

Moreover, a related and emergent topic is that of the role of developing countries in the international division of labour, where native local clusters are often an object of acquisition from MNEs headquartered in advanced economy countries, or are completely created *de-novo* through green field investments (Morrison, Pietrobelli, & Rabellotti, 2008). An open debate is about inequalities connected to the globalization of the economy and how new sustainable patterns of development might be stimulated through private-public partnership initiatives in developing countries, where the cluster model can be sustained as a more conscious way to create wealth for the population. In this case, policy interventions, which involve supra-national entities, are desired to ensure sustainable business models in the global south.

3.7. Environment and sustainability

Sustainability-oriented innovation and technology studies have received increasing attention over the past 10–15 years (Markard, Raven, & Truffer, 2012, p. 955). The importance of sustainable innovation management is growing both in practice and in academia (Schiederig, Tietze, & Herstatt, 2012). Social and environmental issues are increasingly considered pivotal for shaping future trajectories of regional development. Fichter (2005, p. 138) defines sustainable innovation as 'the development and implementation of a radically new or significantly improved technical, organizational, business-related, institutional or social solution that meets a triple bottom line of economic, environmental and social value creation'. The orientation towards sustainability encompasses the concept of innovation, which characterizes new products, new production processes and emergent business models. Strambach (2017) states that 'Novelties that integrate economic, ecological, and social values seem to have the potential to promote complex socio-ecological transformation at the local, regional, or national system level' (Strambach, 2017). These transformations are led by processes of cross-fertilization that include direct/indirect knowledge spillovers to other actors in the economy, through the implementation of business strategies oriented towards a socially desirable outcome.

An interesting emerging strand of research in the debate on sustainability is that of resilience. Over the last few years, the debate on the capacity of local systems – clusters, cities or regions – to continue to grow and compete in response to external disruptions has strongly increased, in particular, since the global financial crisis of 2008. The literature developed onwards has focused especially on the capacity to resist and recover from economic shocks (Martin, 2012). This new line of research has broadened the debate on the economic resilience of systems, proposing a dynamic vision of resilience, where the ability to respond to shocks reorganizing, transforming and innovating has become central (Lazzeretti & Cooke, 2017). But today, in many Western economies, let alone developing ones as in Africa, 'resilience' proves difficult to identify.

However, when talking about clusters and local systems, the ability of responding to recessionary shocks has been a central topic while resilience as a consequence of environmental issues is not discussed enough. This line of research is a cutting-edge topic because a large part of literature recognizes important effects of natural disasters and environmental change on the performance of local systems (Oliva & Lazzeretti, 2017; Pagliacci & Russo, 2016). The study of the inter-relationship between economic resilience, environmental issues and clusters should be engaged in order to contribute to two promising lines of research.

First, a wider investigation is required to understand if and how innovation and new industrial trajectories may emerge as a result of shocks. On the one side, this future line of research should be devoted to understanding how the presence of clusters may encourage technological transition and minimize environmental hazards on territories. On the other side, what is still under-researched is the role of evolution of clusters in contributing to the emergence of new sectors and to the structural change of territories (Iammarino & McCann, 2006).

Second, what is still missing is a strong idea of the determinants of resilience of clusters and local systems. The discussion of how differences in resources endowment, structure of knowledge networks, entrepreneurship and innovation capacity impact on performance of clusters in a disturbed economic environment requires larger investigation. Studies of this kind may be useful for understanding not only what contributes to a successful growth of clusters but also to deep dynamics of clusters decline in an increasing risky environment (Østergaard & Park, 2013).

3.8. Other issues: cluster variety and relatedness

Despite the strong relevance of the issues already discussed there are other themes that deserve attention when talking about cluster research. First of all, it is important to underline that recently, growing attention is paid to the role of diversity, more than to that of specialization, as one of the performance and competitiveness determinants of clusters and districts (Boschma & Frenken, 2009). In fact, the debate on diversification vs. specialization as drivers of the economic development of territories is far from conclusion (Beaudry & Schiffauerova, 2009; Van Oort, 2015). There is still much to do, also in light of the new methods that may help to better understand relations among different sectors and thus capture the 'right distance' that should favour competitiveness of clusters (Quintana-Garcia & Benavides-Velasco, 2008).

In this debate, during the last decade, the concept of related variety emerged (Boschma & Iammarino, 2009; Frenken, Van Oort, & Verburg, 2007), but more recently following the same concept are rising new ideas and methods that may help the debate allowing scholars to better capture the real relatedness between products (Hidalgo, Klinger, Barabási, & Hausmann, 2007) sectors (Innocenti & Lazzeretti, 2019a) or skills of workers (Neffke & Henning, 2013). One other rising theme, firstly developed from Hidalgo and Hausmann (2009) that is recently appearing also on the scene of cluster research (Ketels, 2013), is economic complexity, arguing that those that specialize in more complex products or industries or technologies, are more likely to survive and grow in respect over those that specialize in products and industries that are less complex and thus, suffer from a higher external competition (Hartmann, 2014).

These are two promising fields of research that may be useful to clarify many facets of clusters, and what is more may help understanding of the competitiveness of clusters. In addition, what seems even more interesting is the combination of these two fields. They may help to understand if the competitiveness of the cluster is driven by its specialization in complex sectors or if is enough to be specialized in sectors that are related to complex ones. Many questions may arise from these two concepts and even more, as already said, the methods that may be applied to explore the many facets of cluster research.

4. Structure of the special issue

This Special Issue, beyond this, is composed by 9 articles presented in the first 'Rethinking clusters' International Workshop held at the University of Florence in 2018. All articles deal with the above future trajectories of cluster research, in particular: innovation, internationalization, entrepreneurship, specialization/diversification and finally policies in clusters, regional innovation systems and industrial districts.

The first three papers deal with innovation and radical innovation in clusters and industrial districts, underlining not only that industrial districts and clusters do produce more innovation than other places, but that also radical innovation is boosted in close geographical contexts.

The first paper by Grashof, Hesse, and Fornahl (2019) starts the discussion on radical innovation and clusters. Recently, radical innovations have received increasing attention in order to achieve long-term economic success. Regional clusters, being frequently used as an innovation policy instrument, have been shown to have the potential to support innovations in general. However, it remains unclear whether clusters are really a beneficial environment for the generation of radical innovations. The study aims to shed light on the specific role clusters can play in radical innovation processes. Results show that clusters indeed provide a suitable environment for radical innovations. Furthermore, Authors find that radical innovations rather occur in the periphery of the cluster, where actors tend to be more open to the exchange of external knowledge. This happens in general through linkages with other actors, which we also find to be beneficial for the emergence of radical innovations up to a certain degree. Findings implicate that policy makers should continue to support clusters and further develop funding schemes. Moreover, managers should be open to collaborations with other actors for the cross-fertilization of knowledge to promote radical innovations.

The second paper by Hervas-Oliver, Sempere-Ripoll, Estelles-Miguel, and Rojas-Alvarado (2019) explores and integrates economic geography with innovation literature to shed light on the importance of the role played by Marshallian industrial districts on firms' innovative performance. The study's objective consists of deciphering whether collocation in MIDs, exerts a potential effect on a firm's discontinuous or radical innovative performance. Specifically, authors encompass radical or discontinuous innovation, as opposed to an incremental or imitative one. They build a framework from which MIDs' effect on discontinuous innovation is approached. Using CIS data in Spain in district and non-district firms in a region, results show that: (i) collocated firms' innovative performance is positively related to the District effect, as long as the innovation pursuit is incremental; (ii) collocation in MIDs does not facilitate the pursuit of radical innovation but mainly supports an incremental one, and (iii) district firms show asymmetric capabilities and innovative output, as long as the innovation pursuit is incremental, nor discontinuous. Implications for the MID framework are discussed.

The third paper by Boix, Galletto, and Sforzi (2019) aims to advance in the study of the relationship between industrial districts and innovation. These authors had shown that the industrial districts showed an innovative intensity higher than the national average (Boix & Galletto, 2009; Boix & Trullén, 2010; Galletto & Boix, 2014). This thesis, known as 'I-district effect' or 'i-MID effect' has caused quite a controversy, since a part of the scientific community continues to think of industrial districts as traditional environments, specialized in mature sectors, and with low innovative capacity. This new article introduces the provocative idea of 'the industrial district as an innovation machine', and tests the existence and evolution of the i-MID effect in Spain for a very long period of 24 years (1991–2014) and their behaviour during the phases of economic crisis, recovery and growth. The results reveal that industrial districts innovate more than the average during the entire time span, including both periods of crisis and growth. In fact, they are even more robust than those obtained in previous articles because they place the industrial districts as a true innovation machine, dominant in the quantiles of greater innovative intensity, and as the local productive systems that bring more innovations to the national economy.

The fourth article authored by Grandinetti (2019) continues to focus on industrial districts and deals with the interesting link between industrial district and entrepreneurship. Drawing a distinction between generic entrepreneurship and selective entrepreneurship leads us to acknowledge that a close association between industrial districts as a whole and entrepreneurship is only well-founded if we are speaking of the generic definition of the latter. Burt's theory of structural holes and its application to industrial districts enables us to identify two different types of industrial district, one featuring a high degree of density or closure (P-clusters), the other a high degree of brokerage or (selective) entrepreneurship (SV-clusters). The framework proposed here also suggests a novel interpretation of the transformations that industrial districts of the first type have undergone under the pressure of globalization.

The fifth paper authored by Chaminade, Bellandi, Plechero, and Santini (2019) focuses on regional innovation systems and the possibilities of paths of industrial transformation. Their paper argues that that traditional manufacturing districts, corresponding to specialized RISs and characterized by various nuclei of specialization and know-how, may foster different trajectories in combination with extra-regional networks. In particular, they analyse the interplay between regional and national innovation systems, providing an overview of the effect that different multilevel dynamics have on local trajectories. The cases of the textile industrial districts in Prato (Italy) and Borås (Sweden) show specialized RISs can display not only path extension but also path renewal and creation strategies.

The following two papers introduce the relevant theme of internationalization and global value chain in clusters and industrial districts. The first one (Bettiol et al., 2019) is a bridge between the theme of innovation and internationalization, analysing whether internationalization has an impact on cluster firms' innovation outputs. The second one (Parrilli, 2019) focuses on globalization investigating the challenges that globalization pose to clusters and industrial districts, proposing two factors that may represent crucial conditions for the upgrading of clusters within global markets.

Bettiol et al. (2019) states that innovation in clusters is initially rooted in proximity among specialized actors, but over time it results from an interplay between the local and global levels. For the authors, the internationalization of production and the relocation of cluster manufacturing activities abroad open a debate on the impact of such dynamics on innovation, between knowledge acquisition opportunities and the weakening of local innovation activities. The paper contributes to the debate by empirically testing whether internationalization has an impact on cluster firms' innovation outputs. Based on a survey conducted among 259 Italian cluster firms, the results show that upstream and downstream internationalization *per se* does not impact innovation, measuring product, process, organizational, and marketing innovation outputs. On the contrary, collaboration with external actors, such as designers, research centres or universities, has a positive effect on firms' innovation outputs. This is consistent with the cluster model and with previous studies focusing on innovation in the cluster context. Our analyses show that it is not internationalization that matters when it comes to innovation for cluster firms. Innovation performances are influenced by the relational capabilities of cluster firms to connect and manage collaboration even outside the cluster scale.

The other paper on internationalization and clusters is the one of Parrilli (2019). In this paper, the author aims at discussing the growth potential of clusters in international markets. He states that over the past two decades, clusters and industrial districts have gone under increasing competitive pressure insofar as markets have progressively globalized. Lead companies, either foreign or home-grown multinationals, have globalized their operations while often reducing their commitment (e.g. investments) within clusters and districts. As a result, a number of second, third and fourth tier suppliers disconnect from global value chains coordinated by lead companies, leaving the cluster fractured and jeopardizing local development prospects. Only a small segment of firms in the cluster copes with globalization. This situation represents a challenge that clusters and districts need to take on. Parrilli's paper inquires about the importance of two factors that may represent crucial conditions for the upgrading of clusters within global markets. The long-term commitment of lead companies to the local economy, together with the dense interaction between the regional innovation system and the lead companies and their new global innovation network, are found to be crucial elements for the resilience of clusters/districts and their small and medium-sized firms. A few successful clusters are considered vis-à-vis others that face higher risks of internal fracture. This work analyses relevant cases in Spain, Italy, and Costa Rica.

Finally, the last two papers deal with the concept of relatedness and diversification/specialization of regions. The first one (Innocenti & Lazzeretti, 2019b) presents an empirical analysis of the role of relatedness and knowledge bases for employment growth, while the second one (Hassink & Gong, 2019) focuses on smart specialization strategy proposing six critical questions in order to contribute to its conceptual advancement.

The first paper by Innocenti and Lazzeretti (2019b) adopts an evolutionary economic geography framework to contribute to the literature on the combinatorial dimension of differentiated knowledge bases (KB). Their aim is to determine if there is a pattern of knowledge creation that does not rely on one specific knowledge base, and if the three knowledge bases require the presence of other related sectors to exploit their innovative capacity leading to the growth of the region. They apply Hidalgo et al.'s (2007) methodology of a revealed relatedness measure between sectors, thus measuring the relatedness between the three KB and the relatedness of each KB with all other sectors (outside). The results show how, at the local level, the sectors characterized by synthetic and symbolic knowledge bases in the presence of other sectors with a high degree of relatedness are able to increase the employment growth of the area.

In the last paper, Hassink and Gong (2019) deal with smart specialization strategy. During the last five years, we can observe a soaring academic interest in the concept of smart specialization. A burgeoning literature emerged both conceptually and empirically. In this paper, they pose six critiques so far identified in this emerging literature. The aim is to provide a critical lens for future research on smart specialization strategies and processes. They argue that: (1) Smart specialization is a confusing concept, as what it really means is diversification; (2) It is largely predicated on a conventional science and technology (S&T) model of innovation and regional economic development, whereas socio-ecological innovation and social innovation, have only been implicitly mentioned, at best; (3) It is the continuation of cluster policies, rather than a brand-new policy instrument; (4) It contains a delusional transformative hope, although the entrepreneurial discovery process could very likely lead to lock-ins; (5) Structurally weak regions might be less likely to benefit from smart specialization; and (6) more rigorous measurements of smart specialization are still needed. By engaging systematically with these six issues, they aim to improve the effects of smart specialization as a policy programme and also to contribute to its conceptual advancement.

Notes

1. The conference tracks were the following: (1) Multinationals, clusters and global value chain; (2) Technological change and innovation networks; (3) Clusters and networks in CCIs; (4) Clusters in developing and emerging countries; (5) Cluster life cycle and evolutionary trajectories of local systems; (6) Relatedness, un/related variety and industrial structure; (7) Entrepreneurship in clusters and local systems; (8) Crisis and resilience of clusters and local systems; (9) Research methods on clusters, industrial districts and local systems; (10) Rethinking clusters and industrial districts. Exploring critical issues; (11) Industrial policy, clusters/platforms policy.
2. NVIVO groups together words with the same or similar meaning to that chosen as a label. For instance, the following words were grouped under the term 'Cluster': cluster, clusters, clustered, clustering, 'cluster', clusters', etc.

Disclosure statement

No potential conflict of interest was reported by the authors.

ORCID

L. Lazzeretti ⓘ http://orcid.org/0000-0002-9759-2289
F. Capone ⓘ http://orcid.org/0000-0003-2000-3033
S. R. Sedita ⓘ http://orcid.org/0000-0002-4589-6934

References

Andersson, T., Hansson, E. W., Schwaag-Serger, S., & Sorvik, J. (2004). *The cluster policies Whitebook*. Malmoe: IKED.
Autant-Bernard, C., Billand, P., Frachisse, D., & Massard, N. (2007). Social distance versus spatial distance in R&D cooperation: Empirical evidence from European collaboration choices in micro and nanotechnologies. *Papers in Regional Science, 86*(3), 495–519. doi:10.1111/j.1435-5957.2007.00132.x
Asheim, B. T., Boschma, R., & Cooke, P. (2011). Constructing regional advantage: Platform policies based on related variety and differentiated knowledge bases. *Regional Studies, 45*(7), 893–904. doi:10.1080/00343404.2010.543126
Balland, P. A. (2012). Proximity and the evolution of collaboration networks: evidence from research and development projects within the global navigation satellite system (GNSS) industry. *Regional Studies, 46*(6), 741–756. doi:10.1080/00343404.2010.529121
Balland, P. A., De Vaan, M., & Boschma, R. (2012). The dynamics of interfirm networks along the industry life cycle: The case of the global video game industry, 1987–2007. *Journal of Economic Geography, 13*(5), 741–765. doi:10.1093/jeg/lbs023
Barca, F., McCann, P., & Rodríguez-Pose, A. (2012). The case for regional development intervention: Place-based versus place-neutral approaches. *Journal of Regional Science, 52*(1), 134–152. doi:10.1111/j.1467-9787.2011.00756.x
Bathelt, H., Malmberg, A., & Maskell, P. (2004). Clusters and knowledge: local buzz, global pipelines and the process of knowledge creation. *Progress in Human Geography, 28*(1), 31–56. doi:10.1191/0309132504ph469oa
Bazeley, P., & Jackson, K. (Eds.). (2013). *Qualitative data analysis with NVivo*. London: Sage Publications Limited.
Beaudry, C., & Schiffauerova, A. (2009). Who's right, Marshall or Jacobs? The localization versus urbanization debate. *Research Policy, 38*(2), 318–337. doi:10.1016/j.respol.2008.11.010
Becattini, G. (1979). Dal "settore" industriale al "distretto" industriale. Alcune considerazioni sull'unità di indagine dell'economia industriale. *Rivista di Economia e Politica Industriale, 1*, 7–21.
Becattini, G. (2000). *Dal distretto industriale allo sviluppo locale: Svolgimento e difesa di una idea*. Torino: Bollati Boringhieri.
Becattini, G. (2015a). *La coscienza dei luoghi. Il territorio come soggetto corale*. Roma: Donzelli.
Becattini, G. (2015b). Beyond geo-sectoriality: The productive chorality of places. *Investigaciones Regionales / Journal of Regional Research, 32*, 31–41.
Becattini, G., Bellandi, M., Del Ottati, G., & Sforzi, F. (2003). *From industrial districts to local development*. Cheltenham: Edward Elgar.
Bellandi, M., De Propris, L., & Santini, E. (2019). An evolutionary analysis of industrial districts: the changing multiplicity of production know-how nuclei. *Cambridge Journal of Economics, 43*(1), 187–204. doi:10.1093/cje/bey012
Belussi, F., Caloffi, A., & Sedita, S. R. (2017). MNEs and clusters: The creation of place-anchored value chains. In *Local clusters in global value chains* (pp. 85–107). Cheltenham: Routledge.
Belussi, F., & Rita Sedita, S. (2008). The symbiotic division of labour between heterogeneous districts in the Dutch and Italian horticultural industry. *Urban Studies, 45*(13), 2715–2734. doi:10.1177/0042098008098202
Belussi, F., & Sammarra, A. (Eds.). (2009). *Business networks in clusters and industrial districts: The governance of the global value chain*. Cheltenham: Routledge.

Belussi, F., & Sedita, S. R. (2009a). Life cycle vs. multiple path dependency in industrial districts. *European Planning Studies*, *17*(4), 505–528. doi:10.1080/09654310802682065

Belussi, F., & Sedita, S. R. (2009b). Moving immigrants into Western industrial districts: The 'inverse'delocalization of the leather tanning district of Arzignano. In F. Belussi & A. Sammarra (Eds.), *Business networks in clusters and industrial districts* (pp. 166–175). Cheltenham: Routledge.

Benneworth, P., Danson, M., Raines, P., & Whittam, G. (2003). Confusing cluster? Making sense of the cluster approach in theory and practice. *European Planning Studies*, *11*, 511–520. doi:10.1080/09654310303651

Bettiol, M., Chiarvesio, M., Di Maria, E., & Gottardello, D. (2019). Local or global? Does internationalization drive innovation in clusters? *European Planning Studies*, 1–20. doi:10.1080/09654313.2019.1626806

Boix, R., Capone, F., De Propris, L., Lazzeretti, L., & Sanchez, D. (2016). Comparing creative industries in Europe. *European Urban and Regional Studies*, *23*(4), 935–940. doi:10.1177/0969776414541135

Boix, R., & Galletto, V. (2009). Innovation and industrial districts: A first approach to the measurement and determinants of the I-district effect. *Regional Studies*, *43*(9), 1117–1133. doi:10.1080/00343400801932342

Boix, R., Galletto, V., & Sforzi, F. (2019). Place-based innovation in industrial districts: The long-term evolution of the iMID effect in Spain (1991–2014). *European Planning Studies*, 1–19. doi:10.1080/09654313.2019.1588861

Boix, R., Hervás-Oliver, J. L., & De Miguel-Molina, B. (2015). Micro-geographies of creative industries clusters in Europe: From hot spots to assemblages. *Papers in Regional Science*, *94*(4), 753–772. doi:10.1111/pirs.12094

Boix, R., & Trullén, J. (2010). Industrial districts, innovation and I-district effect: Territory or industrial specialization? *European Planning Studies*, *18*(10), 1707–1729. doi:10.1080/09654313.2010.504351

Borgatti, S. P., Everett, M. G., & Freeman, L. C. (2002). *UCINET for windows: Software for social network analysis*.

Boschma, R. (2005). Proximity and innovation: a critical assessment. *Regional Studies*, *39*(1), 61–74. doi:10.1080/0034340052000320887

Boschma, R., & Fornahl, D. (2011). Cluster evolution and a roadmap for future research. *Regional Studies*, *45*(10), 1295–1298. doi:10.1080/00343404.2011.633253

Boschma, R., & Frenken, K. (2009). Technological relatedness and regional branching. In H. Bathelt, M. Feldman, & D. Kogler (Eds.), *Dynamic geographies of knowledge creation and innovation* (pp. 64–81). Routledge, Taylor and Francis.

Boschma, R., & Iammarino, S. (2009). Related variety, trade linkages, and regional growth in Italy. *Economic Geography*, *85*(3), 289–311. doi:10.1111/j.1944-8287.2009.01034.x

Breschi, S., & Malerba, F. (2005). *Clusters, networks and innovation*. Oxford: Oxford University Press.

Broekel, T., & Boschma, R. (2011). Knowledge networks in the Dutch aviation industry: the proximity paradox. *Journal of Economic Geography*, *12*(2), 409–433. doi:10.1093/jeg/lbr010

Burt, R. S. (2004). Structural holes and good ideas. *American Journal of Sociology*, *110*(2), 349–399. doi:10.1086/421787

Caloffi, A., Lazzeretti, L., & Sedita S. R. (2018). The story of cluster as a cross-boundary concept: From local development to management studies. In F. Belussi & J. Hervas (Eds.), *Agglomeration and firm performance* (pp. 123–137). Springer.

Cantwell, J. A., & Mudambi, R. (2011). Physical attraction and the geography of knowledge sourcing in multinational enterprises. *Global Strategy Journal*, *1*(3–4), 206–232. doi:10.1002/gsj.24

Capone, F. (2016). A bibliometric analysis on tourist destinations research: Focus on destination management and tourist cluster. In *Tourist clusters, destinations and competitiveness* (pp. 29–53). Cheltenham: Routledge.

Capone, F., & Lazzeretti, L. (2017). Inter-organisational networks and proximity: An analysis of R&D networks for cultural goods. *Sinergie Italian Journal of Management*, *34*(101), 53–70.

Capone, F., & Lazzeretti, L. (2018). The different roles of proximity in multiple informal network relationships. Evidence from the cluster of high technology applied to cultural goods in Tuscany. *Industry and Innovation*, 25(9), 897–917. doi:10.1080/13662716.2018.1442713

Chaminade, C., Bellandi, M., Plechero, M., & Santini, E. (2019). Understanding processes of path renewal and creation in thick specialized regional innovation systems. Evidence from two textile districts in Italy and Sweden. *European Planning Studies*, 1–17. doi:10.1080/09654313.2019.1610727

Coleman, J. C. (1988). Social capital in the creation of human capital. *American Journal of Sociology*, 94(1), S95–S120.

Cooke, P. (2018). Responsible research and innovation? From FinTech's 'flash crash' at Cermak to digitech's Willow Campus and Quayside. *European Planning Studies*. doi:10.1080/09654313.2018.1556610

Cooke, P., & Memedovic, O. (2001). *Strategies for regional innovation systems: learning transfer and applications*. Vienna: United Nations Industrial Development Organization.

Cooke, P., & Morgan, K. (1998). *The associational economy: Firms, regions, and innovation*. Oxford: Oxford University Press.

Cooke, P. N., Heidenreich, M., & Braczyk, H. J. (2004). *Regional innovation systems: The role of governance in a globalized world*. London: Psychology Press.

Cooke, P. N., & Lazzeretti, L. (Eds.). (2008). *Creative cities, cultural clusters and local economic development*. Cheltenham: Edward Elgar Publishing.

Crescenzi, R., & Gagliardi, L. (2018). The innovative performance of firms in heterogeneous environments: The interplay between external knowledge and internal absorptive capacities. *Research Policy*, 47(4), 782–795. doi:10.1016/j.respol.2018.02.006

Cruz, S. C., & Teixeira, A. A. (2010). The evolution of the cluster literature: Shedding light on the regional studies–regional science debate. *Regional Studies*, 44(9), 1263–1288. doi:10.1080/00343400903234670

D'Este, P., Iammarino, S., Savona, M., & von Tunzelmann, N. (2012). What hampers innovation? Revealed barriers versus deterring barriers. *Research Policy*, 41(2), 482–488. doi:10.1016/j.respol.2011.09.008

De Marchi, V., Di Maria, E., & Gereffi, G. (Eds.). (2017). *Local clusters in global value chains: Linking actors and territories through manufacturing and innovation*. Cheltenham: Routledge.

De Stefano, D., & Zaccarin, S. (2013). Modelling multiple interactions in science and technology networks. *Industry and Innovation*, 20(3), 221–240. doi:10.1080/13662716.2013.791130

Dunning, J. H. (2009). Location and the multinational enterprise: A neglected factor? *Journal of International Business Studies*, 40(1), 5–19. doi:10.1057/jibs.2008.74

Elola, A., Valdaliso, J., Lopez, S. M., & Aranguren, M. J. (2012). Cluster life cycles, path dependency and regional economic development: Insights from a meta-study on Basque clusters. *European Planning Studies*, 20(2), 257–279. doi:10.1080/09654313.2012.650902

Feldman, R., & Sanger, J. (2006). *The text mining handbook*. New York: Cambridge University Press.

Ferriani, S., Fonti, F., & Corrado, R. (2013). The social and economic bases of network multiplexity: Exploring the emergence of multiplex ties. *Strategic Organization*, 11(1), 7–34. doi:10.1177/1476127012461576

Fichter, K. (2005). *Interpreneurship: Nachhaltigkeitsinnovationen in interaktiven Perspektiven eines vernetzenden Unternehmertums*. Marburg: Metropolis.

Fitjar, R. D., & Rodríguez-Pose, A. (2017). Nothing is in the air. *Growth and Change*, 48(1), 22–39. doi:10.1111/grow.12161

Florida, R. (2002). *The rise of the creative class*. New York: Basic books.

Foray, D., David, P. A., & Hall, B. (2009). Smart specialisation – the concept. Knowledge economists' policy brief, n. 9. Retrieved from http://ec.europa.eu/invest-in-research/pdf/download_en/kfg_policy_brief_no9.pdf

Frenken, K., Van Oort, F., & Verburg, T. (2007). Related variety, unrelated variety and regional economic growth. *Regional Studies*, 41(5), 685–697. doi:10.1080/00343400601120296

Fromhold-Eisebith, M., & Eisebith, G. (2005). How to institutionalize innovative clusters? Comparing explicit top-down and implicit bottom-up approaches. *Research Policy*, *34*(8), 1250–1268. doi:10.1016/j.respol.2005.02.008

Galletto, V., & Boix, R. (2014). Distritos industriales, innovación tecnológica y efecto I-distrito: ¿Una cuestión de volumen o de valor? *Investigaciones Regionales / Journal of Regional Research*, *30*, 27–51.

Garofoli, G. (1991). Local networks, innovation and policy in Italian industrial districts. In E. M. Bergman et al. (Eds.), *Regions reconsidered* (pp. 119–140). London: Mansell.

Gereffi, G. (1999). International trade and industrial upgrading in the apparel commodity chain. *Journal of International Economics*, *48*(1), 37–70. doi:10.1016/S0022-1996(98)00075-0

Gereffi, G., & Bair, J. (2001). Local clusters in global chains: The causes and consequences of export dynamism in Torreon's blue jeans industry. *World Development*, *29*(11), 1885–1903. doi:10.1016/S0305-750X(01)00075-4

Gereffi, G., Humphrey, J., & Sturgeon, T. (2005). The governance of global value chains. *Review of International Political Economy*, *12*(1), 78–104. doi:10.1080/09692290500049805

Gereffi, G., & Kaplinsky, R. (2001). The value of value chain: Spreading the gains from globalisation. *IDS Bulletin*, *32*, 3.

Gereffi, G., & Korzeniewicz, M. (Eds.). (1994). *Commodity chains and global capitalism*. Westport: Praeger.

Gilbert, B. A. (2012). Creative destruction: Identifying its geographic origins. *Research Policy*, *41*(4), 734–742. doi:10.1016/j.respol.2011.11.005

Gilbert, B. A., McDougall, P. P., & Audretsch, D. B. (2008). Clusters, knowledge spillovers and new venture performance: An empirical examination. *Journal of Business Venturing*, *23*(4), 405–422. doi:10.1016/j.jbusvent.2007.04.003

Giuliani, E. (2013). Network dynamics in regional clusters: Evidence from Chile. *Research Policy*, *42*(8), 1406–1419. doi:10.1016/j.respol.2013.04.002

Giuliani, E., & Bell, M. (2005). The micro-determinants of meso-level learning and innovation: Evidence from a Chilean wine cluster. *Research Policy*, *34*(1), 47–68. doi:10.1016/j.respol.2004.10.008

Glänzel, W., Schlemmer, B., Schubert, A., & Thijs, B. (2006). Proceedings literature as additional data source for bibliometric analysis. *Scientometrics*, *68*(3), 457–473. doi:10.1007/s11192-006-0124-y

Glasmeier, A. (1991). Technological discontinuities and flexible production networks: The case of Switzerland and the world watch industry. *Research Policy*, *20*(5), 469–485. doi:10.1016/0048-7333(91)90070-7

Gordon, I. R., & McCann, P. (2000). Industrial clusters: Complexes, agglomeration and/or social networks? *Urban Studies*, *37*(3), 513–532. doi:10.1080/0042098002096

Grabher, G. (1993). The weakness of strong ties. In G. Grabher (Ed.), *The embedded firms* (pp. 255–277). London: Routledge.

Grandinetti, R. (2019). Rereading industrial districts through the lens of entrepreneurship. *European Planning Studies*, 1–19. doi:10.1080/09654313.2019.1614151

Granovetter, M. (1973). The strength of weak ties. *American Journal of Sociology*, *78*(6), 1360–1380.

Grashof, N., Hesse, K., & Fornahl, D. (2019). Radical or not? The role of clusters in the emergence of radical innovations. *European Planning Studies*. doi:10.1080/09654313.2019.1631260

Hartmann, D. (2014). *Economic complexity and human development*. London: Routledge.

Hassink, R., & Gong, H. (2019). Six critical questions about smart specialization. *European Planning Studies*.

Heidenreich, M., & Plaza, B. (2015). Renewal through culture? The role of museums in the renewal of industrial regions in Europe. *European Planning Studies*, *23*(8), 1441–1455. doi:10.1080/09654313.2013.817544

Hervas-Oliver, J., Belussi, F., Sedita, S. R., Caloffi, A., & Gonzalez, G. (2018, April 10–14). *Approaching multinationals in clusters from different perspectives: Making sense of MNEs in geographic spaces*. Paper presented at AAG Annual Meeting, New Orleans.

Hervás-Oliver, J. L., Albors-Garrigos, J., Estelles-Miguel, S., & Boronat-Moll, C. (2018). Radical innovation in Marshallian industrial districts. *Regional Studies, 5*(10), 1–10.
Hervas-Oliver, J. L., Gonzalez, G., Caja, P., & Sempere-Ripoll, F. (2015). Clusters and industrial districts: Where is the literature going? Identifying emerging sub-fields of research. *European Planning Studies, 23*(9), 1827–1872. doi:10.1080/09654313.2015.1021300
Hervas-Oliver, J. L., Sempere-Ripoll, F., Estelles-Miguel, S., & Rojas-Alvarado, R. (2019). Radical vs incremental innovation in Marshallian industrial districts in the Valencian region: What prevails? *European Planning Studies,* 1–16. doi:10.1080/09654313.2019.1638887
Hervas-Oliver, J. L., Sempere-Ripoll, F., Rojas-Alvarado, R., & Estelles-Miguel, S. (2018). Agglomerations and firm performance: Who benefits and how much? *Regional Studies, 52*(3), 338–349. doi:10.1080/00343404.2017.1297895
Hidalgo, C. A., & Hausmann, R. (2009). The building blocks of economic complexity. *Proceedings of the National Academy of Sciences, 106*(26), 10570–10575. doi:10.1073/pnas.0900943106
Hidalgo, C. A., Klinger, B., Barabási, A. L., & Hausmann, R. (2007). The product space conditions the development of nations. *Science, 317*(5837), 482–487. doi:10.1126/science.1144581
Hospers, G. J. (2005). Best practices' and the dilemma of regional cluster policy in Europe. *Tijdschrift voor economische en sociale geografie, 96*(4), 452–457. doi:10.1111/j.1467-9663.2005.00476.x
Hospers, G. J. (2006). Silicon somewhere? Assessing the usefulness of best practices in regional policy. *Policy Studies, 27*(1), 1–15. doi:10.1080/01442870500499934
Iammarino, S., & McCann, P. (2006). The structure and evolution of industrial clusters: Transactions, technology and knowledge spillovers. *Research Policy, 35*(7), 1018–1036. doi:10.1016/j.respol.2006.05.004
Iammarino, S., & McCann, P. (2013). *Multinationals and economic geography: Location, technology and innovation*. Cheltenham: Edward Elgar Publishing.
Innocenti, N., & Lazzeretti, L. (2019a). Do the creative industries support growth and innovation in the wider economy? Industry relatedness and employment growth in Italy. *Industry and Innovation,* 1–22. doi:10.1080/13662716.2018.1561360
Innocenti, N., & Lazzeretti, L. (2019b). Growth in regions, knowledge bases and relatedness: Some insights from the Italian case. *European Planning Studies,* 1–15. doi:10.1080/09654313.2019.1588862
Jones, C., Lorenzen, M., & Sapsed, J. (Eds.). (2015). *The Oxford handbook of creative industries*. Oxford: Oxford University Press.
Ketels, C. (2013). Recent research on competitiveness and clusters: What are the implications for regional policy? *Cambridge Journal of Regions, Economy and Society, 6*(2), 269–284. doi:10.1093/cjres/rst008
Knoben, J., Arikan, A. T., van Oort, F., & Raspe, O. (2016). Agglomeration and firm performance: One firm's medicine is another firm's poison. *Environment and Planning A: Economy and Space, 48*(1), 132–153. doi:10.1177/0308518X15602898
Koschatzky, K. (2012). *Cluster quo vadis? The future of the cluster concept* (No. R1/2012). Working papers firms and region.
Koschatzky, K., Schnabl, E., Zenker, A., Stahlecker, T., & Kroll, H. (2014). *The role of associations in regional innovation systems* (No. R4/2014). Working Papers Firms and Region.
Lazega, E., & Snijders, T. A. (Eds.). (2015). *Multilevel network analysis for the social sciences: Theory, methods and applications*. Dordrecht: Springer.
Lazzeretti, L., Boix, R., & Capone, F. (2008). Do creative industries cluster? Mapping creative local production systems in Italy and Spain. *Industry and Innovation, 15*(5), 549–567. doi:10.1080/13662710802374161
Lazzeretti, L., & Capone, F. (2016). How proximity matters in innovation networks dynamics along the cluster evolution. A study of the high technology applied to cultural goods. *Journal of Business Research, 69*(12), 5855–5865. doi:10.1016/j.jbusres.2016.04.068
Lazzeretti, L., Capone, F., & Innocenti, N. (2017). Exploring the intellectual structure of creative economy research and local economic development: a co-citation analysis. *European Planning Studies, 25,* 1693–1713. doi:10.1080/09654313.2017.1337728

Lazzeretti, L., & Cooke, P. (2017). Responding to and resisting resilience. *European Planning Studies*, *25*(1), 1–9. doi:10.1080/09654313.2016.1270911

Lazzeretti, L., Sedita, S. R., & Caloffi, A. (2014). Founders and disseminators of cluster research. *Journal of Economic Geography*, *14*(1), 21–43. doi:10.1093/jeg/lbs053

Lazzeretti, L., & Vecco, M. (Eds.). (2018). *Creative industries and entrepreneurship: Paradigms in transition from a global perspective*. Cheltenham: Edward Elgar Publishing.

Lee, C. Y. (2018). Geographical clustering and firm growth: Differential growth performance among clustered firms. *Research Policy*, *47*(6), 1173–1184. doi:10.1016/j.respol.2018.04.002

Li, P., Bathelt, H., & Wang, J. (2012). Network dynamics and cluster evolution: Changing trajectories of the aluminium extrusion industry in Dali, China. *Journal of Economic Geography*, *12*, 127–155. doi:10.1093/jeg/lbr024

Lisée, C., Larivière, V., & Archambault, É. (2008). Conference proceedings as a source of scientific information: A bibliometric analysis. *Journal of the American Society for Information Science and Technology*, *59*(11), 1776–1784. doi:10.1002/asi.20888

Loasby, B. (2004). Un distretto industriale. In N. Bellanca, M. Dardi, & T. Raffaelli (Eds.), *Economia Senza Gabbie* (pp. 219–271). Bologna: Il Mulino.

MacKenzie, D. (2008). *An engine, not a camera: How financial models shape markets*. Cambridge: MIT Press.

Markard, J., Raven, R., & Truffer, B. (2012). Sustainability transitions: An emerging field of research and its prospects. *Research Policy*, *41*(6), 955–967. doi:10.1016/j.respol.2012.02.013

Markusen, A. R. (1985). *Profit cycles, oligopoly and regional development*. Cambridge: MIT Press.

Markusen, A., Wassall, G. H., DeNatale, D., & Cohen, R. (2008). Defining the creative economy: Industry and occupational approaches. *Economic Development Quarterly*, *22*(1), 24–45. doi:10.1177/0891242407311862

Martin, R. (2012). Regional economic resilience, hysteresis and recessionary shocks. *Journal of Economic Geography*, *12*(1), 1–32. doi:10.1093/jeg/lbr019

Martin, R., & Sunley, P. (2003). Deconstructing clusters: Chaotic concept or policy panacea? *Journal of Economic Geography*, *3*(1), 5–35. doi:10.1093/jeg/3.1.5

Martin, R., & Sunley, P. (2011). Conceptualizing cluster evolution: Beyond the life cycle model? *Regional Studies*, *45*(10), 1299–1318. doi:10.1080/00343404.2011.622263

Maskell, P., & Kebir, L. (2006). What qualifies as a cluster theory. In *Clusters and regional development: Critical reflections and explorations* (pp. 30–49). Cheltenham: Routledge.

Maskell, P., & Malmberg, A. (1999). Localised learning and industrial competitiveness. *Cambridge Journal of Economics*, *23*(2), 167–185. doi:10.1093/cje/23.2.167

McCann, B. T., & Folta, T. B. (2011). Performance differentials within geographic clusters. *Journal of Business Venturing*, *26*(1), 104–123. doi:10.1016/j.jbusvent.2009.04.004

Metcalfe, J. S. (1994). Evolutionary economics and technology policy. *The Economic Journal*, *104* (425), 931–944. doi:10.2307/2234988

Morrison, A., Pietrobelli, C., & Rabellotti, R. (2008). Global value chains and technological capabilities: A framework to study learning and innovation in developing countries. *Oxford Development Studies*, *36*(1), 39–58. doi:10.1080/13600810701848144

Myles Shaver, J., & Flyer, F. (2000). Agglomeration economies, firm heterogeneity, and foreign direct investment in the United States. *Strategic Management Journal*, *21*(12), 1175–1193. Doi:10.1002/1097-0266(200012)21:12<1175::AID-SMJ139>3.0.CO;2-Q

Neffke, F., & Henning, M. (2013). Skill relatedness and firm diversification. *Strategic Management Journal*, *34*(3), 297–316. doi:10.1002/smj.2014

Oliva, S., & Lazzeretti, L. (2017). Adaptation, adaptability and resilience: The recovery of Kobe after the great Hanshin Earthquake of 1995. *European Planning Studies*, *25*(1), 67–87. doi:10.1080/09654313.2016.1260093

Østergaard, C., & Park, E. K. (2013). Cluster decline and resilience – The case of the wireless communication cluster in North Jutland, Denmark. Retrieved from https://ssrn.com/abstract=2196445

Ostergaard, C. R., & Park, E. (2015). What makes clusters decline? A study on disruption and evolution of a high-tech cluster in Denmark. *Regional Studies, 49*(5), 834–849. doi:10.1080/00343404.2015.1015975

Owen, R., Macnaghten, P., & Stilgoe, J. (2012). Responsible research and innovation: From science in society to science for society, with society. *Science and Public Policy, 39*(6), 751–760. doi:10.1093/scipol/scs093

Ooms, W., Werker, C., & Caniëls, M. (2018). Personal and social proximity empowering collaborations: the glue of knowledge networks. *Industry and Innovation, 25*(9), 833–840. doi:10.1080/13662716.2018.1493983

Pagliacci, F., & Russo, M. (2016). Socio-economic effects of an earthquake: Does sub-regional counterfactual sampling matter in estimates? An empirical test on the 2012 Emilia-Romagna earthquake. *DEMB Working paper series*, 1–27.

Parrilli, M. D. (2019). Clusters and internationalization: The role of lead firms' commitment and RIS proactivity in tackling the risk of internal fractures. *European Planning Studies*, 1–19. doi:10.1080/09654313.2019.1635087

Powell, W. W., Koput, K. W., & Smith-Doerr, L. (1996). Interorganizational collaboration and the locus of innovation: Networks of learning in biotechnology. *Administrative Science Quarterly, 41*(1), 116–145. doi:10.2307/2393988

Powell, W. W., & Grodal, S. (2005). Networks of innovators. In J. Fagerberg, D. C. Mowery, & R. R. Nelson (Eds.), *The Oxford handbook of innovation* (pp. 56–85). Oxford: Oxford University Press.

Pratt, A. C. (2008). Creative cities: The cultural industries and the creative class. *Geografiska Annaler: Series B, Human Geography, 90*(2), 107–117. doi:10.1111/j.1468-0467.2008.00281.x

Quintana-Garcia, C., & Benavides-Velasco, C. (2008). Innovative competence, exploration and exploitation: The influence of technological diversification. *Research Policy, 37*, 492–507. doi:10.1016/j.respol.2007.12.002

UNESCO. (2013). *Creative economy report. Widening local development pathways*. New York: UNESCO.

Richards, G. (2011). Creativity and tourism: The state of the art. *Annals of Tourism Research, 38*(4), 1225–1253. doi:10.1016/j.annals.2011.07.008

Rigby, D. L., & Brown, W. M. (2015). Who benefits from agglomeration? *Regional Studies, 49*(1), 28–43. doi:10.1080/00343404.2012.753141

Robertson, P. L., & Langlois, R. N. (1995). Innovation, networks, and vertical integration. *Research Policy, 24*(4), 543–562. doi:10.1016/S0048-7333(94)00786-1

Salavisa, I., Sousa, C., & Fontes, M. (2012). Topologies of innovation networks in knowledge-intensive sectors: Sectoral differences in the access to knowledge and complementary assets through formal and informal ties. *Technovation, 32*(6), 380–399. doi:10.1016/j.technovation.2012.02.003

Schiederig, T., Tietze, F., & Herstatt, C. (2012). Green innovation in technology and innovation management – An exploratory literature review. *R&D Management, 42*(2), 180–192. doi:10.1111/j.1467-9310.2011.00672.x

Sedita, S. R., Caloffi, A., & Lazzeretti, L. (2018). The invisible college of cluster research: A bibliometric core–periphery analysis of the literature. *Industry and Innovation*, 1–23. doi:10.1080/13662716.2018.1538872

Snijders, T. A., Lomi, A., and Torló, V. J. (2013). A model for the multiplex dynamics of two-mode and one-mode networks, with an application to employment preference, friendship, and advice. *Social Networks, 35*(2), 265–276. doi:10.1016/j.socnet.2012.05.005

Sorenson, O., & Audia, P. G. (2000). The social structure of entrepreneurial activity: Geographic concentration of footwear production in the United States, 1940–1989. *American Journal of Sociology, 106*(2), 424–462. doi:10.1086/316962

Strambach, S. (2017). Combining knowledge bases in transnational sustainability innovation: Microdynamics and institutional change. *Economic Geography, 93*(5), 500–526. doi:10.1080/00130095.2017.1366268

Sunley, P. (1992). Marshallian industrial districts: The case of the Lancashire cotton industry in the inter-war years. *Transactions of the Institute of British Geographers, 17*, 306–320. doi:10.2307/622882

Tallman, S., Jenkins, M., Henry, N., & Pinch, S. (2004). *Knowledge, clusters, and competitive advantage. Academy of Management Review*, 29(2), 258–271. doi:10.2307/20159032

Ter Wal, A. L. (2013). The dynamics of the inventor network in German biotechnology: geographic proximity versus triadic closure. *Journal of Economic Geography*, 14(3), 589–620. doi:10.1093/jeg/lbs063

Van Oort, F. (2015). Unity in variety? Agglomeration economics beyond the specialization-diversity controversy. In C. Karlsson, M. Andersson, & T. Norman (Eds.), *Handbook of research methods and applications in economic geography* (pp. 259–271). Cheltenham: Edward Elgar.

Wang, P., Robins, G., Pattison, P., and Lazega, E. (2013). Exponential random graph models for multilevel networks. *Social Networks*, 35(1), 96–115. doi:10.1016/j.socnet.2013.01.004

Wasserman, S., & Faust, K. (1994). *Social network analysis: Methods and applications*. Cambridge: Cambridge University Press.

Wolfe, D. A., & Nelles, J. (2008). The role of civic capital and civic associations in cluster policy. In C. Karlsson (Ed.), *Handbook of research on innovation and clusters: Cases and policies* (pp. 374–392). Cheltenham: Edward Elgar.

Woolthuis, R. K., Lankhuizen, M., & Gilsing, V. (2005). A system failure framework for innovation policy design. *Technovation*, 25(6), 609–619. doi:10.1016/j.technovation.2003.11.002

Zuboff, S. (2019). *The age of surveillance capitalism*. London: Profile.

Radical or not? The role of clusters in the emergence of radical innovations

Nils Grashof, Kolja Hesse and Dirk Fornahl

ABSTRACT
Recently, radical innovations have received increasing attention in order to achieve long-term economic success. Regional clusters, being frequently used as an innovation policy instrument, have been shown to have the potential to support innovations in general. However, it remains unclear whether clusters are really a beneficial environment for the generation of radical innovations. This study aims to shed light on the specific role clusters can play in radical innovation processes. In order to do this, we apply a quantitative approach on the firm-level and combine several data sources (e.g. AMADEUS, PATSTAT, German subsidy catalogue). Our results show that clusters indeed provide a suitable environment for radical innovations. Furthermore, we find that radical innovations rather occur in the periphery of the cluster, where actors tend to be more open to the exchange of external knowledge. This happens in general through linkages with other actors, which we also find to be beneficial for the emergence of radical innovations up to a certain degree. Our findings implicate that policy makers should continue to support clusters and further develop funding schemes. Moreover, managers should be open to collaborations with other actors for the cross-fertilization of knowledge to promote radical innovations.

1. Introduction

Innovations are commonly accepted to be a key factor for economic growth (e.g. Rosenberg, 2004; Verspagen, 2006). Recently, especially the outstanding opportunities arising from rather radical innovations have been highlighted (Castaldi, Frenken, & Los, 2015). These kinds of innovations combine knowledge pieces that have not been combined before and consequently create something radically new (Fleming, 2001; Nerkar, 2003; Weitzman, 1998). If successful, they can open up completely new markets and industries as well as provide the basis for a long-lasting competitive advantage (Castaldi et al., 2015; Henderson & Clark, 1990; Verhoeven, Bakker, & Veugelers, 2016). From a firm's perspective, they are desirable to enhance their competitiveness (Zhang, Wei, Yang, & Zhu, 2018). Policy makers have also recognized this great economic potential of radical innovations. For instance, in 2019 the German government will establish a public agency for the promotion of radical innovations in Germany (BMBF, 2018).

An already prevalent instrument of innovation policy are regional clusters (Brown, Burgees, Festing, Royer, & Steffen, 2007; Cantner, Graf, & Rothgang, 2018; EFI, 2015; Festing, Royer, & Steffen, 2012), which have been shown to foster the innovativeness of firms (Baptista & Swann, 1998; Bell, 2005). Nevertheless, there also exist contradictory evidence about the effect of clusters on firm's innovativeness (e.g. Pouder & St. John, 1996). It therefore still remains unclear whether clusters are a beneficial environment for innovations in general (Martin & Sunley, 2003) and the generation of radical innovations in particular (Hervás-Oliver, Albors-Garrigos, Estelles-Miguel, & Boronat-Moll, 2018a). In theory, there exist two opposing streams of reasoning in this context. On the one hand, the relatively fast and eased diffusion of knowledge (e.g. via labour mobility), particularly of tacit knowledge, can challenge current thinking, which may result in radical new ideas (Braunerhjelm, Ding, & Thulin, 2017; Mascitelli, 2000; Otto & Fornahl, 2010). On the other hand, firms located within clusters may also be confronted with an inertia regarding potential changes due to uniform thinking and a lack of new challenging external ideas (Boschma, 2005; Martin & Sunley, 2003; Pouder & St. John, 1996). In order to contribute to a clarification, the following research question shall be answered: Does being located in a cluster increase the likelihood to create radical innovations?

By answering this research question in a quantitative way, our study makes a so far pioneering step towards explaining empirically the relationship between clusters and radical innovations. Besides contributing to close a research gap, this paper also has a rather practical meaning for companies as well as policy makers. It does not only show evidence that being located in a cluster can contribute to the emergence of radical innovations, but also deals with the corresponding conditions necessary to generate radical innovations in clusters.

The remainder of this paper is structured in the following way: The subsequent chapter deals with the theoretical background on radical innovations and clusters and combines both strands of literature. Moreover, we embed our hypothesis based on an extensive literature review. In the third section, we describe our data and methodology. After that, the paper turns to the empirical analysis. First, we present some descriptive statistics on our sample and then, we discuss our econometrical results. Finally, the study draws conclusions from our results and points out possible future research endeavours.

2. Theory and hypotheses

During the last decades, it has become common sense that innovations are a core factor for economic growth (Cortright, 2001; Rosenberg, 2004; Verspagen, 2006). In addition, scholars have found evidence that new knowledge, which is transformed into innovations, builds on already existing knowledge pieces. For instance, Weitzman (1998) stated that existing knowledge is recombined in a new way to form new artefacts. Hence, innovative search processes have a cumulative nature (Arthur, 2007; Basalla, 1988).

We can distinguish between two types of new knowledge creation, namely incremental and radical innovations. Most innovations rely on well-defined knowledge pieces, which are recombined repeatedly and hence represent small improvements. These incremental innovations develop mostly alongside well-known knowledge trajectories (Dosi, 1982). On the other hand, search processes that are radical in nature combine knowledge pieces that have not been combined before (Fleming, 2001; Nerkar, 2003; Weitzman,

1998). New combinations then emerge when inventors discover a new purpose for their existing knowledge or they fuse together some external expertise with their own mindset (Desrochers, 2001). A good example is, for instance, the new combination of the technological fields automotive, sensor-based safety systems, communication and high-resolution mapping which are combined for the first time in the self-driving car (Boschma, 2017). Radical innovations are more likely to fail and are accompanied with higher uncertainty in terms of their economic impact in the future (Strumsky & Lobo, 2015). However, if successful, these innovations can bring about a paradigm shift and thus radical change (Dosi, 1982; Verhoeven et al., 2016). This radical change can lead to the formation of new markets and entire industries thereby disrupting old ones (e.g. Henderson & Clark, 1990; Tushman & Anderson, 1986). Radical innovations can introduce a new set of performance features or have a higher functional quality and improve performance significantly (Bers, Dismukes, Miller, & Dubrovensky, 2009). Also, they may reduce cost compared to existing products and may alter the characteristics of the market, such as consumer expectations (Nagy, Schuessler, & Dubinsky, 2016). Hence, radical innovations can help to build a strong competitive advantage (Castaldi et al., 2015) and serve as the basis for future sustainable economic growth (Ahuja & Morris Lampert, 2001; Arthur, 2007).

Scientific literature has used several methodologies to analyse radical innovations empirically mainly based on indicators using forward (e.g. Albert, Avery, Narin, & McAllister, 1991 Trajtenberg, 1990;) and backward (e.g. Rosenkopf & Nerkar, 2001) citations on patents. Recently, approaches following the theoretical concept of recombinant innovation particularly focus on technology classes provided in patent documents to study the nature of radical innovations (e.g. Fleming, 2007; Strumsky & Lobo, 2015; Verhoeven et al., 2016). Our study follows this notion and defines radical innovations as the result of search processes that combine unconnected knowledge domains for the first time (Fleming, 2001, 2007; Rizzo, Barbieri, Ramaciotti, & Iannantuono, 2018). Thus, we focus especially on the emergence of radical innovations, instead of its diffusion. The high degree of radicalness is indicated by the new combination of knowledge. Despite the fact that we cannot predict if these new combinations will have a major impact in the future, we term them 'radical' since they introduce totally novel knowledge combinations (Rizzo et al., 2018; Verhoeven et al., 2016). In line with, e.g. Dahlin and Behrens (2005), we argue that radical innovations have two dimensions (emergence and impact) which are worth inspecting.[1]

In the context of regional clusters, however, the concept of radical innovations has been under-researched (Hervás-Oliver et al., 2018a). This holds especially true for quantitative empirical studies. In light of the popularity and widespread application of the cluster concept, also in terms of policy funding measures, this research gap is particularly astonishing (Brown et al., 2007; EFI, 2015; Martin & Sunley, 2003). In line with Grashof and Fornahl (2017), clusters are here defined as: '[…] a geographical concentration of closely interconnected horizontal, vertical and lateral actors, such as universities, from the same industry that are related to each other in terms of a common resource and knowledge base, technologies and/or product-market' (Grashof & Fornahl, 2017, p. 4).[2] It has been emphasized that clusters can be a preferable environment for fostering firm's innovativeness (Baptista & Swann, 1998; Bell, 2005; Porter, 1998). Although, recently it has been argued that this rather positive relationship between clusters and firm performance also depends on the specific context (e.g. firm and cluster characteristics). Thus, contextual variables, such as cluster size and the industry characteristics, should additionally be considered when investigating firm-specific cluster effects (Frenken, Cefis, & Stam, 2013; Knoben, Arikan, Van Oort, & Raspe, 2015; Rigby & Brown, 2015).

In his pioneering contribution, Marshall (1920) considers the firm-specific advantages of being located in close proximity to similar firms.[3] He emphasized in this context four types of externalities: access to specialized labour, access to specialized inputs, access to knowledge spillovers and access to greater demand by reducing the consumer search costs (Marshall, 1920; McCann & Folta, 2008). Besides promoting innovations in general, these externalities within clusters can likewise provide a fertile ground for the creation of radical innovations in particular. As presented in several case studies dealing with the Silicon Valley (e.g. Brown & Duguid, 2000; Casper, 2007; Saxenian, 1994), the existence of a pooled specialized labour market is beneficial for the emergence of radically new ideas. The pooling of specialized employers and employees in geographical proximity simplifies the search process and strengthens the overall matching quality, leading to an alleviated mobility of employees. The extensive labour mobility is in turn considered to further facilitate localized spillovers of embodied tacit knowledge. The faster diffusion of such knowledge within clusters is essential for collective learning processes and innovation activities of the corresponding firms (Amend & Herbst, 2008; Otto & Fornahl, 2010). This holds particularly true for rather radical innovation activities, as the new knowledge incorporated in local human resources can challenge established processes and ways of thinking, originating potentially radical new insights (Bekkers & Freitas, 2008; Braunerhjelm et al., 2017; Zucker, Darby, & Torero, 2002). In addition to the knowledge diffusion via labour mobility, more generally it has been argued that geographic proximity within clusters can facilitate the transfer of common knowledge (Jaffe, Trajtenberg, & Henderson, 1993) and particularly the dissemination of tacit knowledge due to the higher likelihood of face-to-face contacts, being an efficient medium for the transfer of such knowledge (Daft & Lengel, 1986). This eased knowledge diffusion within clusters, especially the tacit one, is indeed a powerful source for the creation of radical innovations (Audretsch, 1998; Mascitelli, 2000). Glaeser, Kallal, Scheinkman, and Shleifer (1992) connoted in this context that '[...] intellectual breakthroughs must cross hallways and streets more easily than oceans and continents' (Glaeser et al., 1992, p. 1127). By analysing the geographic concentration of superstar patents across U.S. states, Castaldi and Los (2012) empirically confirm this observation. They find evidence that the regional clustering of these superstar patents is much higher than for non-superstar patents. Therefore, companies tend to locate in very specific geographic places for the development of technological breakthroughs, whereas standard innovations seem to happen in many more places (Castaldi et al., 2015; Castaldi & Los, 2012).

Nevertheless, it has also been suggested that over time firms located within clusters may face an inertia regarding market and technology changes, hampering radical innovations. For example, Pouder and St. John (1996) explain the firm performance decline over time with the convergent mental models of managers within the corresponding region, which reinforces old ways of thinking and thereby preventing the recognition of new ideas. Moreover, the exclusive reliance on local face-to-face contacts and tacit knowledge can make local networks especially vulnerable to lock-in situations, enforcing again the inertia of firms located in clusters (Boschma, 2005; Martin & Sunley, 2003). Consequently, it still remains rather unclear whether a cluster can contribute to the creation of radical innovations. Nevertheless, building on the previous theoretical literature contributions, the following hypothesis is proposed:

> **Hypothesis 1:** Being located in a cluster has a positive effect on the emergence of radical innovations in firms.

However, as already indicated, it is reasonable to assume that these potential benefits are not equally distributed (Frenken et al., 2013; Martin, 2009). The established and leading firms in clusters are for example argued to organize the overall knowledge network in a way that guarantees their central position within the corresponding clusters. They only share the specific knowledge, which is necessary to maintain their leading role, with other clustered companies. This directed knowledge exchange may be beneficial for these central actors, but it prevents the recognition of new ideas and thereby promoting an inertia (Hervás-Oliver et al., 2018a; Munari, Sobrero, & Malipiero, 2012). Thus, the following hypothesis is proposed:

> **Hypothesis 2:** A firm's central position in the cluster core has a negative effect on the emergence of radical innovations in this firm.

Besides the position within clusters it may also be crucial for firms to have a sufficiently large number of relationships. The increasing significance and proliferation of inter-firm alliances has promoted the development of the relational view (RV). The main idea of the RV is that internal resources (e.g. financial resources) are not sufficient for the realization of a competitive advantage, but additionally it is essential to consider relational resources, such as inter-firm relationships and routines (Dyer & Singh, 1998; Lavie, 2006; Steffen, 2012). This relational dimension has also been investigated in the context of clusters (Giuliani, 2007; Hervás-Oliver & Albors-Garrigos, 2009). In line with the relational view, it has been highlighted that the number of relationships is positively associated with firm's innovative performance by facilitating local and external knowledge-sharing as well as interactive learning processes (Hervás-Oliver & Albors-Garrigos, 2009; Zaheer & George, 2004). Regarding radical innovations, it can therefore be assumed that by providing access to new knowledge from the local and external environment the number of strategic relationships can mitigate the potential of a lock-in situation within clusters and thereby promote the creation of radical innovations. Nevertheless, it has also been highlighted that after a certain threshold the related costs may outweigh the benefits from collaborating. Engaging in numerous collaborations goes at the cost of intensive coordination expenditures as well as free-riding and unintended knowledge spillovers (Hottenrott & Lopes-Bento, 2016; Kesteloot & Veugelers, 1995). Too many relationships are therefore assumed to hinder the creation of radical innovations. Consequently, the following hypothesis is proposed:

> **Hypothesis 3:** The number of relationships to other organisations asserts an inverted u-shape effect on the emergence of radical innovations in firms, such that a moderate level of relationships is likely to be most beneficial.

Furthermore, the effect of the market and industry environment on firm's innovative performance has been widely acknowledged (Kohlbacher, Weitlaner, Hollosi, Grünwald, & Grahsl, 2013). Building on the theoretical insights proposed by Suarez and Lanzolla

(2005, 2007), dealing with external influences on the first-mover advantage, it is supposed that the pace of technology evolution also affects firm's innovative performance. The pace of technology is captured by technology S curves, depicting the evolution of a technology or the corresponding industry along a particular performance parameter, such as the CPU clock speed in the computer industry. The technology evolution can vary significantly across different industries. While the development of efficiency improvements in the computer industry has been very high, it has only been marginal in the case of the vacuum cleaner industry (Cooper & Schendel, 1976; Suarez & Lanzolla, 2007). In general, it is likely that under a rapid technology evolution firm's current knowledge stock becomes rather unsuitable or even obsolete. The creation of radical innovations is therefore potentially hampered (Suarez & Lanzolla, 2005; Suarez & Lanzolla, 2007). Nevertheless, in clusters a different outcome can be expected. The specific cluster environment, fostering interactions and knowledge spillovers, protects the knowledge stock of the corresponding firms from being outdated. Firms located within clusters are therefore assumed to rather benefit from the new opportunities arising from the fast technology evolution than suffering from its negative accompaniments. Thus, the following hypothesis is proposed:

> **Hypothesis 4:** Firms located in a cluster have advantages in terms of producing radical innovations if the pace of technology evolution of industries is high.

Lastly, the size of the cluster is frequently discussed in the literature as an influential variable for firm's innovativeness (Folta, Cooper, & Baik, 2006; McCann & Folta, 2011). It has been asserted in this context that cluster size has an inverted u-shape effect on firm's innovative performance. Meaning that the marginal firm-specific benefits decline as the cluster grows, providing evidence for size-based negative externalities (Folta et al., 2006; McCann & Folta, 2008). On the one hand, clusters with several different actors provide access to more heterogeneous knowledge than smaller clusters, which is argued to be beneficial for the creation of radically new ideas (Menzel & Fornahl, 2010). On the other hand, at some point a size increase can convert the previously positive aspect of competition into a negative one. The higher density of similar firms encourages the competition within clusters, leading to scarcity of crucial input factors, such as human resources, and significantly higher costs (Folta et al., 2006; McCann & Folta, 2008). Particularly, the lack of adequate input factors can be an enormous obstacle for the development of radical innovations. Thus, the following hypothesis is proposed:

> **Hypothesis 5:** The size of the cluster has a reversed u-shape relation to the emergence of radical innovations in firms.

3. Data and methodology

To construct our final dataset, we employed several databases. The basic database for the empirical analysis providing detailed firm-specific information is the AMADEUS database offered by Bureau van Djik (BvD). It contains extensive firm-level data such as year of establishment, whether the firm is independent and employment data.

For the identification of all relevant clusters in Germany we apply the method by Brenner (2017). Therefore, we calculate a cluster index for each single company on the community level ('Gemeindeebene') based on official IAB employment data from 2012 in three-digit NACE Rev. 2[4] industries. Generally, this actor-based cluster identification offers two main advantages in comparison with more traditional indicators. First, the calculated indicator is free of predefined borders, so that the corresponding cluster identification does not depend on the regional level. Second, the applied index avoids a possible overvaluation of very large companies by using a distance decay function based on travel times (Brenner, 2017).[5] The applied cluster index additionally considers employment in absolute and relative terms. Thus, it accounts for the most central elements of cluster definitions, namely geographical proximity, regional concentration and specialization (Grashof & Fornahl, 2017). The corresponding cluster threshold, indicating whether a company is located in a cluster, has a value of two. It thereby follows the procedure of the European Cluster Observatory (European Cluster Observatory, 2018; European Communities, 2008).[6]

Furthermore, we use patent data retrieved from the European database PATSTAT, to identify radical innovations. We approximate the emergence of radical innovations by new combinations of formerly unconnected technology domains (new dyads). First, we identify all technology combinations proxied by IPC classes mentioned on patents in the years 2012–2014 in Germany. Then, we construct a dataset with all existing IPC combinations between 1983 and one year before the focal year. Subsequently, we compare both datasets to identify new combinations. Hence, a new combination is radical in the sense that it is completely new to Germany (since 1983).[7] Our analysis of IPC combinations is carried out at the four-digit level. This aggregation level is used to have a sufficiently large number of patents in the classes and a maximal number of technologies.

Moreover, patents are used to determine the pace of technology evolution of the corresponding industries (Audretsch & Feldman, 1996; McGahan & Silverman, 2001). By computing the average technological improvement (measured by the weighted number of patents) in three-digit NACE Rev. 2 code industries for a three-year period (2011–2013) it is controlled for possible outlier years. To also consider the industry size, the average technological improvement is then weighted by the size of the corresponding industry, which is measured by the average number of employees.

For the determination of the number of relationships data on subsidized R&D collaborations from the German subsidy catalogue ('Förderkatalog') is used. The German subsidy catalogue comprises approximately more than 160,000 running or already finished R&D projects financed by six different national ministries in the time period between 1960 and 2016 (Roesler & Broekel, 2017). It has been commonly used to capture cooperative relations in knowledge networks and it offers information at an earlier stage than patent data which is why the German subsidy catalogue fits adequately the purpose of this study (Broekel, 2015; Broekel & Graf, 2012). Due to the existing time lag between patents (see the main dependent variable) and received national subsidies, the unweighted number of firm linkages is computed based on all corresponding collaborative R&D projects between 2008 and 2010 (Fornahl, Broekel, & Boschma, 2011).

Regarding a firm's cluster position, various measures have been used (Broekel & Graf, 2012; Lechner & Leyronas, 2012). However, here the already presented cluster index by Brenner (2017) is applied. Apart from the identification of clusters, it also offers information about the position of each company within the corresponding cluster by taking the spatial concentration (in terms of employment) and the geographical distance on the firm-level into account. Hence, the cluster index is also applicable to determine whether a firm is located in the core or periphery of the cluster. Rather low values indicate that companies are located in the periphery, whereas high values emphasize that they are in the centre of the corresponding cluster (Brenner, 2017; Scholl & Brenner, 2016). For the calculation of the cluster size the employment data included in the AMADEUS database is used. In line with most common approaches (McCann & Folta, 2008), cluster size is here computed by the average number of employees within the corresponding cluster between 2012 and 2014.

Additionally, several control variables have been considered. To control for firm-specific influences, firm's age (years since foundation) as well as firm's corporate structure are added. Regarding the corporate structure, based on the AMADEUS database an independence dummy is calculated that indicates whether the corresponding firm is independent and does not belong to a corporate structure. Moreover, on the regional level it is controlled for the regional knowledge base, measured by the weighted number of patents in each administrative community ('Gemeindeebene'). Based on the German research directory ('Research Explorer'), containing information on over 25,000 university and non-university research institutes in Germany, the number of research institutes is additionally calculated on the community level (Research Explorer, 2018). Last, in order to correctly identify research-intensive industries, official data from the German Federal Statistics Office is additionally employed. Based on the corresponding NACE codes, a dummy variable is created that indicated whether an industry is rather research-intensive or not.

For the combination of the different datasets it is required to match the corresponding names of the companies listed in the comprehensive AMADEUS database with the applicants in the patent data and with the grant recipients (executive company) in the German subsidy catalogue, as a comparable identifier is missing.[8] The result of this matching process is a unique firm-level database.

Since our main dependent variable is binary, in line with other contributions (e.g. Hervás-Oliver, Sempere-Ripoll, Alvarado, & Estelles-Miguel, 2018b; McCann & Folta, 2011) we applied logistic regression to test our hypotheses. The logistic regression model has the following form:

$$\text{Logit}(\pi_i) = \beta 0 + \beta 1 \text{ Cluster dummy} + \beta 2 \text{ Central position} + \beta 3 \text{ Relationships} + \beta 4 \text{ Technology evolution} + \beta 5 \text{ Cluster size} + \beta 6 \text{Controls}_i + \varepsilon_i$$

where π is the natural log of the odds for company i to introduce a radical innovation (between 2012 and 2014) and ε represents the corresponding error term.

4. Empirical results and discussion

As can be seen in Table 1, our sample consists of 8404 organizations active in patenting between 2012 and 2014 in Germany. A total number of 365 firms have filed at least one new combination and are considered as radically innovating firms. This represents almost 5% of the total sample, which means that the vast majority of organizations engage in incremental innovating processes. Moreover, 1028 organizations of our sample, corresponding to more than a tenth of all firms, are located in a cluster.

Table 1. Radical innovations and clusters 2012–2014 (own illustration).

	Variable	
	Radical innovation dummy	Cluster dummy
0	8039 (95.66%)	7376 (87.77%)
1	365 (4.34%)	1028 (12.23%)
Total	8404 (100%)	8404 (100%)

Furthermore, we calculated the number of radical innovations per organization based on patent data. Shared patents with more than one applicant where assigned equally to all partners resulting in a variable indicating the number of (radical) patents weighted by the number of co-applicants (Fornahl et al., 2011). The top three firms with the highest number of new combinations are BASF SE (Ludwigshafen), Daimler AG (Stuttgart) and Rehau AG (Hof). The top three industry sectors in terms of new combination amount are manufacture of machinery and equipment (C28), manufacture of chemicals and chemical products (C20) and manufacture of rubber and plastic products (C22). Knowledge-intensive business services also play an important role (e.g. M71, M72).[9] We used the share of radical innovations to analyse the geographical distribution of radical innovations between 2012 and 2014. Based on the firm's address (retrieved from AMADEUS), we assigned all patents to 141 labour market regions as defined by Kosfeld and Werner (2012). We used this definition so that commuter and urban-periphery structures are

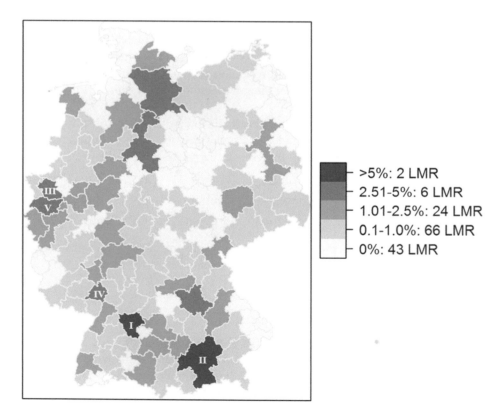

Figure 1. Share of radical innovations in labour market regions 2012–2014 (own illustration).

unlikely to bias the results. As seen in Figure 1, there have not been any radical innovations in one third of the labour market regions. However, the majority of regions (66) at least have a share between 0 and 1%. Overall, the distribution shows that Southern and Western German regions tend to be stronger in radical innovation processes, whereas most regions without radical innovations belong to Eastern Germany. Stuttgart (I) and Munich (II), located in Southern Germany, have the highest share in terms of radical innovations. This is a straightforward observation since both labour market regions are among the economically strongest in the country. The regions include successful firms like Bosch, Daimler and Siemens and are home of some of the most prestigious universities and research institutions like the technical university in Munich and the Fraunhofer Society, Europe's largest application-oriented research organization. The regions Essen (III), Ludwigshafen (IV; South-West) and Dusseldorf (V), lying in the western part of the country, are among the top five regarding the share of radical innovations. Hence, the results show a strong core–periphery disparity, since all these regions include a major city. By contrast, radical innovations are absent mainly in peripheral regions e.g. in Mecklenburg-Western Pomerania, Saxony and Lower Saxony.[10]

To test our main hypotheses, we apply several logistic regression models on the firm-level (see Table 2). For this, we use our full sample of 8404 organizations. In Models 1–4 our dependent variable is a dummy indicating whether a firm is radically innovating (1) or not (0). By investigating the pairwise correlation matrix shown in Appendix 1, one can see that none of our key independent variables are highly and significantly correlated, except for the cluster index and the cluster dummy, which is as expected.

In all models, we find evidence that being located in a cluster indeed has a positive and significant influence on the emergence of radical innovations in firms. This holds true for both indicators, namely the cluster dummy (Model 1, 2, 4) and the cluster index (Model 3 and 4). Hence, we can accept our hypothesis 1. In model 1, the average marginal effect of the cluster dummy is 0.024, which means that being in a cluster increases the probability to produce radical innovations by 2.04 percentage points. The cluster index in model 3 has an average marginal effect of 0.0032, which means that one unit increase in the cluster index

Table 2. Logistic regression results (own illustration).

Radical innovation dummy n = 8404	Model 1	Model 2	Model 3	Model 4
Cluster dummy	0.432***	0.225		0.46*
Cluster index			0.079***	0.302**
Cluster size			0.0005*	0.0005**
Cluster size squared			−1.9e-08	−1.5e-08
Pace of technology evolution	−0.075*	−0.136**	−0.061	−0.062
Number of Linkages	0.064***	0.063***	0.062***	0.061***
Number of Linkages squared	−0.0002**	−0.0002**	−0.0002**	−0.0002**
Research-intensive industry dummy	0.527***	0.615***	0.485***	0.48***
Number of Research Institutes	0.003	0.003	0.003	0.003
Regional knowledge base	0.0001*	0.0001*	0.00008	0.00008
Independence dummy	0.341	0.394	0.302	0.302
Age	0.004**	0.004**	0.004***	0.004***
Cluster dummy*Pace of technology evolution		0.132**		
Cluster dummy*cluster index				−0.254*
Constant	−3.459***	−3.436***	−3.525***	−3.77***
Pseudo R^2	0.021	0.022	0.027	0.028

Significance level: *$p < .10$, **$p < .05$, ***$p < .01$.

and hence, being located in a cluster, increases the probability to produce radical innovations by 0.32 percentage points.

One common concern in this context refers to the existence of a selection bias, meaning that the empirical results become biased as particularly firms with above-average performance choose to locate in clusters. However, in line with the argumentation by McCann and Folta (2011), it is here argued that there are neither theoretically nor empirically justified arguments for the existence of such a positive selection bias. Shaver and Flyer (2000), for instance, find evidence for an adverse selection effect, meaning that very innovative firms have relatively high incentives to avoid collocating in clusters, as the prevailing knowledge spillovers within clusters will especially favour weak innovative firms than the strong ones, which are rather confronted with knowledge drains (negative knowledge spillovers).

Our results also show that the number of formal linkages between organizations has a reversed u-shape relation to the emergence of radical innovations. This outcome is significant throughout all models and supports our hypothesis 3. Thus, we can say that it is favourable for radically innovating firms to collaborate with other firms up to a certain degree. After a turning point, it is probably too much coordination effort to be effective.

In Model 1, the pace of technology evolution has a negative and significant influence at least on the 10% level. Hence, it is more difficult for firms in rapidly developing industries to come up with radical innovations. However, when we include an interaction term between our cluster dummy and the pace of technology evolution in our Model 2, we find evidence, that firms located in clusters can deal with fast developments in their focal industry better and transform them into radically new ideas. This supports our hypothesis 4. At the 5% level we can see, that the interaction term has a positive correlation to the emergence of radical innovations. Hence, under the condition that a firm is located in a cluster, faster technology evolution increases the probability to produce radical innovations. This outcome is also observable if we apply the cluster index instead of the cluster dummy. We also tested, whether it plays a role in this context if the firm is located in the centre or the periphery of the cluster. To do that, we fitted Model 2 with a subsample, including all firms located in clusters, but we did not find a significant difference between firms in the centre and the periphery.[11]

Models 3 and 4 include a cluster size variable to test our hypothesis 5 that the size of a cluster has a reversed u-shape relation to the emergence of radical innovations. Although we find evidence that cluster size is positively related, we do not find proof for the aforementioned assumption.

Model 4 offers additional interesting insights. When we include an interaction term between the cluster dummy and the cluster index, we find a significantly negative influence on radical innovations, which supports our hypothesis 2.[12] The results of the interaction effect suggest that the previously shown positive effect of being located in a cluster on the probability to produce radical innovations is significantly reduced when the value of the cluster index increases.[13] Hence, this suggests that radically innovating firms are more likely to be located in the periphery of a cluster rather than in the centre. We use Figure 2 to illustrate the results of our Model 4. It shows the density of the cluster index (Red – high values to blue – low values). One cluster is represented by the colour tones red to yellow. Firms with a high cluster index are located in the centre of the cluster core and hence would be located in the red part. These firms are less likely to engage in radically innovating processes, because central actors share knowledge

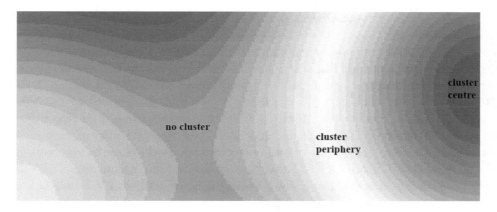

Figure 2. The emergence of radical innovations in clusters – centre vs. periphery (own illustration). The figure is created with kde2d from R package 'MASS'.

only up to a certain degree in order to secure their position in the centre. This, in turn, hinders the opportunities to engage in radical innovation processes. As the cluster index decreases (and the colour tones get cooler), we move towards the periphery of the cluster. Firms located in the yellow part, in the periphery, are more likely to come up with radically new knowledge combinations, since they are more open to new knowledge from outside the firm. Firms located in the blue part have a very low cluster index and are not located in a cluster. Hence, they are less likely to generate radical innovations.

We included several control variables in our models, namely a dummy indicating whether the firm is active in research-intensive industries, the number of research institutes, the regional knowledge base, a dummy whether the organization is independent and firm's age. We find evidence that firms from research-intensive industries are more likely to engage in radical innovations. This finding is highly significant and remains stable over all models. Also, we observe that rather older firms engage in radical innovations, indicated by the (small) positive and significant influence of the variable in all models. The number of research institutes and the independence dummy are both positive but have no significant effect in any of the models. By contrast, the regional knowledge base has a (small) positive and significant influence throughout Models 1 and 2 but loses its explanatory power in Models 3 and 4, which is likely to be driven by the explanatory power of the cluster index.

In sum, based on our empirical findings we can accept four out of five hypotheses. First, being located in a cluster is positively associated with the emergence of radical innovations (hypothesis 1). Second, the centrality of a firms' cluster core position shows a negative relation which means that firms located in the periphery rather engage in radical innovations (hypothesis 2). Third, having a high amount of relationships with other actors has a positive influence on the likelihood to create radical innovations up to a certain degree and afterwards it diminishes (hypothesis 3). Fourth, firms located in clusters can better seize fast technological development in industries to generate radical innovations (hypothesis 4), while the pace of technological evolution in general negatively influences the emergence of radical innovations. Finally, in contrast to our hypothesis 5, the size of the cluster has a positive association with radical innovations. We do not observe a reversed u-shape relation and hence cannot confirm this hypothesis. In the context of radical innovations it thus seems that competition, enhanced by a high geographical concentration of similar firms, rather promotes the creation of radical innovations on the firm-level, as firms recognize the need to be particular innovative in order to differentiate from the nearby competitors and create an competitive advantage (Zhou, Yim, & Tse, 2005).

As robustness checks for our Models 1-4, we also used the amount of radical innovations per firm as dependent variable and fitted a negative binomial regression. We were able to confirm the overall results of our Models 1-4.[14] However, we were not able to find results supporting our hypothesis concerning the negative influence of a firm's central position in the cluster core. Despite the fact that the coefficient is still negative, it is not significant. Thus, with regard to our hypothesis 2, we can indeed observe that rather firms in the periphery of a cluster come up with radically new ideas for the first time. Nevertheless, soon as a firm has had a radical innovation and is trying to produce more the firm's location within the cluster becomes not statistically important anymore.

5. Concluding remarks and outlook

Literature in the recent decades has acknowledged innovation to be a key driver of economic success (e.g. Rosenberg, 2004). In the light of an increasing pace of innovation, innovations that are more radical in nature receive more attention by both managers and policy makers, since they can help to secure long-term economic growth (e.g. Arthur, 2007). While regional clusters are found to be an important factor of inventive activities in general (e.g. Bell, 2005), it remains unclear whether they are also beneficial in terms of radical innovation processes (Hervás-Oliver et al., 2018a). We lack knowledge on whether firms in clusters are more likely to generate radical innovations and which conditions might support this effect. On the one hand, radical new ideas could profit from cross-fertilization of knowledge in clusters and in particular from the exchange of tacit knowledge. On the other hand, clusters could lead to inertia and uniform thinking while hampering the emergence of radical innovations.

The studies' descriptive results show that only a small share of firms is responsible for the emergence of radical innovations. These firms are rather large and are mostly based in urban regions in Southern and Western Germany, while rural regions lag behind. Our regression analysis, which is fitted on a sample of German patenting firms between 2012 and 2014, shows that clusters indeed provide a preferable environment for radical innovations. These results remain stable with various independent variables from different levels of analysis as well as with categorical and continuous dependent variables. Furthermore, we find evidence that radical innovations rather occur in the periphery of the cluster, where actors tend to be more open to the exchange of external knowledge. This happens in general through linkages with other actors, which we also find to be beneficial for the emergence of radical innovations up to a certain degree. Moreover, firms located in clusters are able to seize the fast technology evolution in industries to come up with radically new ideas, whereas this is not the case outside of clusters. Finally, we cannot find evidence that supports a reversed u-shape relation of the size of clusters to the emergence of radical innovations.

Our findings have relevant policy implications. It shows that cluster policy not only supports innovation in general but can also enhance the emergence of radical innovations. Furthermore, it helps firms to deal with fast developments in their focal industry better and transform them into radically new ideas. Policy makers should continue to support clusters and further develop funding schemes. Also, we find that firms in the cluster's periphery are more prone to come up with radically new ideas. However, as soon as there has been a radical innovation in a cluster, the firm's position is however not important anymore. Hence, policy measures could call the attention to radical innovations for all cluster firms in order to promote their emergence. Moreover, our results have implications for managers. In particular, it is beneficial for firms to engage in collaborations with other actors for the cross-fertilization of knowledge (up to a certain degree). Different knowledge pieces hence can be combined and turned into radical innovations. This happens particularly in peripheral regions of a cluster, where firms are more open to the exchange of knowledge.

Our paper does not come without limitations, which offer opportunities for further research: First, our dependent variable is based on new combinations of IPC classes present on patent documents. This only focuses on one dimension of the process, namely the emergence. It could be worthwhile to use other measures, which focus e.g. on the diffusion of the invention (e.g. highly cited patents). Not all new combinations might diffuse successfully. In addition, we could think of using other data (e.g. products) to analyse radical innovations. Second, our analysis does not pay attention to the specific stage clusters are actually in regarding their life cycle. Hence, future studies could try to integrate the cluster life cycle model to analyse whether radical innovations rather occur in young, emerging clusters than in sustaining or declining clusters. Related to this promising area for future research is the use of panel data. While our study is, due to data constraints[15], only based on pooled cross-sectional data[16], raising potential concerns of endogeneity, future studies may apply panel-data to also determine rather dynamic effects. Finally, it could also be interesting to analyse further the inter- and intra-regional linkages.

Notes

1. Although the analysis of our study focuses on invention processes, the paper uses the terms 'innovation' and 'invention' interchangeably.
2. Based on the results of the comparative empirical approach applied in Grashof and Fornahl (2017), highlighting that the spatial connection, the thematic connection and interdependencies are regarded within the literature as the core elements of cluster definitions, industrial districts stressing particularly informal relationships, social capital and trust, are only seen as one specific form of a cluster and hence are not taken explicitly into account here.
3. In line with our cluster definition, we do not consider cities as clusters in this study.
4. A full list of the NACE codes can be found at Eurostat e.g.: https://ec.europa.eu/eurostat/statistics-explained/index.php?title=Glossary:Statistical_classification_of_economic_activities_in_the_European_Community_(NACE).
5. In accordance with the literature, 45 min are here perceived to be an adequate limit for close geographical distance (Brenner 2017; Scholl & Brenner 2016).
6. By using this standard threshold, we avoid to choose arbitrarily a threshold, which constitutes a limitation to several studies dealing with the relationship between clusters and firm performance (e.g. Hervás-Oliver et al. 2018b).

7. Even though patents are commonly used in empirical studies, we still want to acknowledge its flaws. For example, not all innovations are patented and some innovations cannot be patented. For a discussion on shortcomings of patent data, see e.g. Griliches (1990). Nevertheless, patents offer extensive and detailed information on the inventory process such as the date, applicant and technology and over a long time. Hence, it very well fits our empirical approach.
8. A Token algorithm with a log-based weight function has been utilized. It belongs to the group of vectorial decomposition algorithms and compares the elements of two text strings by separating them by their blank spaces (for more information, see e.g.: Raffo 2017; Raffo & Lhuillery 2009).
9. For a detailed overview of the number of radical innovations and the pace of technology evolution by industry, please see Appendix 3.
10. A geographical distribution of the firms in our sample and in total Germany can be found in Appendix 2.
11. The results concerning the application of the cluster index and the interaction term as well as the results of the subsample can be provided by the authors upon request.
12. As indicated by Ai and Norton (2003) problems may raise regarding the interpretation of such an interaction term. However, by using log-odds, we argue that the interpretation problems raised by Ai and Norton (2003) are not that relevant in our case, as the logit model is a linear model in the log odds metric (logit-scale) whereas transformed to the probability scale it indeed becomes nonlinear (Kohler & Kreuter 2008; MacKenzie et al. 2018; UCLA 2018).
13. The cluster index-specific marginal effects of being located in a cluster are illustrated in Appendix 4.
14. Results can be provided by the authors upon request.
15. Particularly referring to the calculation of the cluster index.
16. Since causality is hard to determine with cross-sectional data, in line with Hervás-Oliver et al. (2018b) we claim correlation rather than cause and effect.

Acknowledgements

The authors would like to thank two anonymous referees for comments on an earlier draft and the participants of our presentation at the 1st 'Rethinking Clusters' workshop in Florence. The usual disclaimer applies. The data that support the findings of this study are available from the corresponding author, [NG], upon reasonable request.

Disclosure statement

No potential conflict of interest was reported by the authors.

References

Ahuja, G., & Morris Lampert, C. (2001). Entrepreneurship in the large corporation: A longitudinal study of how established firms create breakthrough inventions. *Strategic Management Journal, 22* (6-7), 521–543. doi:10.1002/smj.176
Ai, C., & Norton, E. C. (2003). Interaction terms in logit and probit models. *Economics Letters, 80* (1), 123–129. doi:10.1016/S0165-1765(03)00032-6
Albert, M. B., Avery, D., Narin, F., & McAllister, P. (1991). Direct validation of citation counts as indicators of industrially important patents. *Research Policy, 20*(3), 251–259. doi:10.1016/0048-7333(91)90055-U
Amend, E., & Herbst, P. (2008). *Labor market pooling and human capital investment decisions* (IAB Discussion Paper 4/2008).

Arthur, W. B. (2007). The structure of invention. *Research Policy*, *36*(2), 274–287. doi:10.1016/j.respol.2006.11.005

Audretsch, D. B. (1998). Agglomeration and the location of innovative activity. *Oxford Review of Economic Policy*, *14*(2), 18–29. doi:10.1093/oxrep/14.2.18

Audretsch, D. B., & Feldman, M. P. (1996). Innovative clusters and the industry life cycle. *Review of Industrial Organization*, *11*(2), 253–273. doi:10.1007/BF00157670

Baptista, R., & Swann, P. (1998). Do firms in cluster innovate more? *Research Policy*, *27*(5), 525–540. doi:10.1016/S0048-7333(98)00065-1

Basalla, G. (1988). *The evolution of technology*. Cambridge, UK: Cambridge University Press.

Bekkers, R., & Freitas, I. M. B. (2008). Analysing knowledge transfer channels between universities and industry: To what degree do sectors also matter? *Research Policy*, *37*(10), 1837–1853. doi:10.1016/j.respol.2008.07.007

Bell, G. G. (2005). Clusters, networks, and firm innovativeness. *Strategic Management Journal*, *26*(3), 287–295. doi:10.1002/smj.448

Bers, J. A., Dismukes, J. P., Miller, L. K., & Dubrovensky, A. (2009). Accelerated radical innovation: Theory and application. *Technological Forecasting and Social Change*, *76*(1), 165–177. doi:10.1016/j.techfore.2008.08.013

BMBF. (2018). Startschuss für Agentur zur Förderung von Sprunginnovationen. Pressemitteilung: 075/2018, Bundesministerium für Bildung und Forschung.

Boschma, R. (2005). Proximity and innovation: A critical assessment. *Regional Studies*, *39*(1), 61–74. doi:10.1080/0034340052000320887

Boschma, R. (2017). Relatedness as driver of regional diversification: A research agenda. *Regional Studies*, *51*(3), 351–364. doi:10.1080/00343404.2016.1254767

Braunerhjelm, P., Ding, D., & Thulin, P. (2017). *Labour mobility, knowledge flows and innovation* (Working Paper No. 54). Swedish Entrepreneurship Forum.

Brenner, T. (2017). *Identification of clusters – an actor-based approach* (Working Papers on Innovation and Space). Philipps-Universität Marburg.

Broekel, T. (2015). The co-evolution of proximities – a network level. *Regional Studies*, *49*(6), 921–935. doi:10.1080/00343404.2014.1001732

Broekel, T., & Graf, H. (2012). Public research intensity and the structure of German R&D networks: A comparison of 10 technologies. *Economics of Innovation and New Technology*, *21*(4), 345–372. doi:10.1080/10438599.2011.582704

Brown, J. S., & Duguid, P. (2000). Mysteries of the region: Knowledge dynamics in Silicon Valley. In C.-M. Lee, W. F. Miller, M. G. Hancock, & H. S. Rowen (Eds.), *The Silicon Valley Edge* (pp. 16–45). Stanford, USA: Stanford University Press.

Brown, K., Burgees, J., Festing, M., Royer, S., & Steffen, C. (2007). The value adding web – a conceptual framework of competitive advantage realisation in clusters. ESCP-EAP Working Paper No. 27.

Cantner, U., Graf, H., & Rothgang, M. (2018). Geographical clustering and the evaluation of cluster policies: Introduction. *The Journal of Technology Transfer*. doi:10.1007/s10961-018-9666-4

Casper, S. (2007). *Creating Silicon Valley in Europe: Public policy towards new technology industries*. Oxford: Oxford University Press.

Castaldi, C., Frenken, K., & Los, B. (2015). Related variety, unrelated variety and technological breakthroughs: An analysis of US state-level patenting. *Regional Studies*, *49*(5), 767–781. doi:10.1080/00343404.2014.940305

Castaldi, C., & Los, B. (2012). Are new 'Silicon Valleys' emerging? The changing distribution of superstar patents across US States. DRUID Summer Conference 2012.

Cooper, A. C., & Schendel, D. (1976). Strategic responses to technological threats. *Business Horizons*, *19*(1), 61–69. doi:10.1016/0007-6813(76)90024-0

Cortright, J. C. (2001). New growth theory, new growth theory, technology and learning: Technology and learning: A practitioner's guide a practitioner's guide. Reviews of Economic Development Literature and Practice No. 4.

Daft, R. L., & Lengel, R. H. (1986). Organizational information requirements, media richness and structural design. *Management Science*, *32*(5), 554–571. doi:10.1287/mnsc.32.5.554

Dahlin, K. B., & Behrens, D. M. (2005). When is an invention really radical?: Defining and measuring technological radicalness. *Research Policy*, *34*(5), 717–737. doi:10.1016/j.respol.2005.03.009

Desrochers, P. (2001). Local diversity, human creativity, and technological innovation. *Growth and Change*, *32*(3), 369–394. doi:10.1111/0017-4815.00164

Dosi, G. (1982). Technological paradigms and technological trajectories: A suggested interpretation of the determinants and directions of technical change. *Research Policy*, *11*(3), 147–162. doi:10.1016/0048-7333(82)90016-6

Dyer, J. H., & Singh, H. (1998). The relational view: Cooperative strategy and sources of interorganizational competitive advantage. *The Academy of Management Review*, *23*(4), 660–679. doi:10.5465/amr.1998.1255632

EFI. (2015). Gutachten zu Forschung, Innovation und Technologischer Leistungsfähigkeit Deutschlands. Expertenkommission Forschung und Innovation.

European Cluster Observatory. (2018). Methodology – indicators. Retrieved from http://www.clusterobservatory.eu/index.html#!view=aboutobservatory;url=/about-observatory/methodology/indicators/

European Communities. (2008). The concept of clusters and cluster policies and their role for competitiveness and innovation: main statistical results and lessons learned. Europe INNOVA / PRO INNO Europe paper N° 9.

Festing, M., Royer, S., & Steffen, C. (2012). Unternehmenscluster schaffen Wettbewerbsvorteile – Eine Analyse des Uhrenclusters in Glashütte. *Zeitschrift Führung und Organisation*, *81*(4), 264–272.

Fleming, L. (2001). Recombinant uncertainty in technological search. *Management Science*, *47*(1), 117–132. doi:10.1287/mnsc.47.1.117.10671

Fleming, L. (2007). Breakthroughs and the 'long tail' of innovation. *MIT Sloan Management Review*, *49*(1), 69.

Folta, T. B., Cooper, A. C., & Baik, Y.-S. (2006). Geographic cluster size and firm performance. *Journal of Business Venturing*, *21*(2), 217–242. doi:10.1016/j.jbusvent.2005.04.005

Fornahl, D., Broekel, T., & Boschma, R. (2011). What drives patent performance of German biotech firms? The impact of R&D subsidies, knowledge networks and their location. *Papers in Regional Science*, *90*(2), 395–418. doi:10.1111/j.1435-5957.2011.00361.x

Frenken, K., Cefis, E., & Stam, E. (2013). *Industrial dynamics and clusters: a survey*. Tjalling C. Koopmans Research Institute, Discussion Paper Series nr: 13-11, Utrecht School of Economics.

Giuliani, E. (2007). The selective nature of knowledge networks in clusters: Evidence from the wine industry. *Journal of Economic Geography*, *7*(2), 139–168. doi:10.1093/jeg/lbl014

Glaeser, E. L., Kallal, H. D., Scheinkman, J. A., & Shleifer, A. (1992). Growth in cities. *Journal of Political Economy*, *100*(6), 1126–1152. doi:10.1086/261856

Grashof, N., & Fornahl, D. (2017). 'To be or not to be' located in a cluster? – A descriptive meta-analysis of the firm-specific cluster effect. Manuscript submitted for publication.

Griliches, Z. (1990). Patent statistics as economic indicators: A survey. *Journal of Economic Literature*, *28*(4), 1661–1707. doi:10.3386/w3301

Henderson, R. M., & Clark, K. B. (1990). Architectural innovation: The reconfiguration of existing product technologies and the failure of established firms. *Administrative Science Quarterly*, 9–30. doi:10.2307/2393549

Hervás-Oliver, J.-L., & Albors-Garrigos, J. (2009). The role of the firm's internal and relational capabilities in clusters: When distance and embeddedness are not enough to explain innovation. *Journal of Economic Geography*, *9*(2), 263–283. doi:10.1093/jeg/lbn033

Hervás-Oliver, J.-L., Albors-Garrigos, J., Estelles-Miguel, S., & Boronat-Moll, C. (2018a). Radical innovation in Marshallian industrial districts. *Regional Studies*, *52*(10), 1388–1397. doi:10.1080/00343404.2017.1390311

Hervás-Oliver, J.-L., Sempere-Ripoll, F., Alvarado, R. R., & Estelles-Miguel, S. (2018b). Agglomerations and firm performance: Who benefits and how much? *Regional Studies*, *52*(3), 338–349. doi:10.1080/00343404.2017.1297895

Hottenrott, H., & Lopes-Bento, C. (2016). R&D partnerships and innovation performance: Can there be too much of a good thing? *Journal of Product Innovation Management*, *33*(6), 773–794. doi:10.1111/jpim.12311

Jaffe, A. B., Trajtenberg, M., & Henderson, R. (1993). Geographic localization of knowledge spillovers as evidenced by patent citations. *Quarterly Journal of Economics*, *108*(3), 577–598. doi:10.2307/2118401

Kesteloot, K., & Veugelers, R. (1995). Stable R&D Cooperation with spillovers. *Journal of Economics & Management Strategy*, *4*(4), 651–672. doi:10.1111/j.1430-9134.1995.00651.x

Knoben, J., Arikan, A. T., Van Oort, F., & Raspe, O. (2015). Agglomeration and firm performance: One firm's medicine is another firm's poison. *Environment and Planning A*, *48*(1), 1–22.

Kohlbacher, M., Weitlaner, D., Hollosi, A., Grünwald, S., & Grahsl, H.-P. (2013). Innovation in clusters: Effects of absorptive capacity and environmental moderators. *Competitiveness Review: An International Business Journal*, *23*(3), 199–217. doi:10.1108/10595421311319807

Kohler, U., & Kreuter, F. (2008). *Datenanalyse mit Stata – Allgemeine Konzepte der Datenanalyse und ihre praktische Anwendung* (3rd ed.). München: Oldenbourg Verlag.

Kosfeld, R., & Werner, A. (2012). Deutsche Arbeitsmarktregionen– Neuabgrenzung nach den Kreisgebietsreformen 2007–2011. *Raumforschung und Raumordnung*, *70*(1), 49–64. doi:10.1007/s13147-011-0137-8

Lavie, D. (2006). The competitive advantage of interconnected firms: An extension of the resource-based view. *The Academy of Management Review*, *31*(3), 638–658. doi:10.5465/amr.2006.21318922

Lechner, C., & Leyronas, C. (2012). The competitive advantage of cluster firms: The priority of regional network position over extra-regional networks – a study of a French high-tech cluster. *Entrepreneurship & Regional Development*, *24*(5–6), 457–473. doi:10.1080/08985626.2011.617785

MacKenzie, D. I., Nichols, J. D., Royle, J. A., Pollock, K. H., Bailey, L. L., & Hines, J. E. (2018). Chapter 3 - Fundamental Principals of Statistical Inference. In D. I. MacKenzie, J. D. Nichols, J. A. Royle, K. H. Pollock, L. L. Bailey, & J. E. Hines (Eds.), *Occupancy Estimation and Modeling* (pp. 71–111). London: Elsevier.

Marshall, A. (1920). *Principles of economics* (8th ed.). London: Macmillan.

Martin, R. (2009). Rethinking regional path dependence: Beyond lock-in to evolution. Papers in Evolutionary Economic Geography (PEEG), No. 910.

Martin, R., & Sunley, P. (2003). Deconstructing clusters: Chaotic concept or policy panacea? *Journal of Economic Geography*, *3*(1), 5–35. doi:10.1093/jeg/3.1.5

Mascitelli, R. (2000). From experience: Harnessing tacit knowledge to achieve breakthrough innovation. *Journal of Product Innovation Management*, *17*(3), 179–193. doi:10.1016/S0737-6782(00)00038-2

McCann, B. T., & Folta, T. B. (2008). Location matters: Where we have been and where we might go in agglomeration research? *Journal of Management*, *34*(3), 532–565. doi:10.1177/0149206308316057

McCann, B. T., & Folta, T. B. (2011). Performance differentials within geographic clusters. *Journal of Business Venturing*, *26*(1), 104–123. doi:10.1016/j.jbusvent.2009.04.004

McGahan, A. M., & Silverman, B. S. (2001). How does innovative activity change as industries mature? *International Journal of Industrial Organization*, *19*(7), 1141–1160. doi:10.1016/S0167-7187(01)00067-4

Menzel, M.-P., & Fornahl, D. (2010). Cluster life cycles – dimensions and rationales of cluster evolution. *Industrial and Corporate Change*, *19*(1), 205–238. doi:10.1093/icc/dtp036

Munari, F., Sobrero, M., & Malipiero, A. (2012). Absorptive capacity and localized spillovers: Focal firms as technological gatekeepers in industrial districts. *Industrial and Corporate Change*, *21*(2), 429–462. doi:10.1093/icc/dtr053

Nagy, D., Schuessler, J., & Dubinsky, A. (2016). Defining and identifying disruptive innovations. *Industrial Marketing Management*, *57*, 119–126. doi:10.1016/j.indmarman.2015.11.017

Nerkar, A. (2003). Old is gold? The value of temporal exploration in the creation of new knowledge. *Management Science*, *49*(2), 211–229. doi:10.1287/mnsc.49.2.211.12747

Otto, A., & Fornahl, D. (2010). Origins of human capital in clusters: Regional, industrial and academic transitions in media clusters in Germany. In D. Fornahl, S. Henn, & M.-P. Menzel (Eds.), *Emerging clusters: Theoretical, empirical and Political Perspectives on the Initial stage of cluster evolution* (pp. 99–139). Cheltenham, UK: Edward Elgar.

Porter, M. E. (1998). Clusters and the new economics of competitiveness. *Harvard Business Review*, 76(6), 77–90. doi:10.1201/b14647-11

Pouder, R., & St. John, C. H. (1996). Hot spots and blind spots: Geographical clusters of firms and innovation. *The Academy of Management Review*, 21(4), 1192–1225. doi:10.5465/amr.1996.9704071867

Raffo, J. (2017). MATCHIT: Stata module to match two datasets based on similar text patterns. Boston College Department of Economics. Retrieved from help file in Stata.

Raffo, J., & Lhuillery, S. (2009). How to play the 'names game': patent retrieval comparing different heuristics. *Research Policy*, 38(10), 1617–1627. doi:10.1016/j.respol.2009.08.001

Research Explorer. (2018). Research Explorer - The German research directory. Retrieved from http://www.research-explorer.de/research_explorer.en.html?

Rigby, D. L., & Brown, M. W. (2015). Who benefits from agglomeration? *Regional Studies*, 49(1), 28–43. doi:10.1080/00343404.2012.753141

Rizzo, U., Barbieri, N., Ramaciotti, L., & Iannantuono, D. (2018). The division of labour between academia and industry for the generation of radical inventions. *Journal of Technology Transfer*. doi:10.1007/s10961-018-9688-y

Roesler, C., & Broekel, T. (2017). The role of universities in a network of subsidized R&D collaboration: The case of the biotechnology industry in Germany. *Review of Regional Research*, 37(2), 135–160. doi:10.1007/s10037-017-0118-7

Rosenberg, N. (2004). *Innovation and economic growth*. Paris: OECD.

Rosenkopf, L., & Nerkar, A. (2001). Beyond local search: Boundary-spanning, exploration, and impact in the optical disk industry. *Strategic Management Journal*, 22(4), 287–306. doi:10.1002/smj.160

Saxenian, A. (1994). *Regional advantage: Culture and competition in Silicon Valley and Route 128*. Cambridge: Harvard University Press.

Scholl, T., & Brenner, T. (2016). Detecting spatial clustering using a firm-level cluster index. *Regional Studies*, 50(6), 1054–1068. doi:10.1080/00343404.2014.958456

Shaver, J. M., & Flyer, F. (2000). Agglomeration economies, firm heterogeneity, and foreign direct investment in the United States. *Strategic Management Journal*, 21(12), 1175–1193. doi:10.1002/1097-0266(200012)21:12<1175::AID-SMJ139>3.0.CO;2-Q

Steffen, C. (2012). How firms profit from acting in networked environments: Realising competitive advantages in business clusters. A resource-oriented case study analysis of the German and Swiss Watch Industry. Schriftenreihe: Internationale Personal- und Strategieforschung.

Strumsky, D., & Lobo, J. (2015). Identifying the sources of technological novelty in the process of invention. *Research Policy*, 44(8), 1445–1461. doi:10.1016/j.respol.2015.05.008

Suarez, F. F., & Lanzolla, G. (2007). The role of environmental dynamics in building a first mover advantage theory. *Academy of Management Review*, 32(2), 377–392. doi:10.5465/amr.2007.24349587

Suarez, F., & Lanzolla, G. (2005). The half-truth of first-mover advantage. *Harvard Business Review*, 83(4), 121–127.

Trajtenberg, M. (1990). A penny for your quotes: Patent citations and the value of innovations. *The Rand Journal of Economics*, 172–187. doi:10.2307/2555502

Tushman, M. L., & Anderson, P. (1986). Technological discontinuities and organizational environments. *Administrative Science Quarterly*, 439–465. doi:10.2307/2392832

UCLA. (2018). Deciphering interactions in logistic regression. Retrieved from https://stats.idre.ucla.edu/stata/seminars/deciphering-interactions-in-logistic-regression/

Verhoeven, D., Bakker, J., & Veugelers, R. (2016). Measuring technological novelty with patent-based indicators. *Research Policy*, 45(3), 707–723. doi:10.1016/j.respol.2015.11.010

Verspagen, B. (2006). Innovation and economic growth. In J. Fagerberg, D. Mowery, & R. Nelson (Eds.), *The oxford handbook of innovation* (pp. 487–513). New York: Oxford University Press.

Weitzman, M. L. (1998). Recombinant growth. *The Quarterly Journal of Economics, 113*(2), 331–360. doi:10.1162/003355398555595

Zaheer, A., & George, V. P. (2004). Reach out or reach within? Performance implications of alliances and location in biotechnology. *Managerial and Decision Economics, 25*(6-7), 437–452. doi:10.1002/mde.1200

Zhang, F., Wei, L., Yang, J., & Zhu, L. (2018). Roles of relationships between large shareholders and managers in radical innovation: A stewardship theory perspective. *Journal of Product Innovation Management, 35*(1), 88–105. doi:10.1111/jpim.12376

Zhou, K. Z., Yim, C. K. B., & Tse, D. K. (2005). The effects of strategic orientations on technology- and market-based breakthrough innovations. *Journal of Marketing, 69*(2), 42–60. doi:10.1509/jmkg.69.2.42.60756

Zucker, L. G., Darby, M. R., & Torero, M. (2002). Labor mobility from academe to commerce. *Journal of Labor Economics, 20*(3), 629–660. doi:10.1086/339613

Radical vs incremental innovation in Marshallian Industrial Districts in the Valencian Region: what prevails?

Jose-Luis Hervas-Oliver, Francisca Sempere-Ripoll, Sofia Estelles-Miguel and Ronald Rojas-Alvarado

ABSTRACT
This study's objective consists of deciphering whether collocation in MIDs, exerts a potential effect on a firm's discontinuous or radical innovative performance. The study explores and integrates economic geography with innovation literature in order to explore the relationship between *Marshalllian Industrial Districts* (MIDs) and firm innovation. Specifically, we encompass radical or discontinuous innovation, as opposed to an incremental or imitative one. We build a framework from which MIDs' effect on discontinuous innovation is approached. Using CIS data in Spain in district and non-district firms in a region, our results show that: (i) collocated firms' innovative performance is positively related to the *District effect*, as long as the innovation pursuit is incremental; (ii) collocation in MIDs does not facilitate the pursuit of radical innovation but mainly supports an incremental one, and (iii) district firms show asymmetric capabilities and innovative output, as long as the innovation pursuit is incremental, nor discontinuous. Implications for the MID framework are discussed.

1. Introduction

This study enters the existent debate (e.g. Gilbert, McDougall, & Audretsch, 2008; Knoben, Arikan, van Oort, & Raspe, 2016; Lee, 2018; Rigby & Brown, 2015) on agglomeration and firm performance but is focused on a particular type of cluster: *socially-based* Marshallian Industrial Districts[1] (MIDs). During the last decades, industrial district literature has been prolific, delivering a very extensive body of knowledge characterizing the pervasive knowledge circulation and the importance of local networks of small firms that simultaneously compete and cooperate (e.g. Becattini, 1990; Belussi & Sedita, 2009; Brusco, 1982; Belussi & Hervás-Oliver, 2017; Hervas-Oliver, Lleo, & Cervello, 2017; Lorenzoni & Lipparini, 1999; Hervas-Oliver & Albors-Garrigos, 2014). Insights on this field have pointed out that firms' capability arises from the knowledge residing both inside and outside organizational boundaries, due to the existence of available knowledge within MIDs. In this chain of thought, we advance the conversation by researching whether this available knowledge, from a prone-to-innovation local environment, fosters incremental or radical innovation. Thus, beyond studying whether collocation in MIDs impacts on a firm's performance, our study goes one step further and seeks to understand that effect through a different lens, assessing *whether* that impact originates a firm's discontinuous or radical innovation. In this study, radical innovation is defined as discontinuous innovation, as opposed to incremental (continuous). For this purpose, CIS (Community of Innovation Survey) definition of *new-to-the market* innovation is utilized, measured as a *significant impact on a market and on the economic activity of firms in that market* (OECD, 2005, p. 58), developing a framework from which to tackle discontinuous innovation in Marshallian Industrial Districts.

At the firm level, we focus on innovation because it is a key organizational capability for sustaining competitive advantage, and because the promotion of an innovative capability is one of the agglomeration-related benefits (e.g. Harrison, Kelley, & Gant, 1996). While most research on MIDs has been conducted applying a framework of incremental or continuous innovation assumption (Robertson & Langlois, 1995), the analysis of the occurrence of radical innovation in MIDs has been reduced to specific case studies (see Hervás-Oliver, Albors-Garrigos, Estelles-Miguel, & Boronat-Moll, 2018) or restricted to how radical innovation was unable to occur, producing instead decline from inertia (e.g. Glasmeier, 1991; Grabher, 1993; Isaksen, 2018; Ostergaard & Park, 2015; Sull, 2001). Going one step further, in this study the (MID) *district effect,* and its impact on a firm's innovative performance, is analyzed, dissecting the different types of a firm's innovation, that is, incremental and radical, in order to empirically assess, through a large-scale dataset, what type of innovation is facilitated by the district. Therefore, this study's objective consists of deciphering whether collocation in MIDs exerts a potential effect on a collocated firm's discontinuous or radical innovative performance.

Theoretically, we set our argument within the agglomeration and firm performance topic (e.g. Lee, 2018), testing whether MIDs facilitate or constrain MID firms from introducing non-incremental discontinuous innovations.

Empirically, we use innovation-based data from the Spanish Community of Innovation Survey, provided by the Spanish Statistical Office (INE) and combine it with other regional datasets in order to determine whether a firm belongs or not to an MID in the Valencia Region. The MIDs we refer to in this study are those that literature has previously identified as socio-economic phenomena (MIDs), consisting of high concentrations of industries in small areas of few neighbouring towns, following a typical pattern of Marshallian districts. Thus, we test our hypothesis on a rich full-scale dataset covering 946 firms. Valencian Region is selected because it presents a high proportion of localization economies in Spain.[2] The paper is organized as follows. The following section details the conceptual framework of our study. Then, in the third section, we elaborate on our data and our empirical design. In the fourth section, the results are presented, together with a brief discussion. Finally, conclusions are developed and some areas for future research are discussed.

2. Literature review

The implications of geography for innovation have been discussed in many strands, suggesting that, generally, collocation in agglomerations is linked to increasing returns and superior innovation because of the potential access to *localization externalities* (e.g.

Audretsch & Feldman, 1996; Marshall, 1890/1920; Saxenian, 1994). Localization externalities[3] are defined as the effects that the concentration of an industry in a region promotes knowledge spillovers between firms and facilitate innovation within that particular industry in that region, promoting learning and access to external knowledge (e.g. Saxenian, 1994), enticing a superior configuration of firms' capabilities and thus improving firms' innovative performance (e.g. Belussi & Sedita, 2009; Hervas-Oliver & Albors-Garrigos, 2009).

Focusing on the particular case of MIDs, there is an additional *social dimension* (e.g. Becattini, 1990; Brusco, 1982) that is based on continuous interactions that promotes trust and a sense of belonging, reducing transaction costs and favouring inter-firm and inter-personal knowledge exchanges. In addition, this model facilitates networking and flexible specialization of production, sustained by extensive and trust-based subcontracting, facilitating the simultaneous co-existence of competition and co-operation that positively impacts innovation and a collective learning (e.g. Belussi & Sedita, 2009; Camagni, 1991; Hervas-Oliver et al., 2017). Therefore, MIDs foster collaboration and generation of knowledge that is available to collocated firms.

Most of the literature on MIDs have pointed out the high circulation of knowledge and information in districts, as well as its collective learning process (e.g. Albino, Garavelli, & Schiuma, 1998; Cainelli & De Liso, 2005; Varaldo & Ferrucci, 1996). Literature, however, has repeatedly stated that innovation is mostly assumed under continuous or incremental innovation frameworks (Bianchi & Giordani, 1993, p. 31; Isaksen, 2018; Ostergaard & Park, 2015; Robertson & Langlois, 1995, p. 558). Creative destruction challenges established paradigms and incumbent technologies in regions, which often lock-in local technological paradigms that prevent the entrance of new ideas or technology. In MIDs there is a strong *collective identity* (see Staber & Sautter, 2011) that favours *homogeneity*, not promoting enough diversity or sufficient heterogeneity to change (see Gilbert, 2012; Glasmeier, 1991; Grabher, 1993). Overall, creative destruction in clusters is said to be very unlikely (see Storper & Walker, 1989).

2.1. Types of innovation in MIDs

The necessary novelty to create discontinuous or radical knowledge in MIDs, however, is not easily generated in MIDs, due to different tensions that might end up provoking lock-in and cognitive inertia (e.g. Glasmeier, 1991; Martin & Sunley, 2006). These tensions, paradoxically, are the quintessential characteristics by which MIDs function and get developed. First, the repetitive and intense interactions among local firms create a sense of community or belonging well manifested in MIDs (e.g. Becattini, 1990). This sense of belonging is fuelled by a *social dimension,* sustained by trust, common language and social norms (e.g. Becattini, 1990; Piore & Sabel, 1984). The reason is based on the fact that existing local networks are vital for agglomerations' functioning (Scott, 1989), in so far as they provide legitimacy to access tacit knowledge (Scott, 1992, p. 16) that is basically exchanged on the basis of trust-based relationships, values, reciprocity and informal norms (Becattini, 1990; Hervás-Oliver, 2016; Saxenian, 1994). As a consequence, collocated firms' thinking similarly may turn a blind eye to different paradigms and changes from the external environment and, eventually, suffer from cognitive inertia (e.g. Martin & Sunley, 2006). Thus, local firms embedded in these environments, tend to focus more on local rivals, exposed to the same type of information, sharing competitive perceptions and likely becoming increasingly homogenous in technology, assumptions, business practices and paradigms. In this context, innovation is primarily driven by incremental changes and imitation (Bianchi & Giordani, 1993; Robertson & Langlois, 1995). Thus, local managers imitate other local managers, creating a generalized biased model inwardly-oriented that prevents looking beyond the local space. As Pouder and St. John (1996, p. 1207) posit:

> Mental models based primarily on local competitors will be biased toward those competitors; at the same time they will direct attention away from outside competitors. Consequently, as local competitors increasingly dominate the perceptions of managers in the hot spot, competitors outside of the industry will be subject to less rigorous scrutiny … ..

Therefore, we expect that:

> Hypothesis 1: District firms are more likely to innovate incrementally than radically.

2.2. MIDs and firm level innovation: asymmetric knowledge and gains

How collocated firms access to and use available local knowledge is well explained in the strategy literature, also intersected with that of economic geography. In short, addressing the firm-level, the idea of *firm competitive heterogeneity*,[4] is well accepted, implying that each collocated firm presents a different way and capabilities to access to and make use of external knowledge, including the social aspects embedded in the territory (see Hervas-Oliver & Albors-Garrigos, 2009; Knoben et al., 2016; Lee, 2018). Put differently, it is generally accepted that firms possess unique capabilities that drive their innovative performance, as recognized in the resource-based view of the firm (e.g. Peteraf, 1993) applied to districts (Hervas-Oliver & Albors-Garrigos, 2009).

In this chain of thought, and following Hervas-Oliver, Sempere-Ripoll, Rojas-Alvarado, and Estelles-Miguel (2018) agglomerations provide a knowledge-abundant context favouring inter-firm knowledge exchange. Externalities and social aspects present in MIDs constitute a knowledge-abundant and rich environment prone to innovation, a kind of district effect. This rich environment, however, cannot be exploited equally by collocated firms. On the contrary, collocated firms perform differently (e.g. Rigby & Brown, 2015). This central tenet is based on the idea that firms are heterogeneous, in line with the resource-based view of the firm (RBV; Nelson & Winter, 1982; Peteraf, 1993). In this chain of thought, each firm has a different stock of capabilities and, therefore, each different absorptive capacity determines a different firm performance. In MIDs, however, access to knowledge is also easy and not all firms invest in developing internal capabilities to access to locally available knowledge that almost freely circulate. Certainly, we posit that in MIDs access to available knowledge is easy, but firms with better capabilities and, therefore, with stronger absorptive capacity, present better access to available knowledge that impacts positively on performance: neither all firms are equal in MIDs, nor all firms access the same type and amount of knowledge in clusters (e.g. Crescenzi & Gagliardi, 2018; Hervas-Oliver, Sempere-Ripoll, et al., 2018; Lee, 2018; McCann & Folta, 2011; Rigby & Brown, 2015). In fact, most of the knowledge circulates unevenly within inter-firm networks and social ties (e.g. Breschi & Lissoni, 2001; Giuliani, 2007). Even assuming that the knowledge is totally available, each firm (heterogeneity) will use it differently. There is a lot of information and also knowledge, but neither all firms are equally using that knowledge, nor all firms can access the same amount and type of knowledge. As Breschi and Lissoni (2001, p. 993) points out: '... *the so-often cited face-to-face contacts may serve only to ease the access to information about who knows what ... which is the only public good. Embodied scientific and technical knowledge remains a private good ... or a club good*'.

Overall, we argue that, as firms are heterogeneous in terms of resources and capabilities (e.g. Peteraf, 1993), therefore, those firms showing higher investment in capability development, can build stronger absorptive capacity and thus access to more available knowledge and thus improve performance (Cohen & Levinthal, 1990). Hereby, we argue that, within MIDs, those firms investing more in developing their internal capabilities will gain the most: better (capabilities) absorptive capacity means better performance (firms are heterogeneous and those with better capability access more knowledge and improve much more performance vis-à-vis those investing less).

Following this chain of thought, firms in MIDs will perform differently, accessing more or less available knowledge for innovation depending on their internal capabilities. Therefore, in line with that *knowledge heterogeneity and innovation asymmetry* tenet within MIDs, originated by a firm's internal resources and capabilities, we expect that:

Hypothesis 2: The district effect on innovation is positively related to firms' capabilities.

3. Introduction to the region and its districts

Our empirical analysis covers firms located in the Valencian Region in Spain. The Valencia Region (VR) presents a relatively independent government structure for specific industrial purposes (regional innovation, cluster development, etc.) like some other regions in Spain (Basque Country, Catalonia, etc.). Why is the VR of interest for studying clusters? In Spain, around 35% of the manufacturing jobs are found in industrial districts (IDs); 70% are small firms and 20% medium-size firms within these IDs. In addition, the IDs have the largest share of Spain's total employment in the sectors of ceramics (over 90%), footwear (around 85.2%), textile and clothing (50.4%), toys (42.3%) and marble (54%), among many others. The highest number of IDs by region in Spain is found in the VR where almost 40% of industrial employment is found in districts,[5] with special mention for the footwear, textile, ceramics, marble and plastics/toys industries that constitute very powerful MIDs in the VR. Table 1 shows a summary of the main MIDs analyzed: ceramics, footwear, toys & plastics, textiles and marble. As it is showed in Table 1, those agglomerations are said to be MIDs, showing the typical dynamics of innovation: a supplier-driven pattern, historical roots, traditional industries and primarily constituted by a constellation of small firms (see e.g. Belso-Martínez, 2010; Expósito-Langa, Molina-Morales, & Capo-Vicedo, 2011; Galletto & Boix, 2014; Hervas-Oliver et al., 2017; Robertson & Jacobson, 2011). These MIDs, in general, have developed a positive lock-in evolution by concentrating efforts in particular products. In all the MIDs we refer to, there is a combination of small and very small firms, along with fewer larger firms. These MIDs are not hub-and-spoke, rather they are network-based and there are leading firms that orchestrate local networks of smaller firms. These MIDs also present specific R&D dynamics (combination of formal and informal innovation, no R&D labs, high dependence of knowledge from equipment suppliers, etc. see Lorenzoni & Lipparini, 1999). In these MIDs there is a high

Table 1. Industries and MIDs involved in the study.

Industry in clusters	Number of firms
Ceramics (MID); High concentration in 3 neighbouring locations (Villareal, Onda and Alcora, around Castellon) of 20 km². More than 90% of the Spanish Production and almost 99% of the Valencian region production. Named a MID (see Gabaldón-Estevan, Manjarrés-Henríquez, & Molina-Morales, 2018; Galletto & Boix, 2014; Hervas-Oliver et al., 2017)	60
Footwear (MID); High concentration in 5 towns (Elche, Elda, Petrer, Villena, Sax) along the Vinalopo Valley. 60% concentration of Spanish production and 90% concentration of Valencian region production. Named a MID (see Belso-Martínez, 2010)	135
Toys & Plastics (MID). High concentration around two neighbouring towns (Ibi and Onil). 70% of the Spanish production and 95% of the Valencian production (see Balland, Belso-Martínez, & Morrison, 2016)	119
Stone & Marble (MID). High concentration around few locations (Novelda, Pinoso). 60% of Spanish production and 99% of Valencian production. Named a MID (see Robertson & Jacobson, 2011)	25
Textiles (MID). High concentration around few neighbouring towns (Alcoi, Ontinyent, Muro, Albaida). 50% of Spanish home textile production and 90% of Valencian production. Name a MID (see Expósito-Langa et al., 2011; Galletto & Boix, 2014)	69
Total sub-sample	408
Industries with lower concentration	
Metallic products	156
Food	119
Furniture	122
Printing	62
Equipment	27
Chemestry	22
Other manufacturing (wood, paper, etc.)	30
Total sample	946

circulation of knowledge and information and a pervasive collective learning process that facilitates innovative behaviour by the collocated firms[6] (e.g. Camagni, 1991).

The VR also hosts a different variety of industries operating in the region, such as metal products, food processing, furniture and other manufacturing industries, although with no high concentration indexes as those MIDs. Table 2 describes the size of the firms analyzed. See Tables 1 and 2.

This study utilizes firm-level and regional variables from two different databases. The firm-level data comes from the Spanish CIS 2006 covering the 2004–2006 period, following traditional CIS structure.[7] Firms in the CIS questionnaire are geographically placed on a regional basis at NUTS 2. We use the latter information in order to connect CIS data with a regional dataset containing localization indicators and NACE codes. The regional level data comes from the INE (Spanish Statistics Institute), the same governmental body which administers the CIS itself and the VR Statistics Office.

First, we have the information of the Valencian industries categorized as MIDs, including localization and NACE codes. Then, we separate firms from the sample that belong to the above MIDs, according to the industries[8] in which the respondent firm is active (based on its 3-digit NACE code) and its location, assigning code 1 ('District') to those firms, and

Table 2. Size of the firms in the sample.

Firms	Size
447	Less than 50 employees
261	50–100 employees
162	100–199
76	From 200 to 250
946	Total

0 to the rest of the firms belonging to other industries ('No District'). Our sample for the VR is composed of 946 firms from which 408 were located in MIDs.

At the firm-level, the CIS questionnaire is very rich, detailing a firm's innovation, separating clearly incremental and non-incremental ones, and providing also a firm's innovation pattern through many variables of interest. Connecting this section to this study's objective of understanding non-incremental, but radical, innovation in MDIs, we follow the Oslo Manual (OECD, 2005, p. 58) that establishes that a *radical innovation is that which presents a significant impact on a market and on the economic activity of firms in that market*; applying this to the Spanish CIS questionnaire and the available data, we refer to radical innovation as that occurring when firms introduce innovations that are *new-to-the-market*, rather than just *new-to-the-company*. This is indicated in Question E.1.4 that offers two dichotomous variables for capturing incremental and radical innovation:

> E.1.4 Regarding the product innovations introduced during the period ….. were they ….1) An innovation only for the company (The company introduced new or significantly improved goods or services for the company, of which the competitors already had one in the market) … YES ….NO.

> Alternatively, … .were they 2) An innovation in the market (The company introduced new or significantly improved goods or services in the market before the competitors … YES … NO.

This study uses variables as follows: *District* variable depicts whether a firm is located in an MID, as defined above. Then, measuring innovative output, through CIS data, *Incremental* is a dependent variable indicating whether an enterprise has introduced a *new-to-the-firm*, capturing incremental or imitative innovation, product or service during the research period. This variable is measured as a dummy variable and has a value of 1 if the firm has introduced a new or improved product and/or service during the studied period, and 0 otherwise. Then, the variable *Radical* is a dependent variable indicating whether a firm has introduced a *new-to-the-market innovation*, also valued as dichotomous as the other variable, both according to E.1.4.

Following similar variables as Hervas-Oliver, Sempere-Ripoll, et al. (2018), the variable *Internal_Capabilities* represents a firm's internal resources of knowledge. The latter is the knowledge base or innovation capability. In constructing this variable we have drawn on the work of Cohen and Levinthal (1990), Escribano, Fosfuri, and Tribó (2009), Lane, Koka, and Pathak and Hervas-Oliver, Garrigos, and Gil-Pechuan (2011) (2006) that emphasize the importance of human resources and R&D activities. Thus, this variable is constructed from a factor analysis that includes R&D internal expenditures, and the percentage of human resources devoted to R&D in relation to total employees. The resulting scores from a principal component analysis (PCA) represent the or internal capabilities[9] to access to external knowledge and innovate. See Appendix I for more information on the construction of this variable. Then, also following Hervas-Oliver, Sempere-Ripoll, et al. (2018), external sources of knowledge (*External_sources*) capture the role of untraded interdependencies or externalities from related industries within value chains without monetary transactions (Saxenian, 1994). These variables arose from the question: *how important have the following information sources been for the innovation activities of your enterprise? This variable is* measured *on a four digit scale from 0 to 3,* including: learning from interactions with *Suppliers* and *Customers,* and/or through *Trade Associations and* participation in *Events*. By focusing on these four knowledge sources we address the external search strategies of firms and/or the external sources of knowledge they accessed. These variables are coded as none (0) to high (3) in a Likert-like scale. We add all of them, by following Laursen and Salter (2006) practice of coding 1 for high (3) and 0 otherwise. In doing so, the scores for the use of the four sources are added up so that each firm gets a score of 0 when no knowledge sources are used to a high degree, while the firm gets the value of 4 when all knowledge sources are used to a high degree (Cronbach's alpha coefficient = 0.74). Control variables are included, such as Size, measured as the total number of employees, *Industry* classification, measured using 2-digit NACE-93 industry classification as dummies, and the OECD's classification of low-, medium-low and medium-high-technology intensive industries, restricted to the type of firms identified.

4. Results

Table 3 shows descriptive statistics and correlation matrix. See Table 3.

Econometrically, hypothesis 2 is measured through the interaction effect of *District* × *Internal_Capabilities*, while hypothesis 1 is captured by the *District* (variable) effect. In both cases, their effects are on innovation, either incremental or radical. As explained below, we use different dependent variables and subsamples in order to provide an accurate and robust set of results for answering (confirming/rejecting) the hypotheses.

Our sample for the VR is composed of 946 firms (408 collocated in MDIS, and 538 non-collocated ones). Out of those 946 firms, 436 are non-innovative ones and 510 innovative. From those innovating (436), 240 manifested solely introducing new-to-the-firm innovation (*Incremental* variable takes 1), 109 indicated solely new-to-the-market innovation (*Radical* variable takes 1) and 161 firms introduced both types simultaneously. In Table 4 three specifications are shown. See Table 4.

As our dependent variables (*Radical vs Incremental*) are binary, therefore, our econometric specifications follow a *logit* model. In Table 4 results from logit analysis testing the introduction of new-to-the-market (*Radical_product*) versus new-to-the-firm (*Incremental*) are presented, using different sub-samples gradually to triangulate results.

According to Table 4, in Model 1 (all innovators vs non-innovators, the latter the baseline; specifications 1 and 2) we observe how the *District* variable is statistically significant and positively related to innovative performance (0.627 and 1.055, both at $p < 0.01$,) respectively for specifications 1 and 2. Hypothesis 1 is confirmed. Then, both *Internal_Capabilities* and *External_Sources* are also statistically significant and positively related to innovative performance (0.778 and 0.699 for Internal Capabilities, specifications 1 and 2, respectively at $p < 0.01$ & 0.192 and 0.191 for External Sources, specifications 1 and 2, respectively at $p < 0.05$). As regards the interaction term between *District* × *Internal_Capabilities*, (1.477 at $p < 0.05$, specification 2), capturing the hypothesis 2, it is significant and positively related to innovative performance in general (containing all types of innovators). Hypothesis 2 is also confirmed.

Then, in the subsequent Models 2 and 3 (specifications 3-to-6), we distinguish between the kind of innovation, being either incremental or radical. As such, in Model 2 (solely incremental innovators vs non-innovators, the latter the baseline; specifications 3 and 4) it is observed that the *District* effect is still positive and significantly (0.609 and 0.960 at $p < 0.01$ in specifications 3 and 4, respectively) related to incremental innovation (those firms that solely introduce incremental, new-to-the-firm, innovation versus non-

Table 3. Correlation Matrix and descriptive statistics.

		Mean	S.D.	Min	Max	1	2	3	4	5	6
1	INNO_PROD	0.539	0.498	0	1						
2	District	0.270	0.444	0	1	0.0429					
3	Internal_Capabilities	0	1	−0.408	21.05	0.0704*	−0.1927*				
4	External_Sources	0.589	0.805	0	4	0.0848*	0.0355	0.0232			
5	Size	3.625	1.101	0	7.135	0.2238*	0.1671*	−0.4449*	0.0112		
6	Low-Med_tech	0.474	0.499	0	1	0.1569*	−0.3884*	−0.0006	0.0346	0.1027*	
7	Medium-High_tech	0.062	0.241	0	1	0.0192	−0.1571*	0.3074*	0.0174	−0.1778*	−0.2451*

Table 4. Logit analysis for different sub-samples and dependent variables.

Model and specifications	Model 1		Model 2				Model 3	
Sub-sample	All innovators (510) vs non-innovators (436); N = 946		Incremental innovators (240) vs non-innovators (436); N = 676		Incremental innovators (240) vs non-innovators (436); N = 676		Radical innovators (109) vs & incremental innovators (240); N = 349	
Variables	1	2	3	4			5	6
Intercept	−2.638***	−2.675***	−2.720***	−2.761***			1.326***	1.331***
	(0.303)	(0.304)	(0.356)	(0.358)			(0.420)	(0.420)
District	0.627***	1.055***	0.609***	0.960***			−0.488*	−0.324
	(0.187)	(0.270)	(0.223)	(0.307)			(0.280)	(0.349)
Internal_Capabilities	0.778***	0.699***	0.420**	0.366**			0.427**	0.379*
	(0.149)	(0.150)	(0.170)	(0.175)			(0.201)	(0.207)
External_Sources	0.192**	0.192**	0.0451	0.0509			0.148	0.147
	(0.0885)	(0.0886)	(0.108)	(0.109)			(0.118)	(0.118)
District × Internal_Capabilities		1.477**		1.153*				0.646
		(0.642)		(0.696)				(0.811)
Inv_mills							−1.100***	−1.115***
							(0.321)	(0.322)
Size	0.600***	0.607***	0.428***	0.436***				
	(0.0776)	(0.0779)	(0.0931)	(0.0934)				
Low-Med_tech	0.871***	0.875***	0.892***	0.895***			−0.708**	−0.706**
	(0.167)	(0.167)	(0.201)	(0.201)			(0.287)	(0.288)
Medium-High_tech	0.697**	0.750**	0.919**	0.961**			−0.978**	−0.955**
	(0.319)	(0.320)	(0.374)	(0.375)			(0.454)	(0.454)
Prob > Chi²	0.000	0.000	0	0.000			0.000	0.000
Psuedo R²	0.0927	0.0928	0.0607	0.0610			0.0586	0.0505
Log-Likelihood	−592,306	−592,271	−413,068	−412,927			−339,999	−338.356

***p < 0.01; p < 0.05; p < 0.1; Industry: low-tech is the baseline; low-med-tech and medium-high-tech, OECD classification. Standard errors into brackets; In model 3 we exclude Size because for the Heckman procedure the independent variables need to vary in the model.

innovators). In addition, the interaction term between *District* × *Internal_Capabilities*, (1.153 at $p < 0.05$, specification 4), is significant and positively related to incremental innovative performance. The result, coincident from both models, (Model 1 and 2, specifications 1-to-4) confirms that, when firms introduce incremental innovation, then the *District* (variable) effect works, improving incremental innovation, offering a robustness check for hypothesis 2.

In addition, and according to the interaction effect obtained in Models 1 and 2 (*District* × *Internal_Capabilities*), the MID effect does not exert the same effect on performance to district firms: depending on each district firm's' internal capability, the innovative performance positively varies. The latter shows the intra-district heterogeneity of capabilities and asymmetric gains. Therefore, according to the results stated in Table 4, we obtain the following insights:

- In MIDs, firms are more likely to innovate incrementally than radically, confirming hypothesis 1.
- The district effect depends on each firm's internal capabilities, that is, firms with higher internal capabilities can exploit better the district effect, confirming hypothesis 2 about knowledge heterogeneity and asymmetric gains.
- The relationship between the district effect on innovation and a collocated firm's capabilities is positive as long as the innovation pursuit is incremental, not radical, refining thus the results.

Results could suffer from additional selection bias. Thepotential problem is tackled as follows: first, the decision to innovate is predicted, and then for the innovators the type of innovation (radical vs incremental innovators) is also predicted. Heckman's two-stage analysis (Heckman, 1979) was run in order to tackle with these selection problems. The inverse Mills ratio obtained was included as an additional independent variable in order to run the regression in Model 3. In Model 3 (radical innovators vs solely incremental, the latter the baseline; specifications 5 and 6) we test the same model on those firms having introduced radical innovation, versus those that have introduced only incremental, addressing specifically hypothesis 2 and double checking for hypothesis 1. Results show (specifications 5 and 6) how the *District* (variable) effect is negative (−0.488 and −0.324, sepcifications 5 and 6, respectively) and non-significant. Similarly, the interaction term (*District* × *Internal_Capabilities*, 0.646 $p > 0.1$, specification 6) is non-significant. Overall, the *District* (variable) effect does not work for radical innovation, nor facilitate the introduction of that type of innovation within MIDs. Firms, therefore, introducing that particular type of innovation do not profit from the collocation and do not invest in absorptive capacity to source local knowledge because the available knowledge circulates within established lock-in paradigms and does not foster radical changes. In other words, MIDs do not facilitate nor constitute a prone-to-innovation context to innovate on a discontinuous basis. Rather, MIDs mainly facilitate and promote incremental or imitative innovation. Alternatively, it can be said that the local and embedded knowledge in those institutional settings primarily foster incremental innovation and, therefore, the local context does not facilitate radical innovation. This result confirms hypothesis 2 and reinforces the previous hypotheses 1. See Table 4.

As regards control variables, Size is positive and statistically significant in all models. Addressing Industry effect dummies, there is strong evidence that medium-low and medium-high are both more (positively) related to innovation (than low-tech, the baseline). For radical innovation the industry effect variable turns out to be insignificant.

5. Conclusions

Addressing the MID effect at the firm level, to the best of our knowledge, there is no study focusing on understanding the relationship between collocation in an MID and the occurrence of radical innovation, at least using a large-scale database beyond anecdotal case studies. In this paper, the focus is on empirically testing whether MID fosters radical innovation, a phenomenon mostly overlooked by scholars. Specifically, this study's objective has consisted of deciphering whether collocation in MIDs exerts a potential effect on a collocated firm's discontinuous or radical innovative performance. Using data from the Spanish CIS and other regional data sets, we tested our predictions on a large sample in the Valencia Region in Spain, covering 946 firms, confirming the three stated hypothesis. Overall, results indicated that collocated firms in MIDs, due to the available prone-to-innovation environment, reinforce their absorptive capacity to access to available knowledge and opportunities, vis-à-vis non-collocated ones, improving thus their innovative performance. Our results have also pointed out that localization externalities from collocation in districts are not related to a firm's new-to-the-market innovative performance, that is, MIDs do not facilitate the occurrence of discontinuous or radical innovations. Rather, the local information and knowledge are mainly devoted to facilitating the introduction of incremental innovation.

Additionally, and looking at interactions, localization externalities in MIDs render a positive effect on innovation depending on each firm's capabilities. That is, not all district firms gain the same. Thus, it is evidenced that the MID effect does not exert the same effect on performance to all district firms: depending on each district firm's' internal capability, the performance varies, signalling an internal-to-the-district firm heterogeneity. This insight shows that it is not only important to compare district and non-district firms, but to understand *intra-district heterogeneity* resulting on asymmetric gains.

Complementary, this study also points out an additional insight. The later results, however, works as long as firms attempt to introduce incremental innovation, reinforcing the idea that MIDs do not facilitate the occurrence of radical innovation. Put differently, radical innovation occurs, indeed, but it is not activated nor facilitated by MIDs that are primarily oriented to generate a positive lock-in around incremental innovation.

Overall, this study contributes to the extensive literature on innovation in MIDs (e.g. Belussi & Sedita, 2009; Brusco, 1982; Cainelli & De Liso, 2005; Hervas-Oliver et al., 2017; Varaldo & Ferrucci, 1996). In particular, it addresses that sub-line of inquiry that, beyond conventional wisdom, argues that knowledge in MIDs flows unevenly and is not always fully accessible to all collocated firms (e.g. Giuliani, 2007). The key contributions to this literature are the insights that point out that, in MIDs, (i) incremental innovation, and not radical, is facilitated and, (ii) there is intra-district firm's heterogeneity. We are not stating that radical innovation does not occur in districts, rather we point out that MIDs primarily facilitate the occurrence of incremental or imitative innovation. In fact, there are firms in district that introduce non-continuous innovation but when this occurs, the MID effect does not exert any positive influence.

Our study has some limitations. First, the results are subjected to a specific region where data has been tested. Second, this study has used product innovation that is new-to-the-market (as opposed to new-to-the-firm) as the dependent variable covering the construct of radical innovation. This has been done in that way because in the Spanish CIS this is the only option to capture non-continuous innovations. For future research the same reasoning and hypotheses need to be replicated in different districts and countries with CIS or other data, in order to test generalization of results and thus to enrich the non-incremental innovation framework in MIDs.

Notes

1. Throughout this paper clusters and Marshallian Industrial Districts are used interchangeably, albeit we do recognize different social mechanisms prevailing in Marshallian Industrial Districts. MIDs in this article refer to *localization advantages* in the sense of Marshall (1890/1920) or Saxenian (1994), due to industry specialization: these localization economies, based on a social dimension, reduce transaction costs, foster knowledge exchange, and facilitate the creation of a network-based model of flexible organization that enables easier innovation and growth.
2. See Galletto & Boix, 2014.
3. Marshall (1890/1920), Arrow (1962), and Romer (1986) put forward a concept, which was later formalized by the seminal work of Glaeser, Kallal, Scheinkman, and Shleifer (1992) and became known as the Marshall–Arrow–Romer (MAR) mode.
4. In strategy and innovation literature, this firm heterogeneity is well accepted, based on the resource-based view of the firm (RBV, e.g. Barney, 1991; Peteraf, 1993).
5. See Galletto & Boix, 2014.
6. For Camagni (1991, p. 130), collective learning is central to milieu or MIDs; 'the local "milieu" may be defined as a set of territorial relationships encompassing in a coherent way a production system, different economic and social actors, a specific culture and a representation system, and generating a dynamic collective learning process'
7. For example, see De-Miguel-Molina, Hervás-Oliver, & Boix, 2019.
8. Obtained from the *Valencia Region Statistical Office* at http://www.pegv.gva.es/es/principales-magnitudes-de-la-industria-en-ambitos-subregionales.
9. The two metric variables generating one single component from the analysis, through its scores, represent the dependent variable which explains 63.26 % of the variance (KMO = 0.69, $p < 0.01$).

Disclosure statement

No potential conflict of interest was reported by the authors.

Funding

This work was supported by Ministerio de Ciencia, Innovación y Universidades [grant number RTI2018-095739-B-100].

References

Albino, V., Garavelli, A. C., & Schiuma, G. (1998). Knowledge transfer and inter-firm relationships in industrial districts: The role of the leader firm. *Technovation*, 19(1), 53–63. doi:10.1016/S0166-4972(98)00078-9

Arrow, K. J. (1962). The economic implications of learning by doing. *The Review of Economic Studies*, 29(3), 155–173. doi:10.2307/2295952

Audretsch, D. B., & Feldman, M. P. (1996). R&D spillovers and the geography of innovation and production. *The American Economic Review*, *86*(3), 630–640.

Balland, P. A., Belso-Martínez, J. A., & Morrison, A. (2016). The dynamics of technical and business knowledge networks in industrial clusters: Embeddedness, status, or proximity? *Economic Geography*, *92*(1), 35–60. doi:10.1080/00130095.2015.1094370

Barney, J. (1991). Firm resources and sustained competitive advantage. *Journal of Management*, *17* (1), 99–120. doi:10.1177/014920639101700108

Becattini, G. (1990). The Marshallian industrial districts as a socio-economic notion. In G. Pike & G. Becattini (Eds.), *Industrial districts and inter-firm cooperation in Italy* (pp. 413–431). Geneva: International Institute for Labour Studies.

Belso-Martínez, J. A. (2010). International outsourcing and partner location in the Spanish footwear sector. *European Urban and Regional Studies*, *17*(1), 65–82. doi:10.1177/0969776409350789

Belussi, F., & Hervás-Oliver, J. L. (Eds.). (2017). *Unfolding cluster evolution*. New York: Routledge.

Belussi, F., & Sedita, S. R. (2009). Life cycle vs. multiple path dependency in industrial districts. *European Planning Studies*, *17*(4), 505–528. doi:10.1080/09654310802682065

Bianchi, P., & Giordani, M. G. (1993). Innovation policy at the local and national levels: The case of Emilia-Romagna. *European Planning Studies*, *1*(1), 25–41. doi:10.1080/09654319308720193

Breschi, S., & Lissoni, F. (2001). Knowledge spillovers and local innovation systems: A critical survey. *Industrial and Corporate Change*, *10*, 975–1005. doi:10.1093/icc/10.4.975

Brusco, S. (1982). The Emilian model: Productive decentralisation and social integration. *Cambridge Journal of Economics*, *6*, 167–184.

Cainelli, G., & De Liso, N. (2005). Innovation in industrial districts: Evidence from Italy. *Industry and Innovation*, *12*(3), 383–398. doi:10.1080/13662710500195991

Camagni, R. (1991). *Innovation networks. Spatial perspectives*. London: Gremi-Belhaven Press.

Cohen, W., & Levinthal, D. (1990). Absorptive capacity: A new perspective on learning and innovation. *Administrative Science Quarterly*, *35*(1), 128–152. doi:10.2307/2393553

Crescenzi, R., & Gagliardi, L. (2018). The innovative performance of firms in heterogeneous environments: The interplay between external knowledge and internal absorptive capacities. *Research Policy*, *47*(4), 782–795. doi:10.1016/j.respol.2018.02.006

De-Miguel-Molina, B., Hervás-Oliver, J.-L., & Boix, R. (2019). Understanding innovation in creative industries: Knowledge bases and innovation performance in art restoration organisations. *Innovation*. doi:10.1080/14479338.2018.1562300.

Escribano, A., Fosfuri, A., & Tribó, J. A. (2009). Managing external knowledge flows: The moderating role of absorptive capacity. *Research Policy*, *38*(1), 96–105.

Expósito-Langa, M., Molina-Morales, F. X., & Capo-Vicedo, J. (2011). New product development and absorptive capacity in industrial districts: A multidimensional approach. *Regional Studies*, *45* (3), 319–331. doi:10.1080/00343400903241535

Gabaldón-Estevan, D., Manjarrés-Henríquez, L., & Molina-Morales, F. X. (2018). An analysis of the Spanish ceramic tile industry research contracts and patents. *European Planning Studies*, *26*(5), 895–914. doi:10.1080/09654313.2018.1427701

Galletto, V., & Boix, R. (2014). Distritos industriales, innovación tecnológica y efecto I-distrito: ¿Una cuestión de volumen o de valor? *Journal of Regional Research*, *30*, 27–51.

Gilbert, B. A. (2012). Creative destruction: Identifying its geographic origins. *Research Policy*, *41*(4), 734–742. doi:10.1016/j.respol.2011.11.005

Gilbert, B. A., McDougall, P. P., & Audretsch, D. B. (2008). Clusters, knowledge spillovers and new venture performance: An empirical examination. *Journal of Business Venturing*, *23*(4), 405–422. doi:10.1016/j.jbusvent.2007.04.003

Giuliani, E. (2007). The selective nature of knowledge networks in clusters: Evidence from the wine industry. *Journal of Economic Geography*, *7*(2), 139–168. doi:10.1093/jeg/lbl014

Glaeser, E., Kallal, H., Scheinkman, J., & Shleifer, A. (1992). Growth in cities. *Journal of Political Economy*, *100*, 1126–1152. doi:10.1086/261856

Glasmeier, A. (1991). Technological discontinuities and flexible production networks: The case of Switzerland and the world watch industry. *Research Policy*, *20*(5), 469–485. doi:10.1016/0048-7333(91)90070-7

Grabher, G. (1993). The weakness of strong ties; the lock-in of regional development in Ruhr area. In G. Grabher (Ed.), *The embedded firm: On the socioeconomics of industrial networks* (pp. 255–277). London: Routledge.

Harrison, B., Kelley, M. R., & Gant, J. J. (1996). Innovative firm behavior and local milieu: Exploring the intersection of agglomeration, firm effects, and technological change. *Economic Geography*, *72*(3), 233–258. doi:10.2307/144400

Heckman, J. J. (1979). Sample selection bias as a specification error. *Econometrica: Journal of the Econometric Society*, *47*(1), 153–161.

Hervás-Oliver, J. L. (2016). What about disruptions in clusters? Retaking a missing debate. In M. D. Parrilli, R. D. Fitjar, & A. Rodríguez-Pose (Eds.), *Innovation drivers and regional innovation strategies* (Vol. 40, pp. 105–121). New York: Routledge.

Hervas-Oliver, J. L., & Albors-Garrigos, J. (2009). The role of the firm's internal and relational capabilities in clusters: When distance and embeddedness are not enough to explain innovation. *Journal of Economic Geography*, *9*(2), 263–283. doi:10.1093/jeg/lbn033

Hervas-Oliver, J. L., & Albors-Garrigos, J. (2014). Are technology gatekeepers renewing clusters? Understanding gatekeepers and their dynamics across cluster life cycles. *Entrepreneurship & Regional Development*, *26*(5–6), 431–452. doi:10.1080/08985626.2014.933489

Hervás-Oliver, J. L., Albors-Garrigos, J., Estelles-Miguel, S., & Boronat-Moll, C. (2018). Radical innovation in Marshallian industrial districts. *Regional Studies*, *52*(10), 1388–1397. doi:10.1080/00343404.2017.1390311

Hervas-Oliver, J. L., Garrigos, J., & Gil-Pechuan, I. J. (2011). Making sense of innovation by R&D and non-R&D innovators in low technology contexts: A forgotten lesson for policymakers. *Technovation*, *31*(9), 427–446. doi:10.1016/j.technovation.2011.06.006

Hervas-Oliver, J.-L., Lleo, M., & Cervello, R. J. (2017). The dynamics of cluster entrepreneurship: Knowledge legacy from parents or agglomeration effects? The case of the Castellon ceramic tile district. *Research Policy*, *46*(1), 73–92. doi:10.1016/j.respol.2016.10.006

Hervas-Oliver, J. L., Sempere-Ripoll, F., Rojas-Alvarado, R., & Estelles-Miguel, S. (2018). Agglomerations and firm performance: Who benefits and how much? *Regional Studies*, *52*(3), 338–349. doi:10.1080/00343404.2017.1297895

Isaksen, A. (2018). From success to failure, the disappearance of clusters: A study of a Norwegian boat-building cluster. *Cambridge Journal of Regions, Economy and Society*, *11*(2), 241–255. doi:10.1093/cjres/rsy007

Knoben, J., Arikan, A. T., van Oort, F., & Raspe, O. (2016). Agglomeration and firm performance: One firm's medicine is another firm's poison. *Environment and Planning A: Economy and Space*, *48*(1), 132–153. doi:10.1177/0308518X15602898

Lane, P. J., Koka, B. R., & Pathak, S. J. (2006). The reification of absorptive capacity: A critical review and rejuvenation of the construct. *Academy of Management Review*, *31*(4), 833–863. doi:10.5465/amr.2006.22527456

Laursen, K., & Salter, A. (2006). Open for innovation: The role of openness in explaining innovation performance among U.K. Manufacturing firms. *Strategic Management Journal*, *27*(2), 131–150. doi:10.1002/smj.507

Lee, C. Y. (2018). Geographical clustering and firm growth: Differential growth performance among clustered firms. *Research Policy*, *47*(6), 1173–1184. doi:10.1016/j.respol.2018.04.002

Lorenzoni, G., & Lipparini, A. (1999). The leveraging of interfirm relationships as a distinctive organizational capability: A longitudinal study. *Strategic Management Journal*, *20*(4), 317–338. doi:10.1002/(SICI)1097-0266(199904)20:4<317::AID-SMJ28>3.0.CO;2-3

Marshall, A. (1890/1920). *Principles of economics*. London: Macmillan.

Martin, R., & Sunley, P. (2006). Path dependence and regional economic evolution. *Journal of Economic Geography*, *6*(4), 395–437. doi:10.1093/jeg/lbl012

McCann, B. T., & Folta, T. B. (2011). Performance differentials within geographic clusters. *Journal of Business Venturing*, *26*(1), 104–123. doi:10.1016/j.jbusvent.2009.04.004

Nelson, R. R., & Winter, S. G. (1982). The Schumpeterian tradeoff revisited. *The American Economic Review*, *72*(1), 114–132.

OECD. (2005). *Oslo manual*. Luxembourg: OECD.

Ostergaard, C. R., & Park, E. (2015). What makes clusters decline? A study on disruption and evolution of a high-tech cluster in Denmark. *Regional Studies, 49*(5), 834–849. doi:10.1080/00343404.2015.1015975

Peteraf, M. A. (1993). The cornerstones of competitive advantage: A resource-based view. *Strategic Management Journal, 14*(3), 179–191. doi:10.1002/smj.4250140303

Piore, M. J., & Sabel, C. F. (1984). *The second industrial divide: Possibilities for prosperity* (Vol. 4). New York: Basic Books.

Pouder, R., & St. John, C. H. (1996). Hot spots and blind spots: Geographical clusters of firms and innovation. *Academy of Management Review, 21*(4), 1192–1225. doi:10.5465/amr.1996.9704071867

Rigby, D. L., & Brown, W. M. (2015). Who benefits from agglomeration? *Regional Studies, 49*(1), 28–43. doi:10.1080/00343404.2012.753141

Robertson, P. L., & Jacobson, D. (Eds.). (2011). *Knowledge transfer and technology diffusion*. Cheltelham: Edward Elgar Publishing.

Robertson, P. L., & Langlois, R. N. (1995). Innovation, networks, and vertical integration. *Research Policy, 24*(4), 543–562. doi:10.1016/S0048-7333(94)00786-1

Romer, P. M. (1986). Increasing returns and long-run growth. *Journal of Political Economy, 94*(5), 1002–1037. doi:10.1086/261420

Saxenian, A. L. (1994). *Regional advantage: Culture and competition in Silicon Valley and route 128*. Cambridge, MA: Harvard University Press.

Scott, A. J. (1989). *New industrial spaces: Flexible production organization and regional development in North America and Western Europe*. London: Pion.

Staber, U., & Sautter, B. (2011). Who are we, and do we need to change? Cluster identity and life cycle. *Regional Studies, 45*(10), 1349–1361. doi:10.1080/00343404.2010.490208

Storper, M., & Walker, R. (1989). *The capitalist imperative*. Oxford: Blackwell.

Sull, D. N. (2001). From community of innovation to community of inertia: The rise and fall of the U.S. tire industry. In *Academy of management proceedings* (Vol. 2001, No. 1, pp. L1–L6). Briarcliff Manor, NY: Academy of Management.

Varaldo, R., & Ferrucci, L. (1996). The evolutionary nature of the firm within industrial districts. *European Planning Studies, 4*(1), 27–34. doi:10.1080/09654319608720327

Appendix I

Internal_Capabilities are constructed by applying a Factor analysis on HRRD (Human Resources on R&D) and Internal R&D (INTEX variable)

Variable. Obs	Mean	Std.	Dev.	Min	Max
HRRD	946	0.0962456	0.1711713	0	1
INTEX	946	0.0929468	1.131605	0	32.2292

After rotating factor loadings (pattern matrix) and unique variances, we got:

Variable	Factor 1	Uniqueness
HRRD	0.7891	0.3774
INTEXT	0.7891	0.3774

Internal Capabilities:
63,26% explained variance
Bartlet test chi-squared: 58,55, *p*-value = 0.00 < 0.05
KMO: 0,69

Place-based innovation in industrial districts: the long-term evolution of the iMID effect in Spain (1991–2014)

Rafael Boix-Domenech ⓘ, Vittorio Galletto ⓘ and Fabio Sforzi ⓘ

ABSTRACT
The innovation-Marshallian industrial district (iMID) effect defines the existence of dynamic efficiency in the Marshallian industrial district (MID) in the form of a positive innovative differential compared to the average of the national economy. Cross-sectional analyses have proven the existence of the iMID effect. Nevertheless, these findings do not provide any evidence on the evolution in the iMID effect over a long period and, in particular, when phases of growth, crisis and economic recovery follow one another, as occurred in the world economy around 1990 and 2007. This paper aims at closing this gap in knowledge by measuring the evolution of the iMID effect for Spain for the period 1991–2014. The measurement is made using an exhaustive database of 143,229 patents and by estimating a knowledge production function for the local production systems (LPSs). The results show that MIDs registered the largest number of patents compared to the other LPSs during the time span considered, that the iMID effect is higher for the highest quantiles of innovative intensity, and that MIDs' innovative intensity has been continuously above the national average, even after the 2007 economic crisis. MIDs are still fundamental for the generation of innovation in the Spanish economy.

1. Introduction

The term 'district effect' was coined by Signorini (1994) to explain the high efficiency rates of firms localized in Marshallian industrial districts (MIDs). Dei Ottati defined the district effect as the 'set of competitive advantages derived from a strongly related collection of economies external to the individual firms but internal to the district' (Dei Ottati, 2006, p. 74).

The empirical research on the district effect has been especially intense in regard to the so-called *static efficiency* – that is, efficiency in costs, productivity and exports-comparative advantages (Boix, Galletto, & Sforzi, 2018).

However, the competitive advantage of the district lies in its *dynamic efficiency*. The introduction of the concept of external economies, 'which arise out of the collective organization of the district as a whole', is due to Alfred Marshall (Marshall, 1930, p. XIII). In the Marshallian theoretical framework, these external economies are nothing but economies of knowledge, and, as such, they support innovation. The dynamic district effect is associated with the production of knowledge and innovation (Becattini, 2004; Bellandi, 1992).

Early on, Russo (1985) documented the dynamic effect and its causes as regards the production of machinery for ceramic tile making in the MID of Sassuolo (Italy). She proved that – without specific research and development (R&D) investment – specific skills, competition among machine producers and the multiplicity of interrelations among producers of machines for tile making and ceramic tile firms led to the intense production and patenting of innovations in the MID. Other researchers have obtained empirical evidence about the dynamic effect for different types of Italian MIDs in regions such as Emilia-Romagna (Leoncini & Lotti, 2004) and Lombardy (Muscio, 2006) although in some cases the findings have been inconclusive (Santarelli, 2004).

Boix and Galletto (2009) made explicit the relationship between innovation and the district effect, coining the term 'innovation-district effect' (I-district effect, or iMID effect). This research introduced several innovative elements. It focused for the first time on an entire country rather than on an individual region or district, on a country other than Italy, using local labour systems (LLSs) as the unit of analysis of innovation – and among these the MIDs, identified according to Sforzi-ISTAT methodology applied to Spain. In addition, it uses an extensive database of patent microdata and other registers of innovation. The research has shown that, despite the very low expenditures in R&D, the MIDs' innovative intensity is much higher than the national average and that, indeed, the Marshallian external economies are behind this fact. This research stream has also addressed critical issues about the robustness of the iMID effect, proving that it is mostly due to the place (the local context) rather than to the specific sectorial specialization (Boix & Trullén, 2010). Moreover, it has proven that MIDs are not only 'weak innovators' – that is, characterized by low-value technological innovation – but that the iMID effect maintains for all types of patents (Galletto & Boix, 2014).

The focus on a short period (2001–2006) is the major limitation of the research stream on the iMID effect. Therefore, the question arises as to how MID innovative capacity changes over a long period and, in particular, whether the iMID effect persists after an economic crisis, such as the crisis the world economy suffered around 2007. Based on the previous literature on the iMID effect and the idea of the MID as an innovation machine, the hypothesis that we explore is that the MID is flexible enough to adapt in the long term and to continue innovating more than the average of the national economy.

The paper makes two contributions. First, it deepens the knowledge on the causes of the iMID effect by developing the idea of the MID as an innovation machine. Second, it advances the knowledge on the iMID by measuring the change of innovation for all the MIDs of a country, Spain, between 1991 and 2014, being the first time that this effect is analysed over such a long period, which includes phases of growth and recession. In addition, this research improves the quality and coverage of the data with respect to previous research and allows comparison with the evolution of the innovative performance of other types of local production systems (LPSs).

Technological innovative intensity is measured for the LPSs of Spain using an exhaustive database of 143,229 applications between 1991 and 2014, which includes utility models and patents from the Spanish Patent and Trademark Office (OEPM), the European Patent Office (EPO) and the United States Patent and Trademark Office (USPTO). The indicator of innovative intensity is aggregated in periods of four years to reduce the annual sensitivity and allows following the evolution of the MID during the different phases of the economic cycle, including the post-2007 crisis. Later, the iMID effect is estimated econometrically using a knowledge production function (KPF).

The paper is structured as follows. Section 2 introduces the theoretical framework, explaining why and how the MID innovates. Section 3 describes the calculation of the indicator for measuring innovative intensity and the categorization of the LPSs into different types, including MIDs. Section 4 accounts for the change of the iMID effect in Spain from 1991 to 2014. Section 5 econometrically models the iMID effect using a KPF. Section 6 draws conclusions.

2. Theoretical background and literature review: the MID as an innovation machine

2.1. Marshallian industrial districts

A population of firms specialized in different phases of the same production process (i.e. phases of processing, parts of a product or products) and embedded in a given local community is what economists call the 'Marshallian industrial district' (MID). Conceptualized in the 1980s by Giacomo Becattini (see Becattini, 2001, 2004), the MID is now, as then, the theoretical benchmark for explaining the economic competitiveness of small and medium-sized enterprises (SMEs).

The source of this competitiveness lies in the ability of district entrepreneurs who work in complementary phases of production to cooperate readily with each other. At the same time, it lies in the ability of entrepreneurs who work in the same phase of production to compete fairly with each other to improve their specialized skills in order to supply products (or phases of processing) at a lower price and better quality compared to other district entrepreneurs.

What holds these multiple networks of inter-firm relationships together – where cooperation and competition coexist – is a widely shared value system and views that permeate the local community and regulate the business relations. Values such as ethic of work and activity, reputation in business, customs of mutual trust, established routines and a view about economic change as a social process define the norms and sanctions that foster cooperation and regulate competition (Becattini, 2004, p. 20).

The segmentation of production into independent firms of phase means that each phase a) has a specific technical culture and b) develops its own market. Therefore, in a textile district, for example, the spinner and the weaver have a scientific-technical approach to their job, whereas the designer of fabrics has an artistic and handicraft-like culture. Likewise, there is a market of spinning, of weaving and of designers of fabric patterns. This plexus of markets also extends to the subsidiary industries that supply the main industry of the district – the textile industry, in this example – with implements, specialized machinery or chemical products for textile processing (Becattini, 2004, pp. 45–46).

As argued by Sebastiano Brusco – a leading economist of the district research in the 1980s – phase entrepreneurs can switch from one to another of the numerous production processes that take place in a MID, and subsidiary entrepreneurs can make or modify their products on demand, thus fostering the circulation and sharing of innovations (Brusco, 1986, pp. 87–88).

The continuous recombination of production relations that occurs within the MID production system breeds a constant stream of innovations and stimulates the tendency to innovate (Becattini, 2004, p. 46).

2.2. Why and how MIDs innovate

What impels district entrepreneurs to innovate derives from the nature of the markets in which they operate and the human desires that the district products satisfy.

The markets for district products are markets with differentiated and variable demand. The demand is differentiated because, as a rule, historical and cultural factors prevent the possibility of selling the same products in different markets – national, regional and even local (Becattini, 1975, p. 27). And it is variable because the satisfaction of the human desires for variety and for social distinction requires a continuous renewal of the sample collection, introducing products that are not only new compared to the previous ones but attractive for their originality.

It should be emphasized that the district production system, not differently from other organizational forms of production that define the capitalist mode of production, such as mass differentiation, does not aim at satisfying human desires but rather at giving rise to new ones.

In the MID world of production, innovation takes the form of modular innovation, referring to the phase in which entrepreneurs specialized in a given (part of) product implement innovation.

These entrepreneurs have both the knowledge of the product component in which they are specialized and the knowledge of the product architecture, i.e. the knowledge about the way in which each component is integrated and linked together in a coherent whole to complete the finished product (Henderson & Clark, 1990).

The fact that innovation proceeds through innovations of phase does not exclude, of course, the possibility that the kick-off of innovation proceeds from the design of the product as a whole to its individual components. In this case, the entrepreneur who designed and engineered the product will entrust the implementation of each component to the phase entrepreneurs constituting his network of collaborators.

Sometimes the engineering of the product requires the involvement of the subsidiary entrepreneur, which contributes with the adaptation of the already-in-place machinery to manufacture the new product or with the construction of ad hoc machinery.

The MID innovation, therefore, is a process of a social and collective nature, the outcome of cooperation and sharing.

The flow of modular or architectural innovations that district entrepreneurs must constantly generate to produce specialized products dedicated to groups of consumers who are demanding and sensitive to novelties, and who sometimes seek novelty for its own sake, could suggest a short life for district innovation, such as to make its intellectual protection unnecessary. If this is partially true, it is equally true that district products adopt or introduce new technological or design solutions that are worth protecting, both when they have already been introduced as a component of the manufacture of a product and when their introduction is still potential.

The protection of innovation through the formal method of patents is an effective indicator of the capacity for the innovation of MIDs although they define it by default.

3. Measurement of the innovative intensity

3.1. Measurement of the technological innovation and the innovative intensity

Boix and Galletto (2009) have stated that the measurement of innovation is a widely discussed topic in the literature although there is no agreement about which indicator is the most appropriate. In this paper, we follow the line started in the previous analyses, so to measure innovation we use indicators based on instruments for the protection of intellectual property related mainly to technology, such as patents and utility models.[1]

As long as patents imply novelty and utility, and an economic expenditure for the applicant, it is supposed that patented innovation has economic value (Griliches, 1990). Furthermore, patent documents contain highly useful data, such as the inventor's name and address as well as the invention's date and technological classification. For these reasons, patent indicators are the most widely employed indicators of innovation (Khan & Dernis, 2006). Therefore, the use of patents offers the additional advantage of allowing one to discuss the results regarding the most extended empirical line. There are two additional reasons for its use: patent microdata cover the entire population and not just a sample and allow for exact georeferencing, which is fundamental when working at a detailed territorial level. The validity and convenience of the use of patents as indicators of technological innovation in MIDs and other LPSs have been profusely discussed in previous research (Boix et al., 2018; Boix & Galletto, 2009; Boix & Trullén, 2010; Galletto & Boix, 2014).

However, in our study we are not interested in patents *per se* but as (technological) innovation indicators.[2] For this reason, patent data are not restricted to a single register or intellectual property office (IPO), as is the usual practice, but rather cover several IPOs to produce a more precise assessment of innovation and the characteristics of different types of LPSs: the OEPM, the EPO and the USPTO. Furthermore, they cover applications with at least one inventor with an address in Spain.[3]

The complete patent database includes 143,229 documents from 1991 to 2014, consisting of the more comprehensive innovation database geocoded at the Spanish municipal level, at least to our knowledge. As is usual in the literature, in cases of multiple inventors a fractional assignation is made to the different municipalities of the addresses.[4]

The selection of the period is marked by the availability of maps of MIDs for Spain since 1991 (Sforzi & Boix, 2019) and the fact that after 2014 the coverage of the innovation registers is not reliable as a result of delays in the publication of data due to secrecy.

To measure local technological innovation, the different sets of data from different IPOs are added to a single indicator related to each year and each municipality so that they can be aggregated by geographical scale and time periods.

In order to avoid yearly fluctuations and to take into account the lags in the outcome of innovation processes, the common practice is to show data on innovation in periods of four to five years (Griliches, 1992). In this research the data are divided into periods of four years. This will allow proper differentiation of the periods of growth and decline of the Spanish economy.

3.2. MIDs and other LPSs in Spain

The relevant territorial units for measuring economic change and innovation processes in MIDs are the LLSs (Boix & Galletto, 2009; Sforzi, 1990). The LLSs and their categorization in LPSs have been recently reworked for Spain (Sforzi & Boix, 2019) for the years 1991, 2001 and 2011 using the well-known Sforzi-ISTAT algorithm (Sforzi, 2009). This elaboration includes a minor correction of the previous LLSs/LPSs identified by Boix and Galletto (2009).

The identification for three time points allows the use of changing units or the constant maintenance of the LPS throughout all the years using a base year. In this case, we have decided to use the LPSs closest to the centre of the period. This solution simplifies the analysis and allows the use of panel methods.

According to their productive characteristics, the procedure allows the identification of up to nine categories of LPSs, which, for parsimony, we have aggregated into six homogeneous types of LPS defined in 2001.[5] They include MIDs (accounting for 215 of total LPSs), manufacturing LPSs of large firms (56), LPSs specialized in agriculture and mining (276), LPSs specialized in construction (42), LPSs specialized in business services (3) and LPS specialized in other services (consumer, social or traditional services) (85).

4. The iMID effect and its evolution in Spain from 1991 to 2014

Innovation has grown during the period 1991–2014 in all the types of LPSs. The impact of the crisis is reflected in the last intervals, when the indicator stagnates.

In the period 2011–2014, MIDs have 26.5% of the total innovations and comprise the greatest innovator of the Spanish economy (in terms of percentage of total innovations) (Table 1). However, this share has decreased during the last two periods, corresponding to the 2007 crisis, due to the higher flexibility of Spanish MIDs – regarding other LPSs – to the cyclical fluctuations of the external demand. The other types of LPSs with high percentages of innovations are the manufacturing LPSs of large firms (26.1%) and LPSs of business services (22.6%) (Table 1).

Innovative intensity is measured using the number of innovations per million employees. During the whole period of 24 years, the innovative intensity has been steady: around 400 annual innovations per million employees (Table 1). This stability can be explained by the simultaneous growth of both innovation and occupation. The aggregated innovative intensity of MIDs during the whole period – the sum of all the innovations in MIDs divided by the total number of employees in MIDs – is approximately 480 innovations per employee. It reaches its maximum in the period 1999–2002 and its minimum during the first years of the crisis (2007–2010) (Table 1).

Figure 1 shows the aggregated innovation intensity of each type of LPS divided by the Spanish average and its evolution. MIDs' innovative intensity is approximately 23% higher

Table 1. Distribution of innovation by type of LPS, 1991–2014.

Number of innovations	1991–1994	1995–1998	1999–2002	2003–2006	2007–2010	2011–2014
Agriculture and mining	746	845	1.103	1.099	1.202	1.188
Construction	236	219	295	294	314	321
Industrial districts	5.948	6.148	7.492	7.908	7.194	7.039
Manufacturing LPSs of large firms	5.987	5.579	6.465	7.555	7.540	6.929
Business services	4.450	4.720	4.688	5.031	6.096	5.993
Other services	2.547	2.967	3.554	4.123	4.349	5.063
Total	19.914	20.479	23.597	26.011	26.694	26.534
Percentage of innovations						
Agriculture and mining	3,7	4,1	4,7	4,2	4,5	4,5
Construction	1,2	1,1	1,3	1,1	1,2	1,2
Industrial districts	29,9	30,0	31,7	30,4	26,9	26,5
Manufacturing LPSs of large firms	30,1	27,2	27,4	29,0	28,2	26,1
Business services	22,3	23,0	19,9	19,3	22,8	22,6
Other services	12,8	14,5	15,1	15,9	16,3	19,1
Total	100	100	100	100	100	100
Innovative intensity (patents per million employees, annual average)[a]						
Agriculture and mining	122	133	167	140	144	158
Construction	160	142	191	155	157	187
Industrial districts	485	482	543	484	426	474
Manufacturing LPSs of large firms	795	712	660	680	652	659
Business services	514	524	430	397	452	477
Other services	184	178	188	169	138	138
Total	404	399	400	375	366	402

[a] For each type of LPS, the indicator is the sum of all the innovations divided by the sum of all the employees.
Source: Authors' elaboration on data from OEPM, EPOBD, PATSTAT, PatentView, USPTO, Ministry of Employment and INE.

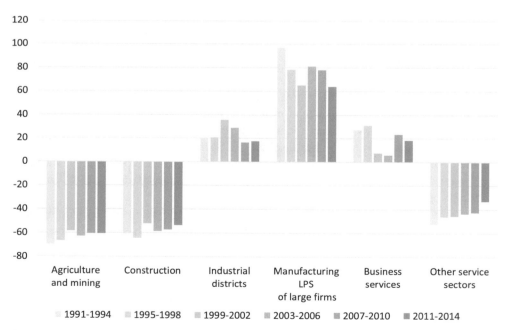

Figure 1. Innovative performance by type of LPS by period. Innovation per million employees, in differences with respect to the average of Spain. Source: Authors' elaboration on data from OEPM, EPOBD, PATSTAT, PatentView, USPTO, Ministry of Employment and INE.

than the Spanish average during the whole period. The greatest difference is achieved between the periods 1999–2002 and 2003–2006 and is reduced by half with the economic crisis. The manufacturing LPSs of large firms show the highest positive difference regarding the national average: approximately 74% more during the whole period. Business services LPSs also show a positive differential of approximately 19%. In the rest of the types of LPSs, the innovative intensity is below the Spanish average. The positive differential for MIDs proves the existence of the iMID effect although it is outpaced by the highest performance of the manufacturing LPSs of large firms. Furthermore, it seems clear that the country is highly polarized between highly innovative and lowly innovative types of LPSs (Figure 1).

The iMID effect is not only confirmed for the aggregate indicator but also when we consider the MIDs individually. Therefore, it is not due to a few MIDs that concentrate large amounts of innovation, but rather it is a generalized fact. During the time span under study (1991–2014), most of the MIDs innovate above the average of LPSs, and they are very important in quantiles of high innovative intensity. Approximately 85% of the MIDs innovate more than the average and approximately 68% more than the median of the LPSs. MIDs are the type of LPSs more represented between the 10% of more innovative LPSs: 39 MIDs (5.7% of the LPSs), followed by the manufacturing LPSs of large firms (18 LPSs and 2.6% of the LPSs). In addition, the number of MIDs innovating more than the median of LPSs has increased from 135 in the period 1991–1994 to 158 in the period 2010–2014.

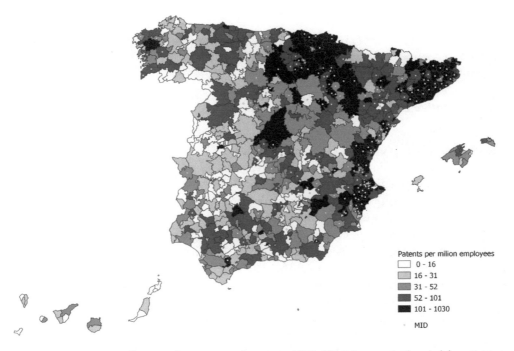

Figure 2. Patents per million employees: annual average 1991–2014. Source: Authors' elaboration on data from OEPM, EPOBD, PATSTAT, PatentView, USPTO and Spanish Ministry of Employment.

This generalized tendency of MIDs to innovate is also observed in Figure 2. It can be seen that higher innovative intensity is located in the MIDs (marked with a white dot on the map) and that most of the MIDs are among the most innovative LPSs.

5. Modelling the iMID effect

5.1. The knowledge production function (KPF)

The KPF (Griliches, 1979; Pakes & Griliches, 1984) relates innovation to R&D inputs. The KPF is modified to incorporate local economic characteristic (Anselin, Varga, & Acs, 2000) which are related to idiosyncratic effects associated to each type of LPSs, denoted by δ (Boix & Galletto, 2009).

Since the effects of R&D on innovation are not immediate (Griliches, 1979; Pakes & Griliches, 1984), the input is lagged a period in the model. As the number of innovations of a place is directly related to the size of the place, the output and the input factors are divided by the total number of employees. The KPF takes the form

$$i_{t,j} = \gamma r_{t-1,j}^{\beta} \delta_{t,k} \varepsilon \qquad (1)$$

where i is the average innovation per employee; r is the average R&D per employee; t refers to the time period; j refers to the LPS; k refers to the type of LPS; γ, β and δ are parameters and ε is a nuisance.

Taking logarithms, the KPF can be transformed into a log-linear expression

$$\log i_{t,j} = \gamma + \beta \log r_{t-1,j} + \delta_{t,k} + \varepsilon \qquad (2)$$

The model, in its form (1) or (2), can be estimated to obtain the effect of the type of LPS on the innovative intensity.

5.2. Innovative outputs and inputs

The dependent variable of the model is the innovation per employee in the LPS aggregated into six periods of four years ($i_{t,j}$) (see section 3).

The indicators of input to the innovative process are the expenditures in R&D per employee in the LPS divided into two categories: firms plus non-profit private institutions and universities plus public sector organizations.

The R&D expenditures of the firms and non-profit private organizations are obtained from the balance sheets of SABI (Bureau van Dijk) and complemented with company reports. The database covers approximately 9,300 firms with R&D expenditures in some year during the period 1991–2014. The R&D expenditures of the universities are obtained by dividing the regional data of expenditures in R&D of the universities (Spanish National Institute of Statistics) by the number of employees per university and campus; the latter are obtained from the Ministry of Education Integrated University Information System (SIUU) and the universities' reports.[6] In the R&D expenditures from the public sector, we take into account only public research organizations (PRO) depending on the central government, for which data are available (Ministry of Education) and assigned by localization.[7]

For all the indicators, the number of employees is obtained from the Social Security registers of the Spanish Ministry of Employment and includes wage-earning employees, self-employees and special regimes.

5.3. Econometric evidence of the iMID effect

The KPF was estimated for the 677 LPSs of Spain in the time span 1991–2014 to test the existence and evolution of the iMID effect. The data were divided into six four-year periods and six types of LPSs (see section 3). Since the R&D of the first period is lagged, the period 1991–1994 is not included in the estimation. The KPF is estimated using two approaches. The first is a parametric fixed effects model with fixed effects for the types of LPSs and period, which makes the results comparable with Boix and Galletto (2009). In the second step, a quantile regression (QR) with fixed effects is used, which relaxes most of the constraints of the parametric linear regression and provides additional information. The correlation matrix and descriptive statistics are provided in the Annex.

5.3.1. Parametric fixed effects

Equation (2) is estimated as a model with fixed effects (Baltagi, 2013; Wooldridge, 2013) by type of LPS and time period. For LPSs without innovation counts the dependent variable cannot be transformed in logarithms, and, to avoid this problem, we consider it to be censured and use Heckman's estimator for panel data (Baltagi, 2013; Wooldridge, 2013). This strategy is similar to that of Boix and Galletto (2009) and makes the results comparable with previous research.[8] The estimation is repeated for each time period to obtain disaggregated information of the evolution of the effect.

The performance and evolution of the iMID effect is evaluated using the estimated effect of the fixed effect for MIDs and can be compared to the other types of LPSs. The fixed effects are expressed as unitary deviations from the averaged group effect such that positive coefficients indicate performance better than the national average.

There is robust and continuous evidence of the iMID effect for the entire period without exception. The estimate for the five periods together is 0.35 and is statistically significant, which means that between 1995 and 2014 the MIDs showed an average innovative intensity 35% higher than the national average (Table 2).

In the independent estimates for each period, the iMID effect oscillates between 30 and 44% above the average (Table 2). The highest positive difference corresponds to the period 2002–2006 (44%). The lowest difference is found in the period 2006–2010 (30%), probably due to the incidence of the 2007 financial crisis.

For the rest of LPSs, a higher territorial effect is found in the manufacturing LPSs of large firms: they show an average innovative intensity 68% higher than the national average, doubling the effect of MIDs (Table 2). The differential effect is also positive for LPSs specialized in business services (approximately 17% more than the average). For the rest of the types of LPSs, the innovative intensity is lower than the average.

Regarding R&D inputs, the results for all the periods show that an increase in 1% in R&D expenditures increases the innovative intensity by 0.036% for firms and non-profit institutions and by 0.022% for universities and the public sector (Table 2). The estimations period by period show that the effect of inputs remains close to those of the periods combined and can be negative or statistically non-significant for a concrete period (Table 2).

Table 2. Estimates of the KPF. The dependent variable is innovation per million employees.

	Dependent variable in logs						Dependent variable in levels			
	Heckman Tobit[a]						Quantile regression[b]			
Period	1995–2014	1995–2014	1995–1998	1999–2002	2002–2006	2006–2010	2010–2014	1995–2014			
Quantile								Q.25	Q.50	Q.75	Q.90
Constant	5.6605 (0.000)	5.2150 (0.000)	4.6700 (0.000)	5.0355 (0.000)	5.0225 (0.000)	4.8139 (0.000)	5.1501 (0.000)				
Log R&D$_{t-1}$ firms and private non-profit institutions	0.0549 (0.000)	0.03631 (0.000)	−0.0266 (0.707)	0.0434 (0.000)	0.0319 (0.000)	0.0472 (0.000)	0.0386 (0.000)	0.0075 (0.319)	0.0286 (0.004)	0.0656 (0.189)	0.0587 (0.000)
Log R&D$_{t-1}$ universities and public sector	0.00005 (0.641)	0.0219 (0.000)	0.0256 (0.075)	−0.0070 (0.534)	0.0284 (0.004)	0.0160 (0.000)	0.0327 (0.000)	25.6194 (0.000)	10.3809 (0.078)	−6.4575 (0.557)	−8.0257 (0.738)
Fixed effect by type of LPS											
– Industrial districts		0.3532 (0.000)	0.3614 (0.000)	0.3218 (0.000)	0.4415 (0.000)	0.3044 (0.000)	0.3427 (0.000)	−0.1964 (0.000)	0.2313	0.3590	0.4127
– Manufacturing LPSs of large firms		0.6810 (0.000)	0.7171 (0.000)	0.6240 (0.000)	0.7463 (0.000)	0.6961 (0.000)	0.6184 (0.000)	0.1846 (0.000)	0.7318	0.8924	0.9575
– Business services		0.1742 (0.000)	0.1652 (0.000)	0.0973 (0.000)	−0.0149 (0.000)	0.1495 (0.000)	0.1721 (0.000)	0.5731 (0.000)	0.5717	0.0042	−0.2357
– Other services		−0.2843 (0.000)	−0.1909 (0.000)	−0.2908 (0.000)	−0.3703 (0.000)	−0.2304 (0.000)	−0.3372 (0.000)	−0.5613 (0.000)	−0.3050	−0.3387	−0.3692
– Agriculture and mining		−0.4443 (0.000)	−0.4760 (0.000)	−0.4334 (0.000)	−0.5011 (0.000)	−0.4353 (0.000)	−0.4091 (0.000)		−0.7365	−0.5539	−0.4922
– Construction		−0.2118 (0.000)	−0.4010 (0.000)	−0.0139 (0.000)	−0.4021 (0.000)	−0.1778 (0.000)	0.0008 (0.000)		−0.4933	−0.3631	−0.2730
Fixed effects by period	Yes	Yes							Yes		
Log-pseudolikelihood	−4627.41	−4395.72	−887.49	−884.45	−877.82	−875.29	−822.00				
Pseudo-R2	0.0982	0.2398	0.1594	0.2271	0.2960	0.2526	0.3015		0.0949		
Number of observations	3385	3385	677	677	677	677	677		3385		

P-values are in parentheses.
[a] Territorial fixed effects provided under the restriction that $\sum \alpha_i = 0$ so that the coefficients are deviations from the averaged group effect.
[b] In the Heckman estimator for panel data (Wooldridge, 2013), the probit is estimated using as explanatory variables the same used in the final model (including dummies by type of LPS and period) plus the number of employees, the density of employees and the lag of innovation per employee in the LPS. Within-group effect model estimates. Bootstrap estandard errors (1,000 replications).
[c] Quantile estimator for panel data by Powell (2015) with Nelder-Mead optimization.

5.3.2. Quantile regression (QR) with fixed effects

The KPF is also estimated using a QR with fixed effects (Powell, 2015). QR estimates the conditional quantiles of the dependent variable (for example, the median). QR is a non-parametrical method and does not make assumptions on the form of the distribution so that it adapts to transformations of the response variable, can handle outliers and extreme values and handles unequal variations due to omitted variables.

By using QR, we can directly estimate the nonlinear form of the KPF (Equation 1) without making any assumption about zeros in the dependent and explanatory variables. The quantile parameter estimates the change of the dependent variable produced by changes in the explanatory variable in a specified quantile. In this way, we can see whether the district effect takes place mainly in districts with low or high innovative intensity.

In QR, the iMID effect is evaluated regarding the median or other quantiles and not with respect to the mean, as in the linear model. The iMID effect is 23% higher than the median (Table 2) (compared to 35% with respect to the mean in the linear estimation). Furthermore, the effect of being an MID increases the extent to which the LPS is innovative: it is low or negative for low innovation intensity MIDs (approximately −19% in the first quantile) and increases up to 41% in the 90th quantile (Figure 3 and Table 2).

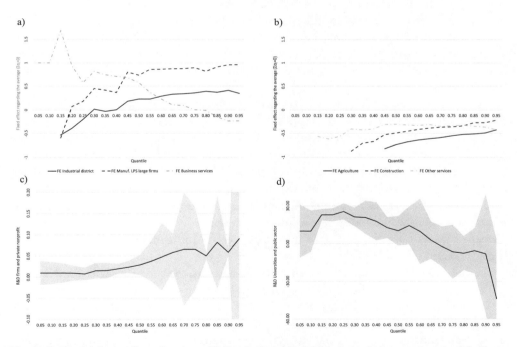

Figure 3. Graph of quantile estimation with fixed effects. Detail for the covariates and territorial effects. Overall 1995–2015. Powell (2015) estimator for fixed effects with Nelder-Mead optimization. (a) Fixed effects. Detail for industrial districts, manufacturing LPSs of large firms and business services. $\sum \alpha_i = 0$. (b) Fixed effects. Detail for agriculture and mining, construction and other (non-business) services LPSs. $\sum \alpha_i = 0$. (c) R&D$_{t-1}$ firms and private non-profit institutions. (d) R&D$_{t-1}$ universities and public sector.

The manufacturing LPSs of large firms follow a similar pattern although, as in the linear estimates, the effect is much higher than for MIDs (Figure 3). Conversely, the effect of being located in LPSs specialized in business services is higher for low innovation intensities and decreases for high innovation rates. In the rest of the LPSs, the fixed effect is below the average, in particular in quantiles where the innovation rate is low.

Regarding the inputs, the effect of the R&D expenditures of firms and private non-profit institutions is larger for percentiles of high innovative intensity (Table 2 and Figure 3). That is, the more innovative LPSs are, the higher the effect of R&D is. The effect of the R&D expenditures of universities and the public sector shows an inverse U curve (Figure 3). This effect is extremely high for quantiles with low innovative intensity and turns negative after the percentile 0.60, probably due to some saturation effect caused by the high concentration of this type of expenditure in a few LPSs.

5.4. Comparability and robustness issues

Our results prove that the innovative intensity of the MIDs during the analysis period is above average and that it is maintained even when the effect of the inputs (R&D) is eliminated. However, some of the above results merit further detail and discussion.

The results can be compared with those of Boix and Galletto (2009), Boix and Trullén (2010), Galletto and Boix (2014) and Boix et al. (2018) for Spain in the periods 2001–2005 and 2001–2006. The estimates of the iMID effect are close to those in these works. In particular, our estimation of 0.44 for the period 2002–2006 is in the range of 0.40–0.49 of previous research. However, we have also found that the response of the manufacturing LPSs of large firms is much greater than that estimated in previous works, and in fact it exceeds that of the MIDs. The response of the innovative intensity with respect to the R&D is lower than in previous research.

The differences regarding previous research are due to the slightly different definition of the types of LPSs (see section 3) as well as the use of raw microdata in the elaboration of both variables,[9] the different elaboration of the R&D expenditures of universities and the public sector (not directly comparable with the previous research) and the higher quality and coverage of our database (mainly in terms of EPO and USPTO patents, represented more in the manufacturing LPSs of large firms and business services).

There are other issues regarding the robustness of the results. First, the iMID effect is robust according to the independence of the type of econometric estimation performed (linear or quantile) and the type of measure used (mean, median) and holds during all the periods under study (Table 2).

Second, only R&D inputs are used as covariates. As explained in Boix and Galletto (2009) and Boix and Trullén (2010), additional inputs are usually related to the type of LPS so that its inclusion could explain the type of LPS (e.g. specialization, value chain suppliers, density, size, etc.), making disappear or distorting the territorial effect associated to those characteristics. Boix and Galletto (2009) and Boix and Trullén (2010) provide more detail about this issue and estimations, including additional covariates and two-way type LPS-specialization estimations.

Third, our KPF estimates assumes that R&D expenditures and the territorial categories are independent. The estimates confirm that the correlation between the inputs and the fixed effects is small. We have tested and found that the mean of the estimates of R&D

for MIDs are not different from the rest. The equality of means cannot be rejected for the R&D expenditures of firms and non-profit institutions (MID mean = 0.040). Equality of means is rejected for R&D expenditures of universities and the public sector (MID mean = 0.007) although these expenditures are more likely to be considered as exogenous since they depend on national and regional governments.

Fourth, the innovation indicator considers that all the patents have the same value, regardless of their characteristics. We have repeated the estimates using the weighted indicator proposed by Galletto and Boix (2014) and Boix et al. (2018). Using the weighted indicator, the iMID effect is reduced slightly in the linear model and is approximately 24% on average and positive in all periods. For the QR, the positive differential effect of the district is only observed after the quantile 70 due to the enormous differential effect of the LPSs specialized in business services up to that quantile.

Fifth, we have used a single indicator based on different types of patents that allows for different local characteristics and innovation modes to be taken into account. Boix and Galletto (2009), Galletto and Boix (2014) and Boix et al. (2018) provide further discussion about the sources and measurement of the iMID effect in terms of knowledge bases, innovation modes, and comparisons with other innovation indicators for different types of LPSs. They conclude that an indicator based on different types of patents is a suitable indicator of technological innovation and that it does not bias in favour of MIDs. Logically, with the limits imposed by a single type indicator.

6. Conclusions

This paper proposes a view of the MID as an innovation machine dedicated to satisfying consumers' desires through constant innovation and change.

We have tested the existence of the iMID in Spain for a long period covering a time span of 24 years, between 1991 and 2014.

The main conclusion is that MIDs maintain an innovative intensity – in terms of patents per (million) persons employed – which is approximately 34% higher than the national average during the entire time span under study. Furthermore, the iMID effect has not reduced significantly over time. MIDs have maintained their innovative capacity after the 2007 economic crisis.

The size of the iMID effect remains significant regardless of different calculation procedures of the indicator and the estimation method, and it is close to that found in previous research (Boix et al., 2018; Boix & Galletto, 2009; Boix & Trullén, 2010; Galletto & Boix, 2014). In addition, MIDs produce the largest number of technological innovations in Spain compared to the national average. Consequently, we can affirm that MIDs are fundamental for the generation of innovation in the Spanish economy.

The research obtains other new and noteworthy results. The first is that the iMID effect is incremental, being higher for the highest quantiles of innovative intensity. The second is that the manufacturing LPSs of large firms show an innovative intensity superior to that of the MIDs, probably because of the combination of economies of scale and scope.

Nevertheless, the interpretation of these results requires caution because of some limitations, which in themselves constitute the purpose of the future investigation.

First, the geographical boundaries of the LPSs/MIDs remained unchanged for the whole period by using the LPSs/MIDs identified at its central point, namely the year

2001. This decision was taken for the sake of simplicity to gain experience in the temporal dynamics of innovation without having to worry about how the limits and types of LPSs changed. However, LPSs/MIDs change over time, so it will be convenient to use dynamic units of analysis in the next phase of the investigation (Sforzi & Boix, 2019).

Second, the determinants of the iMID effect have not been modelled, as was done in previous research (e.g. Boix & Galletto, 2009). Future research should work on how to isolate the effect for each MID and model its determinants over time, which would provide valuable information on the evolution of competitiveness in the MIDs. This is of particular importance since the response of the MIDs to inputs such as R&D expenditures, both private and public, is low, which means that conventional innovation policies have a poor impact on MIDs.

Third, the present study has focused on patents as indicators of technological innovation, but future research will have to incorporate additional intellectual property indicators (industrial designs, trademarks, copyrights, geographical indications and plant variety rights) to cover the different aspects of the innovative processes and the variety of modes of innovation of different types of LPSs.

Finally, note that although this research has focused on MIDs and the generic types of LPSs, its focus, methods and conclusions are also expandable to other categories of territorial innovation models, such as clusters or ecosystems. In the debate about trajectories of change in place-based productive and innovation systems, we have found long-term evidence that some types of LPSs, such as the MIDs, are resilient with respect to the intense challenges coming from the economic and financial crisis, the globalization and the raising competition from developing and emerging countries.

Notes

1. Utility models are granted by the OEPM and are similar to patents although the legal requirements are less strict, and the protection covers only 10 years. Similar figures exist in Austria, Denmark, Finland, Germany, Greece, Italy, Japan, Poland and Portugal. For the sake of simplicity, we will use the term 'patents' also to refer to utility models.
2. There is awareness of the limitation of patents as a measure of innovation since patents are awarded to a new invention, and a new invention may or may not be applied to the manufacture of new products. The fact remains that in the literature patents are widely used as a measure of innovation. In our case, the use of patents is even more significant since they are place-based, meaning that places (MIDs and other LPSs) are conducive to the spread of new ideas.
3. In the case of OEPM records, we had to use the applicant address because it is the only available address for all the years of analysis.
4. The shares of each type of record are as follows: utility models 44%, Spanish patents 31%, European patents 17% and American patents 8%. Duplicate priorities (present in more than one database) are assigned only to the first database in which they are registered. During the 24 years under analysis, utility models decrease their weight from 64% of total innovation in 1991–1994 to 32% in 2011–2014, whereas Spanish and international patents increase their importance from 36% to 68%. This evolution suggests that the Spanish economy experienced an improvement in the quality of innovation and could be interpreted as a reflection of the growing openness of the economy.
5. See Boix and Galletto (2009) and Sforzi and Boix (2019) for more detail. The methodology was originally designed by Sforzi and ISTAT (See Sforzi, 2009) in order to identify Marshallian industrial districts. Once identified the LLSs, there is a four-step algorithm that allows to

single out those with characteristics of MIDs. LLSs are defined as MIDs when they are specialized in manufacturing industry, and have an organization system – in both the LLSs and the production chain – based on SMEs. Boix and Galletto (2009) proposed to assign the remaining LLSs (i.e., those not classified as MIDs) according to the macro-sector in which they are more specialized in the first step of the algorithm, being the macro-sectors defined by ISTAT: agriculture, mining, manufacturing (of large firm if the LLSs are not MIDs), construction, business services, consumer services, social services, and traditional services. For reasons of parsimony, we have grouped agriculture and mining, as well as consumer, social and traditional services. Grouping the macro-sectors does not alter the results of the innovation indicators; it only produces a lower disaggregation of the primary and service sectors. The LPSs specialized in business services are kept separate from other services because they identify large urban areas and therefore have a different behaviour.
6. The INE R&D survey provides data only at the national or regional levels. The expenditures of universities are available by university and item for the more recent years in the SIIU database although not for most of the years used in our analysis. We have chosen to elaborate the indicator in a way that maximizes the temporal coverage, and for this reason the number of employees is used and divided by the regional expenditures. It must be borne in mind that the university centres are very concentrated in a few LPSs, which reduces the measurement error.
7. Other public organizations dependent upon the regions are not included due to the lack of homogeneous data.
8. In the Heckman estimator for panel data (Wooldridge, 2013), the probit is estimated using as explanatory variables the same used in the final model (including dummies by type of LPS and period) plus the number of employees, the density of employees and the lag of innovation per employee in the LPS. On the right-hand side of the equation, it is assumed that each LPS expends at least 1 euro per period in each one of the R&D indicators; this is a reasonable simplification and makes it possible to compute the logarithm.
9. Boix and Trullén (2010) provide estimates of the R&D of firms with the imputed variable ($\beta = 0.26$) and with raw microdata ($\beta = 0.09$). With raw microdata, the elasticity of private R&D tends to be much lower.

Acknowledgements

The authors would like to thank Luciana Lazzeretti, Francesco Capone and the anonymous referees for helpful comments to previous versions of the paper. We benefited from comments and suggestions from participants at the Rethinking Clusters: Critical Issues and New Trajectories of Cluster Research International Workshop held on 2018 at the University of Florence. The authors gratefully acknowledge Jordi Llobet for his support in the elaboration of the databases. The usual disclaimers apply.

Disclosure statement

No potential conflict of interest was reported by the authors.

ORCID

Rafael Boix-Domenech http://orcid.org/0000-0003-0971-3464
Vittorio Galletto http://orcid.org/0000-0003-1709-8000
Fabio Sforzi http://orcid.org/0000-0002-3312-0995

References

Anselin, L., Varga, A., & Acs, Z. J. (2000). Geographic and sectoral characteristics of academic knowledge externalities. *Papers in Regional Science*, 79(4), 435–443. doi:10.1007/PL00011486

Baltagi, B. H. (2013). *Econometric analysis of panel data* (5th ed.). Chichester, UK: Wiley.

Becattini, G. (Ed.). (1975). *Lo sviluppo economico della Toscana, con particolare riguardo all'industrializzazione leggera*. Firenze: Irpet-Guaraldi.

Becattini, G. (2001). *The Caterpillar and the butterfly. An exemplary case of development in the Italy of the industrial districts*. Firenze: Le Monnier.

Becattini, G. (2004). *Industrial districts: A new approach to industrial change*. Cheltenham: Edward Elgar.

Bellandi, M. (1992). The incentives to decentralized industrial creativity in local systems of small firms. *Revue d'Economie Industrielle*, 59, 99–110. doi:10.3406/rei.1992.1406

Boix, R., & Galletto, V. (2009). Innovation and industrial districts: A first approach to the measurement and determinants of the I-district effect. *Regional Studies*, 43(9), 1117–1133. doi:10.1080/00343400801932342

Boix, R., Galletto, V., & Sforzi, F. (2018). Pathways of innovation: The I-district effect revisited. In F. Belussi & J.-L. Hervás-Oliver (Eds.), *Agglomeration and firm performance* (pp. 25–46). New York: Springer.

Boix, R., & Trullén, J. (2010). Industrial districts, innovation and I-district effect: Territory or industrial specialization? *European Planning Studies*, 18(10), 1707–1729. doi:10.1080/09654313.2010.504351

Brusco, S. (1986). Small firm and industrial districts: The experience of Italy. *Economia Internazionale*, XXXIX(2-3-4), 85–97.

Dei Ottati, G. (2006). El 'efecto distrito': algunos aspectos conceptuales de sus ventajas competitivas. *Economía Industrial*, 359, 73–87.

Galletto, V., & Boix, R. (2014). Distritos industriales, innovación tecnológica y efecto I-distrito: ¿Una cuestión de volumen o de valor? *Investigaciones Regionales*, 30, 27–51.

Griliches, Z. (1979). Issues in assessing the contribution of research and development to productivity growth. *Bell Journal of Economics*, 10(1), 92–116. doi:10.2307/3003321

Griliches, Z. (1990). Patent statistics as economic indicators: A survey. *Journal of Economic Literature*, XXVIII, 1661–1707.

Griliches, Z. (1992). The search for R&D spillovers. *Scandinavian Journal of Economics*, 94, 29–47. doi:10.2307/3440244

Henderson, R. M., & Clark, K. B. (1990). Architectural innovation: The reconfiguration of existing product technologies and the failure of established firms. *Administrative Science Quarterly*, 35, 9–30. doi:10.2307/2393549

Khan, M., & Dernis, H. (2006). Global overview of innovative activities from the patent indicators perspective, OECD Science, Technology and Industry Working Papers, 2006/03, Paris: OECD Publishing.

Leoncini, R., & Lotti, F. (2004). Are industrial districts more conducive to innovative production? The case of Emilia-Romagna. In G. Cainelli & R. Zoboli (Eds.), *The evolution of industrial districts: Changing governance, innovation and internationalisation of local capitalism in Italy* (pp. 257–271). Heidelberg and New York: Physica-Verlag.

Marshall, A. (1930). *Principles of economics* (8th ed.). London: Macmillan.

Muscio, A. (2006). Patterns of innovation in industrial districts: An empirical analysis. *Industry and Innovation*, 13(3), 291–312. doi:10.1080/13662710600858860

Pakes, A., & Griliches, Z. (1984). Patents and R&D at the firm level: A first look. In Z. Griliches (Ed.), *R&D, patents and productivity* (pp. 52–72). Chicago: University of Chicago Press.

Powell, D. (2015). Quantile regression with nonadditive fixed effects. RAND Labor and Population Working Paper.

Russo, M. (1985). Technical change and the industrial district: The role of interfirm relations in the growth and transformation of ceramic tile production in Italy. *Research Policy*, 14(6), 329–343. doi:10.1016/0048-7333(85)90003-4

Santarelli, E. (2004). Patents and the technological performance of district firms: Evidence for the Emilia-Romagna Region of Italy. Papers on Entrepreneurship, Growth and Public Policy, # 2904. Jena: Max Planck Institute.

Sforzi, F. (1990). The quantitative importance of industrial districts in Italy. In F. Pyke, G. Becattini, & W. Sengenberger (Eds.), *Industrial districts and inter-firm co-operation in Italy* (pp. 75–107). Geneva: International Institute for Labour Studies.

Sforzi, F. (2009). The empirical evidence of industrial districts in Italy. In G. Becattini, M. Bellandi, & L. De Propris (Eds.), *A handbook of industrial districts* (pp. 327–342). Cheltenham: Edward Elgar.

Sforzi, F., & Boix, R. (2019). Territorial servitization in Marshallian industrial districts: The industrial district as a place-based form of servitization. *Regional Studies, 53*(3), 398–409. doi:10.1080/00343404.2018.1524134

Signorini, L. F. (1994). The price of Prato, or measuring the industrial district effect. *Papers in Regional Science, 73*(4), 369–392. doi:10.1111/j.1435-5597.1994.tb00620.x

Wooldridge, J. M. (2013). *Introductory econometrics: A modern approach* (5th ed.). Mason, OH: South-Western.

Annex 1. **Descriptive statistics and correlation matrix. Aggregated period 1995–2014.**

(a) Descriptive statistics.

Variable	Observations	Mean	Standard deviation	Min	Max
Innovation per million employees	3,385	248.26	402.23	0.0000	6,470.15
R&D$_{t-1}$ firms and private non-profit institutions	3,385	224.66	1,300.48	0.0000	43,446.79
R&D$_{t-1}$ universities and public sector	3,385	0.1257	0.6686	0.0000	15.4119
Log Innovation per million employees	3,385	5.3511	0.9633	1.7088	8.7749
Log R&D$_{t-1}$ firms and private non-profit institutions	3,385	−3.4448	6.2398	−14.4111	10.6793
Log R&D$_{t-1}$ universities and public sector	3,385	−7.6314	2.5686	−12.5170	2.7352

(b) Correlation matrix.

	Innovation per million employees	Log innovation per million employees	R&D$_{t-1}$ firms and private non-profit institutions	R&D$_{t-1}$ universities and public sector	Log R&D$_{t-1}$ firms and private non-profit institutions	Log R&D$_{t-1}$ universities and public sector
Innovation per million employees	1.0000					
Log innovation per million employees	0.7524*	1.0000				
R&D$_{t-1}$ firms and private non-profit institutions	0.0697*	0.1107*	1.0000			
R&D$_{t-1}$ universities and public sector	−0.0054	−0.0151	0.0042	1.0000		
Log R&D$_{t-1}$ firms and private non-profit institutions	0.2288*	0.2436*	0.3167*	0.0961*	1.0000	
Log R&D$_{t-1}$ universities and public sector	−0.0270	0.0292	0.0040	0.6214*	0.0657*	1.0000

* Statistically significant at 5%.

Rereading industrial districts through the lens of entrepreneurship

Roberto Grandinetti

ABSTRACT
This paper analyzes the link between industrial districts and entrepreneurship, building a bridge between the literature on entrepreneurship and the literature on industrial districts. Drawing a distinction between generic entrepreneurship and selective entrepreneurship leads us to acknowledge that a close association between industrial districts as a whole and entrepreneurship is only well-founded if we are speaking of the generic definition of the latter. Burt's theory of structural holes and its application to industrial districts enables us to identify two different types of industrial district, one featuring a high degree of density or closure (P-clusters), the other a high degree of brokerage or (selective) entrepreneurship (SV-clusters). The framework proposed here also suggests a novel interpretation of the transformations that industrial districts of the first type have undergone under the pressure of globalization.

1. Introduction

The discontinuous changes seen in the history of particular industrial districts have been explained on the grounds of an invariant link between two processes: given individuals, or entrepreneurs, develop novel ideas that then spread within the district system (Lazerson & Lorenzoni, 1999). Some innovations become highly visible because of their impact on the district, but many other less remarkable entrepreneurial innovations are destined to go more or less unnoticed. Nevertheless, a look at the ample theoretical literature on industrial districts shows that the concept of entrepreneurship has remained in the shadows. As a matter of fact, entrepreneurship has simply not been among the variables considered by the majority of theoretical studies on industrial districts.

The aim of this theoretical paper is to build a bridge between the literature on entrepreneurship and the literature on industrial districts. To pursue this goal, we must first clarify the ambiguity that accompanies the use of the term 'entrepreneurship', distinguishing between a selective interpretation of the term, i.e. the capacity of certain individuals to identify new business opportunities and exploit their discoveries (Shane & Venkataraman, 2000; Stevenson & Jarillo, 1990), and its more generic meaning, which can be associated with the simple birth of new firms (Section 2). Bearing this distinction in mind, industrial districts can be defined as business incubators for generic entrepreneurship (Section 3). On the other hand, the link between industrial districts and entrepreneurship in the selective sense of the term can be analyzed with the aid of Ronald Burt's theory of structural holes and brokerage (Section 4). This approach leads us to identify two very different types of industrial district, that here we call P-clusters and SV-clusters (Section 5). The conceptual framework that emerges from our analysis helps us to understand the resilience of (some) industrial districts in the era of globalization (Section 6).

As done in numerous theoretical and empirical studies (Lazzeretti, Sedita, & Caloffi, 2014), we use the terms 'industrial district' and 'cluster' here as synonyms. The definition adopted is the one proposed by Porter (2000, p. 15), according to which 'clusters are geographic concentrations of interconnected companies, specialized suppliers, service providers, firms in related industries, and associated institutions (e.g. universities, standards agencies, trade associations) in a particular field that compete but also cooperate'. Clearly, this is a very broad definition that includes very different systems, such as the Prato textile district studied by Becattini (1990), and Silicon Valley studied by Saxenian (1994).

2. Entrepreneurship and its spatial dimension

The term 'entrepreneurship' can be used in a generic or a selective sense (Davidsson, Delmar, & Wiklund, 2006). In its generic sense, entrepreneurship is synonymous with the creation of new firms. Taking this view, a territory in which many firms are born is rich in entrepreneurship. Industrial districts are typically rich in entrepreneurship, as discussed in the next section.

A line of research in management studies that focused specifically on entrepreneurship took shape in the 1990s. While trying to extend the concept to situations other than the creation of new firms, it also attempted to define entrepreneurship more selectively, thereby laying the foundations for a new field of study. One point of arrival along this path is the contribution from Shane and Venkataraman (2000), who link entrepreneurship with opportunity. First of all, an opportunity has to be sought and identified. Then it has to be assessed and exploited. The first phase of the entrepreneurial process – opportunity recognition – assigns an innovative nature to the outcome of this process (Baron, 2006). The other two phases – opportunity evaluation and exploitation – include the expectation that the firm will grow (Davidsson et al., 2006). Such an entrepreneurial process can be developed by an existing firm, taking the form of some sort of renewal occurring within the organization. The alternative is the entrepreneurial spinoff, when ex-employees pursue business opportunities that they have identified within the parent firm. The construct of entrepreneurial orientation, revealed by an organization exhibiting innovativeness, a propensity for taking risks, and proactiveness, is consistent with this interpretation of entrepreneurship (Covin, Green, & Slevin, 2006).

Either way, behind entrepreneurship in the selective sense there are individuals (Alvarez & Busenitz, 2001), whether they are people who set up a new venture or managers whose entrepreneurial behaviour is expressed within the organization where they work (Stevenson & Jarillo, 1990). So, even if organizational studies apply the concept of entrepreneurial orientation to the level of the organization, it is easy to see its elements of innovativeness, risk-taking, and proactiveness on the level of the individuals involved as well (Bolton & Lane, 2012).[1]

Adopting the selective interpretation of entrepreneurship outlined in the specific literature, a territory is rich in entrepreneurship if it has a high density of individuals capable of recognizing and exploiting new business opportunities. Notably, some employees who have this ability at the time t may be independent entrepreneurs by the time $t + 1$. But a territory with a high entry rate of new firms, as is typically the case of industrial districts, is not necessarily rich in entrepreneurship in the selective sense.

3. Industrial districts as business incubators

Industrial districts are localized inter-firm networks (Porter, 1998). A sizable body of literature has explained why firms localized in a district benefit from external economies – outside the firm and inside the district – in addition to the agglomeration advantages that can derive from their mere spatial proximity (Gordon & McCann, 2000). Summarizing the content of these publications, we can say that the relationships between enterprises localized in the same district are influenced by a systemic factor that we call the C-factor for the sake of simplicity. The C-factor is endogenous to a given district and distinguishes it from the rest of the competitive environment.

The C-factor has been given various names. For instance, Porter (2000, p. 241) calls it 'social glue' that 'binds clusters together, contributing to the value creation process'. Dei Ottati (2003) speaks of the 'community market', in the sense of a mechanism governing relationships that comprises a shared language, common values and meanings, and implicit rules of behaviour. These elements facilitate a mutual understanding between people and organizations activating and developing relationships. In essence, these are the same elements that Bell, Tracey, and Heide (2009) include in the 'shared relational macroculture' that they attribute to Silicon Valley and to the Third Italy's industrial districts, unlike the 'shared hierarchical macroculture' identifiable in hub-and-spoke districts.

The C-factor essentially has two types of effect that are important in generating external economies. On the one hand, it reduces the transaction costs associated with inter-organizational relationships, by enabling a buyer firm to deal with a subcontracting firm without stipulating a complicated contract, for instance (Dei Ottati, 2003). On the other, the C-factor facilitates the circulation within the district of information and knowledge, and particularly the tacit knowledge that, by its very nature, is relatively sticky in relation to the organization generating it (Rullani, 2003).

The presence of the C-factor induces us to focus our analysis on the interaction between individuals operating on either side of an inter-organizational relationship. But, in addition to these inter-organizational relationships, certain interpersonal relationships can also have an impact on a district's firms. For instance, two employees working for different, unconnected firms who are relatives or friends may exchange information and knowledge about their work, so their respective firms become indirectly connected (Capone & Lazzeretti, 2018; Sedita, Belussi, & Grandinetti, 2016).

Generally speaking, entrepreneurship cannot be understood regardless of its spatial and social context (Guercini & Cova, 2018; Welter, 2011). Given their distinctive high birth rate, industrial districts can be seen as contexts for the incubation of new firms. Since new ventures are born mainly as spinoffs (Garofoli, 1992; Johannisson, 1988; Patrucco,

2005; Porter, 1998; Saxenian, 1994; Sorenson & Audia, 2000), i.e. as firms set up by ex-employees, individuals who decide to create their own business can take advantage of two incubation contexts, the parent company where they develop their plan, and the district where they wish to change their status from employee to entrepreneur (Camuffo & Grandinetti, 2011). Numerous studies explain this quality of the industrial districts in relation to the presence of the C-factor, which therefore exerts its influence not only on the existing firms, and the direct and indirect relationships between them, but also on the new firms born from them.

Figure 1 illustrates the creation of a new venture via a spinoff as a process involving three phases: the development of a business idea within a parent firm (the incubation phase); the resource assembly phase; and the subsequent start-up phase (Furlan & Grandinetti, 2014). The first phase, in which the business idea is developed, is substantially a learning process. The future entrepreneurs learn partly through inter-organizational relationships in which they are involved at the parent firm, and partly through other, interpersonal relationships based on family ties or friendships, or even of a professional nature (Furlan & Grandinetti, 2016; Hervas-Oliver, Lleo, & Cervello, 2017; Sorenson, 2003). Since the relationships forming part of the future entrepreneur's social capital are embedded in the district context, they are subject to the (cognitive) effect of the C-factor (Furlan & Grandinetti, 2014; Lipparini, 1995). Skipping to the start-up phase, this suffers from a well-known phenomenon, the liability of newness, due to a lesser efficiency and efficacy that not only intra-organizational relationships, but also those with external actors are bound to have during the spinoff's 'running in' phase (Stinchcombe, 1965). Relationships with subcontractors and suppliers, customers and service providers that are established

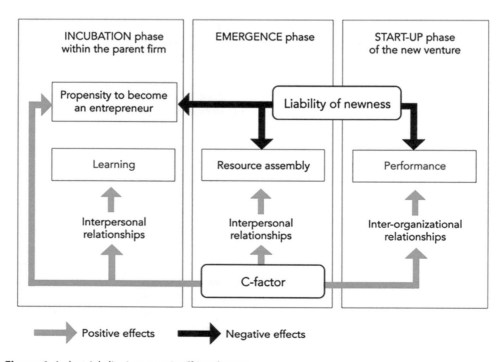

Figure 1. Industrial districts as spinoff incubators.

within a district can still benefit from the C-factor, however (Patrucco, 2005; Solinas, 1996). Going back to the resource assembly phase, this is also burdened with the liability of newness: the people who have the resources the emergent entrepreneur needs (individuals to employ, clients, suppliers of various types of input, including the necessary capital) perceive the difficulties and risks that the new firm may soon face (ex-post liability of newness), and this makes them less likely to engage with the emergent entrepreneur (thus giving rise to an ex-ante liability of newness). The C-factor has an indirect influence on this legitimacy gap: because it reduces the ex-post liability component (as we have seen), it also reduces the ex-ante liability component (Lazerson, 1995; Rocha & Sternberg, 2005). New entrepreneurs must also interact with those who have the external resources they need, and this interaction is often not easy, but the C-factor exerts its positive effect on the contacts needed to complete the resource assembly process too (Sorenson, 2003).

Finally, in addition to the C-factor's impact of the on interpersonal and inter-organizational relationships, we need to remember its influence on an individual's propensity to create a new firm. Employees who break away from an existing district firm to go into business on their own, even in the simple form of self-employment, are not perceived as a negative factor in the district. Their behaviour meets with a broad social approval, as part of the values shared by local firms and people (Garofoli, 1992; Isaksen, 1994; Johannisson, 1988). This effect counteracts the negative influence of the perceived liability of newness on the motivation of would-be entrepreneurs to start their own business (Rocha & Sternberg, 2005).

In short, industrial districts are a fertile terrain for the birth of new firms. If we wish to qualify them as incubators of entrepreneurship, the framework shown in Figure 1 clearly refers to the generic definition of entrepreneurship, according to which the birth of any firm is an expression of entrepreneurship. Some authors have gone a step further, however, claiming that all industrial districts serve as business incubators for entrepreneurship in the selective sense too.

This association is based on the conviction that individuals embedded in a district context have an advantage over those outside such a context when it comes to developing an entrepreneurial idea. Specifically, they would be in a better position to recognize new business opportunities in the industry where they and others work (e.g. Garofoli, 2006; Porter, 1998; Sorenson, 2003; Sternberg, 2009). But innovative ideas that promote firm growth derive more from the exchange and combination of knowledge produced and circulating in a given district with knowledge produced and circulating in other contexts (firms, institutions, other industrial districts) that may even be far removed on the spatial and/or cognitive plane from the district in question. Former (local) knowledge provides an important basis for the emergence of entrepreneurial processes (Hervas-Oliver et al., 2017), but the ability to combine it with the latter is not endemic in industrial districts in general (Camuffo & Grandinetti, 2011). The same reasoning can be extended from the first phase of the entrepreneurial process (opportunity recognition) to the two subsequent phases of opportunity evaluation and exploitation, which demand resources not necessarily available in the district.

Ultimately, industrial districts can be seen as business incubators when we are speaking of generic entrepreneurship, but not when we are dealing with selective entrepreneurship. It is worth noting that the passage from the generic to the selective sense of entrepreneurship leads us to widen the field of observation, adding the existing firms to the new ventures. Since we know that what counts, in both cases, is the individuals involved, this extension does not modify the conclusion to which our analysis leads.

4. Entrepreneurship and structural holes

To identify and conceptualize a connection between industrial districts and entrepreneurship in the selective sense (simply indicated as 'entrepreneurship' from now on) without making the mistake outlined in the previous section, we need to consider entrepreneurship in an appropriate light. The theory of structural holes developed by Burt (1992, 2000) can come to our aid here.

To explain his theory, Burt uses sociograms such as the one shown in Figure 2, where the dots indicate individuals and the lines are relationships. Although at the heart of Burt's analysis there are individuals and their interpersonal relationships (their social capital), the author himself suggests that his concepts can be applied to organizations and inter-

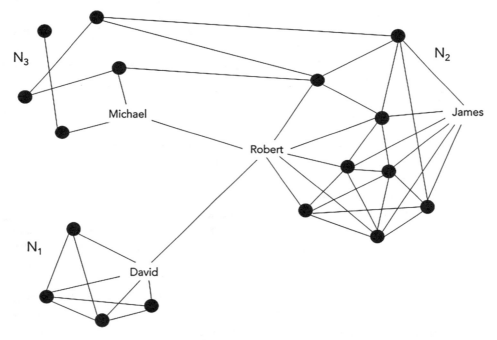

	N_1	N_2	N_3	
N_1	0.90			Network N_1 (5 people and 9 ties)
N_2	0.02	0.58		Network N_2 (10 people and 26 ties)
N_3	0.00	0.07	0.33	Network N_3 (6 people and 5 ties)

Figure 2. Relations within and between networks, and density table.

organizational relationships too. Figure 2 shows three networks (or rather subnetworks within a broader network) of different density. Their density is calculated as the number of actual connections as a ratio of the number of potential connections, and it is indicated by the diagonal of the density table at the bottom of the figure. The densest network is N_1, where nearly everyone is connected to everyone else. The example also includes relationships between networks, the density of which is indicated in the cells outside the diagonal. These density values are distinctly lower than those of the diagonal and they justify the identification of three distinct (sub)networks within the broader network.

Burt describes the network structure in Figure 2 as being rich in structural holes, i.e. holes separating unconnected actors. In such situations, the agents that bridge these structural holes have the opportunity to act as information intermediaries between unconnected actors (brokerage). In Figure 2, as David and Michael are not connected, there is a structural hole between them, and thus between their respective subnetworks N_1 and N_3. Robert bridges the structural hole between N_1 and N_3. His relationship with an individual in N_1 is also a genuine network bridge: break that relationship and there is no connection between N_2 and N_1. If we then compare Robert and James within the subnetwork N_2, we can see that they reach all the other members of their subnetwork through direct relationships or with just one further step (from this point of view, they are both well connected). Robert occupies a better position than James, however, both in relation to the structural holes in their subnetwork and vis-à-vis subnetworks N_1 and N_3, as he is connected with each of the latter through a direct relationship. Robert is unquestionably in an ideal position for brokerage.[2]

Robert's position enables him to operate as an information intermediary, as mentioned earlier, but also to intercept information and knowledge coming from non-redundant sources, 'sources that are more additive than overlapping' (Burt, 2000, p. 353), giving him the opportunity to combine this knowledge to develop good new ideas (Burt, 2004; Caloffi, Rossi, & Russo, 2015; Hargadon, 2002). This second interpretation of brokerage is particularly important in the context of our analysis. In fact, a position with such a vocation for identifying business opportunities leads Burt to define Robert both as a knowledge broker and as an entrepreneur in the literal, selective sense of the word. This definition is consistent with the literature on entrepreneurship (Gedajlovic, Honig, Moore, Payne, & Wright, 2013), although one limitation of Burt's approach lies in seeing a virtually automatic connection between entrepreneurship and the fact of occupying a certain position in the network, a connection that it seems should by no means be taken for granted.[3]

On the other hand, we are interested in Burt's approach not as a theory of entrepreneurship but as a theory of structural holes, which is useful for distinguishing between two types of industrial district. Before moving in this direction, however, we need to recall that Burt's analysis includes two network mechanisms: brokerage and closure. Concerning the second, he goes along with Coleman (1988), who saw networks with closure as creating advantage in two ways: first, closure makes it easier to access information; and second, it facilitates the use of sanctions, making it less risky for people within the network to trust one another and cooperate. The embeddedness theory developed by Granovetter (1985) also arrives at the prediction that dense networks facilitate trust by facilitating effective sanctions.

5. Structural holes and industrial districts

Industrial districts are networks and, as such, Burt's concepts can be applied to them (Molina-Morales, 2005). In some recent works, this has been done on quantitative grounds, and with reference to specific industrial districts (e.g. Boari, Molina-Morales, & Martínez-Cháfer, 2017; Giuliani, 2013; Lechner & Leyronas, 2012). Proceeding along the path charted by these empirical contributions, the aim here is to emphasize how Burt's conceptual framework helps us to improve our understanding of the link between (selective) entrepreneurship and industrial districts. For this purpose, we can modify Figure 2 to obtain Figure 3, where N_1 and N_2 are two industrial districts (the dashed line symbolizes their geographical boundaries), and N_3 is a set of organizations that operate in the same field but are not co-localized. We are speaking of enterprises here but, as we know, the organizational map 'covers' the type of map charted on an individual level in Burt's sociograms.

If we consider industrial districts as localized networks and conceptualize them *à la* Burt, N_1 is characterized by a high density or closure, and N_2 by a significant presence

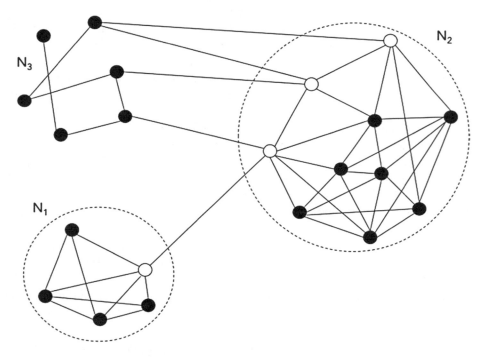

	N_1	N_2	N_3	
N_1	0.90			Network N_1 (5 people and 9 ties)
N_2	0.02	0.58		Network N_2 (10 people and 26 ties)
N_3	0.00	0.07	0.33	Network N_3 (6 people and 5 ties)

Figure 3. Closure and brokerage in industrial districts.

of brokers and entrepreneurs. Removing the automatism that we have seen is characteristic of Burt's view, we can say that the cluster N_1 has a significant presence of brokerage positions (white dots), that can be exploited by agents occupying them in two ways: as knowledge gatekeepers, i.e. absorbing knowledge from the outside of the district and transferring it inside in various ways through relationships that they maintain within the district (Bathelt, Malmberg, & Maskell, 2004; Guercini & Runfola, 2015; Morrison, 2008); and by combining knowledge that they absorb from outside and inside the district to develop entrepreneurial ideas, the implementation of which may then involve within-district actors too (Camuffo & Grandinetti, 2011; Pucci, Brumana, Minola, & Zanni, 2017).

In general, we can now acknowledge differences within the category of industrial districts (as defined in the present contribution) that are due to the degree of these systems' density or closure, and to their greater or lesser abundance of brokerage positions, and particularly of positions that serve as an interface between the cluster and outside networks. Although studies that proposed a typology of industrial districts (Ingstrup & Christensen, 2017; Markusen, 1996; Paniccia, 2006; St. John & Pouder, 2006) did not consider the closure and brokerage constructs, we can extract from the literature two sets of contributions that concern two different types of industrial district or cluster, and their diversity is important in the context of our analysis. These works do not generally refer to Burt's theory of structural holes, but rereading them under the lens of Burt's concepts enables us to distinguish districts with the characteristics of cluster N_1 in Figure 3 from those with the features of cluster N_2. The former are therefore dense, closed, localized networks, that we call P-clusters (where 'P' stands for Prato), while the latter are localized networks relatively rich in entrepreneurial opportunities, or SV-clusters (where 'SV' stands for Silicon Valley).

The two types are illustrated in more detail below. As concerns the studies that enabled us to link industrial districts with Burt's theory of structural holes, it is important to mention that these works generally analyze industrial districts in a given phase of their life cycle. If the analyses conducted in these studies led to the districts in question being grouped among the systems of the former or latter type, this does not necessarily mean that the same industrial districts retained the same distinctive characteristics later on.

5.1. P-clusters: production activities and daily life overlap

The industrial districts of the first type (P-clusters), which have high closure associated with low brokerage, have been labelled to recall the name of one such district, the Prato textile district (Tuscany, Central Italy). This is because it was the case studied by Becattini (1990, 1991), where he found the typical traits of the industrial districts seen by Marshall (1920) in 19th-century England, and something more.

We define P-clusters as Becattini (1991, p. 111) defined the industrial district:

> a socioeconomic entity which is characterized by the active coexistence of an open community of people and a segmented population of firms. Since the community of people and the population of firms live in the same geographical area, they will criss-cross one another. Production activities and daily life overlap.

Clearly, this definition is more specific than the one proposed by Porter (a geographical concentration of interconnected firms), because in 'his' district Becattini finds not only this feature (a segmented population of firms), but also a strong interpenetration between the production domain and the social domain. Looking at the social domain of industrial districts, the 'social glue' (Porter, 2000) appears to be particularly sturdy in P-clusters (Sforzi, 2008).

The idea of an interpenetration between the production and the social domains stems from Becattini's in-depth observation of the Prato textile district begun at the end of the 1970s. During the same period, and even more afterwards, a bevy of scholars recognized the same distinctive traits in many other industrial districts, in Italy and elsewhere in Europe. For instance, in a study on Gnosjö in Sweden, Johannisson (1988) describes this small-business region specializing in low-tech metal manufacturing in much the same way as Becattini describes Prato, albeit without speaking (yet) of industrial districts.

Looking at the neo-Marshallian industrial districts as conceived by Becattini – i.e. P-clusters – in the light of Burt's theory of structural holes, they appear to be localized networks characterized by a particularly high density thanks to the many interpersonal relationships that compound those conveyed by inter-organizational relationships (Becattini, 1990). As a consequence, firms localized in P-clusters benefit from the two types of advantage afforded by network closure, as emphasized by Granovetter (1985) and Coleman (1988): greater access to information and knowledge; and less opportunistic behaviour. The former is due to an amplification of the cognitive effect of the C-factor on within-district relationships: clearly, when inter-organizational relationships are just a subset of the relationships that can convey knowledge, then the probability of this knowledge being transferred increases (Rullani, 2003). The incubator effect is also enhanced in P-clusters, given the role of relationships in the birth of new firms and the propensity of individuals to create a new business (Figure 1). As for the latter type of advantage, a dense context of relationships is characterized by a high informative transparency, and this facilitates the adoption of sanctions, making it more risky for people in the district to behave opportunistically. This is reflected in lower transaction costs and a higher level of relational trust (Dei Ottati, 2003; Mathews & Stokes, 2013). The advantages described explain, for instance, what Becattini (2001) called the 'return' of the industrial districts in Italy in the early 1960s (after the English experience observed by Marshall), and their subsequent golden age up until the 1990s.

While closure makes P-clusters very favourable to the birth of new firms, the dark side of this closure is cognitive lock-in (Belussi & Sedita, 2009; Cooke, 2009; Molina-Morales, 2005). Reasoning along the lines of our framework, the relative poverty of structural holes does not make P-clusters favourable contexts for the emergence of selective entrepreneurship. In particular, as 'natural' incubators, they should facilitate the emergence of replicative spinoffs, rather than entrepreneurial spinoffs. This is confirmed by looking at district spinoffs in Italy: a review of empirical studies on 18 Italian industrial districts (Camuffo & Grandinetti, 2011), all classifiable as P-clusters, shows that firms born as spinoffs generally bear a strong resemblance to their parent companies, or parts of them (as in the case of district firms that outsource a phase of their production process).

Of course, this does not mean that the history of P-clusters has seen no entrepreneurs in the selective sense of the term (Becattini, 2001). In particular, the life cycle of P-clusters is not without discontinuous changes. Analyses on these changes have demonstrated that they can be triggered by one or more brokers, pioneering entrepreneurs who develop a good idea by creating a knowledge bridge between the cluster in which they are embedded and other networks outside (Bellandi, 1996; Camuffo, 2003; Codara & Morato, 2002; Hervas-Oliver, Albors-Garrigos, Estelles-Miguel, & Boronat-Moll, 2018; Isaksen, 1994; Molina-Morales, Martínez-Cháfer, & Valiente-Bordanova, 2017). Interestingly, these pioneers are often misunderstood in the district where they operate, when they first introduce their novel entrepreneurial ideas at least (Grandinetti, 2014; Molina-Morales et al., 2017). In other words, brokerage is not a shared value in P-clusters. It is not part of their C-factor.[4]

5.2. SV-clusters: entrepreneurs and brokerage infrastructure

SV-clusters have a lower density and a relatively large number of brokers, i.e. entrepreneurial human resources who use a selected set of relationships outside the district to discover and exploit new opportunities. Here we have chosen to label clusters of this second type based on the example of Silicon Valley, partly because it is so well known, and partly because studies on this high-tech cluster have documented its entrepreneurial nature in depth (Cohen & Fields, 1999; Klepper, 2010; Saxenian, 1994, 2006). As Silicon Valley became established as a high-tech cluster, it attracted business investments and talented individuals literally from every corner of the world (Cohen & Fields, 1999), and both contributed knowledge and new relationships to the cluster. After a while, some of the immigrants became the new Argonauts described by Saxenian (2006), i.e. individuals creating new ventures in Silicon Valley and others in their own countries of origin (China and India, for example), or returning home and opening ventures while retaining business connections with firms and individuals in Silicon Valley.

A second important aspect from an entrepreneurship perspective concerns the role of various agents other than the semiconductor and computer manufacturers, and the software developers, i.e. the major research universities, venture capitalists, law firms, and knowledge-intensive business services. These actors serve as a brokerage infrastructure, in the sense that they support the emergence of (selective) entrepreneurship by providing not only useful knowledge, but also useful relations with actors and networks far from Silicon Valley. But it would be impossible to explain the copious, uninterrupted flow of entrepreneurial spinoffs studding the history of Silicon Valley without considering the broad base of seed firms, which is the third aspect emphasized in studies on this cluster. Fairchild is the archetype of the countless other seed firms that followed in its wake (Klepper, 2010).

Just as Prato represents clusters of the first type, so Silicon Valley represents those of the second. The clusters described as SV-clusters by the authors who studied them include: the medical technology cluster in the Rhône-Alpes region in France (Andersson, Evers, & Griot, 2013); the biotechnology cluster in Vienna (Trippl & Tödtling, 2007); the life science cluster in Medicon Valley, Scandinavia (Coenen, Moodysson, & Asheim, 2004); the high-tech cluster in Cambridge (Myint, Vyakarnam, & New, 2005); and the Ottawa technology cluster, also known as 'Silicon Valley North' (Harrison, Cooper, & Mason, 2004).

All these SV-clusters operate in fields comprising one or more high-tech sectors. This close association can be explained on the grounds of two interconnected factors. One concerns the distinction between technology clusters and industry clusters as explained by St. John and Pouder (2006). The identity of the former stems from a particular industry anchored to a single market, while that of the latter derives from a specific technology that serves as the basis for diversified applications to different markets or industries. For the purposes of the present analysis, this means that the potential for brokerage in SV-clusters is vastly greater than in P-clusters (Gilbert, 2012). The second factor concerns the fact that the characteristics of high-tech sectors, particularly as concerns their R&D intensity and entrepreneurship, are well suited to that brokerage infrastructure that we have identified as a distinctive trait of SV-clusters (Cooke, 2009). Just to give an example, the likelihood of university research centres interacting with firms is much higher in high-tech sectors (Segarra-Blasco & Arauzo-Carod, 2008).

The crucial importance of the association between diversification and brokerage is demonstrated by the fact that there is not a total overlap between SV-clusters and high-tech sectors. An emblematic case of this is represented by the district of Montebelluna (in north-east Italy) that, after originally specializing in the production of mountain walking boots and ski boots, has gradually extended its range of products in three directions: first, from mountain sports to other sports; then, for a given sport, from footwear to other products dedicated to that particular sport; and third, from sports to a sporty lifestyle. This course of concentric diversification has accompanied the district's evolution from a configuration fully fitting the P-model (Codara & Morato, 2002) to one that has the features of the SV-model instead (Belussi & Sedita, 2009; De Marchi, Gereffi, & Grandinetti, 2018).

Unlike P-clusters, SV-clusters are an ideal setting for the emergence of entrepreneurial spinoffs conceived as a result of a new business opportunity being identified, and created in order to exploit it. Our view of clusters based on the concept proposed by Burt enables a thorough understanding of this peculiarity of the SV-cluster type. Looking first at the parent company (or first-level incubator), all the seed firms (which are common in SV-clusters) are not only particularly endowed with heritable knowledge (Klepper, 2010; Klepper & Sleeper, 2005), but also brokers that intercept knowledge coming from non-redundant sources inside and outside the cluster. In such a situation, good ideas can develop from the combination of such heterogeneous knowledge inside or outside the focal organization, under the initiative of entrepreneurial employees who leave it. The 'outside' outcome has a far from negligible incidence if we bear in mind that the parent firms in question abound with under-exploited knowledge (Agarwal, Audretsch, & Sarkar, 2007). Brokerage can also take the shape of spinoffs from multiple parents, a situation that is not uncommon in SV-clusters (Furlan & Grandinetti, 2016; Harrison et al., 2004). Then, from the cluster (second-level incubator) perspective, the relationships that potential entrepreneurs can develop in such a context enable them to intercept brokerage opportunities. In addition, the C-factor in SV-clusters is permeated by the typical ingredients of an entrepreneurial orientation – innovativeness, a propensity for risk taking, and proactiveness (Covin et al., 2006). Taken together, these values contribute to explaining the SV-clusters' capacity to attract entrepreneurs (or human resources with entrepreneurial characteristics at least) from outside (Cohen & Fields, 1999; Harrison et al., 2004), and they act as a formidable factor of legitimization and stimulus for potential local founders of entrepreneurial spinoffs (Sorenson, 2017).

6. Concluding remarks

The present analysis improves our knowledge of the link between industrial districts and entrepreneurship. Distinguishing between generic entrepreneurship and selective entrepreneurship enabled us to acknowledge that a close association between industrial districts in general and entrepreneurship is only well founded if we are using the generic definition of the concept of entrepreneurship. Burt's theory of structural holes, and its application to industrial districts then led us to identify two different types of industrial district, one characterized by a high degree of closure (P-clusters), the other by a high degree of brokerage (SV-clusters).

The proposed framework offers a novel approach to a topic of considerable importance in the field of research on industrial districts, i.e. the transformations undergone by those with a high degree of density or closure (P-clusters) under the pressure of such a powerful and strongly anti-closure force as globalization.

As mentioned earlier, P-clusters feature an interpenetration of the production domain with the social domain, and this characteristic was fundamental to their success in the second half of the last century. But the advance of globalization has brought a tremendous pressure to bear on both the former and the latter domains, as well as on their interpenetration. From the local society standpoint, generational changes in the native component and the arrival of immigrants (often *en masse*) have eroded the constitutive elements of the C-factor of the past (Bellandi & De Propris, 2017; Dei Ottati, 2009; De Marchi & Grandinetti, 2014). From the local production standpoint, the intensification of the competition on a global scale has forced many district firms to close, while others have relocated their production elsewhere. This has generated a rarefaction of the local relational web, in terms of the interpersonal and inter-organizational relationships with a bearing on the district's specialization at least (Andersen & Bøllingtoft, 2011; McCaffrey, 2013; Rabellotti, Carabelli, & Hirsch, 2009). The districts' loss of weight in the local economies has contributed to the exit of the (P-)clusters from the P-cluster model because an interpenetration between local society and (district) production relies on the latter permeating the former. Returning to the diagram in Figure 1, the combination of these effects on the firm birth rate – or, if you will, on generic entrepreneurship – has been a very evident shrinkage in this type of district (De Marchi, Gereffi, et al., 2018).

The phenomena described have not meant the decline of districts that corresponded to the P-cluster model. Our closure versus brokerage dichotomy prompts us to hypothesize that the P-clusters that have proved resilient are those which have increased their degree of brokerage. No empirical research has adopted this analytical perspective to date, but studies that analyzed the transformations taking place in various districts (certainly of the P-cluster type) as a result of globalization suggest that our hypothesis is promising. Several studies have concluded that the resilience of some districts and the tendency of others to decline are attributable to the presence in the former and the absence in the latter of entrepreneurs acting as brokers. To be specific, there is a need for international or global entrepreneurs capable of identifying and exploiting opportunities on an international scale (or connecting non-redundant sources on an international scale), and involving district resources in the process (Amdam & Bjarnar, 2015; Carbonara, 2018; De Marchi, Di Maria, & Gereffi, 2018; De Marchi & Grandinetti, 2014, 2016; Randelli & Lombardi, 2014). This last aspect is clearly crucial because district firms that become global without maintaining their connections with the district where they are located are of no use for the purposes of the district's reproduction or resilience (Dei Ottati, 2018). Local institutions have a particular part to play here as knowledge gatekeepers – providing knowledge-intensive business services, for instance – to create a bridge between the district firms and networks outside the district (Grandinetti, 2018; Molina-Morales, 2005).

Ultimately, the conceptual framework proposed in this paper can be used to analyze the current evolution of industrial districts by means of qualitative and quantitative studies. As concerns the latter, it should be noted that the brokerage indexes used in social network analysis (such as betweenness centrality) only measure brokerage within the boundaries of a cluster, neglecting the 'white' brokers (Figure 3). It is the white brokers that are the most interesting when it comes to the development of innovation opportunities through knowledge brokerage, but in order to focus on them we need an index of external openness – as proposed, for instance, in the study by Giuliani (2013).

Notes

1. This way of defining entrepreneurship and entrepreneurs is consistent with the literature on entrepreneurship that, after the seminal contribution from Shane and Venkataraman (2000), came to occupy a very important place in the context of management studies. There are other ways to define the concept, however (going beyond its generic meaning). If we consider two scholars who serve as a reference for the literature on industrial districts, the neo-Marshallian Becattini (2006, p. 178) recalls that Marshall saw entrepreneurship as a particular kind of skilled work, consisting of: '(a) the capacity to go straight to the kernel of the practical problems, (b) to see almost instinctively the relative proportions of things, (c) to be a leader of men'. Becattini adds that one of the protagonists of the industrial districts' development in Italy was the small Marshallian entrepreneur.
2. This condition can be measured in various ways. For instance, betweenness centrality is 'an index that measures the extent to which a person brokers indirect connections between all other people in a network' (Burt, 2000, p. 354).
3. This criticism of Burt's idea of entrepreneurship is consistent with the broader analysis conducted by Salancik (1995) on the promise of social network analysis for organizational theory.
4. The rebuttal comes from case studies on 'failing' districts. An emblematic example comes from the way in which Grabher (1993, pp. 262–263) explains the decline of the Ruhr coal, iron and steel district in West Germany in the 1960s: personal cohesiveness and well-established, intensive relations within the cluster 'limited the perception of innovation opportunities and left no room for "bridging relationships" – those that transcend a firm's own narrowly circumscribed group and bring together information from different sources'.

Aknowledgments

The author is in debt to two anonymous reviewers for their valuable comments that have contributed to improve a first version of the paper.

Disclosure statement

No potential conflict of interest was reported by the author.

References

Agarwal, R., Audretsch, D., & Sarkar, M. B. (2007). The process of creative construction: Knowledge spillovers, entrepreneurship, and economic growth. *Strategic Entrepreneurship Journal*, *1*(3-4), 263–286. doi:10.1002/sej.36

Alvarez, S. A., & Busenitz, L. W. (2001). The entrepreneurship of resource-based theory. *Journal of Management, 27*(6), 755–775. doi:10.1177/014920630102700609

Amdam, R. P., & Bjarnar, O. (2015). Globalization and the development of industrial clusters: Comparing two Norwegian clusters, 1900–2010. *Business History Review, 89*(4), 693–716. doi:10.1017/S0007680515001051

Andersen, P., & Bøllingtoft, A. (2011). Cluster-based global firms' use of local capabilities. *Management Research Review, 34*(10), 1087–1106. doi:10.1108/01409171111171492

Andersson, S., Evers, N., & Griot, C. (2013). Local and international networks in small firm internationalization: Cases from the Rhône-Alpes medical technology regional cluster. *Entrepreneurship & Regional Development, 25*(9-10), 867–888. doi:10.1080/08985626.2013.847975

Baron, R. A. (2006). Opportunity recognition as pattern recognition: How entrepreneurs 'connect the dots' to identify new business opportunities. *Academy of Management Perspectives, 20*(1), 104–119. doi:10.5465/amp.2006.19873412

Bathelt, H., Malmberg, A., & Maskell, P. (2004). Clusters and knowledge: Local buzz, global pipelines and the process of knowledge creation. *Progress in Human Geography, 28*(1), 31–56. doi:10.1191/0309132504ph469oa

Becattini, G. (1990). The Marshallian industrial district as a socioeconomic notion. In F. Pyke, G. Becattini, & W. Sengerberger (Eds.), *Industrial districts and inter-firm cooperation in Italy* (pp. 37–51). Geneva: International Institute of Labour Studies.

Becattini, G. (1991). The industrial district as a creative milieu. In G. Benko & M. Dunford (Eds.), *Industrial change and regional development* (pp. 102–114). London: Belhaven Press.

Becattini, G. (2001). *The Caterpillar and the Butterfly: An exemplary case of development in the Italy of the industrial districts*. Florence: Le Monnier.

Becattini, G. (2006). Some notes on the empirical basis of the role attributed to small business and entrepreneurship in the thought of Alfred Marshall. *Foundations and Trends in Entrepreneurship, 2*(3), 178.

Bell, S. J., Tracey, P., & Heide, J. B. (2009). The organization of regional clusters. *Academy of Management Review, 34*(4), 623–642.

Bellandi, M. (1996). Innovation and change in the Marshallian industrial district. *European Planning Studies, 4*(3), 357–368. doi:10.1080/09654319608720351

Bellandi, M., & De Propris, L. (2017). New forms of industrial districts. *Economia e Politica Industriale, 44*(4), 411–427. doi:10.1007/s40812-017-0082-9

Belussi, F., & Sedita, S. R. (2009). Life cycle vs. multiple path dependency in industrial districts. *European Planning Studies, 17*(4), 505–528. doi:10.1080/09654310802682065

Boari, C., Molina-Morales, F. X., & Martínez-Cháfer, L. (2017). Direct and interactive effects of brokerage roles on innovation in clustered firms. *Growth and Change, 48*(3), 336–358. doi:10.1111/grow.12170

Bolton, L. D., & Lane, M. D. (2012). Individual entrepreneurial orientation: Development of a measurement instrument. *Education + Training, 54*(2-3), 219–233. doi:10.1108/00400911211210314

Burt, R. S. (1992). *Structural holes: The social structure of competition*. Cambridge: Harvard University Press.

Burt, R. S. (2000). The network structure of social capital. In R. I. Sutton & B. M. Staw (Eds.), *Research in organizational behavior* (pp. 345–423). Greenwich: JAI Press.

Burt, R. S. (2004). Structural holes and good ideas. *American Journal of Sociology, 110*(2), 349–399. doi:10.1086/421787

Caloffi, A., Rossi, F., & Russo, M. (2015). The emergence of intermediary organizations: A network-based approach to the design of innovation policies. In P. Cairney & R. Geyer (Eds.), *Handbook on complexity and public policy* (pp. 314–331). Cheltenham: Edward Elgar.

Camuffo, A. (2003). Transforming industrial districts: Large firms and small business networks in the Italian eyewear industry. *Industry and Innovation, 10*(4), 377–401. doi:10.1080/1366271032000163630

Camuffo, A., & Grandinetti, R. (2011). Italian industrial districts as cognitive systems: Are they still reproducible? *Entrepreneurship & Regional Development*, 23(9-10), 815–852. doi:10.1080/08985626.2011.577815

Capone, F., & Lazzeretti, L. (2018). The different roles of proximity in multiple informal network relationships: Evidence from the cluster of high technology applied to cultural goods in Tuscany. *Industry and Innovation*, 25(9), 897–917. doi:10.1080/13662716.2018.1442713

Carbonara, N. (2018). Competitive success of Italian industrial districts: A network-based approach. *Journal of Interdisciplinary Economics*, 30(1), 78–104. doi:10.1177/0260107917700470

Codara, L., & Morato, E. (2002). Il distretto di Montebelluna tra locale e globale. In G. Provasi (Ed.), *Le istituzioni dello sviluppo. I distretti industriali tra storia, sociologia ed economia* (pp. 99–143). Rome: Donzelli.

Coenen, L., Moodysson, J., & Asheim, B. T. (2004). Nodes, networks and proximities: On the knowledge dynamics of the Medicon Valley biotech cluster. *European Planning Studies*, 12(7), 1003–1018. doi:10.1080/0965431042000267876

Cohen, S. S., & Fields, G. (1999). Social capital and capital gains in Silicon Valley. *California Management Review*, 41(2), 108–130. doi:10.2307/41165989

Coleman, J. S. (1988). Social capital in the creation of human capital. *American Journal of Sociology*, 94, S95–S120. doi:10.1086/228943

Cooke, P. (2009). Technology clusters, industrial districts and regional innovation systems. In G. Becattini, M. Bellandi, & L. De Propris (Eds.), *A handbook of industrial districts* (pp. 295–306). Cheltenham: Edward Elgar.

Covin, J. G., Green, K. M., & Slevin, D. P. (2006). Strategic process effects on the entrepreneurial orientation–sales growth rate relationship. *Entrepreneurship Theory and Practice*, 30(1), 57–81. doi:10.1111/j.1540-6520.2006.00110.x

Davidsson, P., Delmar, F., & Wiklund, J. (2006). Entrepreneurship as growth: Growth as entrepreneurship. In P. Davidsson, F. Delmar, & J. Wiklund (Eds.), *Entrepreneurship and the growth of firms* (pp. 21–38). Cheltenham: Edward Elgar.

De Marchi, V., Di Maria, E., & Gereffi, G. (Eds.). (2018). *Local clusters in global value chains: Linking actors and territories through manufacturing and innovation*. Abingdon: Routledge.

De Marchi, V., Gereffi, G., & Grandinetti, R. (2018). Evolutionary trajectories of industrial districts in global value chains. In V. De Marchi, E. Di Maria, & G. Gereffi (Eds.), *Local clusters in global value chains: Linking actors and territories through manufacturing and innovation* (pp. 33–50). Abingdon: Routledge.

De Marchi, V., & Grandinetti, R. (2014). Industrial districts and the collapse of the Marshallian model: Looking at the Italian experience. *Competition & Change*, 18(1), 70–87. doi:10.1179/1024529413Z.00000000049

De Marchi, V., & Grandinetti, R. (2016). Industrial districts evolving in glocal value chains: Evidence from the Italian wine industry. *Piccola Impresa/Small Business*, 28(1), 10–36.

Dei Ottati, G. (2003). The governance of transactions in the industrial district: The community market. In G. Becattini, M. Bellandi, G. Dei Ottati, & F. Sforzi (Eds.), *From industrial districts to local development: An itinerary of research* (pp. 73–94). Cheltenham: Edward Elgar.

Dei Ottati, G. (2009). An industrial district facing the challenges of globalization: Prato today. *European Planning Studies*, 17(12), 1817–1835. doi:10.1080/09654310903322322

Dei Ottati, G. (2018). Marshallian industrial districts in Italy: The end of a model or adaptation to the global economy? *Cambridge Journal of Economics*, 42(2), 259–284. doi:10.1093/cje/bex066

Furlan, A., & Grandinetti, R. (2014). Spin-off performance in the start-up phase: A conceptual framework. *Journal of Small Business and Enterprise Development*, 21(3), 528–544. doi:10.1108/JSBED-04-2014-0055

Furlan, A., & Grandinetti, R. (2016). Spinoffs and their endowments: Beyond knowledge inheritance theory. *Journal of Intellectual Capital*, 17(3), 570–589. doi:10.1108/JIC-02-2016-0023

Garofoli, G. (1992). New firm formation and local development: The Italian experience. *Entrepreneurship & Regional Development*, 4(2), 101–125. doi:10.1080/08985629200000006

Garofoli, G. (2006). Strategie di sviluppo e politiche per l'innovazione nei distretti industriali. In B. Quintieri (Ed.), *I distretti industriali dal locale al globale* (pp. 77–114). Rome: Fondazione Manlio Masi.

Gedajlovic, E., Honig, B., Moore, C. B., Payne, G. T., & Wright, M. (2013). Social capital and entrepreneurship: A schema and research agenda. *Entrepreneurship Theory and Practice, 37*(3), 455–478. doi:10.1111/etap.12042

Gilbert, B. A. (2012). Creative destruction: Identifying its geographic origins. *Research Policy, 41*(4), 734–742. doi:10.1016/j.respol.2011.11.005

Giuliani, E. (2013). Clusters, networks and firms' product success: An empirical study. *Management Decision, 51*(6), 1135–1160. doi:10.1108/MD-01-2012-0010

Gordon, I. R., & McCann, P. (2000). Industrial clusters: Complexes, agglomeration and/or social networks? *Urban Studies, 37*(3), 513–532. doi:10.1080/0042098002096

Grabher, G. (1993). The weakness of strong ties: The lock-in of regional development in the Ruhr area. In G. Grabher (Ed.), *The embedded firm: On the socioeconomics of industrial networks* (pp. 255–277). London: Routledge.

Grandinetti, R. (2014). Entrepreneurship, network and community in Marshallian industrial districts. *World Review of Entrepreneurship, Management and Sustainable Development, 10*(4), 449–464. doi:10.1504/WREMSD.2014.064948

Grandinetti, R. (2018). The KIBS paradox and structural holes. *Knowledge Management Research & Practice, 16*(2), 161–172. doi:10.1080/14778238.2018.1442993

Granovetter, M. S. (1985). Economic action and social structure: The problem of embeddedness. *American Journal of Sociology, 91*(3), 481–510. doi:10.1086/228311

Guercini, S., & Cova, B. (2018). Unconventional entrepreneurship. *Journal of Business Research, 92*, 385–391. doi:10.1016/j.jbusres.2018.06.021

Guercini, S., & Runfola, A. (2015). Actors' roles in interaction and innovation in local systems: A conceptual taxonomy. *Journal of Business & Industrial Marketing, 30*(3–4), 269–278. doi:10.1108/JBIM-12-2012-0256

Hargadon, A. B. (2002). Brokering knowledge: Linking learning and innovation. *Research in Organizational Behavior, 24*, 41–85. doi:10.1016/S0191-3085(02)24003-4

Harrison, R. T., Cooper, S. Y., & Mason, C. M. (2004). Entrepreneurial activity and the dynamics of technology-based cluster development: The case of Ottawa. *Urban Studies, 41*(5-6), 1045–1070. doi:10.1080/00420980410001675841

Hervas-Oliver, J. L., Albors-Garrigos, J., Estelles-Miguel, S., & Boronat-Moll, C. (2018). Radical innovation in Marshallian industrial districts. *Regional Studies, 52*(10), 1388–1397. doi:10.1080/00343404.2017.1390311

Hervas-Oliver, J. L., Lleo, M., & Cervello, R. (2017). The dynamics of cluster entrepreneurship: Knowledge legacy from parents or agglomeration effects? The case of the Castellon ceramic tile district. *Research Policy, 46*(1), 73–92. doi:10.1016/j.respol.2016.10.006

Ingstrup, M. B., & Christensen, P. R. (2017). Transformation of cluster specialization in the wake of globalization. *Entrepreneurship & Regional Development, 29*(5-6), 500–516. doi:10.1080/08985626.2017.1298679

Isaksen, A. (1994). New industrial spaces and industrial districts in Norway: Productive concepts in explaining regional development? *European Urban and Regional Studies, 1*(1), 31–48. doi:10.1177/096977649400100104

Johannisson, B. (1988). Business formation: A network approach. *Scandinavian Journal of Management, 4*(3-4), 83–99. doi:10.1016/0956-5221(88)90002-4

Klepper, S. (2010). The origin and growth of industry clusters: The making of Silicon Valley and Detroit. *Journal of Urban Economics, 67*(1), 15–32. doi:10.1016/j.jue.2009.09.004

Klepper, S., & Sleeper, S. (2005). Entry by spinoffs. *Management Science, 51*(8), 1291–1306. doi:10.1287/mnsc.1050.0411

Lazerson, M. (1995). A new phoenix?: Modern putting-out in the Modena knitwear industry. *Administrative Science Quarterly, 40*(1), 34–59. doi:10.2307/2393699

Lazerson, M. H., & Lorenzoni, G. (1999). The firms that feed industrial districts: A return to the Italian source. *Industrial and Corporate Change, 8*(2), 235–266. doi:10.1093/icc/8.2.235

Lazzeretti, L., Sedita, S. R., & Caloffi, A. (2014). Founders and disseminators of cluster research. *Journal of Economic Geography, 14*(1), 21–43. doi:10.1093/jeg/lbs053

Lechner, C., & Leyronas, C. (2012). The competitive advantage of cluster firms: The priority of regional network position over extra-regional networks – A study of a French high-tech cluster. *Entrepreneurship & Regional Development, 24*(5-6), 457–473. doi:10.1080/08985626.2011.617785

Lipparini, A. (1995). *Imprese. Relazioni tra imprese e posizionamento competitivo.* Milan: Etas.

Markusen, A. (1996). Sticky places in slippery space: A typology of industrial districts. *Economic Geography, 72*(3), 293–313. doi:10.2307/144402

Marshall, A. (1920). *Principles of economics* (8th ed.). London: Macmillan.

Mathews, M., & Stokes, P. (2013). The creation of trust: The interplay of rationality, institutions and exchange. *Entrepreneurship & Regional Development, 25*(9-10), 845–866. doi:10.1080/08985626.2013.845695

McCaffrey, S. J. (2013). Tacit-rich districts and globalization: Changes in the Italian textile and apparel production system. *Socio-Economic Review, 11*(4), 657–685. doi:10.1093/ser/mwt005

Molina-Morales, F. X. (2005). The territorial agglomerations of firms: A social capital perspective from the Spanish tile industry. *Growth and Change, 36*(1), 74–99. doi:10.1111/j.1468-2257.2005.00267.x

Molina-Morales, F. X., Martínez-Cháfer, L., & Valiente-Bordanova, D. (2017). Disruptive technological innovations as new opportunities for mature industrial clusters: The case of digital printing innovation in the Spanish ceramic tile cluster. *Investigaciones Regionales, 16*(39), 39–57.

Morrison, A. (2008). *Gatekeepers of knowledge* within industrial districts: Who they are, how they interact. *Regional Studies, 42*(6), 817–835. doi:10.1080/00343400701654178

Myint, Y. M., Vyakarnam, S., & New, M. J. (2005). The effect of social capital in new venture creation: The Cambridge high-technology cluster. *Strategic Change, 14*(3), 165–177. doi:10.1002/jsc.718

Paniccia, I. (2006). Cutting through the chaos: Towards a new typology of industrial districts and clusters. In B. Asheim, P. Cooke, & R. Martin (Eds.), *Clusters and regional development: Critical reflections and explorations* (pp. 90–114). London: Routledge.

Patrucco, P. P. (2005). The emergence of technology systems: Knowledge production and distribution in the case of the Emilian plastics district. *Cambridge Journal of Economics, 29*(1), 37–56. doi:10.1093/cje/bei011

Porter, M. E. (1998). Clusters and competition: New agendas for companies, governments, and institutions. In M. E. Porter (Ed.), *On competition* (pp. 197–287). Boston: Harvard Business School Press.

Porter, M. E. (2000). Location, competition, and economic development: Local clusters in a global economy. *Economic Development Quarterly, 14*(1), 15–34. doi:10.1177/089124240001400105

Pucci, T., Brumana, M., Minola, T., & Zanni, L. (2017). Social capital and innovation in a life science cluster: The role of proximity and family involvement. *Journal of Technology Transfer.* doi:10.1007/s10961-017-9591-y

Rabellotti, R., Carabelli, A., & Hirsch, G. (2009). Italian industrial districts on the move: Where are they going? *European Planning Studies, 17*(1), 19–41. doi:10.1080/09654310802513914

Randelli, F., & Lombardi, M. (2014). The role of leading firms in the evolution of SME clusters: Evidence from the leather products cluster in Florence. *European Planning Studies, 22*(6), 1199–1211. doi:10.1080/09654313.2013.773963

Rocha, H. O., & Sternberg, R. (2005). Entrepreneurship: The role of clusters theoretical perspectives and empirical evidence from Germany. *Small Business Economics, 24*(3), 267–292. doi:10.1007/s11187-005-1993-9

Rullani, E. (2003). The Industrial District (ID) as a cognitive system. In F. Belussi, G. Gottardi, & E. Rullani (Eds.), *The technological evolution of industrial districts* (pp. 63–87). Boston: Springer.

Salancik, G. R. (1995). Wanted: A good network theory of organization. *Administrative Science Quarterly, 40*(2), 345–349. doi:10.2307/2393642

Saxenian, A. (1994). *Regional advantage: Culture and competition in Silicon Valley and Route 128.* Cambridge: Harvard University Press.

Saxenian, A. (2006). *The new Argonauts: Regional advantage in a global economy*. Cambridge: Harvard University Press.
Sedita, S. R., Belussi, F., & Grandinetti, R. (2016). How does a networked business incubator fuel cluster emergence? A theoretical discussion and an empirical illustration. In C. Boari, T. Elfring, & F. X. Molina-Morales (Eds.), *Entrepreneurship and cluster dynamics* (pp. 104–128). New York: Routledge.
Segarra-Blasco, A., & Arauzo-Carod, J. M. (2008). Sources of innovation and industry–university interaction: Evidence from Spanish firms. *Research Policy*, *37*(8), 1283–1295. doi:10.1016/j.respol.2008.05.003
Sforzi, F. (2008). Il distretto industriale: da Marshall a Becattini. *Il Pensiero Economico Italiano*, *16*(2), 71–80.
Shane, S., & Venkataraman, S. (2000). The promise of entrepreneurship as a field of research. *Academy of Management Review*, *25*(1), 217–226.
Solinas, G. (1996). *I processi di formazione, la crescita e la sopravvivenza delle piccole imprese*. Milan: Franco Angeli.
Sorenson, O. (2003). Social networks and industrial geography. *Journal of Evolutionary Economics*, *13*(5), 513–527. doi:10.1007/s00191-003-0165-9
Sorenson, O. (2017). Regional ecologies of entrepreneurship. *Journal of Economic Geography*, *17*(5), 959–974. doi:10.1093/jeg/lbx031
Sorenson, O., & Audia, P. G. (2000). The social structure of entrepreneurial activity: Geographic concentration of footwear production in the United States, 1940–1989. *American Journal of Sociology*, *106*(2), 424–462. doi:10.1086/316962
St. John, C. H., & Pouder, R. W. (2006). Technology clusters versus industry clusters: Resources, networks, and regional advantages. *Growth and Change*, *37*(2), 141–171. doi:10.1111/j.1468-2257.2006.00313.x
Sternberg, R. (2009). Regional dimensions of entrepreneurship. *Foundations and Trends® in Entrepreneurship*, *5*(4), 211–340. doi:10.1561/0300000024
Stevenson, H. H., & Jarillo, J. C. (1990). A paradigm of entrepreneurship: Entrepreneurial management. *Strategic Management Journal*, *11*(Summer Special Issue), 17–27.
Stinchcombe, A. L. (1965). Social structure and organizations. In J. C. March (Ed.), *Handbook of organizations* (pp. 142–193). Chicago: Rand McNally.
Trippl, M., & Tödtling, F. (2007). Developing biotechnology clusters in non-high technology regions: The case of Austria. *Industry and Innovation*, *14*(1), 47–67. doi:10.1080/13662710601130590
Welter, F. (2011). Contextualizing entrepreneurship: Conceptual challenges and ways forward. *Entrepreneurship Theory and Practice*, *35*(1), 165–184. doi:10.1111/j.1540-6520.2010.00427.x

8 OPEN ACCESS

Understanding processes of path renewal and creation in thick specialized regional innovation systems. Evidence from two textile districts in Italy and Sweden

Cristina Chaminade ⓘ, Marco Bellandi ⓘ, Monica Plechero ⓘ and Erica Santini ⓘ

ABSTRACT
The type of regional innovation system (RIS) strongly affects possibilities of paths of industrial transformation. This paper argues that traditional manufacturing districts, corresponding to specialized RISs and characterized by various nuclei of specialization and know-how, may foster different trajectories in combination with extra-regional networks. In particular, the paper analyses the interplay between regional and national innovation systems, providing an overview of the effect that different multilevel dynamics have on local trajectories. The cases of the textile districts in Prato (Italy) and Borås (Sweden) show SRISs can display not only path extension but also path renewal and creation strategies.

1. Introduction

Nowadays a growing number of scholars are interested in understanding the drivers of regional path development and industrial transformation. Some contributions, mainly in the branch of evolutionary economics, focus on the transformation of industries and how their diversification may impact regional paths of transformation (Asheim, Boschma, & Cooke, 2011). Other scholars committed to explore regional innovation systems (RIS) and their dynamics aim instead to understand how the quality and type of RIS affect the development path of clusters and industries within a region (Isaksen & Trippl, 2016).

Within this last strand of literature, scholars agree on the identification of few windows of growth trajectories in thick and specialized RIS (SRIS). SRISs are usually characterized by the existence of one or few very strong industrial clusters or local production systems, specialized support infrastructure and institutions, and the presence of a multitude of clustered small firms. They enjoy classical Marshallian external economies. Some studies argue that the low relational variety that is present in SRIS and the limited diversity of actors may limit the endogenous capability of renewal or transformation of the industrial

This is an Open Access article distributed under the terms of the Creative Commons Attribution-NonCommercial-NoDerivatives License (http://creativecommons.org/licenses/by-nc-nd/4.0/), which permits non-commercial re-use, distribution, and reproduction in any medium, provided the original work is properly cited, and is not altered, transformed, or built upon in any way.

specialization. This type of RIS would have limited endogenous transformative capabilities, low capacity in absorbing extra-regional knowledge, being able at best to go through path extension and at worst path exhaustion (Isaksen & Trippl, 2016). Path renewal (i.e. change to different but related activities) and path creation (i.e. the path of radical change) on the other hand seem to have a better chance to occur in diversified RISs, characterizing, for example, metropolitan areas (Isaksen & Trippl, 2016).

This paper investigates under which conditions path creation and renewal is possible in industrial districts characterizing thick and specialized regional innovation systems (Bailey, Bellandi, Caloffi, & De Propris, 2010; Becattini, 2001; Dei Ottati, 1994). Particular attention will be given to *variety within specialization, extra-regional networks* and to the *role of alignment of policy visions between the actors of regional and national systems* in supporting path renewal and path creation. The relevance of the theoretical framework will be examined by use of two cases of historical textile districts: Prato (Italy) and Borås (Sweden). The main research question of this paper is how can thick and specialized regional innovation systems engage in path renewal and creation. This general question can be divided into the following specific questions:

- What type of path development characterize the textile industry in Prato and Borås?
- What are the historical conditions underlying regional specific path trajectories?

Next section will discuss the main literature linking industrial transformation with the typology of RIS, and bringing concepts from the industrial district literature. It will focus on the intra-regional variety, extra-regional networks, and multilevel policy coordination. Section 3 will present the cases of the two textile districts, after a short overview of the current conditions of the European textile industry. Section 4 will provide a brief conclusion and will discuss some remaining questions related to growth trajectories in SRISs.

2. Regional innovation systems, transformation paths and regional specialization

2.1. Regional innovation systems and transformation paths

An innovation system refers to the set of organizations and institutions engaged in processes of interactive learning and knowledge creation and diffusion (Lundvall, Vang, Joseph, & Chaminade, 2009). Geographical proximity enables interactive learning and innovation through the exchange of both tacit and explicit knowledge among individuals and organizations (Boschma, 2005). This exchange is facilitated by a set of institutions embedded in the territory. Together, the set of organizations and their relations embedded in specific institutional frameworks, are the cornerstone of the regional innovation system (RIS).

RIS is thus defined as 'the wider setting of organisations and institutions affecting and supporting learning and innovation in a region with an explicit focus on competence building and organisational innovations' (Asheim, 2009, p. 28). Higher education and research institutions, funding organizations, bridging institutions, and companies among others interact in production and innovation related activities within highly contextualized institutional frameworks (e.g. culture, values, habit, norms, and regulations).

Considering both the organizational endowment and the degree of specialization Isaksen and Trippl (2016) propose to distinguish between three different types of RIS: (a) Organizationally thick and diversified RIS (DRIS); (b) Organizationally thick and specialized RIS (SRIS); (c) Organizationally thin RIS (TRIS).

DRIS are usually found in metropolitan regions, with a dense and diverse scientific, technological, and productive infrastructure featuring a high density of innovative firms operating in different industrial sectors. On the other side of the spectrum there are TRIS that are typical of peripheral regions with weak innovation and productive infrastructure.

SRIS are usually characterized by the existence of one or few very strong industrial clusters or local production systems, specialized support infrastructure, and institutions that are highly targeted to the specific regional industries. Industrial districts are typically mentioned in the literature in relation to organizationally thick and specialized RISs.[1] Industrial districts are small regions (usually referred in statistical terms to local labour systems) characterized by a main localized industry and the presence of a multitude of specialized firms, usually small-to-medium sized, and independent (Becattini, 2001). Thus, the RIS related to IDs tends to be thick and specialized.[2]

Past and current industrial specialization and institutional frameworks influence the possibilities for future regional development. Isaksen and Trippl (2016) distinguish four different types of regional transformation paths. *Path extension* refers to transformation processes in which regional industries introduce incremental innovations in existing predominant technological paths. In the long term, path extension runs the risk of transforming into path exhaustion as the innovation potential of the local firms decline. *Path renewal* refers to transformations in which local firms switch to different, but often related activities and sectors. *Path creation* refers to the most radical transformation of a regional industry, implying the emergence of new sectors and new types of firms in the region or the introduction of technologies and forms of organization that are radically different from the technical standards in the region.

According to Isaksen and Trippl (2016), path renewal and path creation would occur more often in diversified RIS. Instead, in specialized RIS there would be a high propensity to continue along existing development paths. The strong social capital and the limited variety of knowledge bases that would characterize these types of RIS tend to reinforce existing patterns of behaviour and lock-ins (positive and negative). Path extension would be thus the typical development path followed by a SRIS, unless complemented by external regional sources of knowledge (Trippl, Grillitsch, & Isaksen, 2018).

2.2. Transformation paths and extra-regional networks – exogenous sources of renewal

The role of extra-regional sources of knowledge in processes of regional path creation and renewal has recently been addressed in the literature, particularly in thick and specialized regional innovation systems (Martin, Wiig Aslesen, Grillitsch, & Herstade, 2018; Trippl et al., 2018). The probability to link to external region sources is considered to be a function of the knowledge base prevailing in the regional industries, the specific institutional framework, the organizational infrastructure operating in the system, the embeddedness structure of relations, and the degree of urbanization (Asheim et al., 2011; Sotarauta, Ramstedt-Sen, Seppänen, & Kosonen, 2011). In particular, differences may depend on the types of RIS. Tödtling, Lengauer, and Höglinger (2011), investigating on RIS in Austria, show that while firms in institutionally thin RIS (e.g. Salzburg) tend to establish international linkages more extensively, firms in institutionally thick RIS (e.g. Vienna) tend to limit the establishment of linkages at a domestic level. Plechero and Chaminade (2016) analizing and comparing RIS in emerging and developed economies find similar results. Firms located in SRIS, featured by strong specialization advantages, would rely more on linkages in close proximity (e.g. local or domestic), than on extra-regional linkages. This is particularly evident when a system reaches a mature stage of development where networks stabilized throughout time and 'inertia' can limit exploration strategies (Trippl et al., 2018). The exception could be agglomerations with highly specialized and localized knowledge hard to find anywhere else in the world. Additionally, thick and specialized regions might not have the capacity to tap into, absorb and integrate the knowledge acquired outside the region with the knowledge already available in the region.

However, what such stream of interpretations tends to ignore is the possible heterogeneity within a localized industry and not only in local complementary industries. This is an area well studied within the industrial district literature.

2.3. Transformation paths and intra-regional variety – endogenous sources of renewal

Industrial districts may host a complex array of productive activities, which develop products and services in the area, within the main localized industry, and in the complementary industries. As discussed by Bellandi and Santini (2017), the main industry of an ID and the local complementary industries can be represented, on the cognitive dimension, as a multiplicity of know-how nuclei, each nucleus being a niche of relatively homogenous knowledge, practices, and firms; mainly local SMEs.

Learning and creativity develop within and between the different productive experience of diverse ID nuclei. It is a clear example of what has been called decentralized industrial creativity (see Bailey et al., 2010) or doing-using-interacting mode of innovation (Jensen, Johnson, Lorenz, & Lundvall, 2007), in which innovation takes place thanks to the interactions between users and producers and on-the-job learning.[3] When processes of exploitation of a given pool of knowledge dominate inside the industrial district, the SRIS has limited endogenous dynamic capabilities. Alternatively, given favourable enabling conditions, the proximity[4] between the nuclei might allow exploration processes that bring about the spawning of new complementary or substitutive nuclei. This second type of processes would contribute to the inner differentiation of the traditional main industry through time, outlining two scenarios. When the new nuclei are complementary in productive terms to the traditional nuclei and support their technological and market strength, path extension would be the most likely outcome. Instead, when a decline hits the traditional nuclei, a substitutive function may emerge. Accordingly, some among the new nuclei, having also developed products and market channels independent on the demand of the traditional nuclei, would be able to absorb the local resources made redundant by their decline and start to grow rapidly. This would transform the main specialization of the district, and open up renewed trajectories, possibly categorized as path renewal (see Bailey et al., 2010).

In an evolutionary perspective, the set of nuclei might mutually play a complementary and/or a substitutive role, triggering exploration processes in face of market and technological challenges, also involving non-local sources of knowledge and ideas. A critical issue is understanding how these processes can be nurtured.

2.4. Regional development paths, regional and national policies, and multilevel dynamics

Regional transformations, particularly those involving path renewal and creation, can hardly take place without the support from regional and national policies.

Regional actors and their activities as place leaders are crucial driving forces for sustaining regional transformations (Bailey et al., 2010; Njøs & Fosse, 2018; Sotarauta & Beer, 2017). Therefore, even in regions that are similar in terms of structural preconditions, the type of regional governance makes a difference in regional development path. Specifically, public authorities at the regional level can act as 'proactive facilitators' to face path transformation only when they are positively interrelated with local market-oriented actors and supported by industrial partners (Holmen & Fosse, 2017). This implies an alignment of interests and visions at least between actors at the regional level (Isaksen & Jakobsen, 2017). Alternatively, this alignment would in turn be negative for path renewal and path creation in SRIS, if most of the actors were stuck along an existing development path (Ibid.). On the other side, regional policies are also partly path dependent being more or less embedded in the territory. If not affected by strong path dependency, regional policies could be directed to 'broadening' the scope of the main local industries, supporting crossovers with other related activities in the region, and enable path renewal through the development of related industries (Neffke, Henning, & Boschma, 2011; Njøs & Jakobsen, 2016). However, SRIS might not dispose of the supporting infrastructures needed for regional diversification or some crucial pool of knowledge needed for path renewal and creation. In that case, it has been suggested that effective national policies could provide those infrastructures and support access to such pool of knowledge (Njøs & Fosse, 2018).

National policies might play a fundamental role in shaping the transformation strategies and the regulatory framework of different industries. They support the accumulation of technological competences and the specialization in particular technological fields through the actions of national actors and organizations. They provide as well general 'direction of innovation and competence-building emanating from processes of science-based and experience-based learning' (Lundvall et al., 2009, p. 7). In this perspective, it is important to consider how the different levels of governance could align or could instead generate contradictory effects.[5]

In countries like Finland or Norway, where both State and regional governments share responsibilities for regional development (Njøs & Fosse, 2018), regional actors coordinate constantly with state actors engaging quite efficiently in regional developing strategies. However, the same Norway shows the possible evolution of policies by regional authorities pursuing trajectories that divert from national programmes (Njøs & Jakobsen, 2018). In particular, when policy actions for sustaining industrial regional upgrading are taken at national level, they might be less effective in certain regions with respect to others due to the specific cumulative path of regional choices and the typology of social capital

(Ibid.). Indeed, in the case of IDs, which do not coincide with the administrative boundaries of the region, the dynamics of political interventions at national level directed to new development path may be even more difficult to integrate or align. In Italy, for example, the historical evolution of national policies shows how, in the past, some policy failures of State interventions were due to the difficulty of matching with the specific 'Marshallian capital' of the IDs in which local knowledge, organizational capabilities sediment, and peculiar social governance mechanisms sediment (Bellandi & Caloffi, 2016; Goglio, 2001).

In sum, in the case of high intra-regional variety, such as in industrial districts featuring multiplicity of knowledge nuclei, path renewal processes might be possible, if the most innovative actors receive policy support to develop new activities; but even then, extra-regional networks with external sources of knowledge might be needed. In those cases, as well as in path creation strategies, the coordination between policies by the regional government, by the State and the networks between regional and extra-regional actors might prove crucial. This will be illustrated by looking at different transformation strategies of two regions specialized in traditional manufacturing: the textile districts of Prato (Italy) and Borås (Sweden). We will see how different government mechanisms and multilevel dynamics of policies in the two SRIS, bring about different opportunities.

3. The restructuring of the European textile industry: the path transformation of Prato and Borås districts

This section analyses the emergence of possible traverses to new paths of development in two European industrial districts: Borås in Sweden and Prato in Italy. Both districts have historically specialized in the textile industry, with a somewhat stronger focus on the fashion and clothing subsectors in Prato, and industrial and technical textiles in Borås. The historical development of both districts has been characterized by crises and a consequent industrial re-structuring. The two case studies have been chosen because they illustrate two different trajectories in thick and specialized regional innovation systems. The research reported in next section is based on a combination of previous research by the authors and new secondary and primary data.[6]

3.1. Current trends and path transformation strategies of the textile industry in Europe

The textile industry in Europe has undergone profound changes in the last half-century since it is a sector not only sensitive to the development and stability of the world economy, but it is also highly dependent on technology and demand changes as well as on competition of emerging economies (Wysokinska, 2003). Despite different downturns, recently, the European textile industry and the related clothing industry seem to have found new growth trajectories based on a variety of strategies (European Apparel and Textile Confederation, 2015). The prevalence of strategies aiming at lowering costs, either through the introduction of technologies or through the reconfiguration of value chains and relocation of production facilities, exemplify cases of *path extension*. Digitalization and automatization pervade design and prototyping for reduced time-to-market and fast fashion within existing typologies of products. The introduction of advanced digital manufacturing and the increase in digital trade, as well as of innovative solutions to reduce the environmental impact, may instead express cases of *path renewal*.

As recalled for example by Scheffer (2012), the European industry has its main disadvantages in the low and medium segments of the market. The introduction of digitalized industrial technologies, or the increase of the engineering, and the intangible aspects of products, may guarantee high quality of production and consumption for new personalized customers' needs and new attractive niche markets. The 'artisan' touch, as well as intangible aspects such as reputation, labels, and creative designs, remain crucial both for leading firms and the linked system of suppliers and subcontractors.

New investments in R&D processes and scientific knowledge may support *path creation* that, in the textile industry, appear to be strongly linked to sophisticated technological innovation. They concern for example solutions that improve people quality of life, increase comfort and safety (e.g. fibre material to store energy), or contribute to mitigate health problems (e.g. allergies, pollutions etc.). The dominance of knowledge of more scientific nature is also required to take advantage of cross-fertilization between the textile sector and other sectors and disciplines (medicine, architecture, environmental), involving new chemicals, sensoristics, testing, and measurements methods (Allgemeiner Vliesstoff-Report [AVR], 2013). The technical textiles sector, which today represent the EU part of the industry with stronger linkages to research activities (Scheffer, 2012), appears to provide favourable, though not exclusive, fields for path creation.[7]

Although the heterogeneity in firms' strategies has increased in recent years within IDs, we will see, in the next subsections, that Prato (Italy) seems to be following predominately path extension with a potential for renewal strategies, while Borås to be heading to path creation.

3.2. Path extension and renewal in Prato (Italy)

The textile district of Prato (in the Tuscany region) has been one of the most celebrated Italian industrial districts and one of the main textile districts of Europe (Becattini, 2001). Its area extends to the municipality of Prato (close to Florence) and to other 10 contiguous smaller municipalities.

The local textile industry has a long history that dates back to the Middle Ages. At the beginning of the 1960s, a decentralized industrial organization emerged around the flexible production of a changing variety of carded woollen fabrics and yarns. This drove a fast growth in the number of textile firms, usually SMEs, specialized in single or a few stages of the production processes and employing an increasing number of skilled and semi-skilled workers (Dei Ottati, 1994). Local markets for the exchange of intermediate textile products and operations were integrated by social trust and collective action on contractual norms, territorial and technical infrastructures (e.g. collective industrial purifiers), and by the action of 'open teams of specialised businesses' (Becattini, 2001). Between the 1970s and the 1980s, firms started to work with many different fibres, expanding production across an ever more differentiated range of yarns and fabrics. Various complementary and related production and service activities emerged locally, such as machinery, tools and dyes for the textile industry, clothing, and, later, ICT-enabled solutions for the industry.

In the second half of the 1980s, the local textile industry registered some difficulties of over-production, and the number of textile workers and firms started to decrease. However, the capability of the district to specialize in a rich variety of textile products and services related to the world fashion industry became stronger and confirmed the buoyancy of the district in the 1990s. Technical textiles also expanded without replacing the historical specialization of the district. In the first half of the 2000s, the competition in the yarns and fabrics markets from Asian low- cost producers and international value chains increased, especially because of the reduction of trade barriers and the technological progress in transportation and management systems. This directly impacted the local textile production and the related system of local firms and job markets, even if services and complementary industries kept on growing.

At the same time, since the 1990s and at an increasing pace in the 2000s, the district experienced waves of Chinese immigration, which led to the emergence of a parallel clothing and knitwear business cluster in Prato, led by the Chinese community. Unfortunately, the interplay between the historical textile industry by Italian firms and the new specialization by Chinese companies did not lead to important economic synergies.[8] When the great international crisis exploded in 2007, Prato's industry was under a phase of instability and uncertain transition. This triggered a reshaping of the textile industry[9]:

> The value of textile exports from the Province of Prato between 2001 and 2009 halved (decreasing from 2,412 to 1,026 million euros). As a consequence, the Prato textile system downsized considerably: the number of textile establishments in the Province of Prato fell from 4,976 in 2001 to 2,926 in 2009, while at the same time the number of workers dropped from 32,218 to 18,431 (Dei Ottati, 2014, p. 1258).

Though its local dominance has reduced, the textile core (fabrics, yarns, and other textiles) could still drive the local economy, its competences and knowledge granting a bedrock for a renewal path. As underlined by recent research (Bellandi & Santini, 2019), path renewal would ask active strategies of investments by the more dynamic entrepreneurs, followed by the larger population of artisans, and supported by appropriate knowledge-intensive and institutional services. Specifically, Bellandi and Santini (2019), exploring the transformation of the set of competencies into the district area, suggest that the population of specialized SMEs within the manufacturing core is characterized by a growing heterogeneity in term of firms' capabilities and knowledge nuclei; such heterogeneity could help catch renewed opportunities and the implementation of related strategies. With respect to the challenges coming from digital based processes and organization, the authors identified three main profiles in the population of firms within the core activities of the textile industry:

(a) The Traditional leaders, where the employees are not identified as a crucial source of strategic knowledge, knowledge inputs come from traditional intermediaries working for the manufacturing core, and physical components and outsourcing of material inputs remain central in the organization of production;
(b) The Neo-Makers, quite marginal at the moment, combining artisan approaches to textile products with digital-supported solutions. Employees are identified as a crucial source of strategic knowledge, and knowledge inputs to development projects come predominately from local knowledge intensive service providers (KIBS). Smart/

connectivity components and outsourcing of immaterial inputs are searched at regional but more often at extra-regional level.

(c) A small set of more Vertically integrated firms, led by innovative entrepreneurs with industrial strategies where employees are encouraged to increase their skills, explicitly in technical or scientific fields; knowledge inputs are partially internalized and integrated with manufacturing activities, while high-level knowledge inputs are also searched from relation with universities and international technological networks. For these firms, smart/connectivity components become central, while outsourcing related to material inputs have a lower importance.

The institutional support to the local manufacture appears to have not yet adapted (year 2017) to the exploration of new opportunities opened up by the recent challenges and the possibility of a wave of investments related to the new types of firms and strategies within the core. Therefore, the Neo-Makers and the innovative (relatively) vertically integrated players, which include the germ of path renewal, complain a lack of appropriate local policies and government support. Local support would be at the moment still too much devoted to traditional initiatives of lobbying, mediation, and sectoral training at the local level linked to the main traditional knowledge nuclei.

Inter-sectoral matching platforms, also at cross-scale territorial and sectoral levels, would be needed to strengthen the opportunities of sharing and learning new and diverse knowledge and competencies, and adjust technical standards and contractual expectations in order to reduce transaction costs and conflicts (Bellandi & Caloffi, 2016). But the local support organizations, including policy-makers are still too focused on supporting the traditional knowledge nuclei, rather than on supporting the needs for tapping into new sources of knowledge of the Neo-makers and vertically integrated firms. While the traditional leading players enjoy this kind of traditional institutional support, being strongly reliant on intra-sector relations and initiatives (Bellandi & Santini, 2019), Neo-Makers and Vertically integrated players still remain aside to the system. Path renewal strategies will be unlikely nurtured, and path creation even less so.

The remarks above raise some doubts on the possibility that path renewal or creation in the district could be supported by positive evolutions within the textile core, in particular within fashion specializations characterized by artisan and engineering knowledge or nurtured only by regional policies. National policies aiming at linking the Neo-Makers and the Vertically integrated firms domestically or internationally might be needed.

There is great potential in this strategy. Particularly considering the specificities of the Italian national innovation system characterized by a multitude of industrial districts specialized in different parts of the value chain and with multitude excellence centres often located in large cities.[10] Both Neo-Makers and Vertically integrated firms can potentially take advantage of some external knowledge and service providers, outside the local and often outside the regional borders. In the case of Prato, some of them may be found in the nearby city of Florence, and rarer ones still within national borders, e.g. in Milan, also including a creative advanced service cluster specialized in the fashion industry (Scheffer, 2012). The cognitive and cultural proximity that local actors from Prato have with the upper-regional government (Tuscany region) and with national providers is still at a level in which cooperative activities among the agents are possible, not only because of geographical proximity, but also because actors under the same national identity share the same language and some cultural and social proximity.

The challenge today is for such types of relations to support the exchange of relatively codified but context-dependent pools of engineering and artisan knowledge. There have been attempts in this direction over the last decade, but the results are not yet quite clear (Bellandi & Caloffi, 2016). What is needed are policies that are able to favour extra-regional linkages connecting the emerging niches led by Neo-makers and Vertically integrated firms with the variety of specializations embedded in Italian IDs and cities where complementary (high-tech) services and services devoted to sustain the excellence of made in Italy can be found.

3.3. Path creation in Borås (Sweden)

Borås is the centre of the textile industry located in Western Sweden and has been historically considered the gravitational centre of the textile and apparel industry in Sweden (Lindqvist, Malmberg, & Sölvell, 2008); it is its most important centre even today (Edström, 2018). The textile industry in Sweden is still an important source of manufacturing employment in the country, as compared with other traditional industries.

By the beginning of the twenty-first century, Borås was responsible for half of the Swedish textile exports, a proportion that is maintained today. Despite its apparent current strengths, Borås has been the epicentre of the decline of the traditional textile specialization.

Industrial textile production began in the Borås region in the mid-nineteenth century. Dyers and printers worked primarily with cotton fabrics. Growth continued until the 1950s, when the textile industry suffered its first profound crisis as a consequence of increased international competition. Data from the mid-fifties, before the first crisis hit, shows that 70% of the population was directly or indirectly employed in the textile industry (Edström, 2018). Between the mid-fifties and early seventies, more than half of the industry jobs were destroyed. The trade liberalization that occurred in the seventies and eighties as a consequence of the entry of Sweden in the EU and the Multifibre agreement only aggravated the decline of the industry which could not compete in terms of costs (Ibid.).

The aftermath of the crises brought a profound restructuring of the industry in a process of creative destruction characterized by structural adjustments, bankruptcy of iconic companies, and loss of employment (Gullstrand, 2005), as well as relocation of manufacturing first to other western EU regions, then to Eastern Europe, and finally to Asia – mainly China (Edström, 2018). The major textile, clothing, and knitting companies in the Borås region dealt with this crisis following a similar pattern:

> At first, they purchased modern equipment and outsourced some production. When these measures proved ineffective, they reorganized as holding companies with various activities in other business sectors. Or they created equity portfolios of shares in diverse sectors. Then, as the crisis continued, they sold assets including their trademark brands. Some companies eventually entered bankruptcy or completely restructured. (Edström, 2018, p. 221)

As a consequence, the textile and apparel industry in the Borås region, dominated by small family business with a strongly local entrepreneurship culture, was stripped down to mainly design activities, purchase and retailing, but almost no production. The response by the more dynamic companies, equivalent to the Neo-makers in Prato, was based on three strategies (Edström, 2018; Ljungkvist & Börje, 2016): (1) increased specialization in certain high-added value sub-industries; (2) regional mobilization for the development of skills and competencies in technical textiles, particularly in three focal areas (health and medicine, architecture and construction, and sustainable textiles); and (3) access to public investments for innovations in the area of technical textiles, requiring a coordination of different knowledge at different levels, such as in the case of a fabric that purifies water using solar energy or clothing that measures the heart rate.

Cooperative organization structures are common in Borås, partly due to the large proportion of family-owned companies and relatively few larger companies (Edström, 2018; Ljungkvist & Börje, 2016). But this cooperative spirit is not only limited to companies; in fact, one of the most important initiatives supporting path creation and renewal in the region came from a higher education institution – the Swedish School of Textiles at the University of Borås. In 2006 the University of Borås coordinated a proposal for the renewal of the local textile industry around technical textiles used in industrial applications. The 'Smart Textiles' initiative has as main partners the Swedish School of Textiles, the University of Borås, the SP Technical Research Institute of Sweden, and the incubator of Borås as well as local companies and the local government. The programme received 60 million Swedish crowns (around 6 million Euros) for an 8-year period from VINNOVA, the Swedish Agency for Innovation Systems. Together with local companies, they run around 450 research projects (SmartTextiles, 2017) primarily within three focus areas: Health and Medicine; Sustainable Textiles; and Architecture and Interiors (including sustainable building materials).

The Swedish School of Textiles at the University of Borås, together with local companies and the City of Borås also initiated a project in 2011 to develop a space suitable for the development of spin-off companies from the University. The Textile Fashion Center took form in 2011 and is currently a

> meeting place for businesses that are involved mainly with textiles and clothing [...]. The founding principle of the Textile Fashion Center is that it should provide a platform for the development of new knowledge, new products, and new business opportunities that can strengthen the economy of the Borås region. (Edström, 2018, p. 225)

The path creation and renewal strategies that characterize the transformation and upgrading of the Borås textile and apparel industry were initiated by local actors. However, they would not have been successful without strong support from the national and regional innovation system and policies. On the one hand, in the aftermath of the crises, the City of Borås supported the move to the higher-value parts of the supply-chain by investing in design, education, quality, innovation, marketing and logistics, including fashion e-commerce, which now represents an important source of revenue for the city (UNEP, 2016). The University of Borås, as recalled above, plays a fundamental role in supporting the development of technical and design capabilities in the industry. It employs 700 teachers and researchers and has 12,000 students enrolled in different programmes. Research is conducted in seven areas including Business and IT, and Textiles and Fashion (Design and General), in which they also have a bachelor programme (Edström, 2018).

We have seen as well that significant funding for the upgrading strategy came also through national sources with the Smart Textiles programme. It was funded by VINNOVA in 2006 through the VINNVÄXT-program, which is VINNOVAs main instrument to fund regional initiatives. The programme is a bottom-up project, in which a consortium of regional actors applies for funding to VINNOVA for the implementation of particular upgrading strategy for the region. The programme requires the engagement of companies, researchers and the government, 'which must all work proactively towards a joint strategic concept' (VINNOVA, 2016).

Additionally, the national government has funded the *SP Sveriges Tekniska Forskningsinstitut AB* (the Technical Research Institute of Sweden – TRIS), which is one of the main partners in the Smart Textiles initiative. The TRIS was relocated by the Government from Gothenburg to Borås (Edström, 2018).

The upgrading strategies related to technical textiles in Health and Medicine can be considered a success in terms of research capacity and support from stakeholders. However, the development of sustainable textiles and technical textiles for Architecture and Interiors still suffers from significant limitations. Among them, De Propris et al. (2015) highlight the weak links with the providers of raw materials (notably the forest sector), the end-users, and large-scale retailing companies.

All in all, the Borås case illustrates how more radical strategies of path renewal and path creation strongly rely on investment in R&D and scientific activities, and depend fundamentally on the strength and alignment of the regional and national policies and multi-level government initiatives for its successful deployment. Policy makers play a very important role, not only as providers of funding but also as facilitators of networking space and access to the required knowledge.

A challenge ahead for the industry is to move from innovative specialization in existing or emerging industrial competences to interaction and collaboration between diverse and possibly unrelated actors to address societal challenges (Boschma, Coenen, Frenken, & Truffer, 2017). This is the aim of the new Strategic Innovation programmes that the Swedish government launched in 2012 as a mandate to VINNOVA (Grillitsch, Hansen, Coenen, Miöner, & Moodysson, 2019).

4. Conclusion

The driving question of this paper was to investigate to what extent path extension and renewal strategies could be pursued in thick and specialized regional innovation systems. By combining insights from the regional innovation system literature with that of industrial districts we proposed a framework that considered both endogenous and exogenous sources of renewal.

The Borås case illustrates how more radical strategies of path renewal and path creation in thick and specialized RIS are possible but depend fundamentally on the strength of regional and national policies for its successful deployment. Borås has been the object of successful strategies around shared visions of transformation and coordination between local, regional and national actors and policies. They aimed at path creation in the local industry through the combination of different knowledge across intra and extra-regional networks. State policies play a very important role, not only as providers of funding, but also as facilitators of networking space and access to the extra-regional knowledge required.

The case of Prato suggests that processes of path renewal may be triggered by a more endogenous set of forces. Prato is quite a complex system, hosting many nuclei of know-how within and around the textile specialization with a diverse degree of novelty. Lacking the shared visions and strong multi-level coordination that characterize Borås, path renewal in Prato's textile industry would demand policies supporting local innovative actors, which operate at the fringe of the main industry, and helping them to build or insert into extra-local (national and international) knowledge and trade networks.

These cases illustrate that strategies beyond path extension are possible in thick and specialized RIS but for those strategies to materialize, national and regional policy initiatives should take at least complementary functions. In the case of path creation, when new industries or new activities are to be created, reinforcing policies at national and regional level need to be strongly coordinated along common visions of the new development path, in particular if the regions lack prior industrial preconditions. More research is needed on the interplay of policies at different levels, the degree of alignment or conflict, and their impact.

Policy interventions at different levels should take into consideration the institutional and social conditions which characterize a region as well as its social capital. Furthermore, and in line with recent research (Sotarauta & Beer, 2017), the cases point out to the importance of leadership and agency at multiscale levels – from local, to regional and national. This is an aspect in which more theoretical and empirical work would be dearly needed.

The cases also hint at another important aspect that deserves further research. Strategies of path creation, such as the one pursued in Borås, engaging almost all former actors in the regional industry, if successful, may imply long-term growth for the region. However, if they fail, it might imply the annihilation of the industry in that region. Strategies of path renewal, such as those potentially available in Prato, based both on intra-regional heterogeneity, extra-regional networks and policies, provide experimentation spaces in the fringe of the existing specialization, which might be related to higher degrees of regional resilience. If successful, they eventually grow new local specializations, driving path transformation. If unsuccessful, the traditional specialization – potentially supporting path extension – will remain active, providing source of employment and possibly growth to the region, at least for some time. Therefore, long-term historical analysis of the evolution of different path development strategies in regions should also help to evaluate such different balances of strengths and weaknesses in regional resilience.

Notes

1. It is important to highlight here that IDs *are related* to SRIS but are *not equivalent* to SRIS. While the concept of industrial district refers to the region, RIS refer only to the set of organizations and institutions supporting learning and innovation *in that* region. In other words, SRIS could be understood as a part of an ID comprising those organizations and institutions related more directly to learning and innovation in an ID.
2. In this respect, recent contributions (Gabaldón-Estevan, Manjarrés-Henríquez, & Molina-Morales, 2018 and Gabaldón-Estevan & Ybarra, 2017) suggest to use the term 'District innovation systems' to refer to 'a system of relationships within an industrial district where externalities facilitate firms' innovation processes' (Gabaldón-Estevan et al., 2018, p. 898).

3. Production and innovation activities overlap thus making it difficult to draw clear boundaries between the ID and the SRIS in which it is embedded. Of course, SRIS also includes some institutional actors providing or supporting the provision of crucial specific public goods, such as shared rules on social rewards for innovators, public funding on projects of networks of innovators, or collective laboratories for testing and prototyping, etc.
4. The concept of proximity is a multi-dimensional concept (Boschma, 2005). In the industrial district literature, different forms of proximity (e.g. geographical, institutional, and so on) support also in different times the interplay between the heterogeneity of knowledge. Specifically, a high social or institutional proximity may compensate for low levels of cognitive or organizational proximity, supporting the 'productive chorality' of the system (Becattini, 2015).
5. The perspective of alignment of regional and national levels of governance (Bellandi & Caloffi, 2016; Zukauskaite, Trippl, & Plechero, 2017), could be considered also under the light of the relations between RIS and NIS (national innovation systems). Please refer to Cooke and Morgan (1998) and Chaminade, Lundvall, and Haneef (2018) for some general remarks and examples.
6. We collected primary data through interviews to representatives of 21 institutional agents and 16 firms related to the manufacturing textile core of the district, district experts and policy makers between June 2016 and April 2017. The semi-structured company interviews enquired about the organization's innovation strategies, their innovation activities and knowledge linkages, the use of industry 4.0. technologies and the role of the RIS supporting their innovation strategies.
7. The technical textiles in Europe not only show positive trends but generate today an important part of the industry value (European Apparel and Textile Confederation, 2015).
8. Although it has supported the economic stability of the city and the overall performance of the area (Lombardi & Sforzi, 2016).
9. During the same period, the importance of the clothing and knitwear industry specialization has instead increased in relative and absolute terms, largely pushed by the local Chinese community. The role of the Chinese community in the development of the textile industry in Prato has been discussed extensively by Dei Ottati (2014, 2017), Guercini, Milanesi, and Dei Ottati (2017) and Lazzeretti and Capone (2017). While their economic role in the area is increasingly important, the weakness of industrial interplay with the textile core implies that the three leading profiles in the population of firms of the core, as discussed in the text, are not affected directly.
10. The relations between industrial districts of the made in Italy and larger Italian cities have supported past successes: 'the presence of cities in regions where there is a high intensity of industrial districts' helped the districts to meet easily international buyers of haute couture, branches of multinationals operating in the fashion sectors, design centres or large universities, and take advantage of many fairs or events of the made in Italy. 'On the other hand, without the growth of sets of industrial districts specialized in various parts of the made in Italy, which cannot be explained as a simple effect of the economy of the city, the same cities would not have developed such capabilities' (Bellandi, 2014, Section 4).

Disclosure statement

No potential conflict of interest was reported by the authors.

Funding

This work was supported by Marianne and Marcus Wallenberg Foundation [grant number MMW 2012.0194]; H2020 Marie Skłodowska-Curie Actions [grant number 691192].

ORCID

Cristina Chaminade http://orcid.org/0000-0002-6739-8071
Marco Bellandi http://orcid.org/0000-0002-9044-5630
Monica Plechero http://orcid.org/0000-0001-8854-1343
Erica Santini http://orcid.org/0000-0001-5662-0119

References

Allgemeiner Vliesstoff-Report [AVR]. (2013). Textile research in Europe (2013). Market Overview and Trends. Online publication. Retrieved from http://www.siicex.gob.pe/siicex/documentosportal/alertas/documento/doc/689339046radCE0AC.pdf

Asheim, B. T. (2009). Next generation regional innovation policy: How to combine science and user driven approaches in regional innovation systems. *Ekonomiaz, 70*, 28–43.

Asheim, B. T., Boschma, R., & Cooke, P. (2011). Constructing regional advantage: Platform policies based on related variety and differentiated knowledge bases. *Regional Studies, 45*, 893–904. doi:10.1080/00343404.2010.543126

Bailey, D., Bellandi, M., Caloffi, A., & De Propris, L. (2010). Place-renewing leadership: Trajectories of change for mature manufacturing regions in Europe. *Policy Studies, 31*, 457–474. doi:10.1080/01442871003723408

Becattini, G. (2001). *The caterpillar and the butterfly: An exemplary case of development in the Italy of the industrial districts*. Florence: Felice Le Monnier.

Becattini, G. (2015). *La coscienza dei luoghi. Il territorio come soggetto corale* [The conscience of places. Territory as choral subject] Rome: Saggine- Donzelli Editori.

Bellandi, M. (2014). *Territorial policies for industrial renaissance and innovation*. European Review of Industrial Economics and Policy - ERIEP, Number 7, mis en ligne le 20 décembre 2013. Retrieved from http://revel.unice.fr/eriep/index.html?id=364

Bellandi, M., & Caloffi, A. (2016). Industrial policies in a Marshallian-based multilevel perspective. *European Planning Studies, 24*, 687–703. doi:10.1080/09654313.2015.1125856

Bellandi, M., & Santini, E. (2017). Resilience and the role of arts and culture-based activities in mature industrial districts. *European Planning Studies, 25*(1), 88–106. doi:10.1080/09654313.2016.1268096

Bellandi, M., & Santini, E. (2019). Territorial servitization and new local productive configurations: The case of the textile industrial district of Prato. *Regional Studies, 53*, 356–365. doi:10.1080/00343404.2018.1474193

Boschma, R. (2005). Proximity and innovation: A critical assessment. *Regional Studies, 39*, 61–74. doi:10.1080/0034340052000320887

Boschma, R., Coenen, L., Frenken, K., & Truffer, B. (2017). Towards a theory of regional diversification: Combining insights from evolutionary economic geography and transition studies. *Regional Studies, 51*, 31–45. doi:10.1080/00343404.2016.1258460

Chaminade, C., Lundvall, B.-A., & Haneef, S. (2018). *Advanced introduction to national innovation systems*. Cheltenham: Edward Elgar.

Cooke, P., & Morgan, K. (1998). *The associational economy: Firms, regions, and innovation*. Oxford and New York: Oxford University Press.

De Propris, L., Harmaakorpi, V., Johnston, C., Walter, L., Karlsson, M., Saddler, J., & Held, M. (2015). *Bumpy flight at high altitude? International evaluation of smart textiles, biorefinery of the future and peak innovation*. Online publication. Retrieved from https://www.vinnova.se/globalassets/mikrosajter/vinnvaxt/dokument/international-evaluation-of-smart-textiles.pdf

Dei Ottati, G. (1994). Trust, interlinking transactions and credit in the industrial district. *Cambridge Journal of Economics, 18*, 529–546. doi:10.1093/oxfordjournals.cje.a035289

Dei Ottati, G. (2014). A transnational fast fashion industrial district: An analysis of the Chinese businesses in Prato. *Cambridge Journal of Economics, 38*, 1247–1274. doi:10.1093/cje/beu015

Dei Ottati, G. (2017). Chinese immigrant businesses in the industrial district of Prato and their interpretation. *Chinese Migration and Economic Relations with Europe*. Routledge, *2017*, 79–105.

Edström, A. (2018). Business clusters and organizational resilience. In S. Tengblad & M. Oudhuis (Eds.), *The resilience framework: Organizing for sustained viability* (pp. 197–212). Singapore: Springer.

European Apparel and Textile Confederation. (2015). *European social dialogue 'capacity building' in the textile and clothing industry*. Online publication. Retrieved from http://euratex.eu/projects/completed-projects/

Gabaldón-Estevan, D., Manjarrés-Henríquez, L., & Molina-Morales, F. X. (2018). An analysis of the Spanish ceramic tile industry research contracts and patents. *European Planning Studies, 26*, 895–914. doi:10.1080/09654313.2018.1427701

Gabaldón-Estevan, D., & Ybarra, J.-A. (2017). Innovative culture in district innovation systems of European ceramics SMEs. *European Planning Studies, 25*, 2021–2036. doi:10.1080/09654313.2017.1353591

Goglio, S. (2001). Relazioni Locali e Sovra Locali nell'Industrializzazione Italiana. In G. Becattini, M. Bellandi, G. Dei Ottati, & F. Sforzi (Eds.), *Il Calendoscopio dello sviluppo locale. Trasformazioni economiche nell'Italia contemporanea*, (pp. 67–92). Turin: Rosenberg & Sellier.

Grillitsch, M., Hansen, T., Coenen, L., Miöner, J., & Moodysson, J. (2019). Innovation policy for system-wide transformation: The case of strategic innovation programmes (SIPs) in Sweden. *Research Policy, 48*, 1048–1061. doi:10.1016/j.respol.2018.10.004

Guercini, S., Milanesi, M., & Dei Ottati, G. (2017). Paths of evolution for the Chinese migrant entrepreneurship: A multiple case analysis in Italy. *Journal of International Entrepreneurship, 15*(3), 266–294. doi:10.1007/s10843-017-0209-0

Gullstrand, J. (2005). Industry dynamics in the Swedish textile and wearing apparel sector. *Review of Industrial Organization, 26*, 349–370. doi:10.1007/s11151-004-8115-8

Holmen, A. K. T., & Fosse, J. K. (2017). Regional agency and constitution of new paths: A study of agency in early formation of new paths on the west coast of Norway. *European Planning Studies, 25*(3), 498–515. doi:10.1080/09654313.2016.1276159

Isaksen, A., & Jakobsen, S.-K. (2017). New path development between innovation systems and individual actors. *European Planning Studies, 25*(3), 355–370. doi:10.1080/09654313.2016.1268570

Isaksen, A., & Trippl, M. (2016). Path development in different regional innovation systems. A conceptual analysis. In D. Parrilli, R. Dahl Fitjar, & A. Rodriguez-Pose (Eds.), *Innovation drivers and regional innovation strategies* (pp. 66–84). New York and London: Routledge.

Jensen, M., Johnson, B., Lorenz, E., & Lundvall, B. A. (2007). Forms of knowledge and modes of innovation. *Research Policy, 36*, 680–693. doi:10.1016/j.respol.2007.01.006

Lazzeretti, L., & Capone, F. (2017). The transformation of the Prato industrial district: An organisational ecology analysis of the co-evolution of Italian and Chinese firms. *The Annals of Regional Science, 58*, 135–158. doi:10.1007/s00168-016-0790-5

Lindqvist, G., Malmberg, A., & Sölvell, Ö. (2008). *Swedish cluster maps. Disentangling Clusters, 113*. Stockholm: Center for Strategy and Competitiveness. Online publication. Retrieved from https://www.hhs.se/contentassets/f51b706e1d644e9fa6c4d232abd09e63/swedish_cluster_maps__eng_1.pdf

Ljungkvist, T., & Börje, B. (2016). Structural crisis?: Regional culture and resilience in family business-dominated regions in Sweden. *Journal of Enterprising Communities: People and Places in the Global Economy, 10*, 425–446. doi:10.1108/JEC-05-2015-0030

Lombardi, S., & Sforzi, F. (2016). Chinese manufacturing entrepreneurship capital: Evidence from Italian industrial districts. *European Planning Studies, 24*, 1118–1132. doi:10.1080/09654313.2016.1155538

Lundvall, B.-Å., Vang, J., Joseph, K., & Chaminade, C. (2009). Innovation system research and developing countries. In B.-Å. Lundvall, K. J. Joseph, C. Chaminade, & J. Vang (Eds.), *Handbook of innovation systems and developing countries: Building domestic capabilities in a global setting* (pp. 1–31). Cheltenham: Edward Elgar.

Martin, R., Wiig Aslesen, H., Grillitsch, M., & Herstade, S. J. (2018). Regional innovation systems and global flows of knowledge. In A. Isaksen, R. Martin, & M. Trippl (Eds.), *New avenues for regional innovation systems-theoretical advances, empirical cases and policy lessons* (pp. 127–147). Cham, Switzerland: Springer.

Neffke, F., Henning, M., & Boschma, R. (2011). How do regions diversify over time? Industry relatedness and the development of new growth paths in regions. *Economic Geography, 87*, 237–265. doi:10.1111/j.1944-8287.2011.01121.x

Njøs R., & Fosse J. K. (2018). Linking the bottom-up and top-down evolution of regional innovation systems to policy: Organizations, support structures and learning processes. *Industry and Innovation*, Advanced online publication. doi:10.1080/13662716.2018.1438248

Njøs, R., & Jakobsen, S.-E. (2016). Cluster policy and regional development: Scale, scope and renewal. *Regional Studies, Regional Science, 3*, 146–169. doi:10.1080/21681376.2015.1138094

Njøs R., & Jakobsen S-E. (2018). Policy for evolution of regional innovation systems: The role of social capital and regional particularities. *Science and Public Policy, 45*(2), 257–268. doi:10.1093/scipol/scx064

Plechero, M., & Chaminade, C. (2016). The role of regional sectoral specialization on the geography of innovation networks: A comparison between firms located in regions in developed and emerging economies. *International Journal of Technological Learning, Innovation and Development, 8*, 148–170. doi:10.1504/IJTLID.2016.077106

Scheffer, M. R. (2012). *In-depth assessment of the situation of the T&C sector in the EU.* Prospects Task 7: Synthesis Report for the European Textile and Clothing Sector. Retrieved from https://ec.europa.eu/docsroom/documents/10482/attachments/1/translations/en/renditions/pdf

Smart Textiles. (2017). Online publication. Retrieved from http://smarttextiles.se/en/

Sotarauta, M., & Beer, A. (2017). Governance, agency and place leadership: Lessons from a cross-national analysis. *Regional Studies, 51*, 210–223. doi:10.1080/00343404.2015.1119265

Sotarauta, M., Ramstedt-Sen, T., Seppänen, S. K., & Kosonen, K. J. (2011). Local or digital buzz, global or national pipelines: Patterns of knowledge sourcing in intelligent machinery and digital content services in Finland. *European Planning Studies, 19*, 1305–1330. doi:10.1080/09654313.2011.573139

Tödtling, F., Lengauer, L., & Höglinger, C. (2011). Knowledge sourcing and innovation in 'thick' and 'thin' regional innovation systems. Comparing ICT firms in two Austrian regions. *European Planning Studies, 19*(7), 1245–1276. doi:10.1080/09654313.2011.573135

Trippl, M., Grillitsch, M., & Isaksen, A. (2018). Exogenous sources of regional industrial change: Attraction and absorption of non-local knowledge for new path development. *Progress in Human Geography, 42*(5), 687–705. doi:10.1177/0309132517700982

UNEP - United Nations Environmental Program. (2016). Swedish textile city Borås fashions itself and Viskan River anew. Retrieved December 17, 2017, from http://web.unep.org/stories/story/swedish-textile-city-borås-fashions-itself-and-viskan-river-anew.

VINNOVA. (2016). *Vad är Vinväxt?* Online publication. Retrieved from https://www.vinnova.se/m/vinnvaxt/om-vinnvaxt/

Wysokinska, Z. (2003). Trend analysis of selected segments of the textile-clothing market in the world and Europe: Knitwear, industrial textiles, tapestry and clothing. *AUTEX Research Journal, 3*(2), 46–57.

Zukauskaite, E., Trippl, M., & Plechero, M. (2017). Institutional thickness revisited. *Economic Geography 93*, 325–345. doi:10.1080/00130095.2017.1331703

Local or global? Does internationalization drive innovation in clusters?

Marco Bettiol, Maria Chiarvesio, Eleonora Di Maria and Debora Gottardello

ABSTRACT
Innovation in clusters is initially rooted in proximity among specialized actors, but over time it results from an interplay between the local and global levels. The internationalization of production and the relocation of cluster manufacturing activities abroad open a debate on the impact of such dynamics upon innovation, between knowledge acquisition opportunities and the weakening of local innovation activities. This paper contributes to the debate by empirically testing whether internationalization has an impact on cluster firms' innovation outputs. Based on a survey conducted among 259 Italian cluster firms, the results show that upstream and downstream internationalization *per se* does not impact innovation, measuring product, process, organizational, and marketing innovation outputs. On the contrary, collaboration with external actors, such as designers, research centres or universities, has a positive effect on firms' innovation outputs. This is consistent with the cluster model and with previous studies focusing on innovation in the cluster context. Our analyses show that it is not internationalization that matters when it comes to innovation for cluster firms. Innovation performances are influenced by the relational capabilities of cluster firms to connect and manage collaboration even outside the cluster scale.

1. Introduction

In the past two decades, economic activities have undergone an increasing process of internationalization, with growing fragmentation of value chains at the global level and the shifting of manufacturing processes from Western countries to low-cost countries (Cattaneo, Gereffi, & Staritz, 2010). In this context, even clusters have delocalized their activities (Chiarvesio & Di Maria, 2009) expanding their supply chain beyond the cluster boundaries. Due to the challenges stemming from the international competitive environment, many cluster firms have decided to internationalize their production abroad over the years to take advantage of lower production costs (low-cost markets), better competencies (suppliers in Western countries) or proximity to new emerging markets.

This process has had a number of consequences on the internal structures of inter-firm networks as well as on the cluster system as a whole, also in terms of innovation dynamics (Belussi & Hervas-Oliver, 2017; Camuffo & Grandinetti, 2011; Chiarvesio, Di Maria, & Micelli, 2010; De Marchi & Grandinetti, 2014). Indeed, on the one hand, internationalization – upstream and downstream – offers opportunities to acquire new knowledge from external sources. On the other, when we look at the upstream internationalization in particular, it reduces internal cluster cohesion due to the replacement of local suppliers with international sourcing and potential losses of local competence and knowledge (Crestanello & Tattara, 2011). From this point of view, specifically the internationalization of production (Pickles & Smith, 2011) may diminish innovation processes by decoupling manufacturing and innovation.

This aspect becomes important considering the recent trends connected with the revamping of manufacturing as a source of value and competitive advantage. In fact, recent studies have underlined the risks for companies and countries related to the loss of manufacturing competencies, questioning the idea that value-added activities, such as R&D and marketing, can be detached from product manufacturing (Mudambi, 2008). Co-location of R&D and manufacturing is considered an important driver of innovation, increased quality of products and customization, as new knowledge and innovation activities are possible whenever industrial production occurs, via learning-by-doing processes (Buciuni & Finotto, 2016). Other studies have emphasized the positive linkages between innovation and manufacturing management (Ketokivi, Turkulainen, Seppälä, Rouvinen, & Ali-Yrkkö, 2017; Pisano & Shih, 2012). In the same vein, studies focusing on back-shoring (Fratocchi et al., 2016) underline the need for the co-location of R&D and manufacturing as one of the reasons pushing companies to bring back manufacturing investments and suppliers to the local territory.

In the debate on the evolutionary trends of clusters, the literature pointed out that location decisions concerning manufacturing – implemented through a variety of strategic options (in-house/FDI, global sourcing and non-equity forms of internationalization, collaborative-based forms (Contractor, Kumar, Kundu, & Pedersen, 2010)) – may weaken cluster resilience (Hannigan, Cano-Kollmann, & Mudambi, 2015), as such decisions impact the mechanisms supporting knowledge flows, internally and externally (Belussi, 2018).

However, the question related to the implications of the internationalization of production on the innovation of cluster firms must be further investigated. Moreover, it is worth considering a broader definition of innovation. Innovation, in fact, can assume different forms not only related to science-based and technological factors, but also including other inputs related to customers (users) as well as designers (Jensen, Johnson, Lorenz, & Lundvall, 2007). Consequently, even the innovation outputs may refer to knowledge advancement and applications beyond product (functions and its symbolic/intangible dimensions) and (manufacturing) processes. From this point of view, we can include a large variety of outputs more related to how products are offered to the markets within a marketing perspective (Naidoo, 2010) as well as new organizational processes for efficiency or effectiveness improvement (Armbruster, Bikfalvi, Kinkel, & Lay, 2008).

From this perspective, this paper aims at contributing to the literature understanding how strategies of internationalization influence cluster firms' innovation output. We focused on Italy as an empirical context. This choice is justified by the fact that Italy has been internationally recognized as one of the most relevant countries where the new form of organization of economic activities related to the cluster model has developed (Becattini, Bellandi, & De Propris, 2009; Piore & Sabel, 1984; Porter, 1990). Hence, the analysis is particularly intriguing in this national scenario, taking also into consideration that international competitiveness of Italy is related to manufacturing sectors where the cluster model is dominant (Cucculelli & Storai, 2018). The study of clusters with different degrees of internationalization can support understanding of how different location strategies concerning manufacturing – being this carried out through offshoring and/or global sourcing or the decision to produce domestically, in addition to downstream internationalization strategies – impact firms' innovation performance. In other words, the paper explores whether the internationalization reduces (or enhances) the innovation outputs of the cluster's firms.

2. Clusters between innovation and internationalization

2.1. Innovation in clusters: proximity and connectivity

The literature on the evolution of clusters is vast (Boschma & Fornahl, 2011; Fornahl, Hassink, & Menzel, 2015; Lazzeretti, Sedita, & Caloffi, 2014; Trippl, Grillitsch, Isaksen, & Sinozic, 2015). By analysing the flows of knowledge (Belussi, 2018; Camuffo & Grandinetti, 2011; Lazzeretti & Capone, 2016), several studies focused on the role of geographical proximity in fostering innovation among clusters' firms (Boschma, 2005; Heringa, Horlings, van der Zouwen, van den Besselaar, & van Vierssen, 2014). Firms belonging to a cluster can usually perform better in terms of knowledge acquisition (absorptive capacity) than firms located outside the cluster due to localized learning mechanisms occurring within the cluster's boundaries (Molina-Morales & Martínez-Fernández, 2010). Innovation within clusters is not only a technical fact but has significant social roots related to connections among firms and local institutions as well as social dynamics within the community at the local level (Dei Ottati, 1994). Physical proximity means, above all, cognitive proximity among cluster actors (Boschma, 2005).

The social interaction between key professionals figures sharing the same work practices sparkle innovation at the cluster level (Giuliani, 2005; Lissoni, 2001). Moreover, scholars have described the innovation process occurring at the cluster level as mainly incremental and not formalized. Besides explicit forms of R&D (Hervás-Oliver, Albors-Garrigos, Estelles-Miguel, & Boronat-Moll, 2018; Lee, 2009), many studies on clusters have shown that it is specifically the informal and interconnected nature of the process of knowledge creation that distinguishes cluster firms (Becattini et al., 2009). Furthermore, local social interaction produces a large variety of local expertise, where suppliers – but also business services (KIBS) – specialize in different but interconnected knowledge domains (Camuffo & Grandinetti, 2011).

If geographical proximity is a source of innovation at the cluster level, several authors have pointed out that innovation could rise through the combination of formal (global) knowledge coming from outside the cluster and tacit (local) knowledge coming from inside the cluster (Bathelt, Malmberg, & Maskell, 2004). However, for this combination to happen, as studies on epistemic communities and communities of practice have shown, a common set of norms, values, repertoires and visions have to be shared among actors (Håkanson, 2005). From this perspective, social, and also cognitive, proximity are more relevant than simply spatial proximity (Boschma, 2005).

Recent studies by (Lazzeretti & Capone, 2016) highlight that different forms of proximity (geographical, social, cognitive, organizational, and institutional proximity) play a different role during the cluster life cycle in supporting networks for innovation. In the emergent phase, social proximity is more important than the others, while during the development phase geography and cognitive proximity are key drivers for innovation.

With a similar point of view, Lorenzen and Mudambi (2013) introduce the concept of connectivity to describe the global linkages that sustain knowledge and resources flows at distance, enacting the cluster catching-up dynamics. According to those studies, networking dynamics related to personal as well social connections within the cluster and across locations may assume multiple forms (centralized vs. decentralized), supporting a wide set of alternative options to structure and manage knowledge creation and dissemination. In particular leading cluster firms as well as MNEs subsidiaries represent – among the others – the organizational-based global linkages of clusters.

Before internationalization processes involved clusters, cluster firms mainly relied on local knowledge and on the local socio-economic community to support innovation. With the increased process of openness of cluster boundaries, innovation has increasingly been the result of an interplay between the local and the global (Asheim & Isaksen, 2002) suggesting the relevance for internationalization as a driver of innovation.

2.2. Cluster innovation and forms of internationalization

Clusters are facing multiple evolutionary trajectories influenced by strategies of local actors (cluster lead firms) as well as by global forces, such as the role of global buyers and the intersection of clusters in global value chains (GVCs) (De Marchi, Grandinetti, & Gereffi, 2018).

On the one hand, the increase of lead firms at the cluster level increases internal variety in the local system (De Marchi et al., 2018). The rise of home-grown multinationals (Belussi, 2018) at the cluster level influences the cohesion of the internal cluster but also generates opportunities to benefit from the process of knowledge acquisition from abroad. Studies on internationalization of cluster firms through export and multiple forms of controls market-wise have stressed the positive relationship between firm's cluster location and downstream internationalization (Belso-Martinez, 2006; Chiarvesio et al., 2010). Through the expansion in international markets, cluster firms – especially leading one – can acquire knowledge to be transferred locally by managing internationalization through different forms and level of commitment (Johanson & Vahlne, 2003).

On the other hand, clusters are connected to GVCs due to local investments of global lead firms in terms of sourcing or FDIs, who become another driver of cluster transformation, impacting on the cluster internal cohesion (Giuliani & Rabellotti, 2018). Involving clusters in GVCs opens new opportunities for upgrading and modifying the structure of the cluster model (De Marchi et al., 2018; Giuliani & Rabellotti, 2018).

In this paper, we are interested in exploring the consequences on innovation outputs of multiple forms of internationalization (Contractor et al., 2010; Filatotchev, Stephan, & Jindra, 2008), with a particular attention to manufacturing activities. Studies on outsourcing and offshoring phenomena in clusters show that cluster firms rely mainly on supply networks compared to vertical integration, where the degree of internationalization may vary (Capasso, Cusmano, & Morrison, 2013; Grandinetti & Tabacco, 2015), influencing cluster dynamics over time. Among the different motivations driving internationalization upstream (Chiarvesio, Di Maria, & Micelli, 2013), cluster firms have selected countries of location to benefit mainly from efficiency and cost advantages on the one hand, and market opportunities on the other; however, they have sometimes also considered innovation chances even through sourcing from developing countries. This is consistent with other studies on internationalization that have demonstrated the learning benefits linked to production offshoring and global outsourcing, whereby cost minimization is followed by knowledge acquisition and inputs for innovation (Maskell, Pedersen, Petersen, & Dick-Nielsen, 2007) for cluster firms.

Nevertheless, there could also be negative implications of internationalizing cluster activities from an innovation point of view. One consequence of the internationalization of leading firms is the reorganization of firm networks between the local and the global.. Hence, this could reduce local networks supporting innovation both considering the social and the cognitive aspect of proximity (Lazzeretti & Capone, 2016). Another potential negative result is the increased level of competition related to the entrance of MNEs within the cluster (Belussi, 2018) and their exploitation of knowledge available at the cluster level at a wider, global scale.

Moreover, internationalization can also weaken innovation results due to the decoupling of R&D and manufacturing. This debate can be linked to a recent discussion concerning the reshoring phenomenon developed within international business studies (Fratocchi, Di Mauro, Barbieri, Nassimbeni, & Zanoni, 2014). Among the motivations related to reshoring, the need has emerged for the co-location of innovation and manufacturing activities, suggesting that the advantages in decoupling innovation and production activities should be reconsidered. Specifically regarding R&D activities, studies have stressed that physical proximity allows better coordination between R&D and production, as well as further product innovation (Buciuni & Finotto, 2016).

The need for co-location may depend also on the high level of tacit process knowledge (Gray, Siemsen, & Vasudeva, 2015). In this respect, co-location becomes important if we also consider the cognitive proximity among the actors involved, in which R&D and other business functions must be cognitively close; otherwise, positive results in terms of knowledge development and transfer may not necessarily be achieved (Van den Bulte & Moenaert, 1998). Production carried out distantly from R&D may reduce innovation opportunities, whereas maintaining proximity between development activities and manufacturing at the local (cluster) level sustains positive innovation outcomes (Buciuni & Finotto, 2016).

To sum up, the literature is not conclusive about the relationship between internationalization and innovation in cluster firms. On the one hand, active internationalization may be a fundamental driver for innovation; on the other, especially producing far from the cluster context may impede knowledge creation and sharing. Whenever there is cognitive proximity, distance would not be an issue, but if the reasons for internationalization are more cost-related than interaction-related, then the innovation capabilities of cluster firms may suffer.

One added issue concerns the different forms of innovation. In this respect, research shows that smaller firms are more oriented to product or process innovation with respect to marketing or organizational innovation (Hinteregger, Durst, Temel, & Yesilay, 2018). This is true also for cluster firms, where high specialization and local interaction create peculiar dynamics of innovation allowing obtaining remarkable innovation outputs related to product and process. In this case, scholars stress the role of learning-by-doing despite the limited recourse to formal R&D practices (Hervas-Oliver, Sempere-Ripoll, Boronat-Moll, & Rojas, 2015; Lee, 2009). On the contrary, as regards marketing and organizational innovation, cluster firms cannot leverage on local knowledge and have to look for knowledge coming from outside the cluster (Belussi, 2015; Morone & Testa, 2008).

Within this context, the paper aims at answering to the following questions:

(1) Does internationalization positively influence the innovation outputs of cluster firms?
(2) Which is the relationship between the degree of internationalization both upstream and downstream – captured considering multiple forms of control of foreign activities – and innovation outputs of cluster firms, considering the different forms of innovations?

3. Empirical section

3.1. Data and methodology

3.1.1. Dataset

The target of this study were 1,657 firms located in eight selected Italian clusters extracted from the AIDA – Bureau van Dijk dataset according to industries and municipalities that identify specific clusters (defined by regional laws). The eight clusters considered in this analysis are located in northeast Italy (Veneto and Friuli Venezia Giulia) and are specialized in so-called 'Made in Italy' industries (furniture, mechanics and fashion): furniture clusters in Treviso, Pordenone and Manzano (Udine); mechanics clusters in Vicenza and Pordenone; the Montebelluna sport system; the shoes cluster in Riviera del Brenta; and the eyewear cluster in Belluno.

From the total population (1,657), we selected 1,002 firms which met three criteria: their turnover was above 1 million € in 2014, they specialized in products for final markets or intermediated markets (components), and they were stratified by a 6-digit ATECO code, which considers all the related industries involved in each production process.

The survey was carried out in 2016 through phone interviews based on a structured questionnaire (CATI method). Respondents of the survey were mainly operation managers, entrepreneurs in smaller firms or employees responsible for production management within companies. In the first part of the interview, respondents were asked about the general information of the firm. The second part concerned the organization of the value chain and the production process at the geographic level (cluster, Italy, abroad) as well as ownership versus outsourcing strategies and the adopted supply chain relationships. The third part analysed the innovation strategies of the firms in terms of inputs (R&D) and outputs, forms of collaborations implemented (type of partners and their location) and marketing strategies.

The final sample was composed of 259 firms (return rate 25.8%). Table 1 shows that the firms were equally distributed across three main industry groups based on eight clusters

Table 1. The sample.

Clusters	Cluster firms #	Cluster respondents #	%	Cluster firms by industry %
Furniture Treviso	205	36	14%	33.2
Chair	75	24	9%	
Furniture Pordenone	99	26	10%	
Mechanic Vicenza	198	39	15%	36.3
Mechanic Pordenone Comet	201	55	21%	
Sport system	87	30	12%	30.5
Eyewear	51	19	7%	
Luxury shoes Riviera Del Brenta	86	30	12%	
Total	1,002	259	100	100.0

(33.2% for furniture – Treviso, Pordenone, Manzano; 36.3% for mechanics – Vicenza and Pordenone; and 30.5% for fashion – eyewear, sport system and shoes).

3.1.2. Variables of the analysis

The objective of the analysis was to determine the effects of the upstream and downstream internationalization of production on firms' innovation outputs – considered as a product, process, organizational and marketing innovation. We controlled for the presence of R&D function within the firm as well as collaboration strategies for innovation carried out by the firm within and outside the cluster. Additional controls referred to the position of the firm in the value chain (finished products for final consumers, finished products for other companies or components), its market positioning (high- vs. low-end products), clusters in which the firm was embedded, size and age, business groups and communication strategies. Described below are the four innovation variables (innovation outcomes), the variables related to internationalization and the control variables (Table 2).

3.1.3. Innovation outputs (dependent variables)

Our dependent variable referred to innovation outputs. To determine the factors that could have a determinant effect on innovation, previous research has highlighted the importance of distinguishing and measuring different types of innovation. In this perspective, the measurement of innovations is based on a commonly accepted definition described in the Oslo Manual (2005) and is considered a *s*tandardized testing methodology when surveying enterprises at the European or international level. Thus, we identified product, process, marketing and organizational innovation. Following the Oslo Manual (2005),

- product innovation is the introduction of new or significantly improved goods or services;
- process innovation is focused on the implementation of a new or significantly improved method of production or delivery;
- marketing innovation generates significant improvements in some of the marketing methods, such as product, design, packaging, price, promotion and distribution;
- organizational innovation is centred on the implementation of a new organizational method in a company's business practices, such as the arrangement of the workplace and external relationships.

Table 2. Description of variables considered in the analysis.

Dependent Variables	Measure
Product Innovation	Product or service innovation (1 yes/0 no)
Process Innovation	Innovation in operations, logistics, distributions, ICT, etc. (1 yes/0 no)
Organizational Innovation	Innovation in supply chain management, knowledge management, lean production, etc. (1 yes/0 no)
Marketing Innovation	Innovation in marketing practices, product packaging, etc. (1 yes/0 no)
Internationalization of production	1 if the firm has foreign suppliers and/or productive FDIs, 0 otherwise
Foreign suppliers	% of foreign suppliers (% on total number of suppliers)
Global sourcing	% of total processes or productive activities developed by other companies abroad
Location of suppliers	Place where suppliers are established: No foreign suppliers, suppliers in advanced countries, suppliers in emerging countries or suppliers in both advanced and emerging countries (reference category is: No foreign suppliers)
Experience in global sourcing	Three dummy variables: 1 if the firm has carried out global sourcing strategies with foreign suppliers before 2000; 2 in the period 2000–2007; 3 in the period from 2008 onward (reference category is 'not having had foreign suppliers')
Export (FSTS)	% of foreign sales on total sales
International sales network	1 if the firm has developed a commercial structure or a channel for the distribution of products abroad, 0 otherwise
No collaboration	The firm does not collaborate with design/engineering studios, universities, science parks, research centres, service companies, others
Collaboration inside the cluster	The firm collaborates within the cluster/region with design/engineering studios, universities, science parks, research centres, service companies, others
Collaboration outside the cluster	The firm collaborates outside the cluster with design/engineering studios, universities, science parks, research centres, service companies, others (reference category is: No collaboration)
Cluster	Seven dummy variables: 1 Chair Udine; 2 Furniture Pordenone; 3 Mechanic Vicenza; 4 Mechanic Comet Pordenone; 5 Sport System Montebelluna; 6 Eyewear Belluno; 7 Shoes Riviera (reference category is: Furniture Treviso)
Size	Logarithm of firm turnover 2015
Age	Firm age (current year–foundation year)
Business group	1 if the firm belongs to a business group, 0 otherwise
R&D function	1 if the firm has an internal R&D function, 0 otherwise
Communication	1 if the firm has carried out communication policies to promote firm brands, 0 otherwise
Type of product	Two dummy variables: 1 B2B; 2 component (reference category is B2C)
Product positioning	Two dummy variables: middle, low (reference category is High)

According to our survey, there were four distinct dichotomous variables, which took the value of 1 if the company innovated in any of the four aspects (in the previous 3 years) and 0 otherwise.

3.1.4. Internationalization

Internationalization was measured through a set of different variables through which is articulated the cluster firm's strategy both upstream and downstream. First, we captured production internationalization by measuring any international activities considered through hierarchical investments (presence of FDIs – that is, any investment which entails a lasting control on a foreign enterprise) or global sourcing (presence of foreign suppliers). The variable took the value 1 when we found any of the two strategies in a company, and 0 otherwise. As this represents a very synthetic measure of internationalization of production, we deepened our analysis also considering other variables related to supply chain management (% of foreign suppliers) and its organization at the geographic level between the cluster, domestic and international levels (% of global sourcing), together with a measure of experience in global sourcing (3 dummies measuring the period when the international sourcing started). When considering downstream internationalization, in addition to export (Foreign Sales on Total Sales), we considered any proprietary investments abroad (i.e. retail chain) in order to capture the control over foreign markets the firm can have.

3.1.5. Control variables
A set of common control variables often used in business studies were included (see the description in Table 2 and the descriptive statistics in Table 4): cluster of location (linked with industry specialization) (measured by 7 dummy variables), seniority (age) of the company (current year – foundation year), size (the logarithm of turnover), whether the company was part of a group (dichotomous), type of product (products for other companies, i.e. B2B), products for final markets (B2C component, categorized into 2 dummy variables), product positioning (categorized into 2 dummy variables), presence of a specialized function of R&D (dichotomous) and communication strategies (advertising, public relations, etc.) aimed at enhancing proprietary brands (dichotomous).

Furthermore, as a control variable, the presence of collaboration with other actors capable of supporting firms' innovation, such as universities, research centres, designers, science parks or service companies, was added. This control variable captures companies that collaborate for innovation with any of the partners considered within the cluster or outside the cluster, or that have no collaboration at all. The measurement of all variables used in the study is described in Table 2.

3.1.6. Model
Since the outcomes of interest (the different forms of innovation) were dichotomous, four independent logit models were performed in order to determine the impact of the independent variables. These models were linear and had a logit link function with a binomial probability distribution. For each dependent variable, the equation was as follows:

$$Pr(Y_i = 1) = F(\gamma I_i + \beta' X_i + \varepsilon_i)$$

where Y refers to one of the four outcomes, i refers to the company, F refers to the link function (logit in this case), γ refers to the coefficient of any of the six measures of internationalization I, $\beta'X$ refers to the vector of estimations for the remaining variables working as controls, and ε refers to the error. This model did not allow for the elimination of other possible confounding factors, which were not considered. However, the inclusion of the most common factors used in the literature along with others we considered may have relevant effects in this study, increasing the validity of the estimations of internationalization in innovation.

3.2. Results

3.2.1. Descriptive
More than 57% of the companies in our sample declared that they innovated in at least one of the four dimensions of innovation. As shown in Table 3, product innovation was the most used (83.4%), while marketing innovation was the least used (57.5%). In terms of process and organizational innovation, the percentage of companies that innovated was similar (68.3% and 68.7%, respectively). Only 40% of firms innovated in all four dimensions (not deducible from the table).

Table 3. Firms' innovation strategies and innovation outputs.

	Product innovation	Process innovation	Organization innovation	Marketing innovation
Innovative firms	216	177	178	149
	83.40%	68.34%	68.73%	57.53%
Firms with no innovation	43	82	81	110
	16.60%	31.66%	31.27%	42.47%

$N = 259$ (no missing values).

Table 4 shows the statistics (means with standard deviations or percentages, according to the type of variable) for the independent variables of the model (measures of internationalization). With regard to internationalization of production, we can see that 26.6% of companies have internationalized their production activities through global sourcing and/or FDIs. On average, the percentage of foreign suppliers is 9.3% (considered on the total number of suppliers), while the percentage of global sourcing is 5.3%. As far as the number

Table 4. Descriptive statistics.

Variable	# Firms	Mean/%	Stand. Deviation
Upstream internationalization			
Internationalization of production	259	26.6%	
% foreign suppliers (average # suppliers)	216	9.31%	22.09
% global sourcing	259	5.33%	13.04
% FDIs	259	7.3%	
Location of foreign suppliers			
Suppliers in advanced countries	219	7.8%	
Suppliers in emerging countries	219	11.4%	
Suppliers in both advanced and emerging countries	219	9.1%	
Experience in global sourcing			
Before 2000	219	11.9%	
2000 - 2007	219	9%	
From 2008	219	7.3%	
Downstream internationalization			
% exporters	259	47.1%	
FSTS (%)	252	46.44%	32.98
International sales network	259	54.1%	
No Collaborations (ref.)	259	47%	
Collaborate inside cluster	259	25%	
Collaborate outside cluster	259	28%	
Cluster			
Furniture Treviso (ref.)	259	14%	
Chair	259	9%	
Furniture Pordenone	259	10%	
Mechanic Vicenza	259	15%	
Mechanic Comet Pordenone	259	21%	
Sport system	259	12%	
Eyewear	259	7%	
Luxury shoes (Riviera Del Brenta)	259	12%	
Size (Ml euro)	227	53.27	599.75
Age (year)	255	33.27	21.03
Business group	259	20.8%	
R&D Function	259	52.1%	
Communication strategy	259	36.7%	
Product positioning			
High-medium	259	68.7%	
Medium	259	25.5%	
Medium-low	259	5.8%	
Type product (ref: product for final customer)			
B2B	259	27%	
Components	259	16%	

of firms investing in FDIs, our analysis shows that 7.3% of the sample has manufacturing-related FDIs. Considering companies with foreign suppliers, nearly one-half have internationalized their product processes for almost two decades or more. For 71% of the upstream-internationalized firms, no changes in location strategies for manufacturing activities occurred after they were implemented.

Firms that have developed upstream internationalization are expanding these activities in addition to domestic activities (38.7%) or as replacements in terms of local suppliers (37.1%) or in-house activities (17.7%); 6.5% have invested abroad to exploit country-specific factors (location advantages). Supplier selection in advanced countries is based on competences, reliability and proximity, while for emerging countries efficiency is the main driver. Cluster firms have on average about 46% of export (with high variability though among firms), with a high percentage of proprietary sales networks allowing the cluster firms to control foreign markets (54.1%).

3.2.2. Internationalization and innovation outputs

If we cross the variable measuring internationalization of production with the innovation introduced by the companies, in relation to either the product, the process, the organization or the marketing, in general there are no significant differences. Only in the case of marketing innovation does a statistically significant difference arise, highlighting a correlation between internationalization and marketing innovation, one which should be further explored (Table 5).

To explore whether the internationalization positively influences the innovation outputs of cluster firms, we used different measures of internationalization. Table 6 shows the results derived from the logit model with the first measure of internationalization – that is, through the internationalization of production variable and the selected controls. These results represent the ratio of change in the probability to innovate. When interpreting the binary variables, it is the *discrete change* of probability. When interpreting the quantitative variables, it is the *instantaneous rate of change*. For no one of the four dimensions of innovation did the internationalization variable (captured as the firm having foreign suppliers or FDIs) have a significant effect. Namely, the difference between firms with internationalization of production and the other firms in terms of innovation was null.

Observing controls, a systematic effect on the four dimensions of innovation was observed when considering collaborations with organizations supporting innovation. More specifically, a remarkable effect of collaborations with actors inside the cluster, and especially with regard to organizational (with 23.8% more likely to innovate) and product (with 19.5%) innovation, can be seen. However, for innovation in marketing

Table 5. Internationalization of production and innovation.

	Product	Process	Organizational	Marketing
Firms with internationalization of production	87.0	71.0	70.0	69.6
Firms with no internationalization of production	82.1	67.4	62.5	53.2
Chi-squared	0.86	0.31	0.54	5.57*

Notes: $N = 259$.
*$p < 0.05$.
**$p < 0.01$.
***$p < 0.001$.

Table 6. Logit model results.

	Product innovation	Process innovation	Organization innovation	Marketing innovation
Internationalization of production	−0.015 (0.060)	−0.102 (0.071)	−0.121 (0.071)	0.048 (0.075)
Collaborate inside cluster	0.198 (0.067)**	0.155 (0.070)**	0.236 (0.071)***	0.134 (0.070)*
Collaborate outside cluster	0.091 (0.064)	0.042 (0.071)	0.151 (0.074)*	0.182 (0.073)***
Cluster: Chair	0.017 (0.107)	0.034 (0.114)	−0.095 (0.132)	−0.220 (0.125)
Cluster: Furniture PN	0.035 (0.097)	−0.112 (0.104)	−0.197 (0.119)	−0.144 (0.113)
Cluster: Mechanic	0.1 (0.113)	−0.027 (0.111)	−0.224 (0.117)	−0.073 (0.115)
Cluster: Comet	0.021 (0.086)	0.036 (0.099)	−0.101 (0.132)	−0.230 (0.099)*
Cluster: Sport	−0.101 (0.099)	0.043 (0.121)	−0.209 (0.143)	−0.164 (0.125)
Cluster: Eyewear	0.161 (0.104)	−0.011 (0.134)	−0.126 (0.135)	−0.360 (0.142)*
Cluster: Riviera	0.031 (0.102)	0.103 (0.126)	−0.134 (0.135)	−0.290 (0.123)*
Size (Ml euro)	0.041 (0.33)	0.157 (0.006)***	0.012 (0.033)	0.030 (0.033)
Product average mkt	0.010 (0.052)	−0.198 (0.059)***	−0,001 (0.068)	−0.077 (0.067)
Product low mkt	0.006 (0.090)	−0.143 (0.109)	0.019 (0.126)	0.090 (0.118)
B2B	0.129 (0.057)**	0.062 (0.070)	−0.039 (0.072)	0.010 (0.072)
Component	−0.106 (0.064)	0.059 (0.084)	0.124 (0.093)	0.032 (0.087)
Business group	0.005 (0.076)	−0.138 (0.084)	0.012 (0.089)	−0.183 (0.088)*
R&D function	0.041 (0.053)	0.107 (0.062)	0.113 (0.066)	0.099 (0.064)
Age	0.000 (0.001)	−0.000 (0.001)	−0.002 (0.001)	−0.002 (0.001)*
Communication	0.111 (0.622)	−0.041 (0.06)	0.009 (0.707)	0.300 (0.064)***
LR Chi²	43.94**	53.7**	32.34**	66.07***
N	224	224	224	224

Notes: Presented are the coefficients and the standard error in brackets; Categories of reference for the categoric variables are in Table 2.
*$p < 0.05$.
**$p < 0.01$.
***$p < 0.001$.

aspects, collaborations outside the cluster are more relevant (22.5% and 13.2%, respectively).

Table 7 shows the results derived from the logit model with the other, more detailed measurements of the internationalization of companies identified – this model considers the variety and characteristics of offshoring and global sourcing strategies as well as downstream internationalization – in order to determine whether their effects on innovation are really null. Although all the controls were included in the 4 × 6 = 24 models, only the effects of the internationalization variables are shown (therefore, each variable in the table corresponds to a different model). Little can be said apart from the fact that in none of the specifications were significant effects found.

Table 7. Logit model results with alternative measures of internationalization.

	Product innovation	Process innovation	Organization innovation	Marketing innovation
Models regarding:				
% Foreign suppliers	0	−0.000	−0.001	0.002
	(0.001)	(0.001)	(0.001)	(0.001)
Models regarding:				
Experience global sourcing, before 2000	−0.044	−0.156	−0.051	0.152
	(0.092)	(0.105)	(0.107)	(0.115)
Experience global sourcing, 2000–2007	0.005	−0.078	−0.123	0.018
	(0.098)	(0.113)	(0.109)	(0.116)
Experience global sourcing, from 2008	0.069	−0.038	−0.181	0.140
	(0.101)	(0.114)	(0.110)	(0.127)
Models regarding:				
International sales network	0.051	−0.045	−0.031	−0.007
	(0.052)	(0.064)	(0.068)	(0.065)
Models regarding:				
FSTS	0.000	−0.000	−0.000	−0.000
	(0.000)	(0.001)	(0.001)	(0.001)
Models regarding:				
Suppliers in advanced countries	0.021	−0.079	−0.120	0.123
	(0.108)	(0.114)	(0.110)	(0.125)
Suppliers in emerging countries	−0.057	−0.157	−0.116	0.234
	(0.088)	(0.110)	(0.109)	(0.122)
Suppliers in both advanced and emerging countries	0.124	−0.027	−0.060	−0.059
	(0.131)	(0.119)	(0.113)	(0.114)
Models regarding:				
% global sourcing	0.001	−0.002	−0.002	0.005
	(0.002)	(0.002)	(0.003)	(0.003)

Notes: Presented are the coefficients and the standard error in brackets. Categories of reference for the categorical variables are in Table 2. Sample size is equal to 224 in all regressions.
*$p < 0.05$.
**$p < 0.01$.
***$p < 0.001$.

In terms of controls, the logistic regression confirms (as above) the important effect of collaborations with actors from inside and outside the cluster, depending on the form of innovation analysed. In the case of product innovation, we can also see that firms which produce finished goods for other firms are about 14% less likely to innovate in terms of products than firms that produce goods for the market. In the case of process innovation, firms that produce mid-range products are 20% less likely to innovate in terms of process than firms that produce high-range products. Firm turnover also has influence: For each additional thousand euros, the probability to innovate in terms of process was 2.1% higher. This value should be interpreted as a linear approximation, because it is an interval variable (and, in fact, it is calculated differently from the coefficients of the qualitative variables – the reference is the nearest unit). Regarding marketing innovation, unsurprisingly, firms with already-developed communication strategies were 30% more likely to innovate in marketing than companies without such strategies (further details concerning the empirical analysis is provided in Appendices A1–A3).

4. Discussion and conclusions

Our analyses demonstrate that internationalization has neither positive nor negative impacts as regard to cluster firms' innovation outputs. This result is obtained by exploring the multiple forms of upstream internationalization cluster firms are carrying out as well as also taking into account the control over foreign markets from a commercial point of view. On the contrary, we found the capabilities of cluster firms to connect and manage collaboration inside and even outside the cluster to be more relevant in terms of innovation.

Within the theoretical discussion on the role of proximity and the different forms of connectivity enabling innovation, we can argue that internationalization can provide support to innovation, but also not investing in enlarging upstream or downstream cluster connections may lead to cluster firm' innovation outputs too. Moreover, it is not only a question for cluster firms to be international, but also how they structure their presence abroad.

As far as the downstream part, it arises from our study that controlling more directly the market or exporting does not affect innovation. This result differs from prior studies suggesting value in connecting and controlling foreign markets to learn and have additional inputs to innovation. According to our view, such result can be explained by the role that the cluster still have in suggesting inputs for innovation and it is also related to the relevance of collaboration as the most significant variable innovation-wise. In fact, we should highlight that in many cases the customers served within the cluster are lead firms in their markets (sometimes niche), hence representing valuable sources of knowledge or innovation triggers at the local level. Another possible explanation could be related to the weak capabilities of cluster firms in being visible and present in the final markets. Beyond some (notable) exception, clusters firms rarely were able to develop brand and to market effectively their products internationally.

As far as the upstream internationalization is taken into account, in its multiple forms – from FDI to global sourcing, with different level of commitment and experience – it emerges again its non-significance. This could be related to the motivations supporting such dynamics, where especially global sourcing is not driven by specialization, but more by efficiency. Looking deeper into results, the descriptive statistics show that the drivers of upstream internationalization are mainly related to efficiency factors when addressing emerging markets (the main location for global sourcing), while knowledge-seeking factors are less important and are mainly linked to sourcing from advanced countries. Innovation does not seem to be the first objective when cluster firms internationalize their production.

According to our analysis, the questions literature highlights on the negative consequences of internationalization for cluster firms seem not to be observed in the sample considered. This could be related to the fact that the cluster has still a role in manufacturing for cluster firms, as they do not show a complete process of internationalization of production. Moreover, there is a not negligible percentage of firms that do not internationalize upstream, where the context in which carrying out manufacturing activities is still the cluster.

Consistently with other studies, our analysis shows that collaboration with external partners – not including suppliers – has instead positive relationships with innovation. The localization (inside or outside the clusters) of the partners cluster firms are collaborating with influences the different dimensions of innovation. On the one hand, collaboration with partners localized inside the cluster is more relevant for innovations related to technical elements (product and process innovation) and for organizational innovation. On the other hand, collaboration with partners localized outside the cluster is more relevant for marketing innovation. These different strategies in terms of the selection of an innovation's partner localization seem reasonable if we consider the typology of knowledge available inside or outside the cluster. In fact, knowledge about the technical dimension of the product is more developed and qualified inside than outside the cluster (Dei Ottati, 2018). Therefore, it is unsurprising that firms are working with local partners for product and process innovation. Less clear is the fact that, as our data point out, firms collaborate with partners localized inside the cluster in order to generate organizational innovation (i.e. lean organization). A great degree of organizational innovation almost by definition originates outside the cluster. However, if we consider the specific characteristics of the industries in which clusters are specialized (low-tech, niche production, high-end segments of the market), we must also account for the fact that firms may produce organizational innovation only through an adaptation of the general organizational principle to the specific characteristics of the industry. From this perspective, it is more probable that a partner inside the cluster is able to mediate the general organizational knowledge with the features of local production. In this respect, the role of specialized KIBS is fundamental (Camuffo & Grandinetti, 2011).

Collaboration with partners localized outside the cluster is significant in the case of marketing innovation (Belussi & Sedita, 2009). This sounds reasonable because clusters are specialized in production, and it is difficult to find local, highly specialized competences in marketing. In fact, those competences are usually concentrated in large metropolitan areas (e.g. Milan, Italy); accordingly, if firms wish to innovate in this area, they must connect with partners that are necessarily located outside the cluster.

Our research shows that no matter which is the internationalization commitment of firms in the organization and control of the value chain activities, there are no direct impacts on cluster firms' innovation results. From this perspective, cluster firms seem to adopt the globalization process, managing different geographies of collaboration on the basis of their strategic intent. If firms are seeking a cost advantage, they internationalize; conversely, if they are looking for innovation, they collaborate with specific partners. This does not mean that clusters and local manufacturing are not important. Rather, our research highlights the relevance of local partners as far as product, process and organizational innovation are concerned. If the cluster is active and capable of reproducing specific technical knowledge over time, then the cluster's firms can rely on the local dimension for innovation.

Results of our research provide managerial implications. Clusters firms can support their innovation by combining local and international production – under multiple forms adopted – as well as internationalization downstream. Producing locally may also sustain innovation, whenever the firm is able to exploit the advantages of proximity with other cluster firms and other partners. More importantly, what is relevant in all four models of innovation (product, process, organization, marketing) is a collaboration with partners localized both inside and outside the cluster..

We acknowledge that our work has some limitations. We should extend this study to both Italian and international clusters in order to compare our results. We should also deepen the measures of innovation in a more detailed way, and we should seek a better understanding of the motivation behind internationalization choices, also by considering different forms of governance within the value chain.

Disclosure statement

No potential conflict of interest was reported by the authors.

References

Armbruster, H., Bikfalvi, A., Kinkel, S., & Lay, G. (2008). Organizational innovation: The challenge of measuring non-technical innovation in large-scale surveys. *Technovation*, *28*(10), 644–657. doi:10.1016/j.technovation.2008.03.003

Asheim, B. T., & Isaksen, A. (2002). Regional innovation Systems: The integration of local "sticky" and global "ubiquitous" knowledge. *The Journal of Technology Transfer*, *27*(1), 77–86. doi:10.1023/A:1013100704794

Bathelt, H., Malmberg, A., & Maskell, P. (2004). Clusters and knowledge: Local buzz, global pipeline and the process of knowledge creation. *Progress in Human Geography*, *28*(1), 31–56. doi:10.1191/0309132504ph469oa

Becattini, G., Bellandi, M., & De Propris, L. (Eds.) (2009). *A handbook of industrial districts*. Cheltenham, UK: Edward Elgar Publishing.

Belso-Martinez, A. (2006). Do industrial districts influence export performance and export Intensity? Evidence for Spanish SMEs' internationalization process. *European Planning Studies*, *14*(6), 791–810. doi:10.1080/09654310500496115

Belussi, F. (2015). The international resilience of Italian industrial districts / clusters (ID / C) between knowledge re-shoring and manufacturing off (near) -shoring. *Journal of Regional Research*, *32*(8), 89–113.

Belussi, F. (2018). New perspectives on the evolution of clusters. *European Planning Studies*, *26*(9), 1796–1814. doi:10.1080/09654313.2018.1492059

Belussi, F., & Hervas-Oliver, J-L. (2017). *Unfolding cluster evolution*. Abingdon: Routledge.

Belussi, F., & Sedita, S. R. (2009). Life cycle vs. Multiple path dependency in industrial districts. *European Planning Studies*, *17*(4), 505–528. doi:10.1080/09654310802682065

Boschma, R. (2005). Proximity and innovation: A critical assessment. *Regional Studies*, *39*(1), 61–74. doi:10.1080/0034340052000320887

Boschma, R., & Fornahl, D. (2011). Cluster evolution and a roadmap for future research. *Regional Studies*, *45*(10), 1295–1298. doi:10.1080/00343404.2011.633253

Buciuni, G., & Finotto, V. (2016). Innovation in global value chains: Co-location of production and development in Italian low-tech industries. *Regional Studies*, *50*(12), 2010–2023. doi:10.1080/00343404.2015.1115010

Camuffo, A., & Grandinetti, R. (2011). Entrepreneurship & regional development of Italian industrial districts as cognitive systems: Are they still reproducible? *Entrepreneurship & Regional Development*, *23*(9–10), 37–41.

Capasso, M., Cusmano, L., & Morrison, A. (2013). The determinants of outsourcing and offshoring strategies in industrial districts: Evidence from Italy. *Regional Studies*, *47*(4), 465–479. doi:10.1080/00343404.2011.571668

Cattaneo, O., Gereffi, G., & Staritz, C. (2010). *Global value chains in a postcrisis world*. O. Cattaneo, G. Gereffi, & C. Staritz, (Eds.). Washington, DC: The World Bank. doi:10.1596/978-0-8213-8499-2

Chiarvesio, M., & Di Maria, E. (2009). Internationalization of supply networks inside and outside clusters. *International Journal of Operations & Production Management*, *29*(11), 1186–1207. doi:10.1108/01443570911000186

Chiarvesio, M., Di Maria, E., & Micelli, S. (2010). Global value chains and open networks: The case of Italian industrial districts. *European Planning Studies*, *18*(3), 333–350. doi:10.1080/09654310903497637

Chiarvesio, M., Di Maria, E., & Micelli, S. (2013). Sourcing from Northern and Southern countries: The global value chain approach applied to Italian SMEs. *Transition Studies Review*, *20*(3), 389–404. doi:10.1007/s11300-013-0287-1

Contractor, F. J., Kumar, V., Kundu, S. K., & Pedersen, T. (2010). Reconceptualizing the firm in a world of outsourcing and offshoring: The organizational and geographical relocation of high-value company functions. *Journal of Management Studies*, 47(8), 1417–1433. doi:10.1111/j.1467-6486.2010.00945.x

Crestanello, P., & Tattara, G. (2011). Industrial clusters and the governance of the global value chain: The Romania–Veneto network in footwear and clothing. *Regional Studies*, 45(2), 187–203. doi:10.1080/00343401003596299

Cucculelli, M., & Storai, D. (2018). Industrial districts, district effect and firm size: The Italian evidence. *Cambridge Journal of Economics*, 42, 1543–1566. doi:10.1093/cje/bey021

De Marchi, V., Di Maria, E., & Gereffi, G. (2018). New frontiers for competitiveness and innovation in clusters and value-chains research. In V. De Marchi, E. Di Maria, & G. Gereffi (Eds.), *Local clusters in global value chains linking actors and territories through manufacturing and innovation* (pp. 213–226). Abingdon: Routledge.

De Marchi, V., & Grandinetti, R. (2014). Industrial districts and the collapse of the Marshallian model: Looking at the Italian experience. *Competition & Change*, 18(1), 70–87. doi:10.1179/1024529413Z.00000000049

De Marchi, V., Grandinetti, R., & Gereffi, G. (2018). Evolutionary trajectories of industrial districts in global value chains. In V. De Marchi, E. Di Maria, & G. Gereffi (Eds.), *Local clusters in global value chains. Linking actors and territories through manufacturing and innovation* (pp. 33–50). Abingdon: Routledge.

Dei Ottati, G. (1994). Cooperation and competition in the industrial district as an organization model. *European Planning Studies*, 2(4), 463–483. doi:10.1080/09654319408720281

Dei Ottati, G. (2018). Marshallian industrial districts in Italy: The end of a model or adaptation to the global economy? *Cambridge Journal of Economics*, 42, 259–284. doi:10.1093/cje/bex066

Filatotchev, I., Stephan, J., & Jindra, B. (2008). Ownership structure, strategic controls and export intensity of foreign-invested firms in transition economies. *Journal of International Business Studies*, 39(7), 1133–1148. doi:10.1057/palgrave.jibs.8400404

Fornahl, D., Hassink, R., & Menzel, M.-P. (2015). Broadening our knowledge on cluster evolution. *European Planning Studies*, 23(10), 1921–1931. doi:10.1080/09654313.2015.1016654

Fratocchi, L., Ancarani, A., Barbieri, P., Di Mauro, C., Nassimbeni, G., Sartor, M., … Zanoni, A. (2016). Motivations of manufacturing reshoring: An interpretative framework. *International Journal of Physical Distribution & Logistics Management*, 46(2), 98–127. doi:10.1108/IJPDLM-06-2014-0131

Fratocchi, L., Di Mauro, C., Barbieri, P., Nassimbeni, G., & Zanoni, A. (2014). When manufacturing moves back: Concepts and questions. *Journal of Purchasing and Supply Management*, 20(1), 54–59. doi:10.1016/j.pursup.2014.01.004

Giuliani, E. (2005). Cluster absorptive capacity: Why do some clusters forge ahead and others lag behind? *European Urban and Regional Studies*, 12(3), 269–288. doi:10.1177/0969776405056593

Giuliani, E., & Rabellotti, R. (2018). Italian industrial districts today: Between decline and openness to global value chains. In V. De Marchi, E. Di Maria, & G. Gereffi (Eds.), *Local clusters in global value chains. Linking actors and territories through manufacturing and innovation* (pp. 21–32). Abingdon: Routledge.

Grandinetti, R., & Tabacco, R. (2015). A return to spatial proximity: Combining global suppliers with local subcontractors. *International Journal of Globalisation and Small Business*, 7(2), 139–161. doi:10.1504/IJGSB.2015.071189

Gray, J. V., Siemsen, E., & Vasudeva, G. (2015). Colocation still matters: Conformance quality and the interdependence of R&D and manufacturing in the pharmaceutical industry. *Management Science*, 61(11), 2760–2781. doi:10.1287/mnsc.2014.2104

Håkanson, L. (2005). Epistemic communities and cluster dynamics: On the role of knowledge in industrial Districts. *Industry and Innovation*, 12(4), 433–463. doi:10.1080/13662710500362047

Hannigan, T. J., Cano-Kollmann, M., & Mudambi, R. (2015). Thriving innovation amidst manufacturing decline: The Detroit auto cluster and the resilience of local knowledge production. *Industrial and Corporate Change*, 24(3), 613–634. doi:10.1093/icc/dtv014

Heringa, P. W., Horlings, E., van der Zouwen, M., van den Besselaar, P., & van Vierssen, W. (2014). How do dimensions of proximity relate to the outcomes of collaboration? A survey of knowledge-intensive networks in the Dutch water sector. *Economics of Innovation and New Technology*, 23(7), 689–716. doi:10.1080/10438599.2014.882139

Hervás-Oliver, J.-L., Albors-Garrigos, J., Estelles-Miguel, S., & Boronat-Moll, C. (2018). Radical innovation in Marshallian industrial districts. *Regional Studies*, 52(10), 1388–1397. doi:10.1080/00343404.2017.1390311

Hervas-Oliver, J.-L., Sempere-Ripoll, F., Boronat-Moll, C., & Rojas, R. (2015). Technological innovation without R&D: Unfolding the extra gains of management innovations on technological performance. *Technology Analysis & Strategic Management*, 27(1), 19–38. doi:10.1080/09537325.2014.944147

Hinteregger, C., Durst, S., Temel, S., & Yesilay, R. B. (2019). The impact of openness in innovation in SMEs. *International Journal of Innovation Management*, 23(1), 1950003. doi:10.1142/s1363919619500038

Jensen, M., Johnson, B., Lorenz, E., & Lundvall, B. (2007). Forms of knowledge and modes of innovation. *Research Policy*, 36(5), 680–693. doi:10.1016/j.respol.2007.01.006

Johanson, J., & Vahlne, J.-E. (2003). Business relationship learning and commitment in the internationalization process. *Journal of International Entrepreneurship*, 1, 83–101. doi:10.1023/A:1023219207042

Ketokivi, M., Turkulainen, V., Seppälä, T., Rouvinen, P., & Ali-Yrkkö, J. (2017). Why locate manufacturing in a high-cost country? A case study of 35 production location decisions. *Journal of Operations Management*, 49-51, 20–30. doi:10.1016/j.jom.2016.12.005

Lazzeretti, L., & Capone, F. (2016). How proximity matters in innovation networks dynamics along the cluster evolution. A study of the high technology applied to cultural goods. *Journal of Business Research*, 69(12), 5855–5865. doi:10.1016/j.jbusres.2016.04.068

Lazzeretti, L., Sedita, S. R., & Caloffi, A. (2014). Founders and disseminators of cluster research. *Journal of Economic Geography*, 14(1), 21–43. doi:10.1093/jeg/lbs053

Lee, C.-Y. (2009). Do firms in clusters invest in R&D more intensively? Theory and evidence from multi-country data. *Research Policy*, 38(7), 1159–1171. doi:10.1016/j.respol.2009.04.004

Lissoni, F. (2001). Knowledge codification and the geography of innovation: The case of Brescia mechanical cluster. *Research Policy*, 30(9), 1479–1500. doi:10.1016/S0048-7333(01)00163-9

Lorenzen, M., & Mudambi, R. (2013). Clusters, connectivity and catch-up: Bollywood and bangalore in the global economy. *Journal of Economic Geography*, 13, 501–534. doi:10.1093/jeg/lbs017

Maskell, P., Pedersen, T., Petersen, B., & Dick-Nielsen, J. (2007). Learning paths to offshore outsourcing: From cost reduction to knowledge seeking. *Industry & Innovation*, 14(3), 239–257. doi:10.1080/13662710701369189

Molina-Morales, F. X., & Martínez-Fernández, M. T. (2010). Social networks: Effects of social capital on firm innovation. *Journal of Small Business Management*, 48(2), 258–279. doi:10.1111/j.1540-627X.2010.00294.x

Morone, P., & Testa, G. (2008). Firms growth, size and innovation: An investigation into the Italian manufacturing sector. *Economics of Innovation and New Technology*, 17(4), 311–329. doi:10.1080/10438590701231160

Mudambi, R. (2008). Location, control and innovation in knowledge-intensive industries. *Journal of Economic Geography*, 8(5), 699–725. doi:10.1093/jeg/lbn024

Naidoo, V. (2010). Firm survival through a crisis: The influence of market orientation, marketing innovation and business strategy. *Industrial Marketing Management*, 39(8), 1311–1320. doi:10.1016/j.indmarman.2010.02.005

Pickles, J., & Smith, A. (2011). Delocalization and persistence in the European clothing industry: The reconfiguration of trade and production networks. *Regional Studies*, 45(2), 167–185. doi:10.1080/00343401003601933

Piore, M. J., & Sabel, C. F. (1984). *The second industrial divide: Possibilities for prosperity*. New York, NY: Basic Books.

Pisano, G. P., & Shih, W. C. (2012). Does America really need manufacturing? *Harvard Business Review*, 90(3), 1–14.

Porter, M. E. (1990). *Competitive advantage of nations*. New York, NY: The Free Press.
Trippl, M., Grillitsch, M., Isaksen, A., & Sinozic, T. (2015). Perspectives on cluster evolution: Critical review and future research issues, *23*(10), 2028–2044.
Van den Bulte, C., & Moenaert, R. K. (1998). The effects of R&D team co-location on communication patterns among R&D, marketing, and manufacturing. *Management Science, 44*(11), S1–S18. doi:10.1287/mnsc.44.11.S1

Appendices

Appendix A1. VIF and tolerance

Variable	VIF	TOL
Internationalization of production	1.32	0.755
Collaborate inside cluster	1.48	0.673
Collaborate outside cluster	1.29	0.776
Cluster		
Chair	1.8	0.556
Furniture Pordenone	1.69	0.591
Mechanic Vicenza	1.94	0.516
Mechanic Comet Pordenone	2.22	0.451
Sport system	1.95	0.513
Eyewear	1.49	0.669
Luxury shoes (Riviera Del Brenta)	1.79	0.56
Log Turnover	2.05	0.487
Age (year)	1.2	0.833
Business group	1.45	0.689
R&D Function	1.4	0.713
Communication strategy	1.38	0.725
Product positioning		
Medium	1.14	0.877
Medium-low	1.13	0.881
Type product (ref: product for final customer)		
B2B	1.34	0.747
Components	1.32	0.755

Appendix A2. Pseudo R for the 4 models of innovation

Model 1- Product innovation	
Pseudo R2	0.218
Model 2- Process Innovation	
Pseudo R2	0.202
Model 3-Organization Innovation	
Pseudo R2	0.116
Model 4- Marketing Innovation	
Pseudo R2	0.215

Appendix A3. Correlation matrix

Correlation matrix																						
Internationalization of production	1																					
Product	0.0576	1																				
Collaborate inside cluster	0.0284	0.1419	1																			
Collaborate outside cluster	0.069	0.1642	−0.3664	1																		
Chair	−0.0721	−0.0006	−0.0952	0.0958	1																	
Furniture Pordenone	−0.1141	0.0109	−0.0479	0.0192	−0.1068	1																
Mechanic Vicenza	0.0882	0.0718	0.0015	−0.0478	−0.1346	−0.1406	1															
Mechanic Comet Pordenone	0.0501	0.0287	−0.0003	0.1364	−0.1659	−0.1735	−0.2186	1														
Sport system	0.2458	−0.033	0.0652	−0.0927	−0.1157	−0.1209	−0.1524	−0.1879	1													
Eyewear	−0.0356	−0.0734	−0.0286	−0.0775	−0.0899	−0.094	−0.1185	−0.1461	−0.1018	1												
Luxury shoes (Riviera Del Brenta)	−0.1362	−0.0655	0.0652	−0.1731	−0.1157	−0.1209	−0.1524	−0.1879	−0.131	−0.1018	1											
Log_turnover	0.3639	0.2119	−0.054	0.3358	−0.1061	−0.0319	0.2031	0.0604	−0.1169	−0.0346	−0.1402	1										
Medium Product	−0.0317	−0.0248	0.0037	−0.0512	−0.0341	0.0405	0.0263	−0.0653	−0.0732	0.0394	0.0375	−0.0574	1									
Medium Product	−0.0746	−0.0671	0.0447	−0.0818	−0.0792	0.0272	−0.0582	−0.0075	0.0136	−0.0698	−0.0381	−0.0411	−0.145	1								
B2B	0.08	−0.1212	−0.0018	−0.0579	−0.077	−0.1189	0.0801	0.1888	−0.0602	−0.0733	0.1292	−0.0671	0.0577	−0.0412	1							
Components	−0.1178	−0.0908	−0.1322	0.0104	−0.1021	0.1015	−0.1234	0.1628	−0.0909	−0.0003	−0.0909	0.0195	−0.0594	0.0736	−0.2665	1						
Business group	0.1852	0.0757	−0.1038	0.1855	−0.0329	−0.0449	0.0497	0.1053	−0.0653	−0.1264	0.0743	0.4908	−0.0384	−0.0866	0.1107	−0.0403	1					
R&D Function	0.1929	0.154	0.0461	0.1194	−0.0402	−0.0914	0.1442	−0.0315	−0.0154	0.0621	0.0329	0.3677	−0.1313	−0.1925	0.0518	−0.1561	0.1875	1				
Age (year)	0.061	0.0423	−0.0338	0.1682	0.1225	−0.1316	0.0129	0.0845	−0.1214	−0.0172	0.03	0.2674	−0.0994	−0.0096	−0.0791	0.0134	0.0168	0.0433	1			
Communication strategy	0.2119	0.1673	−0.0222	0.1643	0.116	−0.1209	−0.0068	−0.0622	0.2002	0.0624	−0.0251	0.2121	−0.1141	−0.1201	−0.1444	−0.2203	0.1024	0.2643	0.0458	1		

Clusters and internationalization: the role of lead firms' commitment and RIS proactivity in tackling the risk of internal fractures

Mario Davide Parrilli

ABSTRACT
In this paper, we discuss the growth potential of clusters and industrial districts (CIDs) in international markets. Over the past two decades, CIDs have gone under increasing competitive pressure while markets have progressively globalized. Lead companies, either foreign or home-grown multinationals, have globalized their operations while often reducing their commitment (e.g. investments) within CIDs. As a result, a number of second, third and fourth-tier suppliers disconnect from global value chains coordinated by lead companies, leaving the cluster fractured and jeopardizing local development prospects. Only a few firms in the CID cope with globalization. This situation represents a challenge that CIDs need to take on. In this paper, we inquire about the importance of two factors that may represent crucial conditions for the upgrading of CIDs within global markets. The long-term commitment of lead companies with the local economy, together with the dense interaction between the regional innovation system and the lead companies and their new global innovation network, are found to be crucial elements for the resilience of CIDs and their small firms. A few successful CIDs are considered vis-à-vis others that face higher risks of internal fracture. Relevant cases in Spain, Italy, and Costa Rica are analysed here.

1. Introduction

In this paper we aim at discussing the role of clusters and industrial districts (CIDs) in global markets and global value chains (GVCs) as part of a literature that acknowledge the value of this conceptual and empirical intersection with an explicit focus on the new opportunities offered for local development (De Marchi, De Maria, & Gereffi, 2017; Hervas-Oliver & Boix, 2013; Humphrey & Schmitz, 2002; Parrilli, Nadvi, & Yeung, 2013; Pietrobelli & Rabellotti, 2007). In this work, we use Porter's definition (1998) of clusters as 'interconnected firms and institutions localized in geographical proximity that compete and cooperate', and use industrial districts as a variant of clusters in which a local community actively participate and contribute to the development of a locally-bounded and industry-specific manufacturing production (Becattini, 1990; Markusen, 1996).

Over the past two decades, CIDs have gone under pressure insofar as markets have progressively globalized. Lead companies, either home-grown or foreign multinationals that brand the final product and that coordinate important supply chains within the CID (Belussi, Caloffi, & Sedita, 2017; Hervas-Oliver & Albors-Garrigos, 2008), have globalized their operations while reducing their activities within their home CIDs. As a result, significant numbers of second, third and fourth tier suppliers have increasingly disconnected from global markets, leaving the cluster 'fractured' and with limited prospects of economic development. This situation represents a challenge that several CIDs currently face. In this paper, a detailed discussion is offered as a means to identify the critical conditions for the resilience of CIDs within global markets and lead companies' GVCs, where the latter are intended as supply chains analyzed on the basis of the value adding process across all the different stages of resource extraction, manufacturing production, and commercialization including all pre- and post-production services, e.g. R&D, logistics, operation and maintenance, among others (Gereffi, Humphrey, & Sturgeon, 2005). In these stages different firms are involved, some as lead companies (usually large local or foreign firms) and others as first, second, third and fourth tier suppliers depending on the importance of the component supplied.[1]

In this work, we inquire about the importance of two structural issues that may help explain the success of some clusters vis-à-vis the struggle of others. In particular, we emphasize the role of lead firms and their commitment to the long-term development of the local economy, together with the effort of regional innovation systems (RIS) to support the innovation capacity of local suppliers, mostly small and medium-sized enterprises (SMEs) in a new context in which lead companies tend not to collaborate with them, and instead form their own global innovation networks (GINs). These are networks of innovators formed by a few lead multinationals that aim at collaborating with a handful of the most advanced world technological leaders in relevant segments of production as a means to strengthening their competitive advantage (Ernst, 2009; Parrilli et al., 2013). In our argument, these two elements are likely to be synergic and critical in maintaining cohesive clusters that can compete in the market with good chances of success. In this work we show these dynamics through the study of relevant cases, primarily in Spain, Italy and Costa Rica. This work adds to the literature on regional resilience (Asheim et al., 2011; Boschma, 2015), and in particular purports interpretive keys that pave the way for specific policy actions that may in part be steered by local institutions and actors. Within this stream of the literature, our work addresses the literature on the leadership of 'lead companies' in CIDs (indigenous or home-grown multinationals in Belussi, 2015; Hervas-Oliver & Albors-Garrigos, 2008). In this case the value added consists of considering the corporative commitment they take with the local economy in the context of increasing globalization pressures. Simultaneously, we contribute with the analysis of the interaction between RIS, lead companies and their GIN as a means to produce additional innovation capabilities across local SMEs.

In the next section, selected literature on CIDs is discussed, particularly in relation to their connection to global markets, and the importance of key features of their resilience and competitiveness. After section three on the methodological approach to this study, section four focuses on the empirical evidence provided by selected cases in Europe and

Latin America, where CIDs tend to be common production systems. A section of conclusions and brief policy implications completes the paper.

2. Clusters and industrial districts within global markets

2.1. International dynamics and risk of fracture

The relatively recent challenge of globalization for CIDs has generated an important issue that a few years ago would have been found at the periphery of the invisible college of cluster research (Sedita, Caloffi, & Lazzeretti, 2018). For a period of time, globalization mostly meant the possibility for clustered SMEs to export their production. This was from the 1970s onwards and up until the early 1990s. After this period, it also meant globalization of production (Bailey & De Propris, 2014; Gereffi et al., 2005; Henderson & Nadvi, 2011). Several CID firms started to see Eastern Europe and the Far East as an opportunity to reduce production costs thanks to the possibility to work in contexts earlier used to mass production, e.g. Eastern Europe (Sass & Fifekova, 2014), or oriented to feed a growing urban population in the new poles of industrial production, e.g. China (Altenburg, Schmitz, & Stamm, 2008). The related risk of delocalization has been highly debated over the years (Belussi, 2015; Dunford, 2006; Rabellotti, Carabelli, & Hirsch, 2009).

Simultaneously, another challenge for local development has arisen over the past fifteen years. It is the new competition that happens with new FDI from advanced and emerging economies within the boundaries of former CIDs (Dei Ottati, 2014; Hervas-Oliver & Parrilli, 2017; Pietrobelli, Rabellotti, & Sanfilippo, 2011). In the case of FDI from advanced economies, these investments may lead to dis-anchoring the strategies of lead companies from local development prospects; in the case of emerging countries' FDI (e.g. in European economies) the challenge often comes from new investors that become part of the local SME fabric, and even replace part of it through the adoption of disputed practices and strategies that sometimes rely on exploitation of own workforce (Dametto, 2016; Dei Ottati, 2014).

Both trends meant a new challenge for CIDs as their homogeneity and cohesion cannot be taken for granted anymore. The risk of an internal fracture has been rising as, on the one hand, new internal competitors manage comparative advantages in terms of labour costs, while, on the other, local producers in destination countries (e.g. in China, India and Brazil for the wind energy, Eastern Europe for automotive, footwear and furniture production) find it easier to supply CID's lead companies that enter their national market thanks to their physical proximity and the capacity to exploit economies of scale (Dunning, 1988; Elola, Parrilli, & Rabellotti, 2013).

Overall, we observe the risk of a fracture that can arise within the former CIDs as a consequence of these new globalization strategies of lead firms. Usually these companies are multinationals that focus on their overall profitability, thus may take little commitment towards specific local economies, unless it is convenient for them (Cowling & Sugden, 1997). When they realize that profitable business takes place elsewhere, they move their operations towards these other locations, and re-organize their value chain depending on monopoly power strategies (Cowling & Sugden, 1997), research, production and market opportunities (Cooke, 2013; Henderson & Nadvi, 2011) as well as the related ownership-location-internalization advantages (Dunning, 1988). As a matter of fact, several such companies move their operations around the world while maintaining their headquarters stable (Cowling & Sugden, 1997). Over the past two decades, this process has been seen often with the opening of new production plants in emerging economies. It is the case of Ford in the automotive industry in Mexico (Carrillo, 1995); Intel in electronics in Costa Rica (Alfaro, 2013), Vestas and Gamesa/Siemens in wind energy in China and India (Elola et al., 2013). This strategy has also been developed through the acquisition of important companies within CIDs (e.g. Luxottica purchasing US companies Rayban and Oakley in 1999 and 2007, Siemens purchasing Gamesa in 2016, the Chinese group Dalian Wanda buying out the British Sunseeker in 2013).

The effect of these processes is the formation of new value chains in new production sites and the simultaneous weakening of former value chains in their own countries and CIDs. This is visible in the wind energy industry in the north of Spain (Elola et al., 2013) and in the automotive industry from the US, Japan and the UK to Mexico, China and India (Bailey & De Propris, 2014; Baldwin, 2011; Carrillo, 1995). This situation and trend can lead to the fragmentation of CIDs, especially in countries that do not have a large internal market. Traditional local production systems can disappear in a few years (Isaksen, 2018; Markusen, 1996), wasting competences and skills accumulated over decades of hard work, and leave dwellers, workers and youth with an obscure future ahead.

Within this context, our main research question arises. This is the inquiry about the critical mechanisms that permit CIDs to face these challenges and to activate competitive responses that help them maintain their internal cohesion and international competitiveness. In particular, we hypothesize the relevance of two key elements that have been underlined with different purposes by fellow scholars. Currently, these aspects assume renewed value in relation to the behaviour of lead companies in CIDs. These are: (1) the commitment of lead companies, often indigenous/home-grown multinationals, towards the local economy and society (e.g. Belussi et al., 2017; Hervas-Oliver & Albors-Garrigos, 2008; Hervas-Oliver & Parrilli, 2017, among others), and (2) the proactive interaction between the RIS, its CIDs (Asheim & Gertler, 2005; Cooke, 2001; Isaksen & Trippl, 2016), the lead firms and their GIN (Cooke, 2013; Ernst, 2009). We are going to discuss these aspects in depth in the next subsections.

2.2. Local commitment of lead companies

The first critical aspect refers to the commitment of lead companies in the CID. This is extremely important because it represents the obligation of these companies not to leave the locality, but to find a way to harmonize their international growth aims with synergic ambitions to promote the growth of the local economy where they started their operations. This can be seen in competitive cases such as Luxottica in Belluno's glasses ID (De Marchi et al., 2017), Tecnica in Montebelluna' ski boots ID (Belussi, 2003); Marazzi and Ragno in Sassuolo's tile ID as well as Torrecid in Castellon ceramic ID (Hervas-Oliver & Parrilli, 2017), ST Microelectronics and Gemalto in the microelectronics cluster of Gemenos-Rousset (Longhi, 2016), among others. Here the growth of the CID went hand in hand with the growth of lead companies that continued to rely on their local suppliers in spite of the increasing scope of their international operations.

In the past, there have been cases in which the presence of lead companies was not accompanied by a strong commitment with the local economy. The case of Detroit with GM and Chrysler, and Turin with Fiat automotive seem to represent these situations (Balcet, Commisso, & Calabrese, 2013; Sturgeon & Van Biesebroeck, 2009). In these big cities the main automotive industries downsized while developing an intense FDI campaign abroad in search for cheaper production chains and new markets (e.g. Korea and Europe for GM, Poland and the US for Fiat). As a result, they did not re-activated a florid supply chain in their home locations. In these cases, the size of these companies, their worldwide operations, and the need to respond to the interests of their stakeholders and shareholders, led them to disengage to a significant extent from home value chains. Some scholars may stress the 'size' element in the disconnection from the local originating environment: the larger the lead firm, the higher the risk of delocalization of production activities (Cowling & Sugden, 1997). For others commitment may be related to the difference between foreign multinationals vs. home-grown multinationals (Belussi et al., 2017; Hervas-Oliver & Albors-Garrigos, 2008) as the latter are more likely to maintain their original roots and keep investing in the local economy in the long-term. Other scholars may link commitment to the type of industry technology and market (Turkina & Van Assche, 2018). Finally, some may stress the importance of working within bounded markets (e.g. Europe). In this case assembled products and components could be exported once most part of the production process takes more easily place in the CID. This might be the case of traditional industries (e.g. furniture, footwear and tiles) and industries that target national markets (e.g. fashion, software, among others) as well as European car makers and their strong supply chain in Germany, Check Republic and Hungary (Humphrey & Memedovic, 2003). It is more difficult in the case of more globalized industries such as aircraft, electronics including mobile phones, tablets and PCs, pharmaceuticals, weapons and energy. Here, the norms of national contents, and the weight and difficult transportation of key components create incentives for destination markets to set up their own tier suppliers, thus putting pressure on global lead companies to work with them instead of working with their home suppliers (Elola et al., 2013).

These aspects are likely to be relevant drivers of commitment. However, we stress the importance of critical assets of the local economy, particularly the skills and competences that this is offering to lead companies (Blazek, 2015; Turkina & Van Assche, 2018) as well as the proactivity of local economic and institutional actors to promote long-term local development actions (Rodriguez-Pose, 2013). These key aspects guarantee the lead firm's return on investment in the long term and justify their commitment with the local economy. This is a central issue because without the leadership of one or a few firms, the challenge of joining global markets as a competitive cluster becomes an illusion. As a consequence, crucial questions arise about the key requirements that these lead firms set, the support they deliver, and the performance indicators they adopt to keep these local suppliers integrated in their value chain. In fact, lead companies need to measure and assess the competitiveness of their supply chain, thus even in the case they decide to commit with the local economy, they need to be reassured by positive economic outcomes.

As a result of this discussion and arguments, we argue the following:

Proposition 1: Only lead companies effectively committed with the local economy can avoid internal fractures in the CID and guarantee its long-term development as they do not plan to move their manufacturing and service activities (including R&D) abroad beyond a reasonable extent.

As said, this commitment may be related to a number of factors, but in particular we stress the skills and competences managed by local suppliers as well as the proactivity of local economic and institutional actors to promote actions for the long-term development of the local economy (Rodriguez-Pose, 2013; Blazek, 2015). Overall, we argue that lead firms' commitment is a crucial element for the sustainable development of CIDs. This is a necessary but not sufficient condition. Another element matters, i.e. the capacity of the RIS to work with lead firms and their GIN as a means to help CID firms to meet the requirements of lead firms. It is what we are going to discuss next.

2.3. Regional innovation systems, lead companies and their GIN

The second crucial aspect of the renewed involvement of the local supply chain is related to the innovation capacity and dynamics that occur in the CID. It is long known that innovation is a key asset for the competitiveness of local systems (Cooke, 2001). One condition to maintain a strategic position within the value chain is by preserving and developing skills and competences that promote innovation capacities. This ensures a high quality relation between lead companies and suppliers. Those that manage high competences are invited to join international projects, to establish their bases beside lead companies in new markets, and essentially become first and second tier -thus critical- suppliers for the lead companies. This opportunity implies endeavours that not all firms can undertake. It might be difficult and excessively costly, thus beyond their investment and risk-taking capacity (Chiarvesio, Di Maria, & Micelli, 2010; Elola et al., 2013).

In general, the question is where these firms absorb the advanced knowledge they need to produce innovative and competitive products and technologies. The question needs to find different responses depending on whether lead companies are based in CIDs. The presence of lead firms makes a critical difference. Usually, these firms are large, thus benefit from their dedicated R&D departments. For innovation, they suffice to themselves and do not need to work with innovation systems, while they have recently created alliances with other lead companies worldwide in the form of GINs (Cooke, 2013; Ernst, 2009; Parrilli et al., 2013). In contrast SMEs lack resources and do not manage their own R&D departments, thus rely on research and innovation activities of public bodies, universities, private labs and technology centres (Asheim & Gertler, 2005; Belussi, Sammarra, & Sedita, 2010; Cooke, 2001).

Echoing Cooke (2001, p. 953), RISs are 'proactive regional systems', where a number of 'networked actors' (i.e. firms and organizations) focus on the production of 'new products and processes' by means of 'interactive learning' of skills and capabilities that are embedded within specific 'routines and conventions' applied by firms and interconnected organizations. Without entering the wider debate on the type of RIS best suited for each region (Asheim & Gertler, 2005; Cooke, 2004), or their peculiar development trajectories (Asheim, Lawton-Smith, & Oughton, 2011; Capello & Lenzi, 2018; Isaksen & Trippl, 2016), we stress that in CIDs those five requirements enhance the capacity of local companies that work within the first, second and third tier of supply, thus managing knowledge and competences that make them critical suppliers for lead companies. Due to their smaller size, especially second and third tier suppliers devote fewer resources to R&D and technological development, while need a reliable RIS to monitor and adopt new technologies developed by industry leaders and their GINs (Parrilli et al., 2013; Pietrobelli & Rabellotti, 2011).

As Morrison (2008) clarified, lead firms are crucial 'gatekeepers of knowledge' in CIDs. They have the power to promote knowledge dissemination to local suppliers through their internal and external knowledge and innovation sources, activities and GINs. This opportunity makes a big difference in terms of local development prospects. Some scholars even tend to emphasize the 'compensatory role of GINs in case of institutionally and organizationally non-thick RISs' (Chaminade & Plechero, 2015, p. 215). This is supported by the view that GINs work best in the context of thick local buzz and very small local clusters with little innovation capacity (Morrison, Rabellotti, & Zirulia, 2013).

However, engagement with GINs cannot be taken for granted as lead companies might not be interested in sharing knowledge with local suppliers beyond a certain extent. The commitment of these lead firms comes once again under scrutiny. Moreover, in our view compensation is never complete and tend to respond to whether lead companies work within the most advanced research and technology settings (e.g. aircraft and pharma industry), and want to disseminate their knowledge to their suppliers as part of their competitive value chains, or alternatively work in medium technology settings (e.g. renewable energies and shipbuilding), and are not particularly interested in pursuing a strong engagement of the local supply chain that is often used for cost reduction purposes (Blazek, Natsuda, & Sykora, 2018). For these reasons, local lead companies may lose their original connection to their RIS, and replace it with their brand-new GIN. In this case, a gap may arise between technology developments promoted by these lead companies, and what the RIS and the local SMEs can develop autonomously. This situation may create a fracture that weakens the CID.

In response, the RIS and its CIDs need to work in synergy and proactively to develop the capacity to monitor and absorb the technological and market changes brought about by lead companies and their GINs. This requires long-term investments so as to maintain the capacity (in terms of human capital and physical infrastructure) to develop advanced R&D activities in pro of local production and innovation (Asheim, Boschma, & Cooke, 2011, Asheim, Lawton-Smith, et al., 2011; Lundvall, 2007; Parrilli et al., 2013). As a result of this discussion and arguments, we support the following:

Proposition 2: Only CIDs that rely on both: i) the sharp and proactive contribution of their RIS, and ii) knowledge transfer produced by lead companies and their GIN, are likely bolster their innovation capacity and remain important localized supply chains for lead companies, thus reducing the scope for internal fractures.

In synthesis, when the RIS and lead companies (and their GIN) work together, the CID can benefit from the above-mentioned double flow of knowledge that enhances the capabilities of the local SMEs/suppliers: (i) knowledge produced by the RIS (Asheim & Gertler, 2005; Cooke, 2001; Hervas-Oliver & Parrilli, 2017); (ii) knowledge produced by lead firms and their GIN (Cantwell, 2009; Morrison, 2008; Turkina & Van Assche, 2018).

Overall, propositions 1 and 2 help us study key elements of the resilience and sustainable development of CIDs in a context of increasing global competition and dynamic industry transformations.

3. Methodology

We work through a set of cases that are representative of the challenges that we envisage: the scope of the CID internal fracture between lead companies and first tier suppliers that internationalize their operations on the one hand, and most other suppliers that focus on local production on the other. The latter face the risk of being driven out of global value chains and of their expanding market.

In particular, we have identified four CIDs on which a long-term meta-study and appraisal is built thanks to the work of a number of scholars and organizations. Some of these CIDs are undergoing an unstable growth path, while others are on a steady growth path -a situation that may change in the future-. These different cases help to analyze the role of lead firms' commitment, as well as the RIS engagement with CIDs on the one hand, and lead firms and their GIN on the other. As a result, we should be able to answer the question of whether these two elements represent crucial assets for a cohesive growth of CIDs.

The CIDs are selected on the basis of representative features (Yin, 2003). In Table 1 the key aspects of the selected CIDs are presented. In all cases it is a selection of CIDs that contain the following aspects: (i) critical mass of firms and production volumes. They have all been active for at least two decades; therefore show an evolutionary process that includes periods of expansion and recession (Menzel and Fornahl, 2010), which help to get the wider picture of the competitive capacity of these CIDs. (ii) Inclusion of one or more lead companies. This means that we are considering hub-and-spoke clusters where the current and future presence of lead firms is strategic (Cantwell, 2009; Markusen, 1996). (iii) Selected CIDs and lead firms have a clear global orientation. In some cases, it is in terms of export and production markets, in other cases also in terms of knowledge generation processes. (iv) Innovation is a key aspect of the success of these CIDs. This lends to the discussion of whether the innovation outcome is produced on the basis of local firms' efforts, the lead company's or the RIS'. (v) Not all these CIDs are positioned in high technology industries; two clusters are in traditional industries (i.e. furniture/upholstery), one in intermediate technologies (i.e. wind energy), while the fourth is in high-tech industries (i.e. electronics and ICTs). In our analysis, this aspect should help us understand whether technology intensity matters for the growth of cohesive clusters (Turkina & Van Assche, 2018). (vi) Geographically, these CIDs are selected from three countries, two in Europe

Table 1. Key constructs and variables, and assessment.

Constructs	Variable 1	Variable 2	Variable 3	Overall assessment
A. Commitment of lead companies	Physical investment	Investment in human capital (training, education, etc.)	Contribution to local strategic planning	High: 1 + 2+3 Medium: 1 + 2 Low: 1 None: 0
B. Innovation collaborations	Internal R&D in lead companies and SME suppliers	Active RIS and relevant projects with 1st, 2nd, 3rd, and 4th tier suppliers	Interaction and joint projects between RIS, CID, lead firms and their GIN	High: 1 + 2+3 Medium: 1 + 2 Low: 1 None: 0
Risk of fracture	A1 + B1	A2 + B2	A3 + B3	Max: 0 High: 1 Medium: 1 + 2 Low: 1 + 2+3

Source: own elaboration.

(Italy and Spain) and one from Latin America (Costa Rica). The latter is rather homogeneous with the former group as Costa Rica represents a quite developed economy (63th position within the category of High Human Development, 2019). It is positioned before Turkey that is typically assimilated to European standards. Moreover, this Costa Rican cluster is representative of an economy that relies on SME competitiveness as most European economies.

These representative case studies are selected on the basis of key aspects that we plan to analyze (Yin, 2003). We refer to: (1) large firm commitment with the local economy; (2) whether CIDs interact more or less actively with RIS agents, or they also rely on exchanges with lead companies and their global knowledge community in their specific industry (GIN). For the first aspect and research proposition, we focus on lead companies' physical investments (variable 1), the interaction that they maintain with the local firms and institutions to promote human capital, e.g. in training courses, education prizes, investment decisions (variable 2), and the lead firms' interest in joining forums and actions with local partners around local development plans and strategies (variable 3). In relation to the second proposition, we focus on the existence of internal R&D within lead companies and SME suppliers (variable 1), whether small firms develop innovation collaborations with RIS organizations (e.g. investment in small firms, innovation projects with local universities –variable 2-), or RIS and SMEs are integrated in more open initiatives that include technology transfers from lead firms' GIN to the RIS and the local businesses (variable 3).

This approach helps us understand whether there is the effective risk of a fracture within the CIDs as the lead companies move towards international markets, and in doing so they are concerned about taking with them their local suppliers. For this study, we rely on own studies over a long period of time (mid-2000s up to now), and complete the relevant information with other studies developed by fellow scholars that have analysed these cases over time. Technical reports, consultancy and policy documents about recent development of these CIDs are also considered. All these form a bulk of specialized information that helps triangulate information, and study the way these CIDs cope with the challenges of internationalization.

4. The competitiveness of clusters within global markets

4.1. Local commitment of lead firms

As per Table 2, the four CIDs have a history in which some lead firm promoted the growth and internationalization of local industrial activities. In some of these CIDs, these firms show an orientation to maintain their competitiveness insofar as to promote the growth of a significant local supply chain; in others they exhibit a more ambiguous approach to the local supply chain. Table 3 shows the key traits of these CIDs and their firms in relation to their commitment to promote the growth of the local economy by means of engaging with a dense network of local suppliers and institutions.

The unsteady growth cases of Forli-Italy and Bilbao-Spain represent CIDs that are striving to maintain their position in international markets. A few large lead firms work here and compete in international markets. These firms have developed successful strategies (e.g. Poltrone&Sofa through their large set of retail shops across Italy and France; Iberdrola through their world leadership in renewable energy distribution). In both

Table 2. Selected cluster case studies in the UK, Italy, Spain and Costa Rica.

	Upholstery, Forli, Italy	Wind energy Bilbao, Spain	Furniture, Azpeitia, Spain	Electronics & Software, S. Jose, Costa Rica
Size & growth	100+ firms; 5,000 employees; €169 million export	100+ firms and 16,000 workers; 7.3 billion turnover and increasing	200 firms & 5,500 employees; €1.2 billion turnover & increasing	900 firms; $3 billion of export in 2016 and increasing
Lead company	Large local firm (Poltrone&Sofa)	Large local firms (Iberdrola & Gamesa)	Medium-sized firms (FMG-MCG)	Large foreign firm (Intel)
Internationalization	Export	Export + FDI	Export	Export
Innovation	Incremental	Radical and incremental	Radical and incremental	Radical and incremental
Type of Industry	Traditional industry	Intermediate technology industry	Traditional industry	High technology industry
Potential for an internal fracture	Risky position	Risky position	Current success	Current success
Main sources of information	Intesa San Paolo, 2017; Dametto, 2016; Parrilli, 2009	Cluster Energia webpage 2018; Parrilli et al., 2013	Cluster Habic webpage 2018; Parrilli and Zabala, 2014; Parrilli et al., 2010	Camtic webpage, 2018; Alfaro, 2013; Ciravegna, 2011; Parrilli and Sacchetti 2008

Source: own elaboration.

cases, these large firms are also embedded in the local cluster. For instance, Iberdrola built its headquarters skyscraper in Bilbao in 2011–2013 giving a clear sign of its long-term commitment to this cluster. Notwithstanding these relevant elements, these CIDs and their lead firms also show some weak elements. For instance, Poltrone&Sofa is an outsider in Forli. They come from Parma (around 200 kilometres up north in Emilia-Romagna), although they decided to exploit the tradition of upholstery production of Forli, and set their main manufacturing bases here. This cluster hosts a number of migrant-led small firms that tend to operate as cost subcontractors for Poltrone&Sofa and for other local medium-sized companies (Dametto, 2016). This situation weakens the internal cohesion of the district as many other local SMEs struggle to achieve the cost competitiveness of these new subcontractors. Moreover, no particular actions are undertaken by the lead company to stir joint investments in human capital or joint local development plans in collaboration with local government and business associations (Dametto, 2016).

In the case of Bilbao, the cluster has grown over the past fifteen years thanks to the growth of two large lead companies, and the proactive regional cluster policy that supports joint projects among businesses and other regional organizations (Aranguren, De la Maza, Parrilli, Vendrell, & Wilson, 2014). In this wind energy cluster, Iberdrola is leader in the

Table 3. Lead firms' commitment.

CID	Lead firm	Internationalization	Commitment	Growth
Upholstery Forli, Italy, Upholstery	Poltrone&Sofa	Only Export	Low	Unsteady growth
Bilbao, Spain, Wind Energy	Iberdrola & Gamesa	Export and overseas production	Medium	Unsteady growth
Azpeitia/Azkoitia, Spain, Furniture	FMG/MCG	Only export	High	Sustained growth
San Jose, Costa Rica, Electrons. & Software	Intel	Export	High	Sustained growth

Source: own elaboration.

distribution of renewable energy, although it does not produce components. Instead, the leading manufacturing company is Gamesa. This company grew quickly in the early 2000s and became the fourth manufacturing wind energy company worldwide (Elola et al., 2013). However, the enlargement of its international operations led to the dismissal of around 3000 employees in 2013 (Gamesa webpage 25 April 2019), but also made this company appealing to other multinationals. In fact, in 2016 it has been taken over by the giant Siemens. Since most local suppliers produce manufacturing inputs (e.g. nacelles, generators and transformers, pitch drives, among others), this decision may jeopardize the future of this cluster as the strategy of this MNC is decided from outside the cluster and may lead to substantial relocations depending on the future main markets of this company. Gamesa's decision to create a set of R&D centres in destination markets (e.g. China and India) as well as the closure or sale of some local companies in recent years exhibit this risk. Only recently there have been some preliminary efforts of the new Siemens-Gamesa to promote –with the regional government- a set of development programmes around the supply chain, the digitalization and innovation of this industry (Siemens-Gamesa webpage, 25 April 2019). However, these are just preliminary intentions that need to be corroborated by facts.

In contrast to these cases, we have also identified two CIDs that show a steadier growth path: the electronics and software cluster of San Jose/San Pedro in Costa Rica, and the furniture cluster of Azpeitia/Azkoitia in the North of Spain. In the first case the cluster has a clear leader; Intel in San Jose/San Pedro. This company accepted the financial and economic incentives provided by the Costa Rican government, and set up an important manufacturing plant in 1997. In the mid-2000s, Intel also set up the Latin American Electronic Study Centre (LAES) as a means to develop innovations in the country (Camtic website). Simultaneously, Intel invested resources in the local/national universities to strengthen the supply of skilled electronic and software engineers for the local job market (Parrilli & Sacchetti, 2008). At first, they hired a significant number of local employees for the manufacturing plant (around 2,000), all in technical positions, thus leading to a technology transfer process that improved the local human capital. In recent years, the company decided to sell its manufacturing plant and to increase its investment in the research centre. As a result, the jobs in the manufacturing plant were progressively lost, while a large number of qualified jobs (i.e. engineering) were opened in the research centre that currently employs 1900 people (Camtic website). These decisions and investments represent long-term commitments of Intel that give stability to the local economy, promote new business opportunities for the local skilled workforce, and bolster a steady demand for qualified jobs in the company. In a few years, a significant number of local companies arose in the software industry (around 900), focusing on specific ICT and software niches, and on different international markets (Alfaro, 2013; Camtic website; Parrilli & Sacchetti, 2008).

The CID of Azpeitia/Azkoitia is different to a certain extent as no very large firm is based there. However, two local companies (Fagor and Danona) reached a relevant size (small among the large-sized companies) and led the development process of this cluster for a long period. Being part of the large Mondragon Cooperative Group (MCG), these companies always showed a strong commitment to the local economy. They never planned to leave the cluster, although the group developed FDI in China. As a result, once the crisis arrived (in the late-2000s), these firms suffered the effects and merged with one another while downsizing operations. With their local suppliers and the local development agency they set up a local forum to plan recovery actions. They lost the local leadership that was assumed by the new cluster organization Habic, which in collaboration with local firms developed a quite novel and complex cluster that reactivated production and development prospects in the mid-2010s (Habic website; Parrilli & Zabala, 2014). Simultaneously, MCG cooperative group actively pursues actions related to the development of human capital, in particular through their own local university (Mondragon University) and local training institutions.

Overall, these four CIDs do not seem to justify the idea that the home-grown origin of the lead companies matters much for the growth opportunities of the local supply chain. The size also seems not to matter as this latter case does not entail the current leadership of a large lead firm. However, the long-term commitment of the lead company/organization matters, particularly for the investment they make in critical local assets that ensure progress and good prospects in the future. This is the case of Intel's investment in human capital and education infrastructure/universities in Costa Rica (Alfaro, 2013; Camtic website; Parrilli & Sacchetti, 2008), and the proactive and coordinating role taken by the new cluster organization in the furniture CID of Azpeitia-Azkoitia which stirs the effort of local firms to develop a number of innovation-led initiatives, e.g. turnkey solutions for hotels and restaurants, schools and health clinics (Parrilli & Zabala, 2014). In contrast, the former intermediate cases show mixed features that include: (i) positive aspects such as the location of lead firms in the cluster, but also (ii) lower investment scope as no specific programmes are designed to stir new skills and capabilities there, and (iii) risks connected to the takeover of some of these local lead firms that may promote a footloose approach of these businesses to the cluster, thus weakening local strategic plans and jeopardizing future growth prospects.

4.2. Clusters, innovation systems and global innovation networks

The second key aspect in our analysis is the relation between the RIS, the clustered SMEs and the lead companies and their GIN. In advanced economies, innovation is an essential ingredient for competitiveness. For small firms that do not invest in R&D, external sources of innovation are essential, either in the form of supply chain-based interactions, or through the support of science and technology-based organizations including universities (Jensen, Johnsson, Lorenz, & Lundvall, 2007). In the case of lead firms that have their own R&D facilities and skilled human capital, the RIS is not a critical asset. They tend to work through their GINs with other selected lead companies and organizations worldwide (Chaminade & Plechero, 2015; Cooke, 2013; Ernst, 2009; Parrilli et al., 2013). However, this autonomy of large firms may lead to a fracture with smaller suppliers, as lead firms invest resources wherever they find it convenient, thus may skip the RIS (unless it is leading in science). As a consequence the RIS organizations need to make additional efforts to monitor and test new technologies and supply local SMEs with relevant knowledge so as to make them appealing to lead firms in their production and innovation activities. This effort and its outcome are not to be taken for granted. A relevant appraisal is required to understand whether the RIS works effectively or not, and how to improve its capacity to supply firms with appropriate knowledge and innovation opportunities (Asheim, Lawton-Smith, et al., 2011) (Table 4).

Table 4. Local lead firms, local SMEs, RIS and GIN.

	Type of industry	Internal R&D	Collaborations RIS with CID	Interaction RIS&CID with lead firms & GIN	Overall assessment & performance
Forli, Italy, Upholstery	Traditional	Low	Low	Low	Low
Bilbao, Spain, Wind Energy	Intermediate technology	High (lead and 1st tier suppliers)	High (1st tier suppliers only)	Medium	Medium
Azpeitia, Spain Furniture	Traditional	Medium	High	High (MCG)	High
San Jose, Costa Rica, Software & Electronics	High technology	High (lead and 1st tier suppliers)	High	High	High

Source: own elaboration. Note for overall assessment: High = 3; Medium = 2; Low = 1 (see Table 1).

The CIDs with risky prospects present special features. In Forli ID, the RIS is not self-evident. Emilia-Romagna RIS is focused on a medium-high technology sectors (e.g. motor industry, biotech and machinery and equipment, among others), while a large part of the CIDs focus on traditional productions (clothing, footwear, furniture). Here CIDs benefit from the formation (in the 1980s) of specific cluster organizations (e.g. CITER in the clothing CID of Carpi). In Forli there are no such catalysts of industry innovation apart from the major regional organizations (ASTER for technological development), which are located away from actual production, thus leading to poor interaction with SMEs (Dametto, 2016; Parrilli, 2009). For this reason, the firms in these industries depend on their incremental innovation activities (i.e. design). Neither information is found about the existence of a GIN linked to the lead company here, nor evidence is discovered about a significant interaction for innovation between CID firms and the lead firm (Poltrone&Sofa). This overall picture leaves the CID in a quite weak position vis-à-vis future challenges from global competitors that join this market with cost effective solutions.

In the wind energy industry in Bilbao, the lead company Iberdrola has formed its own GIN with lead international companies from the US, Holland and Singapore. Simultaneously, Iberdrola has maintained relationships with RIS agents (e.g. technology centres Tecnalia and IK4), which is a key step to help the latter monitor the current scientific and technological advances. However, in the manufacturing area the lead company Gamesa has progressively disconnected from the RIS, while focusing on creating its R&D centres in India, China, and the US (Elola et al., 2013). This trend may even increase with the recent takeover by Siemens in 2016. Overall, fear exists that the involvement of the (generally strong) RIS with the SMEs of the wind energy industry cluster in Bilbao may deteriorate, opening a gap between the knowledge managed by lead companies, and that available to second, third and fourth tier local suppliers.

These cases exhibit clear dissimilarities vis-à-vis the following CIDs where the RIS exists and operates more effectively. In the steadier growth case of Azpeitia/Azkoitia furniture cluster, the RIS proves to be active as the new cluster organization Habic has been able to reactivate the interest of the local technology centre Cidemco and the local training institute Urola-LH so as to produce new projects (e.g. EU-Interreg 'Woodtech') in search for better technologies and a more advanced combination of components and products for new markets abroad, e.g. restaurant and hotel chains, health and education facilities (Parrilli & Zabala, 2014; Habic website). For the peculiarity of this region (i.e. homogeneous population and culture), lead companies work directly with the RIS. Simultaneously, members of the cluster and of MCG have built up international innovation networks in relation to EU Interreg projects and other international knowledge sources (e.g. German engineers invited to discuss design innovation for the cluster since 2013–2014). As a result, a collective effort is organized by agents of this cluster (led by the cluster organization) that promotes an innovation and technology transfer between GIN and RIS that cross-fertilizes all firms in this CID.

In San Jose/San Pedro, the linkage between the cluster and the RIS is guaranteed by the important efforts of Intel. In 2013, this company removed its manufacturing plant from Costa Rica, but simultaneously strengthened its research and development centre (LAES) that currently employs 1,900 workers (Camtic website). In addition, Intel maintains its collaboration with the University of Costa Rica (UCR) and the Technological Institute of Cartago for the formation of engineers and technicians in electronics. This helps to transfer knowledge from the lead company and its GIN to the local economy. Several local ICT and software firms benefit from these activities and from a range of public and private labs dedicated to experimentations and trials in electronics and ICT (Alfaro, 2013; Camtic website). The government keeps developing financial lines that benefit the autochthonous ICT industry so as to promote the continuous growth of this diverse and competitive industry. Overall, the connection between clustered firms and the RIS is sound.

Overall, these cases show that where the lead firms have built their own GINs and do not ensure a similar collaboration with the RIS, the risk of a disconnection between lead firms and local SME suppliers grows. Instead, when the RIS actively engages with the lead firm and its GIN in the process of innovation, the local suppliers are more likely to benefit from voluntary knowledge transfer and technology spillovers that put them in the best position to follow the lead companies in their internationalization strategies. This is shown by Table 5.

Table 5. Synthetic results.

	Commitment	Innovation collaborations (RIS/CID-lead firm/GIN)	Type of industry	Success of the CID
Forli, Italy, Upholstery	Low	Low	Traditional	Unsteady
Bilbao, Spain, Wind Energy	Medium	Medium	Intermediate technology	Unsteady
Azpeitia, Spain Furniture	High	High	Traditional	Steady
San Jose, Costa Rica, IT & Electronics	High	High	High technology	Steady

Source: own elaboration.

5. Conclusions

In this paper, we provide evidence on two drivers that are very likely to affect the capacity of CIDs to develop cohesively in spite of the new globalization challenges. The risk of internal fractures is visible in cases of growing separation between lead firms and their local suppliers due to the low resources the latter invest in innovation. This risk increases with the globalization of lead companies that might find convenient to replace their local suppliers with scale economies-led suppliers in the countries where they develop FDIs and internationalization strategies (Bailey & De Propris, 2014; Belussi, 2015; Elola et al., 2013).

Based on previous scholarly work on the role of home-grown/indigenous multinationals in CIDs (Belussi et al., 2010; Hervas-Oliver & Albors-Garrigos, 2008; Sedita et al., 2013), here we identified the 'commitment' of these lead companies with their CIDs as a key for local resilience and sustainable success (Asheim, Lawton-Smith, et al., 2011; Boschma, 2015). This commitment can be seen in renewed investments in physical (e.g. R&D labs, production plants) and intangible assets (e.g. training courses, university programmes) as well as in participation to local development plans with local stakeholders. Moreover, their commitment is essential to promote knowledge transfer from their GIN to the pre-existent RIS in a way that allows the RIS and in particular local SMEs to be nourished with advanced knowledge, thus maintaining an appeal for the lead companies. These are the key aspects and approach of this paper that represent an original contribution to the strand of research on the importance of RISs for SME innovation in CIDs (Asheim & Gertler, 2005; Belussi et al., 2010; Cooke, 2001; Isaksen & Trippl, 2016) and on the role of home-grown multinationals for local development more in general (Belussi, 2015; Hervas-Oliver & Albors-Garrigos, 2008; Morrison, 2008; Sedita et al., 2013).

The evidence that we have provided shows a range of CIDs, some of which are competitive though also present risks of internal fractures due to the lower commitment of lead firms to the strengthening of the local supply chain. We also identified a couple of success cases in which their steady growth path is linked to the effort of lead companies to continuously invest in the development of a significant local supply chain, also by means of promoting significant investments in the RIS while simultaneously investing in the formation of their own effective GIN (Parrilli et al., 2013).

These findings offer relevant indications for both practice and policy-making as the commitment of lead companies can be assessed and promoted through policy actions and incentives (e.g. joint effort by Intel and the Costa Rican government for the promotion of specialized human capital; Parrilli & Sacchetti, 2008; Camtic website). In addition, the synergies between GINs and RISs (mediated by the lead company) can also be assessed and bolstered, provided they are inserted within well-planned development strategies that include technological developments as well as public investments in innovation infrastructures such as universities, labs, science and technology parks, business incubators, among others (Asheim, Boschma, et al., 2011, Asheim, Lawton-Smith, et al., 2011; Morrison, 2008; Parrilli et al., 2013).

This work presents limitations that can be addressed through further studies. The set of cases is limited, thus a larger number of applications would be useful as a means to verify the importance of those critical drivers (commitment and GIN-RIS interaction) across a wider set of cases. The study of CID failures could also help to achieve consistency. Moreover, it would be interesting to study more cases in which leadership and commitment are not in the hands of a lead company as in hub-and-spoke clusters, but also shared across larger sets of SMEs (Marshallian industrial districts). In effect, commitment is essential, and yet does not need to be concentrated in one or few companies only.

Note

1. This structure has been long analyzed in the context of the automotive industry, where brand manufacturers are the lead companies, while for instance engines and gearboxes are produced by first tier suppliers, steering wheels by second tier, windscreens and seats by third tier, and raw materials and generic components by fourth tier suppliers; see for instance Grabher (1993).

Acknowledgements

The author thanks the colleagues for their insightful comments on earlier versions of the paper, and in particular those received by Luciana Lazzeretti, Editor of the special issue of EPS on "Rethinking Clusters", and the reviewers of this paper. The usual disclaimers apply.

Disclosure statement

No potential conflict of interest was reported by the author.

ORCID

Mario Davide Parrilli http://orcid.org/0000-0002-1210-403X

References

Alfaro, L. (2013). *La industrial del software en Costa Rica: un exitoso resultado desde la universidad publica*. San Jose: Centro Internacional de Politica Economica, Universidad Nacional de Costa Rica.
Altenburg, T., Schmitz, H., & Stamm, A. (2008). Breakthrough: China's and India's transition from production to innovation. *World Development, 36*, 325–344. doi:10.1016/j.worlddev.2007.06.011
Aranguren, M. J., De la Maza, X., Parrilli, M. D., Vendrell, F., & Wilson, J. (2014). Evaluation of cluster policy. *Regional Studies, 48*, 1547–1562. doi:10.1080/00343404.2012.750423
Asheim, B., Boschma, R., & Cooke, P. (2011). Constructing competitive advantage: Platform policy based on related variety. *Regional Studies, 45*, 893–904. doi:10.1080/00343404.2010.543126
Asheim, B., & Gertler, M. (2005). The geography of innovation: Regional innovation systems. In *The Oxford handbook of innovation* (pp. 291–317). New York: Oxford University Press.
Asheim, B., Lawton-Smith, H., & Oughton, C. (2011). Regional innovation systems: Theory, empirics and policy. *Regional Studies, 45*, 875–891. doi:10.1080/00343404.2011.596701
Bailey, D., & De Propris, L. (2014). Mannufacturing reshoring and its limits: The UK automotive case. *Cambridge Journal of Regions, Economy and Society, 7*, 379–395. doi:10.1093/cjres/rsu019
Balcet, G., Commisso, G., & Calabrese, G. (2013). Structuring and restructuring FIAT-Chrysler: Can two carmakers jointly survive in the new automotive arena?. *International Journal of Automotive Technology and Management, 13*, 183–197. doi:10.1504/IJATM.2013.052995.
Baldwin, R. (2011). *Trade and globalization after gobalisation 2nd unbundling: how building and joining a supply chain are different* (NBER Working Papers 17716). Cambridge MA.
Becattini, G. (1990). Industrial district as a socioeconomic notion. In F. Pyke, G. Becattini, & W. Sengenberger (Eds.), *Industrial districts and interfirm cooperation* (pp. 37–51). Geneva: ILO.
Belussi, F. (2003). 11. The changing governance of IDs: The entry of multinationals in local nets. In B. T. Asheim, & Å Mariussen (Eds.), *Innovations, regions and projects: Studies in new forms of knowledge governance* (pp. 317–346). Stockholm: Nordregio.
Belussi, F. (2015). The international resilience of Italian industrial districts/clusters between knowledge re-shoring and manufacturing off (near)-shoring. *Investigaciones Regionales, 32*, 89–113. http://hdl.handle.net/10017/26698.
Belussi, F., Caloffi, A., & Sedita, S. (2017). MNEs and clusters. In V. De Marchi, E. Di Maria, & G. Gereffi (Eds.), *Local clusters in global value chains* (pp. 71–93). Abingdon: Routledge.
Belussi, F., Sammarra, A., & Sedita, S. (2010). Learning at the boundaries in an open regional innovation system: Innovation in Emilia-Romagna life science industries. *Research Policy, 39*, 710–721. doi:10.1016/j.respol.2010.01.014
Blazek, J. (2015). Topwards a typology of repositioning strategies of GVC/GPN suppliers. *Journal of Economic Geography, 16*, 849–869. doi:10.1093/jeg/lbv044

Blazek, J., Natsuda, K., & Sykora, J. (2018). Entrance-exit dynamics of supplier and the repercussions for reshaping the structure of GVC/GPNs. *European Planning Studies, 26*, 2364–2386. doi:10.1080/09654313.2018.1533529

Boschma, R. (2015). Towards an evolutionary perspective on regional resilience. *Regional Studies, 49*, 733–751. doi:10.1080/00343404.2014.959481

Cantwell, J. (2009). Location and the multinational enterprise. *Journal of International Business Studies, 40*, 35–41. doi:10.1057/jibs.2008.82

Capello, R., & Lenzi, C. (2018). Structural dynamics of regional innovation patterns in Europe: The role of inventor's mobility. *Regional Studies, 53*, 30–42. doi:10.1080/00343404.2017.1379600

Carrillo, J. (1995). Flexible production in the auto sector: Industrial reorganization at Ford, Mexico. *World Development, 23*, 87–101. doi:10.1016/0305-750X(94)00108-B

Chaminade, C., & Plechero, M. (2015). Do regions make a difference? Regional innovation systems and global innovation networks in the IT industry. *European Planning Studies, 23*, 215–237. doi:10.1080/09654313.2013.861806

Chiarvesio, M., Di Maria, E., & Micelli, S. (2010). Global value chains and open networks: The case of Italian IDs. *European Planning Studies, 18*, 333–350. doi:10.1080/09654310903497637

Ciravegna, L. (2011). FDI, social ties and technological learning in new Silicon Valleys clones: Evidence from the Costa Rican ICT cluster. *Journal of Development Studies, 47*, 1178–1198. doi:10.1080/00220388.2010.547935

Cooke, P. (2001). Regional innovation systems, clusters and the knowledge economy. *Industrial and Corporate Change, 10*, 945–971. doi:10.1093/icc/10.4.945

Cooke, P. (2004). Introduction. In P. Cooke, M. Heidenreich, & H. Braczyck (Eds.), *Regional systems of innovation* (pp. 1–18). London: Routledge.

Cooke, P. (2013). From global production networks to global innovation networks in ICTs: Stability versus growth. *European Planning Studies, 21*, 1081–1094. doi:10.1080/09654313.2013.733854

Cowling, K., & Sugden, R. (1997). *Beyond capitalism*. London: Pinter.

Dametto, F. (2016). *Caso Poltrone-Sofa: l'artigianalita' nella produzione su larga scala* (BA dissertation). Universita' di Padova.

De Marchi, V., De Maria, E., & Gereffi, G. (Eds.). (2017). *Local clusters in global value chains: Linking actors and territories through manufacturing and innovation*. London: Routledge.

De Marchi, V., Gereffi, G., & Grandinetti, R. (2017). Evolutionary trajectories of industrial districts in global value chains. In V. De Marchi, E. Di Maria, & G. Gereffi (Eds.), *Local clusters in global value chains* (pp. 33–50). Abingdon: Routledge.

Dei Ottati, G. (2014). A transnational fast-fashion industrial district: Analysis of the Chinese businesses in Prato. *Cambridge Journal of Economics, 38*, 1247–1274. doi:10.1093/cje/beu015

Dunford, M. (2006). Industrial districts, magic circles and the restructuring of the Italian textile and clothing chain. *Economic Geography, 82*, 27–59. doi:10.1111/j.1944-8287.2006.tb00287.x

Dunning, J. (1988). The eclectic paradigm of international production. *Journal of International Business Studies, 19*, 1–31. doi:10.1057/palgrave.jibs.8490372

Elola, A., Parrilli, M. D., & Rabellotti, R. (2013). The resilience of clusters under increasing globalization: The Basque wind energy value chain. *European Planning Studies, 21*, 989–1006. doi:10.1080/09654313.2013.734456

Ernst, D. (2009). *A new geography of knowledge in the electronics industry? Asia's role in global innovation networks* (Pol Stud no. 54). Honolulu: East-West Center.

Gereffi, G., Humphrey, J., & Sturgeon, T. (2005). The governance of global value chains. *Review of International Political Economy, 12*(1), 78–104. doi:10.1080/09692290500049805

Grabher, G. (Ed.) (1993). *The embedded firm*. New York: Routledge.

Henderson, J., & Nadvi, K. (2011). Greater China: The challenges of global production networks and the dynamics of transformation. *Global Networks, 11*, 285–297. doi:10.1111/j.1471-0374.2011.00326.x

Hervas-Oliver, J. L., & Albors-Garrigos, J. (2008). Local knowledge domains and the role of MNE affiliates in bridging and complementing a cluster's knowledge. *Entrepreneurship & Regional Development, 20*, 581–598. doi:10.1080/08985620802462231

Hervas-Oliver, J. L., & Boix, R. (2013). The economic geography of meso-global spaces: Integrating MNCs and clusters. *European Planning Studies*, *21*(7), 1064–1080. doi:10.1080/09654313.2013.733853

Hervas-Oliver, J. L., & Parrilli, M. D. (2017). Networks of clusters within GVCs: The European ceramic tile industry in Italy and Spain. In V. De Marchi, E. Di Maria, & G. Gereffi (Eds.), *Industrial districts, clusters and global value chains: Toward an integrated framework* (pp. 175–192). Cheltenham: Elgar.

Humphrey, J., & Memedovic, O. (2003). *The global automotive industry value chain*, UNIDO Report, Vienna.

Humphrey, J., & Schmitz, H. (2002). How does insertion in global value chains affects upgrading in clusters? *Regional Studies*, *36*, 1017–1027. doi:10.1080/0034340022000022198

Isaksen, A. (2018). From success to failure, the disappearance of clusters: a study of a Norwegian boat-building cluster. *Cambridge Journal of Regions, Economy and Society*. doi:10.1093/cjres/rsy007.

Isaksen, A., & Trippl, M. (2016). Path development in different regional innovation systems, a conceptual analysis. In M. D. Parrilli, R. Fitjar-Dahl, & A. Rodriguez-Pose (Eds.), *Innovation drivers and regional innovation strategies* (pp. 66–84). New York: Routledge.

Jensen, M., Johnsson, B., Lorenz, E., & Lundvall, B. A. (2007). Forms of knowledge and modes of innovation. *Research Policy*, *36*, 680–693. doi:10.1016/j.respol.2007.01.006

Longhi, C. (2016). Building high-tech clusters: The case of the competitiveness clusters "secure communicating solutions" in the French Provence-Alpes-Cote d'Azur Region. In M. D. Parrilli, R. Fitjar-Dahl, & A. Rodriguez-Pose (Eds.), *Innovation drivers and regional innovation strategis* (pp. 123–141). New York: Routledge.

Lundvall, B.A. (2007), National innovation systems: Analytical concept and development tool. *Industry and Innovation*, *14*, 95–119.

Markusen, A. (1996). Sticky places in slippery space: A typology of industrial districts. *Economic Geography*, *72*, 293–313. doi:10.2307/144402

Menzel M.P., & Fornhal, D. (2010), Cluster life cycles: Dimensions and rationale of cluster evolution, *Industrial and Corporate Change*, *19*, 205–238.

Morrison, A. (2008). Gatekeepers of knowledge within industrial districts: Who they are, how they interact? *Regional Studies*, *42*, 817–835. doi:10.1080/00343400701654178

Morrison, A., Rabellotti, R., & Zirulia, L. (2013). When do global pipelines enhance the diffusion of knowledge in clusters? *Economic Geography*, *89*, 77–96. doi:10.1111/j.1944-8287.2012.01167.x

Parrilli, M. D. (2009). Collective efficiency, policy-inducement and social embeddedness: Drivers of ID development. *Entrepreneurship & Regional Development*, *21*, 1–24. doi:10.1080/08985620801886513

Parrilli, M. D., Nadvi, K., & Yeung, H. W. (2013). Local and regional development in global value chains, production networks and innovation networks: A comparative review and the challenges for future research. *European Planning Studies*, *21*(7), 967–988. doi:10.1080/09654313.2013.733849

Parrilli, M. D., & Sacchetti, S. (2008). Linking learning with governance in networks and clusters: Key issues for analysis and policy. *Entrepreneurship & Regional Development*, *20*, 387–408. doi:10.1080/08985620801886463

Parrilli, M. D., & Zabala, J. M. (2014). Interrelated diversification and internationalization: Critical drives of global industries. *Revue d'économie industrielle*, *145*, 63–93.

Pietrobelli, C., & Rabellotti, R. (Eds.). (2007). *Upgrading to compete*. New York: Harvard University Press.

Pietrobelli, C., & Rabellotti, R. (2011). Global value chains meet innovation systems: Are there learning opportunities for developing countries?. *World Development*, *39*, 1261–1269. doi:10.1016/j.worlddev.2010.05.013

Pietrobelli, C., Rabellotti, R., & Sanfilippo, M. (2011). Chinese FDI strategy in Italy: The Marco Polo effect. *International Journal of Technological Learning Innovation and Development*, *4*, 277–291. doi:10.1504/IJTLID.2011.044138

Porter, M. (1998), Clusters and the new economics of competition, Harvard Business Review, Nov-Dec Issue. Retrieved from https://hbr.org/1998/11/clusters-and-the-new-economics-of-competition.

Rabellotti, R., Carabelli, A., & Hirsch, G. (2009). Italian industrial districts on the move: Where are they going?. *European Planning Studies, 17,* 19–41. doi:10.1080/09654310802513914

Rodriguez-Pose, A. (2013), Do institutions matter for regional development?. *Regional Studies, 47,* 1034–1047.

Russo, M. (2004). *The ceramic industrial district facing the Chinese challenge.* Dept. of Social, Cognitive and Quantitative Sciences, Modena: University of Modena and Reggio Emilia.

Sass, M., & Fifekova, M. (2014). Offshoring and outsourcing business services to central and Eastern Europe: Some empirical and conceptual considerations. *European Planning Studies, 19,* 1593–1609. doi:10.1080/09654313.2011.586196

Sedita, S.R., Caloffi, A., & Belussi, F. (2013), *Heterogeneity of MNEs entry modes in industrial clusters, 35th DRUIDS conference,* June 17–19, Barcelona.

Sedita, S. R., Caloffi, A., & Lazzeretti, L. (2018). The invisible college of cluster research. *Industry and Innovation.* doi:10.1080/13662716.2018.1538872.

Sturgeon, T., & Van Biesebroeck, J. (2009). *Crisis and protection in the automotive industry, Policy Research Working Papers.* Retrieved from https://doi.org/10.1596/1813-9450-5060.

Turkina, E., & Van Assche, A. (2018). Global connectedness and local innovation in industrial clusters. *Journal of International Business Studies,* 49(6), 706–728. doi:10.1057/s41267-018-0153-9

Yin, R. (2003). *Case study research, third edition.* London: Sage Publications.

Websites

S Jose-Costa Rica

https://www.intel.com/content/www/us/en/jobs/locations/costa-rica/sites/heredia.html

https://www.camtic.org/wp-content/uploads/2017/06/CAMTIC-Mapeo-Sectorial.pdf

https://www.larepublica.net/noticia/el-sector-tic-costarricense-datos-y-relevancia-2018-06-14-11-32-26

Bilbao-Spain

https://www.energias-renovables.com/eolica/aerogeneradores-de-mas-de-20-megavatios-sobre-20180802

https://redclustercolombia.com/assets/multimedia/Presentaci-n-Cluster-de-Energ-a-Colombia.pdf

https://www.siemensgamesa.com/es-es/sala-de-prensa/2018/05/mou-gobierno-vasco

Forli-Italy

http://www.fc.camcom.it/download/studiestatistica/documento/il-mobile-imbottito-di-forli-studio.pdf?DWN=10069 Forli

https://www.forlitoday.it/tag/mobile-imbottito/

https://www.group.intesasanpaolo.com/scriptIsir0/si09/contentData/view/esempio_MonDis_02.pdf?id=CNT-04-0000000042FF2&ct=application/pdf

Azpeitia-Spain

http://www.clusterhabic.com/Wood/Noticia.aspx?id=401

http://www.elmundoempresarial.es/noticias/es/1506/2/4087/El-centenar-de-empresas-del-Cl%C3%BAster-Habic-espera-seguir-su-crecimiento-este-a%C3%B1o-a-un-ritmo-del-5.htm

https://www.naiz.eus/es/hemeroteca/gara/editions/2015-12-30/hemeroteca_articles/el-fondo-maecenas-kapital-adquiere-fagor-grupo-mueble-fgm-de-azpeitia

Growth in regions, knowledge bases and relatedness: some insights from the Italian case

Niccolò Innocenti and Luciana Lazzeretti

ABSTRACT
The present work uses an evolutionary economic geography framework to contribute to the literature on the combinatorial dimension of differentiated knowledge bases (DKB). The aim is to determine if there is a pattern of knowledge creation that does not rely on one specific knowledge base, and if the three knowledge bases require the presence of other related sectors to exploit their innovative capacity leading to the growth of the region. We apply Hidalgo, Klinger, Barabási, and Hausmann's [2007. The product space conditions the development of nations. *Science*, 317(5837), 482–487.] methodology of a revealed relatedness measure between sectors, thus measuring the relatedness *between* the three KB and the relatedness of each KB with all other sectors (*outside*). The results show how, at the local level, the sectors characterized by synthetic and symbolic knowledge bases in the presence of other sectors with a high degree of relatedness are able to increase the employment growth of the area.

Introduction

In recent literature on economic development and the role of externalities, the attention devoted to diversity as a performance determinant of regions, clusters and districts is growing (Boschma & Frenken, 2009; Cooke, 2012; O'Connor, Doyle, & Doran, 2018; Pede, 2013).

When discussing diversity, it is important to refer to the seminal contribution of Jane Jacobs (1969), which explains how urban environments that are rich in terms of variety have a strong ability to generate knowledge spill-overs, innovation and growth. However, the debate on the leading importance of diversity or specialization is still open and far from its conclusion (Beaudry & Schiffauerova, 2009). In this direction, the contribution of Van Oort (2015) suggests that there is no unique answer to whether diversification or specialization is more important for the growth of a region, but both strategies matter depending on the context of analysis. In fact, new developing theories are contributing to this issue, introducing methods that capture both sides of the story. They suggest that a driver of growth must have a fair degree of diversity and specialization between industries or technologies or ideas, using the concept and methods of related variety (Boschma & Iammarino, 2009; Frenken, Van Oort, & Verburg, 2007) or knowledge coherence (Nesta & Saviotti, 2005; Quatraro, 2010) to explain the growth of regions. However, there is wide consensus that specialization is more dangerous than diversification as it exposes the region to higher risks of external shocks, while a more diversified region may have a portfolio effect that helps resist sector-specific shocks (Frenken et al., 2007; Sedita, De Noni, & Pilotti, 2017).

The most interesting results regarding growth, resilience, innovation and learning are highlighted when enterprises in the regions have a relatedness that facilitates exchanges and cross-connections, even at the level of technological knowledge bases (KB) (Fitjar & Timmermans, 2018; Grillitsch, Martin, & Srholec, 2017; Sedita et al., 2017). This combinatorial approach is becoming more important for this field (Asheim, Grillitsch, & Trippl, 2017; Boschma, 2018; Manniche, Moodysson, & Testa, 2017).

In recent years, the role of differentiated knowledge bases (DKB) as drivers of innovation and growth in the area have gathered growing attention (Asheim, Coenen, Moodysson, & Vang, 2007a; Asheim et al., 2017; Aslesen & Freel, 2012). The idea is that regions dominated by one of the three knowledge bases (analytical, synthetic and symbolic) tend to behave differently in respect to the knowledge use, knowledge creation and type of innovations that will emerge in the region, leading to different capacities to innovate (Grillitsch et al., 2017; Herstad, Aslesen, & Ebersberger, 2014; Květoň & Kadlec, 2018), grow (Hájková & Hájek, 2014; Isaksen & Trippl, 2017) and resist external shocks (Sedita et al., 2017). However, these are obviously diverse, not specialized regions, and these studies fit in the debate about specialization and diversification by increasing the arguments in favour of the need for variety in the region. Recently, as suggested by Boschma (2018), we are moving to the second level of DKB, called DKB 2.0, where the roles of relatedness and proximity are gathering more attention, suggesting a combinatorial approach between innovation studies and evolutionary concepts (Fitjar & Timmermans, 2018; Grillitsch & Trippl, 2014; Strambach & Klement, 2012).

The aim of the present work is to determine if a DKB search for combinations outside or between, rather than within, is able to promote growth. We search for a pattern of knowledge creation that does not rely on one specific knowledge base and to determine whether the three knowledge bases require the presence of other related sectors to exploit their innovative capacities to increase the growth of the region.

In the literature, we may find a lot of measures for variety (Frenken et al., 2007; Glaeser, Kallal, Scheinkman, & Shleifer, 1992) and relatedness (Boschma, Minondo, & Navarro, 2013; Essletzbichler, 2015; Hidalgo et al., 2007); in this work, we used the relatedness measure proposed by Hidalgo et al. (2007), which has been recently applied to many studies about economic development and technological diversification (Balland, Boschma, Crespo, & Rigby, 2018; Boschma et al., 2013; Boschma, Balland, & Kogler, 2014; Neffke, Henning, & Boschma, 2011; Petralia, Balland, & Morrison, 2017; Rigby, 2015). We apply this measure to define relatedness among industrial sectors. Then, we focus on the relatedness of industrial categories belonging to different knowledge bases (analytical, synthetic and symbolic), each with all other industrial categories, measuring how those industries are connected in every Italian province in terms of relatedness. This measure can enter a regression and could show the relationship between employment growth in the wider economy and the concentration of workers of different knowledge bases with other highly related sectors.

On the one hand, the results show how, at the local level, the sectors characterized by synthetic and symbolic knowledge bases in the presence of other sectors with a high degree of cognitive proximity/relatedness are able to increase employment growth. On the other hand, high levels of specialization accounted for all sectors are associated with lower employment growth in the area.

The paper is structured as follows. The second section briefly outlines the role of relatedness and its importance for differentiated knowledge bases. The third section discusses the research design and the construction of variables to understand the impact of DKB for growth. In the fourth section, the results of the analysis are reported. The fifth section discusses the results and concludes the paper.

Theoretical background

The debate on the role of externalities is still wide open, and there is increasing consensus on the leading importance of diversification or specialization (Beaudry & Schiffauerova, 2009). In this debate, the seminal work of Frenken et al. (2007) has strongly projected the concept of related variety and how it could be particularly relevant to examine relatedness among industries as leading factors for the innovation and growth of regions. Since then, studies following this approach have flourished, and many scholars worked to explain the determinants of the innovation and growth of regions. Among them, relevant attention has been devoted to the role of knowledge bases (Asheim & Gertler, 2005) as one of these determinants, first assessing that the prevalence of one of the three KB influences the way regions innovate and thus their growth capacity. More recently, DKB literature has come closer to evolutionary conceptualization, expanding upon the ideas of related variety, relatedness and proximity (Boschma, 2018). The first work that directly links them is by Asheim, Boschma, and Cooke (2011), who built a policy model that mainly relies on three strands of literature: the relatedness theme (Boschma et al., 2014; Frenken et al., 2007), the one connected with the type of knowledge of the area that tends to vary by industrial sector (Asheim & Gertler, 2005; Dosi, 1988; Pavitt, 1984) and the concept of policy platforms (Cooke, 2007). This paper focusses on the first two issues, combining them to determine if the relations among sectors belonging to different knowledge bases favour knowledge creation, innovation and growth in the region.

The classification followed here is developed from Asheim and Gertler (2005), who distinguished between analytical and synthetic knowledge bases, which are then extended to the symbolic knowledge base (Asheim et al., 2007a; 2011). This distinction is particularly interesting because it considers many characteristics of particular industrial categories, such as the tacitness of knowledge, the most frequent type of innovation, the role of geographical proximity and so on.

Analytical knowledge indicates economic activities where knowledge is more formal and where a strong importance of codified knowledge is present. In this case, the knowledge is mainly related to scientific activities, and innovations take the form of discoveries or inventions.

The second type of knowledge, called synthetic, is concerned with economic activities where the innovations are mainly incremental and reach through the recombination of already existing knowledge, leading to fewer breakthrough innovations. In this type of knowledge, tacitness is more important because the knowledge is usually acquired from experience and is also connected with the wide literature on learning by doing, using and interacting DUI (Jensen, Johnson, Lorenz, & Lundvall, 2007; Johnson, Lorenz, & Lundvall, 2002) that involves knowledge recombination among diverse knowledge in a process that is practice driven (Cooke, 2013).

The last category is symbolic knowledge and is related to the aesthetic attributes of products. This type of knowledge relates to the creative capacity of the individual and is not merely a matter of physical production but is in large part dedicated to the generation of new ideas and images. Innovation is usually incremental and is often in the form of aesthetic attributes or unusual re-combinations of existing knowledge. This explains the necessity of interacting and cooperating with others in sectors characterized by this type of knowledge.

The combination in a region of different knowledge bases influences the innovative capacity and growth of the area (Hájková & Hájek, 2014; Herstad et al., 2014), and as Asheim et al. (2017) stated, ' … their combination is feasible and often essential, in particular, for more radical innovations and new regional industrial path development.' (p. 431). This is strongly connected to the main idea of studies involving the measurement of relatedness between different sectors. Many prior studies explain how technological variety is necessary for the development of new ideas and products, although it is frequently defined as a matter of the right distance and generally emphasised as a need for – not too much – diversity.

The role of agglomeration economies and studies on the importance of variety were also applied to the concepts of KB, starting from Asheim et al. (2011), but other works used those concepts to study the importance of KB combination and variety for the innovation, growth or resilience of regions. There is a wide consensus on the importance of this combinatorial approach from a theoretical perspective (Boschma, 2018; Fitjar & Timmermans, 2018; Isaksen & Trippl, 2017), while empirical and systematic tests of these hypotheses are still underdeveloped.

However, scholars have recently developed systematic studies on the role of related variety and KB, achieving interesting results. Concerning the resilience of regions, Sedita et al. (2017) showed how in Italian local systems there is an increasing effect of related variety in improving the resilience of the area due to the combination of synthetic and symbolic KB in the local system.

Another interesting study concerning the innovation of regions (Grillitsch et al., 2017) found a positive impact of analytical KB on the innovative performance of Swedish regions; however, they confirmed that a balanced presence (i.e. 'variety') of the three KB is the most beneficial for firms' innovativeness. Other studies focus on the role of variety within single KB to determine the impact on the innovation and growth of regions (Innocenti & Lazzeretti, 2019; Klement & Strambach, 2019; Lazzeretti, Innocenti, & Capone, 2017), while other studies search for different impacts of knowledge bases for the development of cities (Hájková & Hájek, 2014).

A large part of the literature follows a strand of research based on the concept of related variety. Because of this, they present the same problem of considering two industries to be more or less related based on the number of digits shared. This ex-ante definition of relatedness, of course, presents some limitations, and recently interest is growing toward a different way of viewing the relatedness between industries, technologies or products by methods based on revealed relatedness. These new methods, firstly developed by Hidalgo et al. (2007), allow the measurement of relatedness between product classes based on the idea that two products are more or less related depending on how many countries co-export them. Accordingly, if a country is a strong exporter (exports with a value higher than the world average) of two products, there may be reason to produce them together (similar capabilities, similar resources, similar technologies, etc.), and if this happens often (the two products are co-exported by many countries) there might be a reason, and thus they are considered to be more related. This way of looking at relatedness could be particularly useful when determining relatedness not only within DKB (as the majority of previous empirical works did) but, as in this case, more specifically between them or even outside.

The first analysis using this method to understand relatedness between industries belonging to DKB was by Fitjar and Timmermans (2018), who examined the combinatorial dimension of DKB in Norway, showing high relatedness outside each KB. However, this study did not examine the effect in terms of the innovation or growth of different relatedness settings of regional KB and the surrounding industrial composition.

The following step is to use the different knowledge bases as separate categories and apply the relatedness methodologies to capture the need for combinations of specialization or diversification of knowledge to foster innovation and growth in the area.

2. Research design

2.1 Data source

This study concerns the totality of Italian provinces corresponding to the NUTS-3 classification of the European Union, representing the 110 Italian provinces. The data to construct the relatedness measures are drawn from the ISTAT[1] Census 2011 and are about the number of employees subdivided by NACE code, up to the four-digit level of detail.

Other data used to construct the control variables are drawn from different sources (EUROSTAT and EPO), all provided or recollected for the same unit of analysis NUTS-3 (110 provinces).

To attribute the NACE categories to the different knowledge bases, we followed previous classification (Aslesen & Freel, 2012; Sedita et al., 2017) derived from the Constructing Regional Advantage (CRA) report of the European Commission (EC, 2006). Table 1 shows which NACE categories are attributed to each knowledge base. Of course, the attribution of NACE categories to a particular knowledge base has some limits; in fact, nearly all industries are composed of all three types of knowledge bases. The idea is to associate an industry with the prevailing knowledge base that most characterizes the industry (Asheim & Hansen, 2009; Martin, 2012).

Table 1. NACE categories assigned to each knowledge base.

KB	NACE code
Analytical	2011–2211; 2611–2680; 7211–7220
Synthetic	1011–1920; 2219–2599; 2711–3320; 6419–6832; 7711–7740
Symbolic	5811–6020; 6201–6399; 9001–9329

2.2 Methodology

Recently, many measures of relatedness have been developed (Frenken et al., 2007; Hidalgo et al., 2007; Neffke et al., 2011), and the present work follows one of the most interesting methods to define the relatedness between industrial categories (Hidalgo et al., 2007). This method is particularly interesting in this context because it allows us to measure the relatedness between industries following a co-occurrence analysis without relying on the number of digits shared to define the relatedness between sectors. Due to these important characteristics, it has been used in many fields, not only to study the relatedness between products (Donoso & Martin, 2016) as in the original work but also between technologies (Kogler, Rigby, & Tucker, 2013; Rigby, 2012) and industries (Boschma, Minondo, & Navarro, 2012).

Here, the original methodology of Hidalgo et al. (2007) is followed and applied to the industrial categories, thus building up an industry space[2] (Innocenti & Lazzeretti, 2019; Neffke et al., 2011).

For this purpose, a measure of Relative Comparative Advantage[3] (RCA) is computed for each industrial category in each Italian province. Then, the relatedness between every pair of industrial categories is measured as the minimum of the conditional probability for every Italian province to find an RCA in industrial category i, given that the province already exhibits an RCA in category j. Thus, the relatedness is computed as follows:

$$\varphi_{i,j,t} = \min\{P(RCAx_{i,t}|RCAx_{j,t}), (RCAx_{j,t}|RCAx_{i,t})\}$$

The result is an n^*n matrix, where n represents the number of industrial categories considered, represented in this case by each NACE category disaggregated at the four-digit level of detail, and each cell contains the measure of relatedness between two industrial categories.

The aim is to determine if the concentration in an area of a high level of proximity among the aggregation considered and all the other industrial categories is a driver for the employment growth of the region. Values of relatedness among industrial categories are used to compute a measure of relatedness of the different aggregations (in this case, the three KB) and all the other sectors for each Italian province in 2011:

$$Relatedness_{pt} = \sum_{s=1}^{S} R_{aw}\left(\frac{n_{ap} + n_{wp}}{N_p}\right)$$

where p represents the province, R_{aw} is the index of relatedness between the sector a appertaining to the KB that we are working on and the sector w that is not one of the sectors of that KB, n_{ap} indicates the number of employees in the sector a of the province p, while n_{wp} is the number of the employees of the sector k for the same province. N represents the total number of workers of the considered province.

This indicator allows us to have a value of provincial relatedness among the sectors of interest (all sectors belonging to each knowledge base) and all the other sectors weighted for the reciprocal concentration of employees as an indicator of the interaction opportunities between the KB of interest and the surrounding industrial environment.

In this work, some control variables are included in the models. The first is *population density*, used to control for urbanization levels and measured as the population and area ratio of provinces. A variable *patent* related to the innovation in each province is added and computed as the number of patents per million inhabitants from 2006 to 2011 using an obsolescence rate of 10% every year $E_{i,t} = h_{i,t} + (1 - \delta)E_{i,t-1}$, where $h_{i,t}$ is the flow of regional patent applications and δ is the rate of obsolescence (Quatraro, 2010). This variable is useful for the assessment of the innovation capability of the area and for the stock of knowledge of the area that could foster or inhibit employment growth.

To account for the level of formal education of each province, a *human capital* variable is added to the models. This is computed as the number of residents holding a third-level instruction in the total active population. This variable is added to account for highly educated inhabitants, which are often associated with increased innovation, productivity and growth.

3. Relatedness and growth

This section presents the results of the estimation. Table 2 presents the descriptive statistics for the variables included in the models; the variables of employment variations are drawn from the ISTAT database and are computed as the variation of employment in the period 2011–2014.

There are some high values of correlation between the variables, but they are related to variables that will be included in different models, while the values of variables present in the same model are not worrisome. However, further tests on multicollinearity have been performed using Variance Inflation Factors (VIF) without problems; the average VIF is reported at the end of each model in Table 3, showing values below 2.

In this work, a cross-section analysis is performed using multivariate regression OLS following a step-wise approach to identify the relationship between the measures of employment growth and the different measures of relatedness.

The structure of the models is as follows:

$$\Delta y_{i\,t} = \beta_1 + \beta_2 Relatedness_{i\,t} + \beta_3 Pop.Density_{i\,t} + \beta_4 Patent_{i\,t} + \beta_5 Hum\,Cap_{i\,t} + \epsilon_{i\,t} \tag{1}$$

$\Delta y_{i\,t}$ is the employment growth rate between t and t_1, then every model includes the variable of interest *relatedness* in different forms and the control variables.

Since growth models use regional or provincial data, as in this case, the presence of spatial autocorrelation (Anselin, 1988) may be a misspecification of the model; here,

Table 2. Descriptive statistics.

	N of cases	Min	Max	Mean
Emp Grow.	110	−0.179	0.073	−0.033
Rel. All sectors	110	144.64	98.976	133.019
Rel. Analytic & All	110	2.353	7.150	3.292
Rel. Synthetic & All	110	23.621	52.406	39.279
Rel. Symbolic & All	110	4.010	7.062	5.022
Rel. Analytic & Symb.	110	0.043	0.341	0.120
Rel. Analytic & Synt.	110	0.383	2.976	1.094
Rel. Synthetic & Symb.	110	0.794	1.927	1.327
Pop. Density	110	30.912	2591.288	257.940
Patent	110	0	1145.951	192.833
Human Capital	110	0.057	0.163	0.101

Source: Authors' elaboration

Table 3. Estimation results

Variables	Model 1 Emp. Grow. 20011-14 Coeff	Std Err	Model 2 Emp. Grow. 2011-14 Coeff	Std Err	Model 3 Emp. Grow. 2011-14 Coeff	Std Err	Model 4 Emp. Grow. 2011-14 Coeff	Std Err	Model 5 Emp. Gr. Ind. 2011-13 Coeff	Std Err	Model 6 Spatial Lag Emp. Gr. Serv. 2011-13 Coeff	Std Err
Rel. All sectors	**−0.0180***	0.0039	**−0.0137***	0.0045	**−0.0149***	0.0046	**−0.0123***	0.0047	0.0191	0.0184	**−0.0213***	0.0060
Rel. Analytic & All	0.0083	0.0051							**−0.0222°**	0.0125	**0.0147°**	0.0079
Rel. Synthetic & All	**0.0126***	0.0057							0.0046	0.0225	**0.0132°**	0.0079
Rel. Symbolic & All	**0.0105***	0.0051							0.0052	0.0236	**0.0122***	0.0061
Rel. Analytic & Symb.			**0.0100°**	0.0052								
Rel. Analytic & Synt.					**0.0118***	0.0053						
Rel. Synthetic & Symb.							**0.0138***	0.0061				
Pop. Density	0.0001	0.0001	0.0001	0.0001	0.0001	0.0001	0.0001	0.0001	0.0001	0.0001	0.0001	0.0001
Patent	−0.0001	0.0001	−0.0001	0.0001	−0.0001	0.0001	−0.0001	0.0001	**0.0001***	0.0001	−0.0001	0.0001
Human capital	0.3186	0.3861	0.1246	0.3364	0.4278	0.3375	0.2979	0.2933	−0.6482	1.018	0.5651	0.4775
Constant	**−0.0332***	0.0077	**−0.0469***	0.0221	**−0.0658***	0.0282	**−0.0393***	0.0076	−0.0454	0.0212	−0.0182	0.0130
W_Emp. Growth											**0.2199***	0.1145
LM (error)	0.0144		0.8582		0.4550		0.0732		0.6571		1.3871	
LM (lag)	1.9987		5.3552		3.7725		3.5030		0.2477		**3.7725***	
Log-Likelihood	192.976		189.704		192.524		191.173		53.302		158.494	
Akaike	−369.951		−367.408		−371.048		−370.346		−90.603		−300.988	
Schwarz	−348.347		−351.205		−352.144		−354.143		−69.001		−279.384	
R-Squared adj. (Pseudo)	0.3198		0.3195		0.3223		0.2894		0.0330		(0.2610)	
Vif Av.	1.84		1.59		1.90		1.81		1.84		1.84	
N. of Cases	110		110		110		110		110		110	

Significant at: °$p<0.1$, * $p<0.05$, ** $p<0.01$, *** $p<0.001$. The values of the LM error and LM lag for model 6 are from the respective OLS model.
Source: Authors' elaboration.

spatial controls are performed using a first-order contiguity matrix, the Lagrange Multiplier (LM), for the spatial lag and the error term to test if there are spatially related variables or a spatial dependence in the errors. In case some spatial autocorrelation is detected, the model that better estimated the phenomenon is then used.

The general structure of the model (1) in the case of spatial lag becomes the following:

$$y = \rho W y + X \beta + u \qquad (2)$$

where X represents the independent variables, Wy is the matrix of the spatially lagged dependent variable and ρ is the parameter that measures the spatial autocorrelation.

In the case of the error term:

$$y = X \beta + \lambda W \varepsilon + u \qquad (3)$$

$W\varepsilon$ is the matrix of the spatially lagged error, u is the independent error term, ε is a spatially autoregressive error term and λ is the parameter that measures the strength of spatial autocorrelation in the error term.

The results of the estimations are reported in Table 3, where the dependent variable is the growth of employment in the period 2011–2014 for the first four models, while model 5 is the growth of employment only in industrial sectors in the period 2011–2013,[4] and model 6 is the growth of employment in service sectors only during the same period.

The results of the first model clearly show the negative impact of over-relatedness between all sectors; this is in line with the hypothesis and follows the theories assessing that a certain degree of variety and diversity to foster innovation and economic development is needed (Boschma, 2005; Boschma et al., 2012). Two of the variables of interest show positive and significant effects on employment growth, with a high value for the synthetic knowledge base, indicating an important impact on the employment growth of Italian provinces after three years. The value of the symbolic knowledge base is lower but still positive and significant, while the analytic knowledge base is not significant. However, it is interesting that for two of the three KB the presence of highly related workers in the area is a relevant factor able to foster innovation and employment growth.

Models 2, 3 and 4 present the results for the same period using the same dependent variable (employment growth). However, as variables of interest, instead of looking at the relatedness of each KB with all other sectors, the relatedness between pairs of KB in each model is added (we were not able to add all pairs of KB in one model because this would have caused multicollinearity problems).

The three models show interesting results. As in model 1, the variable accounting for the relatedness of all sectors retains a negative sign and a high level of significance. In model 2, the relatedness among analytic and symbolic KB is added, revealing a positive effect on the employment growth of the area. This implies that the interaction among workers in sectors driven by analytic and symbolic KB leads to a higher level of innovation and thus higher employment growth.

Even in model 3, the results show the same direction; in this case, the variable accounting for relatedness is computed among analytic and symbolic KB. The sign is still positive, while the coefficient of the variable is even higher, showing a strong impact of the interaction among workers of these KB that are able to generate stronger synergies and more employment.

In the fourth model, the last pair of KB is analysed, and the results are significant and in the same direction, showing that among the three pairs of KB, the most relevant effect is found when the interaction among workers in sectors driven by symbolic and synthetic KB is considered.

The last two models are added to determine if there is a different impact on the employment growth in industrial or service sectors; due to data availability, the period of analysis is different, and the employment growth is computed in a shorter period from 2011–2013.

The results related to employment growth in the industrial sectors are shown in model 5 and strongly differ from those of the previous models. In fact, the variable accounting for the relatedness among all sectors is not significant. Among the three variables of interest, the only significant result (but with a negative sign) is the relatedness between analytic KB and all other sectors. This implies that a high concentration of relatedness between workers in sectors driven by this KB and other workers negatively affect occupation in industrial sectors.

Finally, model 6 tests the impact of different KB on employment growth in service sectors. In this case, the results are in line with those of model 1. In fact, employment growth is negatively affected by the variable accounting for the relatedness concentration among all sectors, while a positive impact is found between all three variables accounting for the relatedness of each KB and all other sectors, confirming the positive role of this kind of relatedness for employment growth in service sectors. In this case, the spatial tests reveal that the LM for the spatial lag is significant, and thus the model specification can be improved by adding the spatial lag of the dependent variable (the average employment growth in service sectors of each province's neighbouring provinces). In addition, the spatial lag of the dependent variable is significant and positive, meaning that there is a positive relationship between neighbouring provinces in terms of employment growth in the service sectors.

4. Discussion and conclusions

The results of this study allow us to argue that differentiated knowledge bases, if supported by the presence of related sectors, are dynamic for employment growth in the area. This is probably due to cross connections with related sectors that are able to promote innovation and thus employment growth.

This is not the case when there is a high level of relatedness between all sectors, indicating too much specialization in the area. In this case, over-relatedness among all sectors (too high specialization) of the area leads to a decrease in employment. This could be due to lock-in effects because if cognitive proximity is too high (over-specialized regions leading to cognitive dissonance), there is no opportunity for knowledge exchange, and the innovation capacity of the area is inhibited, resulting in lower employment growth (Van Oort, 2015).

The KB that seems to be the most relevant in a short-run analysis, as in this case, is synthetic. It is characterized by economic activities where innovation is mainly incremental and reached through the recombination of already existing knowledge, so the needs of related sectors is much more important, following path-dependent trajectories (Asheim, Coenen, & Vang, 2007b; Boschma, 2018). Innovations in these activities are practice driven and in this case, DUI model is particularly relevant (Cooke, 2013). In fact as suggested by this literature, DUI modes would be significantly connected to synthetic KB and partly also to the symbolic one, because they rely on tacit processes of learning and based on interacting and experience (Asheim, 2012).

Symbolic KB still plays an important role in favouring the employment growth of the area, even if to a lesser extent, and this is interesting considering that the total number of workers in these sectors[5] is relatively low, accounting in Italy for approximately 5% of employees. This is probably due to the characteristics of the sectors driven by this kind of knowledge, related to the aesthetic attributes of products and the creative capacity of the individual. Even in this case, innovations are usually incremental and are often in the form of aesthetic attributes or unusual re-combinations of existing knowledge, explaining the need of sectors characterized by this type of knowledge to interact and cooperate with other sectors (Lazzeretti et al., 2017) that in the standard classifications (such as NACE) are usually considered unrelated, but that with this methodology (Hidalgo et al., 2007) are found to be related and able to favour innovation and employment growth.

The analytic KB does not show any effect on employment growth. It appears that as this kind of KB indicates economic activities where knowledge is mainly formal and characterized by codified knowledge, innovations in sectors characterized by this KB usually take the form of discoveries or inventions and, for this reason, are better captured in a long-run analysis. This means, for example, in scientific knowledge where codification is formalized in a scientific publication, methodology or patent, those who have expertise can understand it more or less directly. In fact, further explanation of this result is related to the codified knowledge that characterizes these activities and leads to lesser importance of geographical proximity (Maskell & Malmberg, 1999). In fact, such collaborations could occur easily and more frequently than with the other two kinds of KB at a higher distance (through ICT, for example). Accordingly, the benefits in terms of innovation and employment growth (Boschma, 2018) may also be split and occur in different regions.

When analysing interactions among the pairs of KB, the results lead to similar conclusions. The strongest results are found when there is high relatedness between workers of synthetic and symbolic KB, while growth is the least (even if still positive) impacted when considering the relatedness between analytic and symbolic KB. In our opinion, this is for two main reasons. First is the already acknowledged lower importance of geographical proximity when accounting for the codified knowledge that strongly characterizes analytic KB. Second, the dimensions of the sectors are considered because the workers in sectors characterized by analytic and symbolic KB account for less than those belonging to synthetic. This could influence the capacity to favour the growth of the overall economy.

Our findings provide useful insights for policy makers. In terms of policy implications, this study suggests that it is necessary for policy makers to consider the importance of promoting the development of synergetic skills and not building 'cathedrals in the desert' that do not allow for the necessary interactions between sectors that have a strong need to interact with each other. According to the results of this study, policies aimed at the development of the DKB need to be viewed from a broader perspective. It is therefore necessary for policy makers to adopt policies that favour the development of the DKB in conjunction with those sectors that have high relatedness that allows them to interact and encourage the innovative process. In fact, the mere presence of specialization in one of the DKB is not enough to foster the innovative process or the resultant growth of the area. Policy makers should keep in mind the possible synergies and the need for collaboration between the DKB and firms in related sectors (despite apparently belonging to different sectors) to foster cross-fertilization and the unusual connections that appear to be important drivers of innovation and growth. More than specialization, is variety but in related sectors able to favour the growth of the area.

The present study comes with a number of limitations. First, the short period of the analysis could lead to positive results mainly driven by incremental innovation and usual connections rather than by unrelated connections that in the long run could produce breakthrough innovations. Regarding the period analysed, there could be a bias connected to the impact of the economic crisis that strongly affected Italy during the period under study.

Another limitation is the identification of the sectors with a specific KB, which is a simplification. In fact, nearly all industries are composed of all three types of knowledge bases, but when the analysis is not performed at the individual level, it is impossible to attribute each worker to the real function they belong to. Thus, the idea is to associate an industry with a knowledge base that best characterizes the industry.

In terms of future research, it could be interesting to better connect and directly investigate the relation of KB relatedness and innovation both formal and informal. Of particular interest is the role of institutions in the development of clusters and the interaction with particular KB settings in favouring growth and innovation. Following this direction, it is important to add to the present framework a third fundamental issue for KB described by Asheim et al. (2011), namely policy platforms.

Despite the acknowledged limitations, this work shows how, when discussing the combinatorial nature of DKB, it is important to examine the relatedness outside each KB rather than focussing only within each KB, as many previous works did. This could lead to a more conscious comprehension of the interactions between sectors belonging to different KB and also externally.

In conclusion, the results emphasise the disadvantages of over-specialization for the growth of the area and the need for a certain degree of variety in the territory. The presence of DKB and related sectors is relevant and may favour cross-connections and new combinations leading to innovation and growth.

Notes

1. Italian National Institute of Statistics.
2. The use of industry data instead of export data is due to the specific focus of this research, namely DKB, as many of the categories belonging to DKB are not likely to export, mainly those related to the analytical and symbolic KB.
3. If a province exhibits a concentration of employees higher than the national average in an industrial category, it is then considered to have an RCA in that sector.
4. The shorter period of analysis for the last two models is due to the availability of employment data at the moment of the analysis; employment data divided between industry and service are available only until 2013.
5. The sectors are those reported in Table 1: Publishing, motion picture, photography, computer programming, music, museums and performing arts.

Disclosure Statement

No potential conflict of interest was reported by the authors.

ORCID

Niccolò Innocenti http://orcid.org/0000-0001-8421-5479
Luciana Lazzeretti http://orcid.org/0000-0002-9759-2289

References

Anselin, L. (1988). *Spatial Econometrics: Methods and models*. Dordrecht, The Neederlands: Kluwer Academic Publishers.
Asheim, B. (2012). The changing role of learning regions in the globalizing knowledge economy: A theoretical re-examination. *Regional Studies*, 46(8), 993–1004. doi:10.1080/00343404.2011.607805
Asheim, B., Boschma, R., & Cooke, P. (2011). Constructing regional advantage: Platform policies based on related variety and differentiated knowledge bases. *Regional Studies*, 45(7), 893–904. doi:10.1080/00343404.2010.543126
Asheim, B., Coenen, L., Moodysson, J., & Vang, J. (2007a). Constructing knowledge-based regional advantage: Implications for regional innovation policy. *International Journal of Entrepreneurship and Innovation Management*, 7(2-5), 140–157. doi:10.1504/IJEIM.2007.012879
Asheim, B., Coenen, L., & Vang, J. (2007b). Face-to-Face, Buzz and knowledge bases: Socio-spatial implications for learning, innovation and innovation policy. *Environment and Planning C: Government and Policy*, 25(5), 655–670. doi:10.1068/c0648
Asheim, B., & Gertler, M. (2005). The geography of innovation: Regional innovation systems. In J. Fagerberg, D. C. Mowery, & R. R. Nelson (Eds.), *The Oxford handbook of innovation* (pp. 291–317). Oxford: Oxford University Press.
Asheim, B., Grillitsch, M., & Trippl, M. (2017). Introduction: Combinatorial knowledge bases, regional innovation, and development Dynamics. *Economic Geography*, 93(5), 429–435. doi:10.1080/00130095.2017.1380775
Asheim, B., & Hansen, H. (2009). Knowledge bases, talents and contexts: On the usefulness of the creative class approach in Sweden. *Economic Geography*, 85(4), 425–442. doi:10.1111/j.1944-8287.2009.01051.x
Aslesen, H., & Freel, M. (2012). Industrial knowledge bases as drivers of open innovation? *Industry and Innovation*, 19(7), 563–584. doi:10.1080/13662716.2012.726807
Balland, P., Boschma, R., Crespo, J., & Rigby, D. (2018). Smart specialization policy in the European Union: Relatedness, knowledge complexity and regional diversification. *Regional Studies*. Advance online publication. doi:10.1080/00343404.2018.1437900
Beaudry, C., & Schiffauerova, A. (2009). Who's right, Marshall or Jacobs? The localization versus urbanization debate. *Research Policy*, 38(2), 318–337. doi:10.1016/j.respol.2008.11.010
Boschma, R. (2005). Proximity and innovation: A critical assessment. *Regional Studies*, 39(1), 61–74. doi:10.1080/0034340052000320887
Boschma, R. (2018). A concise history of the knowledge base literature: Challenging questions for future research. In A. Isaksen, R. Martin, & M. Trippl (Eds.), *New Avenues for regional innovation systems - theoretical Advances, empirical cases and policy Lessons* (pp. 23–40). New York: Springer.
Boschma, R., Balland, P., & Kogler, D. (2014). Relatedness and technological change in cities: The rise and fall of technological knowledge in US metropolitan areas from 1981 to 2010. *Industrial and Corporate Change*, 24(1), 223–250. doi:10.1093/icc/dtu012
Boschma, R., & Frenken, K. (2009). Technological relatedness and regional branching. In H. Bathelt, M. Feldman, & D. Kogler (Eds.), *Beyond territory: Dynamic Geographies of knowledge creation and innovation* (pp. 64–68). London: Routledge.

Boschma, R., & Iammarino, S. (2009). Related variety, Trade Linkages, and regional growth in Italy. *Economic Geography*, 85(3), 289–311. doi:10.1111/j.1944-8287.2009.01034.x

Boschma, R., Minondo, A., & Navarro, M. (2012). Related variety and regional growth in Spain. *Papers in Regional Science*, 91(2), 241–256.

Boschma, R., Minondo, A., & Navarro, M. (2013). The emergence of new industries at the regional level in Spain. A proximity approach based on product-relatedness. *Economic Geography*, 89(1), 29–51. doi:10.1111/j.1944-8287.2012.01170.x

Cooke, P. (2007). To construct regional advantage from innovation systems first build policy platforms. *European Planning Studies*, 15(2), 179–194. doi:10.1080/09654310601078671

Cooke, P. (2012). Transversality and Transition: Green innovation and New regional path creation. *European Planning Studies*, 20(5), 817–834. doi:10.1080/09654313.2012.667927

Cooke, P. (2013). Towards DUI regional innovation systems. *Papers in Evolutionary Economic Geography*, 13.21, University of Utrecht, Urban & Regional Research Centre, Utrecht.

Donoso, V., & Martin, V. (2016). Product relatedness and economic diversification in the USA: An analysis at the state level. *The Annals of Regional Science*, 56(2), 449–471. doi:10.1007/s00168-016-0747-8

Dosi, G. (1988). Sources, procedures, and microeconomic effects of innovation. *Journal of Economic Literature*, 26(3), 1120–1171.

Essletzbichler, J. (2015). Relatedness, industrial branching and technological cohesion in US metropolitan areas. *Regional Studies*, 49(5), 752–766. doi:10.1080/00343404.2013.806793

European Commission. (2006). *Constructing Regional Advantage. Principles, Perspectives, Policies*. Final Report, DG Research, Brussels.

Fitjar, R., & Timmermans, B. (2018). Knowledge bases and relatedness. A study of labour mobility in Norwegian regions. In A. Isaksen, R. Martin, & M. Trippl (Eds.), *New Avenues for regional innovation systems - theoretical Advances, empirical cases and policy Lessons* (pp. 149–171). New York: Springer.

Frenken, K., Van Oort, F., & Verburg, T. (2007). Related variety, unrelated variety and regional economic growth. *Regional Studies*, 41(5), 685–697. doi:10.1080/00343400601120296

Glaeser, E., Kallal, H., Scheinkman, J., & Shleifer, A. (1992). Growth in cities. *The Journal of Political Economy*, 100(6), 1126–1152. doi:10.1086/261856

Grillitsch, M., Martin, R., & Srholec, M. (2017). Knowledge base combinations and innovation performance in Swedish regions. *Economic Geograpy*, 93(5), 458–479. doi:10.1080/00130095.2016.1154442

Grillitsch, M., & Trippl, M. (2014). Combining knowledge from different sources, Channels and geographical Scales. *European Planning Studies*, 22(11), 2305–2325. doi:10.1080/09654313.2013.835793

Hájková, V., & Hájek, P. (2014). Efficiency of knowledge bases in urban population and economic growth–evidence from European cities. *Cities*, 40(A), 11–22. doi:10.1016/j.cities.2014.04.001

Herstad, S., Aslesen, H., & Ebersberger, B. (2014). On industrial knowledge bases, commercial opportunities and global innovation network linkages. *Research Policy*, 43(3), 495–504. doi:10.1016/j.respol.2013.08.003

Hidalgo, C., Klinger, B., Barabási, A., & Hausmann, R. (2007). The product space conditions the development of nations. *Science*, 317(5837), 482–487. doi:10.1126/science.1144581

Innocenti, N., & Lazzeretti, L. (2019). Do the creative industries support growth and innovation in the wider economy? Industry relatedness and employment growth in Italy. *Industry and Innovation*. Advance online publication. doi:10.1080/13662716.2018.1561360

Isaksen, A., & Trippl, M. (2017). Exogenously Led and policy-supported New path development in Peripheral regions: Analytical and synthetic Routes. *Economic Geography*, 93(5), 436–457. doi:10.1080/00130095.2016.1154443

Jacobs, J. (1969). *The economy of cities*. New York: Vintage.

Jensen, M., Johnson, B., Lorenz, E., & Lundvall, B. (2007). Forms of knowledge and modes of innovation. *Research Policy*, 36(5), 680–693. doi:10.1016/j.respol.2007.01.006

Johnson, B., Lorenz, E., & Lundvall, B. (2002). Why all this fuss about codified and tacit knowledge? *Industrial and Corporate Change*, 11(2), 245–262. doi:10.1093/icc/11.2.245

Klement, B., & Strambach, S. (2019). Innovation in creative industries: Does (related) variety matter for the Creativity of urban Music Scenes? *Economic Geography*. Advance online publication. doi:10.1080/00130095.2018.1549944

Kogler, D., Rigby, D., & Tucker, I. (2013). Mapping knowledge space and technological relatedness in US cities. *European Planning Studies*, *21*(9), 1374–1391. doi:10.1080/09654313.2012.755832

Květoň, V., & Kadlec, V. (2018). Evolution of knowledge bases in European regions: Searching for spatial regularities and links with innovation performance. *European Planning Studies*, *26*(7), 1366–1388. doi:10.1080/09654313.2018.1464128

Lazzeretti, L., Innocenti, N., & Capone, F. (2017). The impact of related variety on the creative employment growth. *The Annals of Regional Science*, *58*(3), 491–512. doi:10.1007/s00168-016-0805-2

Manniche, J., Moodysson, J., & Testa, S. (2017). Combinatorial knowledge bases: An Integrative and dynamic approach to innovation studies. *Economic Geography*, *93*(5), 480–499. doi:10.1080/00130095.2016.1205948

Martin, R. (2012). Measuring knowledge bases in Swedish regions. *European Planning Studies*, *20*(9), 1569–1582. doi:10.1080/09654313.2012.708022

Maskell, P., & Malmberg, A. (1999). Localised learning and industrial competitiveness. *Cambridge Journal of Economics*, *23*(2), 167–185. doi:10.1093/cje/23.2.167

Neffke, F., Henning, M., & Boschma, R. (2011). How do regions diversify over time? Industry relatedness and the development of new growth paths in regions. *Economic Geography*, *87*(3), 237–265. doi:10.1111/j.1944-8287.2011.01121.x

Nesta, L., & Saviotti, P. (2005). Coherence of the knowledge base and the Firm's innovative performance: Evidence from the U.S. Pharmaceutical industry. *The Journal of Industrial Economics*, *53*(1), 123–142. doi:10.1111/j.0022-1821.2005.00248.x

O'Connor, S., Doyle, E., & Doran, J. (2018). Diversity, employment growth and spatial spillovers amongst Irish regions. *Regional Science and Urban Economics*, *68*, 260–267. doi:10.1016/j.regsciurbeco.2017.11.002

Pavitt, K. (1984). Sectoral patterns of technical change: Towards a taxonomy and a theory. *Research Policy*, *13*(6), 343–373. doi:10.1016/0048-7333(84)90018-0

Pede, V. (2013). Diversity and regional economic growth: Evidence from US Counties. *Journal of Economic Development*, *38*(3), 111–12.

Petralia, S., Balland, P., & Morrison, A. (2017). Climbing the ladder of technological development. *Research Policy*, *46*(5), 956–969. doi:10.1016/j.respol.2017.03.012

Quatraro, F. (2010). Knowledge coherence, variety and economic growth: Manufacturing evidence from Italian regions. *Research Policy*, *39*(10), 1289–1302. doi:10.1016/j.respol.2010.09.005

Rigby, D. (2012). The geography of knowledge relatedness and technological diversification in US cities. *Papers in Evolutionary Economic Geography*, *12*(18), 1–33.

Rigby, D. (2015). Technological relatedness and knowledge space: Entry and exit of US cities from patent classes. *Regional Studies*, *49*(11), 1922–1937. doi:10.1080/00343404.2013.854878

Sedita, S., De Noni, I., & Pilotti, L. (2017). Out of the crisis: An empirical investigation of place-specific determinants of economic resilience. *European Planning Studies*, *25*(2), 155–180. doi:10.1080/09654313.2016.1261804

Strambach, S., & Klement, B. (2012). Cumulative and combinatorial micro-dynamics of knowledge: The role of space and place in knowledge integration. *European Planning Studies*, *20*(11), 1843–1866. doi:10.1080/09654313.2012.723424

Van Oort, F. (2015). Unity in variety? Agglomeration economics beyond the specialization–diversity controversy. In C. Karlsson, M. Andersson, & T. Norman (Eds.), *Handbook of research methods and applications in economic geography* (pp. 259–271). Cheltenham: Edward Elgar.

Six critical questions about smart specialization

Robert Hassink ⓘ and Huiwen Gong ⓘ

ABSTRACT
During the last five years, we can observe a soaring academic interest in the concept of smart specialization. A burgeoning literature emerged both conceptually and empirically. In this paper, we pause for a while and take stock of six critiques so far identified in this emerging literature. The aim is to provide a critical lens for future research on smart specialization strategies and processes. We argue that: (1) Smart specialization is a confusing concept, as what it really means is diversification; (2) It is largely predicated on a conventional science and technology (S&T) model of innovation and regional economic development, whereas socio-ecological innovation and social innovation, have only been implicitly mentioned, at best; (3) It is the continuation of cluster policies, rather than a brand-new policy instrument; (4) It contains a delusional transformative hope, although the entrepreneurial discovery process could very likely lead to lock-ins; (5) Structurally weak regions might be less likely to benefit from smart specialization; and 6) more rigorous measurements of smart specialization are still needed. By engaging systematically with these six issues, we not only aim to improve the effects of smart specialization as a policy programme, but also to contribute to its conceptual advancement.

1. Introduction

Regional innovation policy has a long tradition in Europe and academic research on it has started in the 1990s (Cooke & Morgan, 1998; Hassink, 1992; Landabaso, 1997). During a relatively long time, clusters and regional innovation systems were the main conceptual foundations of this policy, but most recently smart specialization, has become increasingly prominent. Mainly developed by Foray (2015), smart specialization has in fact two meanings, namely a conceptual one and a policy strategy one.

Smart specialization has received strong academic and political attention recently (Fellnhofer, 2018; Radosevic, Curaj, Gheorghiu, Andreescu, & Wade, 2017), not only in Europe, but also internationally thanks to support from the OECD (2013) and the World Bank (Aprahamian & Correa, 2015). Within a few years, the number of publications has exploded, both concerning policy reports, white papers with recipes on how to develop a smart specialization strategy, books, as well as journal articles. This paper will neither give a complete overview of the literature (for a recent bibliometric analysis, see Fellnhofer,

2018), nor will it repeat a mere description of the strategy and its background (see Foray, 2015). Instead, our intention is to step aside for a while from the emerging maelstrom of smart specialization literature and focus on six critical questions that have been raised in the literature (for an early critique, see Cooke, 2012). These questions deal with the confusion around the concept, the embeddedness of smart specialization within existing regional innovation policy, the distinction between smart specialization and cluster policy, the wishful policy thinking of transformative hope, its effects on structurally weak regions, as well as the indicators in measuring such smart specialization effects. The aim of the paper, thus, is to provide a critical lens and based on that to come to questions for future research on smart specialization strategies and processes. This future research is not only supposed to lead to improving the effects of smart specialization as a policy programme, but also to contribute to conceptual advancements around smart specialization, as theoretical concepts and policy strategies are inter-related and mutually influence each other through learning processes (Hassink & Lagendijk, 2001). Before focusing on the critical questions, we will first give a short introduction into smart specialization as a concept and policy strategy.

2. Smart specialization: a short introduction

As has been stated in the introduction, smart specialization has a conceptual and policy strategy meaning. First, it has a conceptual meaning, that is 'the capacity of an economic system (a region for example) to generate new specialities through the discovery of new domains of opportunity and the local concentration and agglomeration of resources and competences in these domains' (Foray, 2015, p. 1). Secondly, it is foremost an influential policy strategy, which emerged due to thoughts developed by the Knowledge for Growth Expert Group (Foray, David, & Hall, 2009) on how to explain and reduce the productivity gap between the USA and the EU. They identified two main weaknesses in Europe: first, national-level fragmentation of public research systems, and secondly, duplication of knowledge bases (every region focusing on the same high-tech industries) (Foray, 2015, p. 10, 11). The rationale of smart specialization is to build on existing structures and to transform them with the help of new, but related explorative, research activities (Foray, 2015, p. 11). The latter should have the potential to transform existing regional economic structures. That is to say, smart specialization is not about more of the same, but more about R&D and innovation in existing sectors (Foray, 2015, p. 11). The strategy is defined as a policy process that should lead to the selection and prioritization of domains (fields or areas) that are part of a cluster in which entrepreneurs play a key role as they are supposed to discover the appropriate domains for the future (Foray, David, & Hall, 2011, p. 7). In a similar vein, Foray (2015, p. 2) states that punctual and targeted governmental intervention is key in this process as it is supposed to select the most promising new activities, which should lead to spillovers and structural changes in the regional economy. It is not only about having an important industry in a regional economy (such as the Alpine industry in a tourism region), but about smart diversification with the help of general-purpose technologies, so that existing industries get more competitive (e.g. ICT application in the Alpine industry) (Foray, 2015).

These strategies, officially called Research and Innovation Strategies for Smart Specialisation (RIS3) and being an ex-ante condition for receiving support from European Structural and Investment Funds (Landabaso, 2014), were introduced as a way to achieve a paradigm shift in the structure of regional innovation policies. Each region should 'identify transformation priorities that reflect and amplify existing local structures and competences, and thus produce original and unique competitive advantages' (Foray, 2015, p. 2). They emerged in the increasingly popular framework of place-based policies (Barca, McCann, & Rodríguez-Pose, 2012), in which geographical context, consisting of social, cultural and institutional elements, matters and policy intervention should include the participation of a broad group of actors, avoiding social exclusion and unevenness. They potentially can solve the problem of too standardized, one-size-fits-all regional innovation policies (Tödtling & Trippl, 2005). They therefore consist of an integrated, place-specific and place-sensitive agenda for economic change, focusing on specific strengths, competitive advantages and the performance potential of a country or region as a starting point, trying to strengthen regional diversity and take into account the differences between 'leader' vs. 'follower regions' (Foray et al., 2009, p. 27). They are also open to support for all sorts of innovation (beyond just technological) and the involvement of a broad range of innovation actors in the strategy development and priority setting. The entrepreneurial discovery process is a core element of the strategy.

Having briefly introduced the notion of smart specialization and its policy concern, we now look carefully into the six questions that are critical for advancing smart specialization, both as a policy instrument and a conceptual notion.

3. Is smart specialization about specialization or diversification?

Smart specialization is closely related to a set of other theoretical concepts around regional agglomerations and territorial innovation models (Moulaert & Sekia, 2003). Although many authors adopted the term smart specialization in their publications, it is argued by many scholars, that smart specialization is not about specialization as we know from previous Porter-like cluster strategy. Rather it is about 'diversified' specialization (Asheim, Grillitsch, & Trippl, 2017), or, smart diversification (Balland, Boschma, Crespo, & Rigby, 2018; Boschma & Gianelle, 2013; Piirainen, Tanner, & Alkærsig, 2017), where regions identify areas or domains of existing or potential competitive advantage, and differentiate themselves from others. In economic geography, an increasing number of notions such as relatedness (Balland et al., 2018; McCann & Ortega-Argilés, 2015), branching (Boschma & Gianelle, 2013), variety (Frenken, Van Oort, & Verburg, 2007), etc., have been discussed under the so-called smart specialization umbrella, which makes it look confusing and conceptually chaotic. Such fuzziness is particularly problematic when the concept is put into policy practice. According to several evaluation reports on the early implementation of the smart specialization strategies in regions (Capello & Kroll, 2016; Gianelle, Guzzo, & Mieszkowski, 2019; McCann & Ortega-Argilés, 2015), many local actors, be they entrepreneurs, policy makers or opinion leaders, had difficulties in fully understanding the concept. Misinterpreting smart specialization for further specialization in regional economies that so far suffered from it, such as mono-structural old industrial areas and company towns, could lead to the wrong strategies strongly negatively affecting the prospects of those economies. Therefore, the plurality of terms used in the literature and particularly the lacking distinction between specialization and diversification will only lead to further confusion, as most policy implementers lack the capability to interpret or translate them correctly (Hassink & Lagendijk, 2001).

4. How well is smart specialization embedded in existing regional innovation policies?

The current hype around smart specialization should not blind us for the fact that the strategies are part of a broader and much older set of measures of regional innovation policies (McCann & Ortega-Argilés, 2013; Rodríguez-Pose, 2018; Uyarra, Flanagan, Magro, Wilson, & Sotarauta, 2017), as well as broader trends in innovation policies in general.

Regional innovation polices have developed strongly in large parts of Europe and other industrialized countries since the mid-1980s (McCann & Ortega-Argilés, 2013; OECD, 2011). In economic geography, strong contributions have been made by scholars working on regional innovation systems (RISs) (e.g. Asheim & Coenen, 2005; Cooke, Uranga, & Etxebarria, 1997; Isaksen, Martin, & Trippl, 2018). This surge of interest in regional innovation policies is mainly due to the increasing importance of the regional level with regard to diffusion-oriented innovation support policies (Asheim, Isaksen, Nauwelaers, & Tödtling, 2003; Fritsch & Stephan, 2005; OECD, 2011; Prange, 2008). Partly supported by national and supranational support programmes and encouraged by strong institutional set-ups found in successful regional economies such as Baden-Württemberg in Germany and Emilia-Romagna in Italy, many regions in Europe had been setting up regional innovation policies. They consist of the following measures: science parks, technopoles, technological funding schemes, innovation support agencies, community colleges, cluster policies and most recent initiatives to support the smart specialization of industries (McCann & Ortega-Argilés, 2013). The central aim of these regional innovation policies is to support regional endogenous potential by encouraging the diffusion of new technologies both from universities and public research establishments to small and medium-sized enterprises (SMEs), between SMEs and large enterprises (vertical co-operation) and between SMEs themselves (horizontal co-operation). Smart specialization policies are just part of these broader regional innovation policies and often we find several cluster and smart specialization initiatives under the roof of one regional innovation policy. Scholars in favour of a place-based approach towards regional development policy (Barca et al., 2012; OECD, 2011) have recently taken up the arguments in favour of regionalization and unfolding endogenous potential in regions again. Moreover, concerning the broader trends in innovation policies in general, Schot and Steinmueller (2018) have recently summarized three frames of innovation policy during the last few decades. Innovation policy 1.0 refers to the post-war science and R&D innovation policy, whereas innovation policy 2.0 is about the systems of innovation model since the 1980s, and the current socio-ecological innovation policy 3.0 is supposed to solve grand challenges and lead to sustainable transformation. Recently, the turn to more sustainable modes of production and consumption has been high on the policy agenda. Innovation policy 3.0 started to pay increasing attention to challenges such as climate change, ageing societies, the refugee crisis, food and energy security, etc. (Coenen, Hansen, & Rekers, 2015; Schot & Steinmueller, 2018). It addresses the issues of sustainable and inclusive societies at a more fundamental level than previous framings or their associated ideologies and practices (Coenen & Morgan, 2019). It can also be related to recent discussions on so-called 'mission-oriented' innovation policy (Mazzucato, 2018) and social innovation (Moulaert, 2013). In contrast to previous generations of innovation policies, which contain a strong motivation to resolve all sort of structural failures (e.g. Coenen et al., 2015), innovation policy 3.0 involves the explicit mobilization of science, technology and innovation for meeting societal needs and addressing the United Nation's Sustainable Development Goals (Schot & Steinmueller, 2018).

As a policy instrument that pays substantial attention to regional innovative capability, how well is smart specialization embedded in (and informed by) the recent generation of innovation policies? Although the guide to smart specialization (Foray et al., 2009) was largely predicated on a conventional science and technology (S&T) model of innovation (innovation policy 1.0 and 2.0), another model of innovation – that is, the socio-ecological model has been less highlighted. In facing the grand challenge to transform to a sustainability society, this implicit model deserves more prominence in smart specialization policies, because its ends are very different to the S&T model (Coenen & Morgan, 2019). In a recent paper, Foray (2018) has argued that smart specialization policy can be well positioned in the mission-oriented policy category, due to its non-neutral (preferential intervention) nature, and its relevance for moving from the 'old' to 'new' types of missions. However, the strong focus on science and technology (S&T) models of innovation and entrepreneurial activities has led to doubts about whether sustainability transition can be achieved by implementing smart specialization strategies. Particularly, what should policy makers do when the pursuing of economic competitiveness contradicts with other aspects of social well-being (e.g. environmental cleanness, ecological integrity)? So far, this issue has been largely overlooked. All in all, although the smart specialization strategies draw a lot from the previous generations of innovation policy, its connections to social-ecological innovation that can lead to sustainable transition needs to be more carefully examined.

5. From cluster to smart specialization policy: really something new or more of the same?

Arguably, of all existing concepts and policy strategies clusters are the closest to smart specialization. In many publications and white papers about smart specialization, clusters are regarded as important building blocks of smart specialization. In an OECD report, for instance, it is written that

> some case studies in the OECD appear to interpret smart specialization as necessarily involving prioritizing 'sectoral cluster', 'sectoral strategic plans' or 'cluster strategy', for example, the Photonics Cluster (Gwanju, Korea); Automotive Cluster (East Marmara, Turkey and West Midlands, United Kingdom); Aeronautics Cluster (Andalucía, Spain) (OECD, 2013, p. 50).

Moreover, Aranguren and Wilson (2013) asked themselves what we could learn from cluster policies for fostering regional smart specialization, but the question that needs to be asked first is: is there added value of RIS3 policies compared to cluster policies? This critique mainly stems from the lacking arguments in favour of the value added of the new smart specialization policies in comparison to existing regional innovation policies, such as cluster policies (see also Kiese, 2013).

Even Foray (2015, p. 82) admits that one failure many regional policy-makers make when thinking about a smart specialization strategy is that they ' … simply recycle cluster programmes'.[1] Also Morgan (2017) stresses that smart specialization does not start from scratch: due to policy path dependence and cognitive lock-ins among policy-makers, they are often relabel former cluster policies (see also Pugh, 2018; Valdaliso, Magro, Navarro, Aranguren, & Wilson, 2014).

Foray (2015) does as if, so far, regional innovation policy has only consisted of horizontal measures (financial aid schemes, SME support, technology transfer), whereas smart specialization is the first vertical measure, selecting promising activities in a non-neutral manner. However, cluster policies have been doing just that. In fact, according to Foray (2015, p. 15) smart specialization strategies can be seen as a continuation of cluster policies as they focus on existing structures. These existing structures could well be supported by cluster policies, so should regional policy-makers get rid of existing cluster policies and replace them with a smart specialization strategy? Why should they? Other similarities with cluster policies include the level of granularity, which is neither the sectoral nor the individual level ('mid-grained level of aggregation'), as well as its inclusive nature: each sector and each territory has a chance to be included: no longer a rigid line between traditional and modern sectors (Foray, 2015, p. 3). Moreover, both cluster and smart specialization policies encourage concentration, which is regarded as crucial, as through concentration, critical mass (scale) and agglomeration economies and knowledge spillovers can be achieved.

However, in some aspects smart specialization strategy can also be considered as a break with cluster policies, such as the particularity of the early effort and how new activities and domains are opened (Foray, 2015). This early effort should avoid the herd instinct effect of following best practices that has been criticized about cluster policies (Kiese, 2013). The entrepreneurial discovery process, in particular, started by entrepreneurs and researchers is seen as the main source of information, not administrators, politicians and policy-makers (Foray, 2015, p. 3). However, in principle, this could also be the procedure of bottom-up cluster policy initiatives (Fromhold-Eisebith & Eisebith, 2005).

6. Entrepreneurial discovery process: a transformative hope or a lock-in trap?

According to smart specialization, countries and regions should identify strategic 'domains' of existing and/or potential competitive advantage, where they can specialize and create capabilities in a different way compared to other countries and regions (Asheim, 2019), which should lead to structural change. According to Foray, David, and Hall (2011), such structural change takes four forms: transition, modernization, regional diversification and radical formation. Transition refers to the fact that a new domain can emerge from the existing industrial commons (the collective R&D, engineering and manufacturing capabilities that sustain innovation). Modernization refers to the development of specific applications of a general-purpose technology that have a significant impact in terms of efficiency and quality in an existing sector. Regional diversification indicates the development of a new line of productive activity based on regional assets. A fourth pattern involves the radical formation within the region of an entirely new and distinct domain of enterprise. Such radical foundation involves the co-emergence of an R&D/innovation activity and the related business activity.

Therefore, transforming the economic structure of a region is one of the key aims of the smart specialization strategy. The transformative hope of smart specialization, according to Foray (2015), lies in the potential of individual entrepreneurial discovery processes to contribute to the rest of the regional economy with the help of knowledge spillovers. Entrepreneurial discovery is defined as a process in which entrepreneurial actors (both firms and non-firms actors, such as researchers at universities and public research establishments) in a region explore and discover new and innovative activities, which is called a domain, which in turn leads to innovation and transformation of the regional economy. In some cases, this involves a strategic interaction between the government and the private sector (Foray et al., 2009, p. 26; Aranguren, Magro, Navarro, & Wilson, 2019). Regional actors involved in an entrepreneurial discovery process can stem from a certain cluster or industry, but not necessarily so.

If used properly, the entrepreneurial discovery process is a useful tool for identifying sectoral comparative advantages in regions. In reality, however, such a transformative hope towards a better economic structure is most often turned into a delusion if one considers: (1) the vested interest groups that need to be incorporated in this process, and (2) the geographical diversity of entrepreneurship in many countries and regions (Fritsch & Storey, 2014; Stuetzer et al., 2016). According to Sotarauta (2018), selecting entrepreneurial discovery processes is not just a technological process that aims at selecting industries that contain competitive advantages, but it is a very complicated social and political process, where issues such as power, vested interests of different groups, etc., need to be taken into account (see also Magro & Wilson, 2018). Similarly, Grillitsch (2016, p. 22) states that 'picking winners, rent-seeking behaviour, corruption and lock-ins … are typically associated with place-based policies, such as smart specialisation'. A lack of hard institutions, good governance and political goodwill, will jeopardize the good intention of the smart specialization policy (Rodríguez-Pose, 2013). Moreover, the presence of regional differences in terms of entrepreneurial culture, as well as the dynamics of new firm formation within Europe and beyond also make the transformation in certain regions with low level of entrepreneurial activities very difficult (Audretsch, Belitski, & Desai, 2018; Dodd, Jack, & Anderson, 2013; Down, 2013; Goldschlag & Tabarrok, 2018).

The second critical aspect concerning entrepreneurial discovery process is whether this process will lead regions to lock-out from negative path dependence (Martin & Sunley, 2006) or regional lock-ins (Hassink, 2010; Martin, 2010). While the RIS3 consist of wishful thinking that entrepreneurial discovery process will lead regions to lock out of negative path dependence, the decision-making and domain-selection activities of local stakeholders are often influenced by rent-seeking behavior and hence lead to negative lock-ins (Boschma, 2014). The latter threat is particularly existent due to the focus of smart specialization on pre-existing economic structures. This could not only be researched in the USA, to which Foray (2015) refers in his conceptual work (Sull, 2001), but also in Europe, in which there are plenty of examples of old industrial areas, which have been suffering from all kind of lock-ins hindering transformation, diversification and modernization (Hassink, 2010, 2017). Potentially negative lock-ins might be worsened by local myopia (see Uyarra, Marzocchi, & Sorvik, 2018) and this shows why non-local resources are key to avoid them (Boschma, 2014, p. 7). In theory, local stakeholders are supposed to look for resources, technologies and competences both within and outside of the region. This is also stressed by Rodríguez-Pose, Di Cataldo, and Rainoldi (2014, p. 10) as they state: the smart specialization approach is expected to help 'inefficient regional administrations become accustomed to external connections and be confronted with practices and experience coming from outside, challenging inertia and clientelism which prevail in locked-in systems'. Even though geographical openness (pipelines) is potentially important for the entrepreneurial discovery process, in practice, however, the geography of smart specialization is still very local. This is because local political stakeholders are supposed to strengthen existing structures and have a strong vested interest in keeping the money in the region (this is similar to cluster policy, see Schmidt, Müller, Ibert, & Brinks, 2018). Moreover, many local political stakeholders lack sufficient knowledge about the international competitive position of local activities, leading to suboptimal decisions from an international, competitive point of view. Recent empirical research confirms the problem of local myopia. Iacobucci and Guzzini (2016) found that inter-regional connections between the chosen domains was a neglected area of analysis in smart specialization documents. According to Radosevic and Stancova (2018), there is both a poor understanding of the opportunities offered by trans-regional cooperation, as well as insufficient interest or capacity to explore and support trans-regional cooperation.

Thirdly, and related to the earlier discussion on lock-outs and lock-ins, it is questionable if structural change should only be achieved by incremental structural change that is related to existing structures. In fact, recent literature on unrelated variety and unrelated knowledge combination both in peripheral and core regions provides some counter evidence (e.g. Asheim, 2019; Asheim et al., 2017; Lo Turco & Maggioni, 2018; Neffke, Hartog, Boschma, & Henning, 2018; Trippl, Grillitsch, & Isaksen, 2018; Zhu, He, & Zhou, 2017). Neffke et al. (2018), for instance, argue that the related unrelated diversification required for structural change mostly originated via new establishments, especially via those with nonlocal roots. Asheim (2019) claims that a long-term perspective is necessary to promote fundamental structural changes in the economy through transformative activities as part of a RIS3 strategy. Only applying a short- and medium-term perspective limits the scope for new policy initiatives. It thus limits the scope for promoting economic activities that have higher knowledge and technology complexity than previous industries but have lower relatedness to the region's existing knowledge base. Moreover, the applications of general-purpose technologies, such as artificial intelligence, to (traditional) economic sectors are in many cases still in an embryonic stage, and hence not fully occupied by core regions yet, leaving the windows of opportunity open for all regions. The recent sustainability transition literature has supported this argument. In the case of solar thermal energy in China, Dezhou, which is a latecomer city, was able to leapfrog to environmentally friendly technologies as they are less locked in by existing technological regimes (Yu & Gibbs, 2018). In addition to supporting vertical smart specialization, therefore, lagging regions should also have policy portfolios to support their horizontal research and innovation capabilities, so that they would not run the risk of further lagging behind in the current and future rounds of the digital and knowledge economy.

Overall, while entrepreneurial discovery process is in principle a good tool to select regional sectoral priorities, we argue that the vested interest groups included and the related rent-seeking behavior, as well as the strong dependence on pre-existing economic structures and conditions, and the consequential high risk of lock-ins, make the entrepreneurial discovery process a rather delusional hope.

7. Which type of region tends to benefit from smart specialization?

Smart specialization is claimed to be beneficial to all types of region, be they global metropolitan regions, specialized old industrial areas or structurally weak peripheral regions. However, most illustrative examples of smart specialization are located in structurally strong regions. Foray (2015), for instance, presents several cases with the typical phenomena of smart specialization, namely entrepreneurial discovery and spillovers, agglomeration effects, leading to structural changes, in economically strong regions in Switzerland or France. This is a little bit like looking at Silicon Valley to learn something about clusters.

Moreover, the successful examples chosen by smart specialization proponents also tend to be located in relatively small regions, which might implicitly indicate that structural change is more possible in relatively small regional economies where a successful entrepreneurial discovery process can really lead to a transformation of an existing cluster. However, in large regional economies, such as Baden-Württemberg, such a process might very likely resemble a drop in the ocean. Therefore, in this sense, size really matters. Moreover, as observed by Trippl, Zukauskaite, and Healy (2019), while organizationally thick regions may be better prepared for smart specialization, these regions also face difficulties to make tough choices as regards to whom to include in the smart specialization practice and how to balance the needs and ideas of a large number of capable actors.

Whilst the logic of smart specialization seems to work well in the context of developed regions, its application in peripheral regions has proven more challenging, suggesting a persistence of the so-called European regional innovation paradox (Uyarra et al., 2018). The latter refers to the mismatch between the large need for innovation in structurally weak regions and their low absorptive capacity to use innovation funds (Hassink & Marques, 2016; Marques & Morgan, 2018; Muscio, Reid, & Rivera Leon, 2015; Oughton, Landabaso, & Morgan, 2002; Papamichail, Rosiello, & Wield, 2019). Therefore, smart specialization might only be successful in regions where the right horizontal measures are in place. However, smart specialization is supposed to boost the economy of structurally weak regions, as it is an ex-ante condition for receiving support from European Structural and Investment Funds (Landabaso, 2014).

The key question, however, is: do structurally weak regions also benefit from smart specialization? There are several reasons why one might be sceptical. First, the existing structures on which the smart specialization builds might be too weak in structurally weak regions. Therefore, it might be no coincidence that most successful cases presented in the theoretical literature are located in structurally strong regions (Foray, 2015). Secondly, the strategy puts high demands on the institutional capabilities in regions to select the right entrepreneurial discovery processes (Capello & Kroll, 2016; Kroll, 2015), as well as to guarantee that both sleeping giants, excited goblins and hungry dwarfs are included.[2] However, one might doubt whether one can find these capabilities to a satisfactory extent in structurally weak regions. Moreover, Foray (2015, p. 56) stresses the complementarity between smart specialization strategy and horizontal instruments with the general regional innovation policy that is available in a region. That means, however, that if structurally weak regions have only weakly developed horizontal measures, which is often the case, they will not be able to develop complementary smart specialization strategies. Recent research has shown that institutional and governance capabilities are particularly weak in the structurally weak regions in Southern and Eastern Europe

(Rodríguez-Pose & Garcilazo, 2015), which casts doubts about their capability to devise a sound smart specialization strategy. This issue is related to the literature on the innovation paradox, mentioned earlier. Capello and Kroll (2016) summarize these obstacles as lack of interest, lack of ability and general politics. However, while in general structurally weak regions are not fully capable of doing the smart specialization as prescribed by the EU, recent evidence has shown that they benefit from policy learning and system building efforts (Trippl et al., 2019). In a similar vein, Kroll (2015) also argues that the main merit of RIS3 processes may lie in their contribution to changing routines and practices of governance. In sum, although smart specialization strategies are supposed to boost the economies of structurally weak regions, we doubt whether they will be able to achieve this aim.

8. How to measure the effects of smart specialization?

Measurements are important for smart specialization both to assess the potential in a regional economy to set up a strategy and its core entrepreneurial discovery process, but also to evaluate the effects of a strategy after it has been carried out. According to Foray (2015, p. 6, 7) specialization is not simply about location quotients, but it is about the regional concentration of knowledge and competences that gives rise to locational effects. Analyzing the indicators used in the literature, there is so far a strong focus on using patent data, as well as other quantitative indicators, such as surveys, to measure both the potential and the effects of the strategies (see Balland et al., 2018; D'Adda, Guzzini, Iacobucci, & Palloni, 2018; Kogler, Essletzbichler, & Rigby, 2017; Kroll, 2015; Varga, Sebestyén, Szabó, & Szerb, 2018). While such quantitative measures might be useful in indicating the outcomes of the policy, qualitative methods are essential, since smart specialization and particular the entrepreneurial discovery process is a qualitative concept, as also becomes clear from cases described by Foray (2015). To use employment data in order to judge structural changes in a regional economy is also problematic, since structural changes taking place within an industry might not be revealed just by analyzing these quantitative data (see for instance the case of the textile industry in Westmünsterland, Germany, in Hassink, 2007). Therefore, to fully understand the features of entrepreneurial discovery processes, as well as structural change in the regional economy we also need qualitative methods (Grillitsch & Asheim, 2018). Innovation biography, for instance, could be an appropriate qualitative method to soundly analyze an entrepreneurial discovery process, taking into account the main actors, the origin of their ideas and the development of the process in different steps (see Butzin & Widmaier, 2016; Manniche & Testa, 2018). Overall, we are convinced that a clever method mix is necessary to assess and measure both the potential for smart specialization in a regional economy, the actual emergence and development of an entrepreneurial discovery process and the overall effect of the strategy on structural change in a regional economy.

9. Conclusions

As stated in the introduction, recently both policy-makers and academics have paid much attention to smart specialization. It represents an explicit, place-based and place-sensitive approach, emphasizing prioritization and selectively through non-neutral, vertical policies aiming at diversified specialization. The aim of this paper was to pause for a moment and contemplate on the maelstrom of literature on this concept and strategy. To be fair, smart specialization as a policy strategy has been developed in a very short time period (Foray, 2015, p. 7). Therefore, there has been little time between conceptualization and implementation.

We agree with Boschma (2014) that smart specialization has many positive characteristics as a place-based and place-sensitive regional innovation policy strategy. It focuses on knowledge and innovation and stresses that one-size-fits-all policy and starting-from-scratch are wrong. It also takes region-specific needs and resources into account. Moreover, it emphasizes local demand (needs and potentials) as a potential driver for innovation and expedites agglomeration processes by reducing double investments. It also encourages regional players, particularly regional governments to particularize themselves, leading to a concentration of resources in those areas or activities that are likely to effectively transform the existing economic structure through R&D and innovation. Finally, it encourages the participation of a large group of different regional actors (beyond just firms) in entrepreneurial discovery processes.

However, as we have pointed out in this paper, there are six critical questions deserving more examination. These six questions, which are inter-related to each other, can be seen as a constructive critique, from which we can draw questions for future research.

First, since scholars have been discussing many related terms (e.g. diversification, regional branching, relatedness, variety, etc.) under the umbrella of smart specialization, conceptual confusion and fuzziness have been increasing. Particularly the lacking distinction between specialization and diversification has been problematic. What does the smart specialization concept offer compared to these other concepts? Why should all regional economies further specialize, whereas in some cases diversification might the better strategy?

Second, smart specialization strategies and their value added have been insufficiently discussed in a broader framework of regional innovation policies and trends in innovation policy in general. How do smart specialization strategies fit into overall regional innovation policies? To what extent do these strategies complement existing regional innovation policies? To what extent do smart specialization strategies aim at tackling grand challenges such as sustainability transitions?

Thirdly, and related to the second question, to what extent do smart specialization strategies differ from cluster policies? Are they really new and a break with the past or just a continuation of existing cluster policies under a new label?

Fourthly, entrepreneurial discovery processes have been questioned as a tool to set in motion structural changes of a regional economy. Can they really lead to an economic structural change, or are they putting a region in various lock-in risks, given the focus on existing structures and the potential influence of vested interests on key decisions about priorities? In addition, which kind of institutional conflicts can emerge because of the tension between locking in and locking out?

Fifthly, since most structurally weak regions have a weak existing structure and limited institutional capabilities, they might lack enough potential to develop promising entrepreneurial discovery processes. This, in turn, might increase instead of reducing regional economic inequalities. So the key question for future research is: what exactly hinders smart specialization strategies from being successful in structurally weak regions? And are there differences between different kind of structurally weak regions, such as peripheral, sparsely populated regions and old industrial regions?

Sixthly and finally, we have expressed doubts about the focus on quantitative indicators and data, such as patent data, in measuring the effects of what can be regarded a qualitative concept and strategy. So future research might tackle questions such as: what alternative measures and indicators are available to measure the effects of smart specialization strategies, in general, and entrepreneurial discovery processes, in particular? What is the ideal mix of quantitative and qualitative methods to assess the effects of smart specialization strategies on structural change in a regional economy?

On a more fundamental level, two additional issues should be raised. First, the sole focus on entrepreneurship, though broadly defined, might be questioned, as in fact, co-operatives are recently discussed in the literature as an alternative, promising form of regional economic development (Nicholls, 2012). Secondly, although smart specialization cherishes high hopes for linking existing economic structures in structurally weak regions with several general-purpose technologies and key enabling technologies, such as ICT, in fact, the European Union lacks competitive strength in exploiting many of these technologies. It shows that smart specialization can only be successful if it is carried out in tandem with policies fostering the explorative as well as the exploitative subsystems of the innovation systems (Asheim, 2019).

To address many of these issues in future research requires a rethinking of the theoretical embedding of the smart specialization concept. Foray (2015, p. 16) considers particularly the paradigm of evolutionary economic geography (Boschma & Frenken, 2018) as the theoretical paradigm behind smart specialization. However, in order to deal with most of the issues raised in this paper, we would suggest to embed smart specialization in a broader set of theories and paradigms of economic geography (Hassink, Klaerding, & Marques, 2014). They can namely provide better answers to questions about power relations, governance issues and the evolution of networks, as well as co-evolution (Gong & Hassink, 2019).

Overall, we are sympathetic to most of the elements of smart specialization. However, we have also detected several critical issues, such as vested interests, the weak institutional capacities of structurally weak regions, the limited attention paid to extra-regional sources and the strong overlap with cluster policies. In our view, these critical issues should deserve special attention in future research on the concept of smart specialization and smart specialization strategies.

Notes

1. There still seems to be confusion on how smart specialization strategies differs from cluster policy. One of the authors, for instance, asked at the Kick-off Conference of Maritime Stakeholder Platform in the Baltic Sea Region, supported by the European Commission, in Kiel, 26–27 March 2015, in a Session on Smart Specialization what smart specialization could add to existing cluster policies around the Baltic Sea and nobody could give a satisfying answer.
2. Regional institutional capacity is influenced by national political-administrative systems, giving regions in federal systems more autonomy and often a stronger capacity than regions in centralized systems (see Baier, Kroll, & Zenker, 2013).

Disclosure statement

No potential conflict of interest was reported by the authors.

ORCID

Robert Hassink ● http://orcid.org/0000-0001-7524-4577
Huiwen Gong ● http://orcid.org/0000-0002-4764-6867

References

Aprahamian, A., & Correa, P. G. (eds.). (2015). *Smart specialization in Croatia: Inputs from Trade, innovation, and productivity analysis. Directions in development – countries and regions*. Washington, DC: World Bank.

Aranguren, M. J., Magro, E., Navarro, M., & Wilson, J. R. (2019). Governance of the territorial entrepreneurial discovery process: Looking under the bonnet of RIS3. *Regional Studies*, *53*, 451–461. doi:10.1080/00343404.2018.1462484

Aranguren, M. J., & Wilson, J. R. (2013). What can experience with clusters teach us about fostering regional smart specialisation. *Ekonomiaz*, *83*, 126–145.

Asheim, B., Grillitsch, M., & Trippl, M. (2017). Introduction: Combinatorial knowledge bases, regional innovation, and development dynamics. *Economic Geography*, *93*, 429–435. doi:10.1080/00130095.2017.1380775

Asheim, B. T. (2019). Smart specialisation, innovation policy and regional innovation systems: What about new path development in less innovative regions? *Innovation: The European Journal of Social Science Research*, *32*, 8–25. doi:10.1080/13511610.2018.1491001

Asheim, B. T., & Coenen, L. (2005). Knowledge bases and regional innovation systems: Comparing Nordic clusters. *Research Policy*, *34*, 1173–1190. doi:10.1016/j.respol.2005.03.013

Asheim, B. T., Isaksen, A., Nauwelaers, C., & Tödtling, F. (2003). *Regional innovation policy for small-medium enterprises*. Cheltenham: Edward Elgar.

Audretsch, D. B., Belitski, M., & Desai, S. (2018). National business regulations and city entrepreneurship in Europe: A multilevel nested analysis. *Entrepreneurship Theory and Practice* (forthcoming). doi:10.1177/1042258718774916

Baier, E., Kroll, H., & Zenker, A. (2013). *Regional autonomy with regard to innovation policy: A differentiated illustration of the European status quo*. Karlsruhe: Working Papers Firms and Region, No. R3/2013.

Balland, P. A., Boschma, R., Crespo, J., & Rigby, D. L. (2018). Smart specialization policy in the European Union: Relatedness, knowledge complexity and regional diversification. *Regional Studies* (forthcoming). doi:10.1080/00343404.2018.1437900

Barca, F., McCann, P., & Rodríguez-Pose, A. (2012). The case for regional development intervention: Place-based versus place-neutral approaches. *Journal of Regional Science*, *52*, 134–152. doi:10.1111/j.1467-9787.2011.00756.x

Boschma, R. (2014). Constructing regional advantage and smart specialisation: Comparison of two European policy concepts. *Scienze Regionali*, *13*, 51–68. doi:10.3280/SCRE2014-001004

Boschma, R., & Frenken, K. (2018). Evolutionary economic geography. In G. Clark, M. Gertler, M. P. Feldman, & D. Wójcik (Eds.), *The New Oxford Handbook of economic geography* (pp. 213–229). Oxford: Oxford University Press.

Boschma, R., & Gianelle, C. (2013). *Regional branching and smart specialization policy*. JRC technical reports, (06/2104).

Butzin, A., & Widmaier, B. (2016). Exploring territorial knowledge dynamics through innovation biographies. *Regional Studies*, *50*, 220–232. doi:10.1080/00343404.2014.1001353

Capello, R., & Kroll, H. (2016). From theory to practice in smart specialization strategy: Emerging limits and possible future trajectories. *European Planning Studies*, *24*, 1393–1406. doi:10.1080/09654313.2016.1156058

Coenen, L., Hansen, T., & Rekers, J. V. (2015). Innovation policy for grand challenges: An economic geography perspective. *Geography Compass*, 9, 483–496. doi:10.1111/gec3.12231

Coenen, L., & Morgan, K. (2019). Evolving geographies of innovation: Existing paradigms, critiques and possible alternatives. *Norsk Geografisk Tidsskrift*.

Cooke, P. (2012). *Complex adaptive innovation systems: Relatedness and transversality in the evolving region*. London: Routledge.

Cooke, P., & Morgan, K. (1998). *The associational economy: Firms, regions, and innovation*. Oxford: Oxford University Press.

Cooke, P., Uranga, M. G., & Etxebarria, G. (1997). Regional innovation systems: Institutional and organisational dimensions. *Research Policy*, 26, 475–491. doi:10.1016/S0048-7333(97)00025-5

D'Adda, D., Guzzini, E., Iacobucci, D., & Palloni, R. (2019). Is smart specialisation strategy coherent with regional innovative capabilities? *Regional Studies*, 53, 1004–1016. doi:10.1080/00343404.2018.1523542

Dodd, S. D., Jack, S., & Anderson, A. R. (2013). From admiration to abhorrence: The contentious appeal of entrepreneurship across Europe. *Entrepreneurship & Regional Development*, 25, 69–89. doi:10.1080/08985626.2012.746878

Down, S. (2013). The distinctiveness of the European tradition in entrepreneurship research. *Entrepreneurship & Regional Development*, 25, 1–4. doi:10.1080/08985626.2012.746876

Fellnhofer, K. (2018). Visualized bibliometric mapping on smart specialization: A co-citation analysis. *International Journal of Knowledge-based Development*, 9, 76–99. doi:10.1504/IJKBD.2018.090502

Foray, D. (2015). *Smart specialisation: Opportunities and challenges for regional innovation policy*. Abingdon: Routledge/ Regional Studies Association.

Foray, D. (2018). Smart specialization strategies as a case of mission-oriented policy – a case study on the emergence of new policy practices. *Industrial and Corporate Change*, 27, 817–832. doi:10.1093/icc/dty030

Foray, D., David, P. A., & Hall, B. H. (2009). Smart specialisation: The concept. In E. Commission (Ed.), *Knowledge for growth: Prospects for science, technology and innovation* (pp. 25–29). Brussels: European Commission. DG Research.

Foray, D., David, P. A., & Hall, B. H. (2011). Smart specialization. From academic idea to political instrument, the surprising career of a concept and the difficulties involved in its implementation. MTEI-working paper, November 2011, Lausanne.

Frenken, K., Van Oort, F., & Verburg, T. (2007). Related variety, unrelated variety and regional economic growth. *Regional Studies*, 41, 685–697. doi:10.1080/00343400601120296

Fritsch, M., & Stephan, A. (2005). Regionalization of innovation policy – introduction to the special issue. *Research Policy*, 34, 1123–1127. doi:10.1016/j.respol.2005.05.013

Fritsch, M., & Storey, D. J. (2014). Entrepreneurship in a regional context: Historical roots, recent developments and future challenges. *Regional Studies*, 48, 939–954. doi:10.1080/00343404.2014.892574

Fromhold-Eisebith, M., & Eisebith, G. (2005). How to institutionalize innovative clusters? Comparing explicit top-down and implicit bottom-up approaches. *Research Policy*, 34, 1250–1268. doi:10.1016/j.respol.2005.02.008

Gianelle, C., Guzzo, F., & Mieszkowski, K. (2019). Smart specialisation: What gets lost in translation from concept to practice? *Regional Studies* (forthcoming). doi:10.1080/00343404.2019.1607970

Goldschlag, N., & Tabarrok, A. (2018). Is regulation to blame for the decline in American entrepreneurship? *Economic Policy*, 33, 5–44. doi:10.1093/epolic/eix019

Gong, H., & Hassink, R. (2019). Co-evolution in contemporary economic geography: Towards a theoretical framework. *Regional Studies*, 53, 1344–1355. doi:10.1080/00343404.2018.1494824

Grillitsch, M. (2016). Institutions, smart specialisation dynamics and policy. *Environment and Planning C: Government and Policy*, 34, 22–37. doi:10.1177/0263774X15614694

Grillitsch, M., & Asheim, B. (2018). Place-based innovation policy for industrial diversification in regions. *European Planning Studies*, 26, 1638–1662. doi:10.1080/09654313.2018.1484892

Hassink, R. (1992). *Regional innovation policy: Case-studies from the Ruhr area, Baden-Württemberg and the North East of England*. Utrecht: Nederlandse Geografische Studies.

Hassink, R. (2007). The strength of weak lock-ins: The renewal of the Westmünsterland textile industry. *Environment and Planning A, 39*, 1147–1165. doi:10.1068/a3848

Hassink, R. (2010). Locked in decline? On the role of regional lock-ins in old industrial areas. In R. Boschma & R. Martin (Eds.), *Handbook of evolutionary economic geography* (pp. 450–468). Cheltenham: Edward Elgar.

Hassink, R. (2017). Cluster decline and political lock-ins. In F. Belussi & J.-L. Hervas-Oliver (Eds.), *Unfolding cluster evolution* (pp. 190–202). London: Routledge.

Hassink, R., Klaerding, C., & Marques, P. (2014). Advancing evolutionary economic geography by engaged pluralism. *Regional Studies, 48*, 1295–1307. doi:10.1080/00343404.2014.889815

Hassink, R., & Lagendijk, A. (2001). The dilemmas of interregional institutional learning. *Environment and Planning C, 19*, 65–84. doi:10.1068/c9943

Hassink, R., & Marques, P. (2016). The regional innovation paradox revisited. In U. Hilpert (Ed.), *Routledge Handbook of politics and technology* (pp. 120–131). Abingdon: Routledge.

Iacobucci, D., & Guzzini, E. (2016). Relatedness and connectivity in technological domains: Missing links in S3 design and implementation. *European Planning Studies, 24*, 1511–1526. doi:10.1080/09654313.2016.1170108

Isaksen, A., Martin, R., & Trippl, M. (2018). *New avenues for regional innovation systems: Theoretical Advances, empirical cases and policy lessons*. Cham: Springer.

Kiese, M. (2013). Von Clusterpolitik zur intelligenten Spezialisierung: Ein Schritt in die richtige Richtung? Presentation at Workshop 'Ist Spezialisierung intelligent?' Frankfurt am Main, 18 December 2013.

Kogler, D. F., Essletzbichler, J., & Rigby, D. L. (2017). The evolution of specialization in the EU15 knowledge space. *Journal of Economic Geography, 17*, 345–373. doi:10.1093/jeg/lbw024

Kroll, H. (2015). Efforts to implement smart specialization in practice – leading unlike horses to the water. *European Planning Studies, 23*, 2079–2098. doi:10.1080/09654313.2014.1003036

Landabaso, M. (1997). The promotion of innovation in regional policy: Proposals for a regional innovation strategy. *Entrepreneurship & Regional Development, 9*, 1–24. doi:10.1080/08985629700000001

Landabaso, M. (2014). Guest editorial on research and innovation strategies for smart specialisation in Europe: Theory and practice of new innovation policy approaches. *European Journal of Innovation Management, 17*, 378–389. doi:10.1108/EJIM-08-2014-0093

Lo Turco, A., & Maggioni, D. (2018). Local discoveries and technological relatedness: The role of MNEs, imports and domestic capabilities. *Journal of Economic Geography* (forthcoming). doi:10.1093/jeg/lby060

Magro, E., & Wilson, J. R. (2018). Policy-mix evaluation: Governance challenges from new place-based innovation policies. *Research Policy* (forthcoming). doi:10.1016/j.respol.2018.06.010

Manniche, J., & Testa, S. (2018). Towards a multi-levelled social process perspective on firm innovation: Integrating micro, meso and macro concepts of knowledge creation. *Industry and Innovation, 25*, 365–388. doi:10.1080/13662716.2017.1414746

Marques, P., & Morgan, K. (2018). The heroic assumptions of smart specialisation: A sympathetic critique of regional innovation policy. In A. Isaksen, R. Martin, & M. Trippl (Eds.), *New avenues for regional innovation systems-theoretical advances, empirical cases and policy lessons* (pp. 275–293). Cham: Springer.

Martin, R. (2010). Roepke lecture in economic geography-rethinking regional path dependence: Beyond lock-in to evolution. *Economic Geography, 86*, 1–27. doi:10.1111/j.1944-8287.2009.01056.x

Martin, R., & Sunley, P. (2006). Path dependence and regional economic evolution. *Journal of Economic Geography, 6*, 395–437. doi:10.1093/jeg/lbl012

Mazzucato, M. (2018). Mission-oriented innovation policies: Challenges and opportunities. *Industrial and Corporate Change, 27*, 803–815. doi:10.1093/icc/dty034

McCann, P., & Ortega-Argilés, R. (2013). Modern regional innovation policy. *Cambridge Journal of Regions, Economy and Society, 6*, 187–216. doi:10.1093/cjres/rst007

McCann, P., & Ortega-Argilés, R. (2015). Smart specialization, regional growth and applications to European Union cohesion policy. *Regional Studies, 49*, 1291–1302. doi:10.1080/00343404.2013.799769

Morgan, K. (2017). Nurturing novelty: Regional innovation policy in the age of smart specialisation. *Environment and Planning C, 35*, 569–583. doi:10.1177/0263774X16645106

Moulaert, F. (2013). *The international handbook on social innovation: Collective action, social learning and transdisciplinary research*. Cheltenham: Edward Elgar.

Moulaert, F., & Sekia, F. (2003). Territorial innovation models: A critical survey. *Regional Studies, 37*, 289–302. doi:10.1080/0034340032000065442

Muscio, A., Reid, A., & Rivera Leon, L. (2015). An empirical test of the regional innovation paradox: Can smart specialisation overcome the paradox in Central and Eastern Europe? *Journal of Economic Policy Reform, 18*, 153–171. doi:10.1080/17487870.2015.1013545

Neffke, F., Hartog, M., Boschma, R., & Henning, M. (2018). Agents of structural change: The role of firms and entrepreneurs in regional diversification. *Economic Geography, 94*, 23–48. doi:10.1080/00130095.2017.1391691

Nicholls, A. (2012). Editorial: 'The world turned upside down'. *Journal of Social Entrepreneurship, 3*, 1–5. doi:10.1080/19420676.2012.665633

OECD. (2011). *Regions and innovation policy, OECD Reviews of regional innovation*. Paris: Author.

OECD. (2013). *Innovation-driven growth in regions: The role of smart specialisation*. Paris: Author.

Oughton, C., Landabaso, M., & Morgan, K. (2002). The regional innovation paradox: Innovation policy and industrial policy. *The Journal of Technology Transfer, 27*, 97–110. doi:10.1023/A:1013104805703

Papamichail, G., Rosiello, A., & Wield, D. (2019). Capacity-building barriers to S3 implementation: An empirical framework for catch-up regions. *Innovation: The European Journal of Social Science Research, 32*, 66–84. doi:10.1080/13511610.2018.1537844

Piirainen, K. A., Tanner, A. N., & Alkærsig, L. (2017). Regional foresight and dynamics of smart specialization: A typology of regional diversification patterns. *Technological Forecasting and Social Change, 115*, 289–300. doi:10.1016/j.techfore.2016.06.027

Prange, H. (2008). Explaining varieties of regional innovation policies in Europe. *European Urban and Regional Studies, 15*, 39–52. doi:10.1177/0969776407081276

Pugh, R. (2018). Questioning the implementation of smart specialisation: Regional innovation policy and semi-autonomous regions. *Environment and Planning C, 36*, 530–547. doi:10.1177/2399654417717069

Radosevic, S., Curaj, A., Gheorghiu, R., Andreescu, L., & Wade, I. (eds.). (2017). *Advances in the theory and practice of smart specialization*. London: Academic Press.

Radosevic, S., & Stancova, K. C. (2018). Internationalising smart specialisation: Assessment and issues in the case of EU new member states. *Journal of the Knowledge Economy, 9*, 263–293. doi:10.1007/s13132-015-0339-3

Rodríguez-Pose, A. (2013). Do institutions matter for regional development? *Regional Studies, 47*, 1034–1047. doi:10.1080/00343404.2012.748978

Rodríguez-Pose, A. (2018). The revenge of the places that don't matter (and what to do about it). *Cambridge Journal of Regions, Economy and Society, 11*, 189–209. doi:10.1093/cjres/rsx024

Rodríguez-Pose, A., Di Cataldo, M., & Rainoldi, A. (2014). *The role of government institutions for smart specialisation and regional development*. Publications Office of the European Union.

Rodríguez-Pose, A., & Garcilazo, E. (2015). Quality of government and the returns of investment: Examining the impact of cohesion expenditure in European regions. *Regional Studies, 49*, 1274–1290. doi:10.1080/00343404.2015.1007933

Schmidt, S., Müller, F. C., Ibert, O., & Brinks, V. (2018). Open region: Creating and exploiting opportunities for innovation at the regional scale. *European Urban and Regional Studies, 25*, 187–205. doi:10.1177/0969776417705942

Schot, J., & Steinmueller, W. E. (2018). Three frames for innovation policy: R&D, systems of innovation and transformative change. *Research Policy, 47*, 1554–1567. doi:10.1016/j.respol.2018.08.011

Sotarauta, M. (2018). Smart specialization and place leadership: Dreaming about shared visions, falling into policy traps? *Regional Studies, Regional Science, 5*, 190–203. doi:10.1080/21681376.2018.1480902

Stuetzer, M., Obschonka, M., Audretsch, D. B., Wyrwich, M., Rentfrow, P. J., Coombes, M., … Satchell, M. (2016). Industry structure, entrepreneurship, and culture: An empirical analysis using historical coalfields. *European Economic Review, 86,* 52–72. doi:10.1016/j.euroecorev.2015.08.012

Sull, D. N. (2001). From community of innovation to community of inertia: The rise and fall of the US tire industry. *Academy of Management Proceedings, 2001,* L1–L6. doi:10.5465/apbpp.2001.6132933

Tödtling, F., & Trippl, M. (2005). One size fits all? Towards a differentiated regional innovation policy. *Research Policy, 34,* 203–1219. doi:10.1016/j.respol.2005.01.018

Trippl, M., Grillitsch, M., & Isaksen, A. (2018). Exogenous sources of regional industrial change: Attraction and absorption of non-local knowledge for new path development. *Progress in Human Geography, 42,* 687–705. doi:10.1177/0309132517700982

Trippl, M., Zukauskaite, E., & Healy, A. (2019). Shaping smart specialization: The role of place-specific factors in advanced, intermediate and less-developed European regions. *Regional Studies.*(forthcoming). doi:10.1080/00343404.2019.1582763

Uyarra, E., Flanagan, K., Magro, E., Wilson, J. R., & Sotarauta, M. (2017). Understanding regional innovation policy dynamics: Actors, agency and learning. *Environment and Planning C, 35,* 559–568. doi:10.1177/2399654417705914

Uyarra, E., Marzocchi, C., & Sorvik, J. (2018). How outward looking is smart specialisation? Rationales, drivers and barriers. *European Planning Studies, 26,* 2344–2363. doi:10.1080/09654313.2018.1529146

Valdaliso, J. M., Magro, E., Navarro, M., Aranguren, M. J., & Wilson, R. J. (2014). Path dependence in policies supporting smart specialisation strategies: Insights from the Basque case. *European Journal of Innovation Management, 17,* 390–408. doi:10.1108/EJIM-12-2013-0136

Varga, A., Sebestyén, T., Szabó, N., & Szerb, L. (2018). Estimating the economic impacts of knowledge network and entrepreneurship development in smart specialization policy. *Regional Studies.* (forthcoming). doi:10.1080/00343404.2018.1527026

Yu, Z., & Gibbs, D. (2018). Sustainability transitions and leapfrogging in latecomer cities: The development of solar thermal energy in Dezhou, China. *Regional Studies, 52,* 68–79. doi:10.1080/00343404.2016.1260706

Zhu, S., He, C., & Zhou, Y. (2017). How to jump further and catch up? Path-breaking in an uneven industry space. *Journal of Economic Geography, 17,* 521–545. doi:10.1093/jeg/lbw047

In response to 'Six critical questions about smart specialization'

Dominique Foray

ABSTRACT
This paper has been written as a response to « Six critical questions about smart specialization » by R. Hassink and H. Gong. The paper starts with a reminder of what has not changed in terms of the basic principles and *raison d'être* of smart specialization. Then it proceeds to identifying what we have learned since 2014 and on this basis it will address the six critical questions posed by Robert and Huiven.

Introduction

In 'Six critical questions about smart specialization', Robert Hassink and Huiven Gong (2019) give a very good explanation of the origin of the concept of Smart Specialisation Strategies (S3) and its application within the framework of European regional policies as from 2014, while formulating a series of pertinent questions. These questions essentially reflect and clearly express a sort of discrepancy between what was at this time an incomplete concept – and a massive and immediate implementation of the prescriptions formulated by this concept. The questions posed by Robert and Huiven are therefore very pertinent and I thought it would be interesting to attempt to answer them, based on what we have learnt since 2014, at the end of a period of implementation and interactions between practice and theory. This massive implementation has in fact constituted a vast field of more or less successful experimentation – that academic researchers have been able to observe and whose results have been integrated into the 'models' – a rapid and parallel learning process thanks to which – it seems to me – we are better prepared to answer the questions raised by Robert and Huiven. I admire Hirschman's epistemology, so well expressed in 'Development Projects Observed' (1967). Today this is the one that I endeavour to follow – in all modesty: the meticulous and systematic observation of smart specialization experiments, in Europe and beyond, based primarily on a form of participative research, allows us to propose a more robust and simple concept, whose implications regarding implementation are much more obvious and easy for the regions concerned.

With this in mind, I will start with a reminder of what has not changed in terms of the basic principles and *raison d'être* of smart specialization. Then I will identify what we have learned since 2014 and on this basis, I will address the six critical questions posed by Robert and Huiven.

I. Raison d'être and basic principles still valid !

The S3 approach focuses on the deployment of innovative activity and the establishment of new connections within and beyond the region, enabling the region concerned to transform itself and develop new competitive advantage based on these transformations. The other *raison d'être* of S3 is to encourage regions to build competitive advantage on their specific strengths, potentials and opportunities, rather than doing as others do. Thus they avoid doing the same 'good' things as others, which in the end will in many cases prove inconsistent and unrelated to the region's existing assets and potentials and does not provide any comparative advantage. Instead, the region achieves the specific critical mass needed for a significant change in the regional economy.[1]

To attain these very general objectives, the principles identified in 2009 remain valid (Foray, David, & Hall, 2009):

- *Concentrate on certain priorities*. This principle aims to generate a certain density of actors and projects that are 'related' as they are dedicated to the same priority – an imperative condition to benefit from the resulting synergies, complementarities and agglomerations, which are essential determinants of innovation, creativity and R&D productivity. This is also an important condition for a government to be able to reach the level of input 'specificity' required to innovate in a given industrial or technological domain. This has been a constant argument by Hausman and Rodrik (2006) – that 'the public inputs that innovators require tend to be highly specific in the area in question. There are really very few truly generic inputs for innovation'. But governments cannot address all specific innovation infrastructures and specific services for all markets and activities. Government capacities both in terms of information (what does each industry need in terms of specific inputs?) and resources (can we afford the provision of all industry-specific public inputs for all sectors?) are indeed limited. They need to choose.
- *Concentrate not on structures (for example the region's three most important industries) but on the transformation of these structures*. Each priority includes one or several sectors as well as a direction of change. If both elements are combined and sufficiently well defined to create the density effects mentioned above, they build a priority area, a cornerstone of a smart specialization strategy.
- *Favour an entrepreneurial discovery logic,* which means simply that the targeted transformation will not follow a path that is decided from the top but will be discovered as the process unfolds. There is therefore no *ex ante* plan, but rather a permanent process of navigation in line with the transformation objectives, which implies rigorous feedback, monitoring and flexibility mechanisms. This does not mean that objectives should not be set but rather they should be pursued and adjusted in line with emerging evidence and experience.

The S3 approach is thus marked on the one hand by a high level of intentionality and strategic focus on priorities. On the other hand, it is characterized by a high level of self-discovery and initiative by the actors of the innovation process. It is this combination of two policy logics – a planning logic and a self-discovery logic, frequently opposed in the literature and in practice – that constitutes its trademark! As so well expressed by Paul

David – one of the concept's three originators – S3 is neither totally top down nor purely bottom up. 'The S3 approach is about designing an intermediate process aiming to enhance entrepreneurial efforts and coordination within a framework (a strategic priority) structured by the government'.[2]

II. We are better at 'doing' an S3 nowadays

Thanks to the massive exercise of implementation since 2014 and the first lessons learned from it, we are now able to refine the process of design and implementation. Although the rationale is intact and the general principles remain in place, we can identify certain conditions or provisions that at the time seemed absolutely vital for the success of the approach but that henceforth seem less necessary or even useless and harmful.[3] We can consequently propose a simpler and more obvious process that regions will find easier to implement, while its effectiveness will no doubt be greater. In this section, we want to briefly discuss three issues – the three steps needed for the design and implementation of an S3; the data needed to support the policy process and whose nature changes according to the three steps; the governance mechanisms, which also evolve according to the three steps.

A. Three steps for policy actions

Instead of talking of a large number of stages within a rigid process that must be respected at all costs, it is undoubtedly wiser to suggest just three steps to regions, which they can then conduct as they like:

A. Identifying thematic priority areas
B. Translating these priority areas into transformational roadmaps
C. Implementing the transformational activities with an action plan

i. Identification of thematic priority areas

This is the starting point and must include one (or several) sector(s) with a clear direction of change. Only the subject of change (e.g. one or several sector(s)) and a direction of change together build what is called a priority area in S3.

The implication of such a definition is that not all actors will be part of S3 simply because they belong to the sector concerned. They need to belong to the sector 'while' being involved in and committed to the transformation process, which is part of the definition of the priority area. There is therefore a delicate balance to be found between a too broad and too narrow definition of the priority area. A too broad area (e.g. digitalization of healthcare) will make it difficult to generate the density and agglomeration effects, one of the crucial objectives of an S3. A too narrow area (e.g. the development of certain types of medical devices) will result in excluding some actors who were ready to be involved in some kind of transformation and thus in concentrating resources and efforts on a too small number of predetermined champions.

This identification naturally remains based on a considerable effort to acquire statistical knowledge of the economy, assess its competitive position and define the innovation capacities of the region. Furthermore, the identification relies on a participatory process aimed at bringing together a maximum number of public and private stakeholders who are best placed to know where the growing markets are and what research would best satisfy the business and societal needs of a region.

There are two important points here that we have learned and which can now help us to propose a more simple and obvious process.

First, it was argued that the priority areas should be chosen through an entrepreneurial discovery process. This provision was very difficult to follow and generated a high level of stress within the community of regional policymakers. And this was unnecessary. It is important here to avoid a classic confusion between a participatory process and entrepreneurial discovery. This point was very well expressed by our colleague M. Navarro –

> Certainly, priorities are the result of a participatory process. But not all participatory processes involve a logic of entrepreneurial discovery. In almost all the territories we have analysed the government has been the actor that has led the prioritisation process, and the role of other actors has been small or almost testimonial. In short top-down processes have prevailed over bottom-up processes in the setting of priorities.[4]

Indeed, there is not really any entrepreneurial discovery at this stage and what is needed is a more 'simple' participatory process. Having no entrepreneurial discovery here is not a problem because, as already stated, the S3 design is structured to involve two logics of policy actions – a planning mode and a self-discovery mode. Clearly, the first step (selecting a few priority areas) has a planning aspect while the second and third ones will be profoundly influenced by the entrepreneurial discovery process (below). There is therefore no room or need for an entrepreneurial discovery process at the priority area selection stage. But just wait! The entrepreneurial discovery will very quickly materialize during the following two phases.

Secondly, it was argued that regions need to identify and select region-specific priority areas and that too many cross-regional similarities at this level (many regions choosing similar priorities) were an indication of failure. Recent lessons tell us that this is not true! Priority areas can to a great extent be similar from one region to another – after all, the potential for solutions in terms of structural change is not infinite and regions characterized by the same provisions of natural resources and the same economic specializations will tend to want the same types of transformation. And now we think that it is not a big problem because regional differentiation will happen later in the process. In fact similar priorities will lead to specific solutions and transformational roadmaps because capacities, potentials and opportunities are region-specific. The translation of the priority into a transformative activity (the second step) enables regional differentiation to occur.

These two points (priorities can be similar – entrepreneurial discovery is not the right word to describe what is happening at step one) help to show how we can make the concept more obvious and simple – by helping regions to get rid of unnecessary provisions that were very detrimental to starting the process.

ii. The translation of a priority area into a transformational roadmap

This step involves the definition of the nature, scope and meaning of the investments for transformation and transition within the considered sector(s). It is important to emphasize this step because it has been observed that many regions that had correctly conducted their prioritization task found it very difficult to concretize and implement these priorities.

And yet this is the crucial phase: 'the conversion of each priority into a more concrete transformational roadmap' – a set of projects and actors – all committed to following the same direction of change – and thus linked by this common direction. The crucial and possibly only common link among projects and actors is 'to be involved in the same direction of change'. But this is enough to obtain coordination and agglomeration effects from a set of related projects and actors.

This conversion process from priority area to transformational roadmap is the most difficult one and it cannot happen if the direction of change is not known. The problem can be expressed thus: an identified priority targets a certain transformation of one or several industries – e.g. the transition of the electromechanical sector towards industry 4–0. Before S3 is designed and implemented, we are at a certain level of technology, employment and qualification, business model and performance where we are aiming to move to a higher level of digital innovation in this industry. This requires a full understanding of the obstacles to this transformation: Why haven't we already reached this level? What constraints, market and coordination failures, obstacles of all kinds prevented this evolution? How can it work? All the identified projects and actors are going to address these problems and constraints that concern 'not only R&D but enterprises with their suppliers and clients, with the need for new skills and qualifications, new forms of management and logistics, specific public goods (specialized services), and adoption of certain key technologies (diffusion)'. Here, in the identification and search for resolutions to these obstacles, is where entrepreneurial discovery kicks in.

All of these diversified projects will eventually constitute the transformative activity. The definition of a transformative activity is very simple:

> It is neither an individual project nor a sector as a whole but a collection of related capacities, projects, activities and people that have been 'extracted', as it were, from an existing structure or several structures, to which can be added extra-regional capacities and that is oriented towards a certain direction of change.

This translation of a priority into transformational roadmap in order to build and develop a transformative activity is the key transition. It enables many of the S3 objectives to be attained.

It concretizes a certain **direction** of change, initially expressed by the priority, and reveals guidelines concerning the course of action to achieve this change.

It enables the transition from priorities, which can to a great extent be similar from one region to another, to a broad regional **differentiation**. In fact, similar priorities will lead to different transformative activities as the latter are designed as a specific response to problems and opportunities that are specific to the particular region.

This is the missing link between a priority area and the individual projects. The transformative activity is a collection of related 'projects' – linked by the fact that they all contribute in one way or another to the same structural transformation in the priority area. It thus creates relational **density** and the chance to reap the benefits of a certain coordination between the projects and actors involved in this transformation. The transformative activity covers a large number of factors, including the formation of human capital, corporate management, adoption of new technologies, etc. It is therefore a collection of **distributed** capacities and projects, which cannot be reduced to the notion of a single major project (like the creation of a new specialized R&D institute, frequently destined to become the proverbial white elephant).

This is the preferred framework for entrepreneurial **discovery**. At the end of the priority definition phase, it is impossible to know what the outlines and content of the transformative activities will be. They are built and developed on the basis of the entrepreneurial discovery process.

Therefore this translation phase produces the good properties of an S3 approach, designed to transform the structures of the regional economy, and which we have grouped under the heading the **5 Ds**:

Direction of change
Relational **D**ensity
Regional **D**ifferentiation
Entrepreneurial **D**iscovery
Distributed capacities

We can add one important effect of this translation phase. It operates as a feedback mechanism to verify the pertinence of the priorities. If the transformational roadmap comprises only a few projects, projects that are not very innovative or unconnected, etc., this is an indication that the priority was perhaps badly formulated or premature. We should go back to square one and discuss the pertinence of the priority in question again.

iii. Implementation with an action plan
The action plan step centres on the implementation of the transformative activity. It involves mobilizing and coordinating financial instruments, which often have different objectives (R&D, training, infrastructures), evaluating projects regarding their financing, designing feedback mechanisms, monitoring and flexibility to maximize the informational effects and spillovers of entrepreneurial discovery – more important than ever at the transformative activity development stage.

iv. More a script than the 10 Commandments!
It is therefore quite obvious that an S3 must not rely on an immutable formula that everyone must adhere to in order to avoid failure – like the 10 Commandments! Let's leave the regions the freedom to invent their own approach, while still insisting on the necessity of adhering to the three stipulated phases. Here we can be inspired by the idea of a script: a set of simple rules like those the theatrical director gives the actor he is asking to improvise concerning a certain theme.

B. Governance

If we go back to M. Navarro's reflection, it is clear that the prioritization phase is determined by a logic of top-down governance – which does not exclude a participatory and collaborative process between all the stakeholders and in no way detracts from the evidence-based character of this prioritization process either. This means simply – as

P. A. David wrote (above) – that the framework within which the entrepreneurial discovery will take place is constructed from the top.

On the other hand, the two following phases are extremely decentralized. For each identified priority there must be a corresponding coordination and investment board that will deal with the execution of phase 2 – the conversion of the priority into transformation roadmap – and phase 3 – the elaboration of the plan of action and its implementation for the development of the transformative activity in question. This decentralization is important so that the monitoring, information and flexibility mechanisms can be as efficient as possible. Phases 2 and 3 actually correspond to an ARPA- type form of governance, featuring principles such as general organizational flexibility, bottom-up programme design, discretion regarding project selection and active project management – all these features relying on highly talented, independent and empowered programme staff (Azoulay, Fuchs, Goldstein, & Kearney, 2018).

III. On the six critical questions

We can now address the six critical questions posed by Robert and Huiven.

A. Is smart specialization about specialization or diversification?

The first lesson to be learned from this experience is that you must think twice before deciding on the title of your article! Most of the time, it's not very important, but in some cases, it matters terribly! The term 'specialization' is probably not appropriate. There is indeed the idea of concentrating, focalizing on some areas – for the two reasons mentioned in Section I. But if the idea is to concentrate, it is to better achieve transformations, and hence to avoid a specialization in technologies and business models that are soon outdated. The important thing therefore is to insist on this duality between 'specialization' (concentration of resources and choice of priorities) and transformation (diversification, transition, modernization,...). This is the essence of our concept. However, it is not well captured by the expression 'smart specialization'. We had quite quickly confided our doubts to the Commission concerning the suitability of the term – arguing that the concept of specialization in economics has a relatively negative connotation – but it was already too late!

B. How well is smart specialization embedded in existing regional innovation policies?

It seems to me that the S3 concept is a 'recombinant innovation' – in other words, its newness originates from the combination of concepts that already existed.

The K4G Group was a group composed only of innovation economists, macroeconomists working on endogenous growth and econometricians specializing in the measurement of R&D and productivity (to name a few: Aghion, David, Hall, Licht, Mairesse, Marimon, Metcalfe, Van Ark, Veugelers). This does not mean that these economists were not interested in the spatial dimension of innovation! Of course not, since the spatial dimension lies at the heart of innovation conditions and procedures and thus constitutes an integral part of the research programme of innovation economists. But this does mean that the regional system and regional governance dimensions were missing.

This is why, very rapidly, experts on regional economies and policies improved the approach – particularly as from the practical implementation phase – and among these brave pioneers, we must of course mention McCann and Ortega-Argiles (2015), Morgan (2017), Rodrigues Pose, Di Cataldo, and Rainoldi (2014), who insist especially on the constraints and limits of the regions in terms of institutional capacity to design and apply relatively sophisticated policies.

But the approach has also been considerably strengthened by the work concerning industrial and development policy developed primarily by Hausman and Rodrik (2006) – whose arguments and developments very quickly proved to be incredibly pertinent for the consolidation of the S3 approach. I am thinking particularly of the emphasis placed on the importance of specific (*versus* generic) inputs and capacities required in order to innovate – which entails a government making choices, as it cannot address all the specific capacity and infrastructure problems in all sectors.

Finally, the work carried out on related variety – notably by Boschma and Gianelle (2014) or Frenken, Van Oort, and Verburg (2007) – has led *ex post* to a significant theoretical basis for the fundamental idea that regions had to imagine and build their future using existing capacities and structures. It remains a very significant contribution even if I do not think that this work can be used prescriptively in relation to the concrete implementation of an S3.

I am deliberately omitting work concerning national/regional innovation systems (from Freeman to Lundvall) – that has not radically influenced this approach, and it is useful to recall that another report from the K4G Group expressed criticism of these approaches – criticism with which to a great extent I agree (David & Metcalfe, 2009).

Any combination of knowledge can cause a breakthrough and in our case, I think that it is the combination of two policy logics – a planning logic and a self-discovery logic, frequently opposed in the literature and in practice – that constitutes a breakthrough. There is also this idea of a concentration of resources, not on a structure but on a transformation process.

C. From cluster to smart specialization policy: really something new or more of the same?

The third question comes at just the right moment! Breakthrough? But how can we talk of breakthrough when the concept of cluster policy emerged well before that of S3? Let's go back to the second basic principle (Section I). The concentration of resources and prioritization must be not on a structure but on a transformation process. But in the minds of the originators of S3, a cluster is a structure – quite a favourable and productive structure, at least we hope so, but it's not certain, and it remains a structure. The structure must change, transform itself when new opportunities arise. And yet a cluster's capacity to transform itself – like Silicon Valley – can certainly not be taken for granted (Hassink, 2017). From this point of view, the S3 approach becomes a mechanism that can enable this transformation to occur. A cluster is thus both a possible starting point (if the cluster exists but has lost its initial dynamism) and a desirable point of arrival for the

S3 approach. A successful S3 always leads to the formation of a cluster – a collection of related projects and actors, all involved in a certain transformation.

S3 is also the response to the collapse of certain cluster policies – that do not understand that the real formation process of the cluster by a collective involvement of actors and projects in a defined direction – possibly stimulated by S3 – is far more important that its administrative creation.

D. Entrepreneurial discovery process (EDP): a transformative hope or a lock-in trap?

Robert and Huiwen actually ask a lot of questions here! I think that it is on this level – the role and meaning of the EDP concept in the theory and practice of S3 – that we have made most progress. The main function of the concept is to introduce a bottom-up component in a process that also has a top-down component. As already emphasized: the main characteristic of S3 as policy process is the combination between a planning logic and an entrepreneurial discovery logic. The entrepreneurial discovery process does not take place at the step of priority area choice (as was previously thought) – and here a participative process (always important as from the first phase) must not be confused with an entrepreneurial discovery process that will only take place afterwards in the way in which the transformative activity is constructed and developed – in response to the priorities considered (see M. Navarro, above).

This improved specification of the scope of the EDP is very useful and very productive. It relieves the regions of a great deal of pressure, while providing this entrepreneurial discovery logic with its true field of operation: the identification, implementation and evolution of a collection of projects – all moving in the same direction of transformation. The very notion of entrepreneurial discovery implies the production of information concerning these projects – the successes, the failures, the surprises – which obviously requires monitoring and flexibility mechanisms – with the aim of maximizing the social value of the information produced.

So here we are talking about discovering, on the one hand, the path to transformation and, on the other, the characteristics and properties of the projects that have been identified and selected. Is the term EDP appropriate? Yes, probably, even if Kirzner (1997) would certainly not acknowledge it – and it's possible that the expression coined by Hirschman (1967) – 'a voyage of discoveries' – is more suitable.

Two difficult questions remain. Of course, the choice of priorities and then the selection of projects can be subjected to policy capture and in that case there is a risk of public funds being monopolized by a small number of regulars (i,e., vested interests). The only answer here is belief in the possibility of establishing more transparent and robust processes, and delegating certain tasks of selection and choices to external committees of experts. This answer is only partially satisfactory but I think it's the only possible one when confronted with those who would like to throw out the baby (here any form of industrial policy) with the bathwater!

Can the process as a whole foster breakthroughs and radical innovations? There is no proof to the contrary. A lock-in trap is created precisely when a structure becomes incapable of transforming itself – and S3 concentrates precisely on transformation. But what degree of radicalness can be attained with this approach with regard to transformation is a relatively academic question. The ultimate decider should be the growth of productivity. Indeed we observe significant effects of productivity created by a transformation consisting essentially of processes of development and adoption of generic technologies invented elsewhere. This is the profound contribution of the analytical framework of general purpose technologies. Within this framework, the horizontal propagation of a generic technology – in other words, the development of new applications adapted to more-or-less traditional sectors and the formation of new capabilities (skills, management) – represents a key factor of productivity (Bresnahan, 2010). Indeed, with respect to regional development, breakthrough innovation and frontier research cannot be viewed as the only sources of productivity, growth and development. There are many types of innovation-related actions that are relevant for productivity and growth, such as building up human capital, adopting (not inventing) new technologies, diffusing novel management practices, generating complementarities between key enabling technologies and traditional sectors as well as developing social innovations. All these activities are important in order to strengthen capabilities and lever the growth and development potential of a regional economy; and all need to be included in any S3 exercise as important drivers of innovation, growth and structural change. As the great innovation economist Manuel Trajtenberg (2010) wrote a few years ago: 'They are perhaps less exciting and flamboyant than high-tech and world-class science, but they ultimately represent the key to economy-wide growth in most regional economies.'

E. Which type of region tends to benefit from smart specialization?

I no longer think that S3 can be beneficial for all regions! Incidentally, one of the first three autors – Bronwyn Hall – had mentioned her scepticism concerning the most advanced and largest regions in terms of GDP per capita.[5] The reason is well expressed by Robert and Huiwen who refer to 'a drop in the ocean': it doesn't make much sense to ask a region like Baden-Württemberg to choose and prioritize – whereas that is the very essence of S3. At the other end of the spectrum, it is clear that less advanced regions will have great difficulties in acquiring the minimum of entrepreneurial and institutional capacities necessary for the implementation of the concept in accordance with the three steps. But there are still all the intermediate regions – for which the concept and its implementation really do make sense. I have just returned from two experiences – one in Sfax (Tunisia) and the other in Curitiba (Brazil) – and I observed to what extent the founding principles of S3 were well understood and the tools provided for its implementation well used. It is certainly regrettable that there was an initial attempt to affirm a 'one size fits all' logic that was not pertinent. The disappearance of the ex ante conditionality principle regarding the next budgetary period will resolve this problem as each region will be totally free to choose whether or not to implement an S3 concept.

F. How to measure the effects of smart specialization?

The measurement of the effects is obviously a considerable challenge. Clearly, we will not reach the highest scientific standard to discern causality and the reasons are many: no pure treatment effect, complexity, time lags in realizing benefits. However, it is not because application of the most rigorous and academically recognized methods (e.g. to isolate the treatment effect and discern causality) is not possible that all attempts at assessment should be abandoned.

The crucial issue is to correctly understand what we wish to measure, and clearly distinguish between intermediate outcomes (particularly the development of the transformative activity) and true and final impact.

The way in which the transformative activity develops within the framework of a priority area and creates innovations and structural transformations must be observed, measured and monitored. The different dimensions of the transformative activity (R&D projects, training programmes, service platforms, start-ups) entail the development of specific metrics and the mobilization of third-party data. Those metrics that offer a data-intensive and timely view of each component of the transformative activity provide 'a real-time barometer' of the development of the activity that can be used as a starting point for understanding the dynamics of transformation and the degree to which there is progress or an indication that something warrants further investigation (Feldman et al., 2014).

IV. Conclusion

The 'Six critical questions' article is very useful at the dawn of a new budgetary period concerning regional policies, during which regions are invited to reconsider their choices of growth and innovation policy. These questions neatly summarize all the problems and uncertainties posed by the S3 concept. But today these questions cannot be answered as if we were still in 2010 or 2012, as if we have learned nothing.

The unique experience of S3 over the past few years has led to an enormous learning process regarding the design of strategies, preconditions and procedures required for effective implementation. Thanks to an impressive collective effort between academic researchers and policymakers at European, national, regional and local levels significant progress has been made. This progress has concerned the academic aspect; thus the innovation policy research domain has changed considerably within a few years (particularly thanks to the work on S3) (Foray, 2018a, 2018b, 2019; Morgan, 2017; Radosevic, Curaj, Gheorgiu, Andreescu, & Wade, 2017). But it has concerned especially the practical aspect as the S3 community of practice that has developed an implementation concept, which is consistent with theory, ambitious and whose feasibility has been demonstrated. The result is that the most recent national/regional S3 initiatives to strengthen research, development and innovation are far better conducted than they were a few years back.

This is why it seems to me that it is easier to elucidate the questions posed by Robert and Huiwen today than it was yesterday, even if there is still a lot to learn. Their article provided a magnificent opportunity to demonstrate this, and I thank them for it.

Notes

1. See the recent paper by Foray, Morgan, and Radosevic (2018) for an analysis of S3 within the broader research and innovation policies landscape of the EU.
2. P. David (personal communication, 2011).
3. On this subject, the famous guide mentioned by Robert and Huiwen, to which I contributed like many others, is no doubt a model of what must not be done when one wishes to convince

public agencies and regional governments regarding the implementation of a policy concept. It presented an incredibly complex process, displayed a certain rigidity and was ultimately counterproductive. That's my opinion !
4. M. Navarro (personal communication, 2016).
5. B. Hall (personal communication, 2010).

Acknowledgment

I thank Robert Hassink and Phil Cooke for their encouragements and support to write this reply.

Disclosure statement

No potential conflict of interest was reported by the author.

References

Azoulay, P., Fuchs, E., Goldstein, A., & Kearney, M. (2018). *Funding breakthrough research: Promises and challenges of the "ARPA model"* (Working Paper 24674). Cambridge: NBER.
Boschma, R., & Gianelle, C. (2014). *Regional branching and smart specialisation policy* (JRC Technical Reports, n°06/2014). Joint Research Centre.
Bresnahan, T. (2010). General purpose technologies. In *Handbook of the economics of innovation* (Vol. 2, pp. 761–791). Amsterdam: North-Holland.
David, P. A., & Metcalfe, S. (2009). How the universities can best contribute to enhancing Europe's innovative performance. *Knowledge for growth: Prospects for science, technology and innovation*. EUR 24047, European Commission.
Feldman, M., Lanahan, L., Kemeny, T., McGarrah, S., Polly, A., Neulist S., … Ethridge, F. (2014). *Stage IV: The 21st century economic development evaluation system*. Chapel Hill: Carolina Institute for Public Policy, University of North Carolina.
Foray, D. (2018a). Smart specialization as a case of mission-oriented policy – a case study on the emergence of new policy practices. *Industry and Corporate Changes*, *27*(5), 817–832, special issue on *Mission oriented innovation policy*.
Foray, D. (2018b). Smart specialization strategies and industrial modernization in European regions – theory and practice. *Cambridge Journal of Economics*, *42*(6), 1505–1520, special issue – *The dynamics of industrial and economic renewal in mature economies*.
Foray, D. (2019). On sector-non-neutral innovation policy: Towards new design principles. *Journal of Evolutionary Economics*, special issue on evolutionary innovation policy. doi:10.1007/s00191-018-0599-8
Foray, D., David, P., & Hall, B. (2009). Smart specialisation: The concept. *Knowledge for growth: Prospects for science, technology and innovation*. EUR 24047, European Commission.
Foray, D., Morgan, K., & Radosevic, S. (2018). *The role of smart specialisation in the EU Research and Innovation policy landscape* (Working paper). DG Regio.
Frenken, K., Van Oort, F., & Verburg, T. (2007). Related variety, unrelated variety and regional economic growth. *Regional Studies*, *41*(5), 685–697. doi:10.1080/00343400601120296
Hassink, R. (2017). Cluster decline and political lock-ins. In F. Belussi & J. L. Hervas Oliver (Eds.), *Unfolding cluster evolution* (pp. 190–202). London: Routledge.
Hassink, R., & Gong, H. (2019, August). Six critical questions about smart specialization. *European Planning Studies*. doi:10.1080/09654313.2019.1650898
Hausman, R., & Rodrik, A. (2006). *Doomed to choose: Industrial policy as predicament*. Cambridge, MA: Center for International Development, Harvard University.
Hirschman, A. O. (1967). *Development projects observed*. Washington, DC: Brooking Classic.
Kirzner, I. (1997). Entrepreneurial discovery and the competitive market process: An Austrian approach. *Journal of Economic Literature*, *35*,(1) 60–85.

McCann, P., & Ortega-Argiles, R. (2015). Smart specialization, regional growth and applications to European Union cohesion policy. *Regional Studies, 49*, 1291–1302. doi:10.1080/00343404.2013.799769

Morgan, K. (2017). Nurturing novelty: Regional innovation policy in the age of smart specialisation. *Environment and Planning C, 35*, 569–583.

Radosevic, S., Curaj, A., Gheorgiu, R., Andreescu, L., & Wade, I. (Eds.). (2017). *Advances in theory and practice of smart specialization*. London: Academic Press.

Rodrigues Pose, A., Di Cataldo, M., & Rainoldi, A. (2014). *The role of government institutions for smart specialization and regional development*. Brussels: Publications Office of the Eropean Union.

Trajtenberg, M. (2010). Development policy: An overview. In D. Foray (Ed.), *The new economics of technology policy*. Cheltenham: Edward Elgar.

Index

Page numbers in **bold** refer to tables and those in *italic* refer to figures.

adaptive system 6
aeronautics cluster 175
agglomeration economies 159, 176
agglomerations 8–9, 46–50, 83, 103, 159, 172, 173, 176, 179, 181, 189, 190, 192
Albors-Garrigos, J. 49, 52
Alfaro, L. **146**
Allgemeiner Vliesstoff-Report (AVR) 106
AMADEUS database 31, 33
analytical knowledge 158
applied index 31, 33, 34
Aranguren, M. J. 6–7, 175
'artisan' touch 106, 107
Asheim, B. T. 158, 159, 167, 178
automotive cluster 175
Azpeitia/Azkoitia cluster **146**, 147–9, **149, 150**

Barabási, A. L. 17, 157, 160, 161
Bathelt, H. 6
Becattini, G. 64, 82, 89, 90
Behrens, D. M. 28
Bellandi, M. 15, 103, 107
Bell, S. J. 83
Belussi, F. 6, 11, 12, 15
Bettiol, M. 16
bibliometric analysis 2, **3**, 171–2
Boix, R. 8, 15, 63, 66, 67, 71, 74, 75
Boronat-Moll, C. 49, 52
Boschma, R. 157–9, 167, 178, 181, 195
Brenner, T. 31, 32
Breschi, S. 50
brokerage **3**, 15, 82, 87, **88**, 89, 91–4
Brusco, S. 65
Bureau van Djik (BvD) 31, 70, 122
Burt, R. S. 86, 87
Burt's theory 15, 82, 89, 90, 93
business incubators 81–2, 115; C-factor 83, 84; incubation of new firms 83; industrial districts, spinoff incubators 84, *84*; inter-firm networks 83

calculated indicator 32
Caloffi, A. 3, 4, 12, 15

Capello, R. 180
Capone, F. 8
Castaldi, C. 29
CATI method 122
C-factor 83–5, 90, 92, 93
Chaminade, C. 15, 103
Chiarvesio, M. 16
Chinese immigration 107
Ciravegna, L. **146**
civic society 11
cluster existence argument 7
cluster life cycle 6–7
clusters and industrial districts (CIDs) 10, 138–9, 150; case studies 145; constructs and variables, and assessment 144, **144**; Costa Rican cluster 145; global markets and GVCs 137; lead firms' commitment 144; technical reports, consultancy and policy documents 145; *see also* global markets
clusters firms 119, 130, 131
Cohen, W. 52
Coleman, J. S. 87, 90
Community of Innovation Survey (CIS) 15, 47, 51, 52, 57, 58
Constructing Regional Advantage (CRA) report 160
control variables 33, 37, 53, 57, 123, 125, 160–2
Cooke, P. 142, 158, 159, 167
cooperative organization structures 110
correlation matrix 136; and descriptive statistics 53, **54**, 71, **80**; independent variables 35
creative cities analysis 7
creative class analysis **3**, 7
'creative entrepreneurship' 8
creativity and clusters 7–8
cross-fertilization process 12, 14, 38, 39, 106, 167
cultural and creative industries (CCIs) 7, 8
cultural and creative tourism 8

Dahlin, K. B. 28
Dametto, F. **146**
dataset 32, 33, 47, 51, 122–3, **123**
data source 160, **160**

David, P. A. 176, 193–4
De Miguel-Molina, B. 8
De Noni, I. 159
De Propris, L. 111
descriptive statistics 52, **54**, 71, 125, **126**, 130, 162, **162**; and correlation matrix 80
'Development Projects Observed' (1967) 188
Di Cataldo, M. 177, 195
differentiated knowledge bases (DKB): analytical, synthetic and symbolic 157; evolutionary conceptualization 158; firms 167; innovation studies and evolutionary concepts 157; in Norway 160; path-dependent trajectories 165; sector-specific shocks 157
digitalization and automatization 105
Di Maria, E. 16
distributed capacities and projects 192–3
district effect 15, 47, 49, 50, 53, 56, 62, 63, 73
district variable 52, 53
diversified RIS (DRIS) 101, 102
DKB 2.0 157
DUI model **3**, 159, 165–6
dynamic efficiency 63

Eastern Europe 109, 139, 179–80
econometric evidence: parametric fixed effects 71, **72**; QR with fixed effects **73**, 73–4
Elola, A. 6–7
entrepreneurial discovery process (EDP) 17, 173, 176–82, 191–3, 196–7
entrepreneurship: business opportunities 83; employees 85; external resources 85; former (local) knowledge 85; generic/selective sense 82; phases 82; structural holes theory 86, 86–7; venture/managers 82
ERGM models 9
Escribano, A. 52
Estelles-Miguel, S. 49, 52
EU projects 9–10
European Apparel and Textile Confederation (2015) 105
European Cluster Observatory procedure 32
European Patent Office (EPO) 64, 66, 74, 160
European regional innovation paradox 179
European Structural and Investment Funds 172–3
European textile industry *see* Prato and Borås districts
extensive labour mobility 29
externalities, types of 29
extra-regional networks 15, 101–3, 111, 112

Fichter, K. 12
Finland 104
firms' innovation strategies and outputs 16, 118, 123, 125, **126**
first-generation countries 8
Fitjar, R. 160
Flyer, F. 36
Folta, T. B. 36
Foray, D. 171, 175–7, 179, 180, 182

foreign clients/suppliers 7
'formal' relationships 9–10
Fornahl, D. 6, 14, 28
forward and backward citations on patents 28
Fosfuri, A. 52
Frenken, K. 158, 195
furniture clusters 122, 147, 149

Galletto, V. 15, 63, 66, 67, 71, 74, 75
German Federal Statistics Office 33
German subsidy catalogue 32, 33
Gertler, M. 158
Gianelle, C. 195
Giuliani, E. 94
Glaeser, E. L. 29
global innovation networks (GINs) 138, 142, 143, 148–51
global markets: international dynamics and risk of fracture 139–40; local commitment of lead companies 140–2, **146**, 146–8
global value chains (GVCs) 11–12, 120, 137, 138
Gong, H. 188, 196, 197
Gonzalez, G. 15
Gottardello, D. 16
governance 4, 104, 105, 131, 177, 179–80, 182, 190, 193–5
Grandinetti, R. 15
Granovetter, M. 10, 87, 90
Grashof, N. 14, 28
Grillitsch, M. 159
Guzzini, E. 178

Hall, B. H. 176, 197
Harmaakorpi, V. 111
Hartog, M. 178
Hassink, R. 17, 188, 196, 197
Hausmann, R. 17, 157, 160, 161, 189, 195
Health and Medicine 110, 111
Healy, A. 179
Heckman's two-stage analysis 56
Heide, J. B. 83
Held, M. 111
Henning, M. 178
Hervás-Oliver, J. L. 8, 15, 49, 52
Hesse, K. 14
Hidalgo, C. A. 17, 157, 160, 161
Hirschman, A. O. 188, 196
Höglinger, C. 103
human capital variable 162

Iacobucci, D. 178
'I-district effect' 15, 63
'i-MID effect' 15
incremental innovations 9, 27–8, 102, 149, 167; *see also* Marshallian Industrial Districts (MIDs)
incubator effect 90
independent logit models 125
industrial districts (IDs) 50; Burt's concepts 88; closure and brokerage 88, *88*; description 81; knowledge gatekeepers 89; *see also* business

incubators; innovation-Marshallian industrial district (iMID) effect; structural holes theory
'informal' relationships 10
information and communication technologies (ICT) 7, 8, 106, **124**, 144, 147, 150, 166, 172, 182
Innocenti, N. 17
innovation in clusters: internationalization forms 120–2; proximity and connectivity 119–20
innovation-Marshallian industrial district (iMID) effect: business services 69; comparability and robustness issues 74–5; innovation by type of LPS, 1991–2014 67, **68**; innovative performance 67, *68*; patents per million employees 69, 70; robustness 63; *see also* econometric evidence; modelling, iMID effect
innovation outputs (dependent variables) 123–4
innovation policy 6, 11, 14, 27, 171, 172, 174–6, 179, 181, 198
innovative intensity: and LPSs in Spain 67; and technological innovation 66–7
innovative outputs and inputs 70–1
inter-connection of papers and macro-themes 5
internationalization drive innovation: firm turnover 129; global sourcing 124; internal cluster cohesion 118; logit model results 127, **128, 129**; production and innovation 127, 127; upstream and downstream 118, 124; *see also* innovation in clusters
internationalization of clusters 11
internationalization-related keywords 5
inter-sectoral matching platforms 108
intra-regional variety 103–4
Isaksen, A. 102

Jacobs, J. 156
Johannisson, B. 90
John, C. H. St. 29, 49, 91
Johnston, C. 111

Kallal, H. D. 29
Karlsson, M. 111
K4G Group 194, 195
Kirzner, I. 196
Klinger, B. 17, 157, 160, 161
knowledge bases (KB) 16–17, 75, 102, 164–6, 172; *see also* differentiated knowledge bases (DKB)
Knowledge for Growth Expert Group 172
knowledge-intensive business services 34, 91, 93–4
knowledge intensive service providers (KIBS) 107, 119, 131
knowledge networks 2, **3**, 9–10, 13, 30, 32
knowledge production function (KPF) 64, 70, 71, **72**, 73, 74
Koka, B. R. 52
Koput, K. W. 9
Kosfeld, R. 34
Kroll, H. 180

Lagrange Multiplier (LM) 162, 164
Lane, P. J. 52
Lanzolla, G. 30–1
Latin American Electronic Study Centre (LAES) 147, 150
Laursen, K. 53
Lazzeretti, L. 3, 4, 8, 17
lead companies 16, 138–46, 148–51
Lengauer, L. 103
Levinthal, D. 52
Li, P. 6
Lissoni, F. 50
Loasby, B. 7
localization externalities 47–8, 57
local labour systems (LLSs) 63, 67, 102
local production systems (LPSs) 11, 63, 64, 66, 67, **68**, 69, 70, **72**, 73, 74–6, 100, 102, 140
local support 108
logistic regression model 33, 35
logit analysis 53, **55**
Lopez, S. M. 6–7
Lorenzen, M. 120
Los, B. 29

macro-themes 3–6, **3**, *4*
'Made in Italy' industries 122
marketing innovation 16, 123, **124**, 125, **126**, 127, **128, 129**, 130–1, 135
Marshall, A. 29, 63, 89
Marshallian Industrial Districts (MIDs) 9, 15; artistic and handicraft-like culture 64; asymmetric knowledge and gains 49–50; creative destruction challenges 48; district effect 47; economic competitiveness, SMEs 64; entrepreneurs 64; innovation 65–6; social dimension 48; socio-economic phenomena 47; types of innovation 48–9; values 64
Martin, R. 6
McCann, B. T. 36
McCann, P. 195
mechanics clusters 122
mental models 29, 49
Ministry of Education Integrated University Information System (SIUU) 70
'mission-oriented' innovation policy 174, 175
modelling, iMID effect: innovative outputs and inputs 70–1; KPF 70
modernization 176, 177, 194
Mondragon Cooperative Group (MCG) **146**, 147, **149**, 150
Montebelluna sport system 122
Morgan, K. 175, 195
Morrison, A. 143
Mudambi, R. 120
multinational enterprises (MNEs) **3**, 7, 12, 120, 121

NACE categories 160, **160**
NACE codes 33, 51, 160
Nadvi, K. **146**
national policies 104–5, 108, 111

Navarro, M. 191, 193
Neffke, F. 178
neo-makers 107–10
network-related and innovation-related keywords 4
Norway 104, 160
NUTS 2 codes 51
NUTS-3 classification of European Union 160
NVIVO software 3

organizational innovation 121–3, **124**, 125, 130, 131
Ortega-Argiles, R. 195
Oslo Manual 52, 123
Ottati, D. 62, 83

pace of technology evolution 30–2, **35**, 36
Parrilli, M. D. 16, **146**
patents or publications 9–10
patent variable 162
Pathak, S. J. 52
path creation 101, 102, 104–6, 108–12
path extension 16, 101–3, 105–9, 111, 112
path renewal 16, 101, 102, 105–9; *see also* transformation paths
PATSTAT, European database 32, *68*, *69*
P-clusters 15, 82, 89–93
Photonics Cluster 175
Pilotti, L. 159
Plechero, M. 15, 103
policy actions: action plan step 193; 10 commandments 193; priority area translation, transformational roadmap 191–3; thematic priority areas 190–1
policy and social issues 10–11
policy makers 11, 14, 26, 27, 38, 39, 108, 111, 166–7, 173, 175, 176, 180
policy platforms concept 158
policy-related keywords 5
population density 161–2
Porter, M. E. 82, 83, 89–90, 137
Pouder, R. W. 29, 49, 91
Powell, W. W. 9
Prato and Borås districts: current trends and path transformation strategies 105–6; historical development 105
Prato textile district 82, 89, 90, 107
pre- and post-production services 138
principal component analysis (PCA) 52
'proactive facilitators' 104
process innovation 7, 121–3, **124, 126, 128, 129**, 130, 131
product innovation 52, 58, 121, 123, **124**, 125, **126, 128**, 129
pseudo R for 4 models of innovation 135
public research organizations (PRO) **54**, 70

quantile regression (QR) 71, **72**, *73*, 73–4

radical innovations 28; centre *vs.* periphery 36, *37*; and clusters 2012–2014 33, **34**; emergence of 30, 36; firms location in cluster 31; inverted u-shape effect 30–1; labour market regions 2012–2014 *34*, 35; logistic regression results 35, **35**; on patent data 34; PATSTAT, European database 32; Southern Germany 35
Radosevic, S. 178
Rainoldi, A. 177, 195
R&D and manufacturing: co-location 118; science-based and technological factors 118
R&D partnerships 9–10
regional actors 104, 105, 111, 177, 181
regional clusters 14, 27–9, 38, 146
regional differentiation 191–3
regional diversification 104, 176
regional economies 17, 172–4, 176–7, 179–82, 189, 193, 195, 197
regional innovation policy 171, 172, 174, 176, 179, 181
regional innovation systems (RIS) 138, 142–3, 148–50, 174; defined 101; types 102; *see also* transformation paths
regional transformations 102, 104
relatedness: and cluster variety 13–14; and growth **162**, 162–5, **163**; method 161–2; variety and entrepreneurship 5
relational density 192, 193
relational view (RV) development 30
Relative Comparative Advantage (RCA) 161
Research and Innovation Strategies for Smart Specialization (RIS3) 172, 175, 177, 178, 180
'Research Explorer,' German research directory 33
Rodríguez-Pose, A. 177, 195
Rodrik, A. 189, 195
Ron Boschma, R. 6
Russo, M. 63

Sacchetti, S. **146**
Saddler, J. 111
Salter, A. 53
Santini, E. 15, 103, 107
SAOM/SIENA models 9
Saxenian, A. 82, 91
Scheffer, M. R. 106
Scheinkman, J. A. 29
Schot, J. 174
science and technology (S&T) model 17, 148, 151, 175
Sedita, S. R. 3, 4, 6, 11, 12, 15, 159
Semantria software 2–4
Sforzi, F. 15, 74, 75
Sforzi-ISTAT algorithm 63, 67
Shane, S. 82
Shaver, J. M. 36
Shleifer, A. 29
Signorini, L. F. 62
'Silicon Valley North' 91
small and medium-sized enterprises (SMEs) 64, 103, 106, 107, 138, 139, 142, 143, 145, 146, 148, 149, 151, 174
smart specialization 5, 7, 17; academic and political attention 171; cluster policy concept 195–6;

concentrate not on structures 189; concentrate on certain priorities 189; defined 172; or diversification 173; EDP (*see* entrepreneurial discovery process (EDP)); entrepreneurial discovery logic 189; entrepreneurs 172; innovative activity deployment 189; 'leader' *vs.* 'follower regions' 173; measurement of effects 197–8; measurements 180; regional innovation policies 194–5; region tends 197; specialization/diversification 194; structurally weak regions 179; typical phenomena 179; weaknesses in Europe 172
'Smart Textiles' initiative 110
Smith-Doerr, L. 9
social and business networks 6
social and environmental issues 12
social dimension 48
social innovation 8, 17, 174, 197
Sotarauta, M. 177
Spain: iMID effect 1991 to 2014, 67–70, **68**, *68*, *69*; LPSs in 67
Spanish Patent and Trademark Office (OEPM) 64
specialized RIS (SRIS) 15, 16, 100–5, 111, 12
Stancova, K. C. 178
state interventions 105
static efficiency 62
Steinmueller, W. E. 174
Strambach, S. 12
strategic innovation programmes 111
structural holes theory: Burt's analysis 86, 87; density values 87; non-redundant sources 87; relations within and between networks, and density table *86*, 87; unconnected actors 87; *see also* P-clusters; SV-clusters
Suarez, F. F. 30–1
Sunley, P. 6, 7
supra-national entities 12
'Surveillance Capitalism' 7, 11
sustainability-oriented innovation 12–13
SV-clusters 15, 82, 89, 91–3
symbolic knowledge 17, 158, 159, 164, 166
synthetic knowledge 158–9, 164

tacit knowledge 27, 29, 38, 48, 83
Technical Research Institute of Sweden (TRIS) 102, 111
technical textiles sector 106, 107
technological innovative intensity 64
The Textile Fashion Center 110
textual analysis 2
thin RIS (TRIS) 102, 103
Third Italy's industrial districts 83
three-digit NACE Rev. 2 code industries 32
Timmermans, B. 160

Tödtling, F. 103
Tracey, P. 83
traditional leaders 107
traditional local production systems 140
Trajtenberg, M. 197
transformation paths: DRIS, SRIS and TRIS 102; and extra-regional networks 102–3; geographical proximity 101; and intra-regional variety 103–4; *see also* Prato and Borås districts
Tribó, J. A. 52
Trippl, M. 102, 159, 179
Trullén, J. 74
2-digit NACE-93 industry classification 53
two-way type LPS-specialization estimations 74

UCINET-Netdraw software 6
United Nation's Sustainable Development Goals 175
United States Patent and Trademark Office (USPTO) 64, 66, *68*, *69*, 74
The University of Borås 110
University of Costa Rica (UCR) 150
University of Florence in 2018 2, 14

Valdaliso, J. 6–7
Valencian region (VR): CIS questionnaire 52; databases 51; industries and MIDs 50, **51**; R&D dynamics 50; size of firms in sample 51, **51**; in Spain 50; variety of industries 51
Van Oort, F. 156, 158, 195
variables of analysis 123, **124**
variance inflation factors (VIF) 135, 162
variety/knowledge coherence 156–7
Venkataraman, S. 82
Verburg, T. 158, 195
vertically integrated firms 108, 109
VIF and tolerance 135
VINNOVA, Swedish Agency 110, 111
VINNVÄXT-program 111

Walter, L. 111
Wang, J. 6
Weitzman, M. L. 27
Werner, A. 34
Western countries 117
Wilson, J. R 175
word cloud, cluster research 3, *4*
World Bank 171

Yeung, H. W. **146**

Zabala, J. M. **146**
Zuboff, S. 7
Zukauskaite, E. 179